# CONTEMPORARY PERSPECTIVES ON RATIONAL SUICIDE

# SERIES IN DEATH, DYING, AND BEREAVEMENT
## ROBERT A. NEIMEYER, CONSULTING EDITOR

Nord—*Multiple AIDS-Related Loss: A Handbook for Understanding and Surviving a Perpetual Fall*
Harvey—*Perspectives on Loss: A Sourcebook*
Davies—*Shadows in the Sun: The Experiences of Sibling Bereavement in Childhood*
Werth—*Contemporary Perspectives on Rational Suicide*

*FORMERLY*

### SERIES IN DEATH EDUCATION, AGING, AND HEALTH CARE
HANNELORE WASS, CONSULTING EDITOR

Bard—*Medical Ethics in Practice*
Benoliel—*Death Education for the Health Professional*
Bertman—*Facing Death: Images, Insights, and Interventions*
Brammer—*How to Cope with Life Transitions: The Challenge of Personal Change*
Cleiren—*Bereavement and Adaptation: A Comparative Study of the Aftermath of Death*
Corless, Pittman-Lindeman—*AIDS: Principles, Practices, and Politics, Abridged Edition*
Corless, Pittman-Lindeman—*AIDS: Principles, Practices, and Politics, Reference Edition*
Curran—*Adolescent Suicidal Behavior*
Davidson—*The Hospice: Development and Administration, Second Edition*
Davidson, Linnolla—*Risk Factors in Youth Suicide*
Degner, Beaton—*Life-Death Decisions in Health Care*
Doka—*AIDS, Fear, and Society: Challenging the Dreaded Disease*
Doty—*Communication and Assertion Skills for Older Persons*
Epting, Neimeyer—*Personal Meanings of Death: Applications of Personal Construct Theory to Clinical Practice*
Haber—*Health Care for an Aging Society: Cost-Conscious Community Care and Self-Care Approaches*
Hughes—*Bereavement and Support: Healing in a Group Environment*
Irish, Lundquist, Nelsen—*Ethnic Variations in Dying, Death, and Grief: Diversity in Universality*
Klass, Silverman, Nickman—*Continuing Bonds: New Understanding of Grief*
Lair—*Counseling the Terminally Ill: Sharing the Journey*
Leenaars, Maltsberger, Neimeyer—*Treatment of Suicidal People*
Leenaars, Wenckstern—*Suicide Prevention in Schools*
Leng—*Psychological Care in Old Age*
Leviton—*Horrendous Death, Health, and Well-Being*
Leviton—*Horrendous Death and Health: Toward Action*
Lindeman, Corby, Downing, Sanborn—*Alzheimer's Day Care: A Basic Guide*
Lund—*Older Bereaved Spouses: Research with Practical Applications*
Neimeyer—*Death Anxiety Handbook: Research, Instrumentation, and Application*
Nord—*Multiple AIDS-Related Loss: A Handbook for Understanding and Surviving a Perpetual Fall*
Papadatou, Papadatos—*Children and Death*
Prunkl, Berry—*Death Week: Exploring the Dying Process*
Ricker, Myers—*Retirement Counseling: A Practical Guide for Action*
Samarel—*Caring for Life and Death*
Sherron, Lumsden—*Introduction to Educational Gerontology. Third Edition*
Stillion—*Death and Sexes: An Examination of Differential Longevity, Attitudes, Behaviors, and Coping Skills*
Stillion, McDowell, May—*Suicide Across the Life Span—Premature Exits*
Vachon—*Occupational Stress in the Care of the Critically Ill, the Dying, and the Bereaved*
Wass, Corr—*Childhood and Death*
Wass, Corr—*Helping Children Cope with Death: Guidelines and Resource. Second Edition*
Wass, Corr, Pacholski, Forfar—*Death Education II: An Annotated Resource Guide*
Wass, Neimeyer—*Dying: Facing the Facts. Third Edition*
Weenolsen—*Transcendence of Loss over the Life Span*
Werth—*Rational Suicide? Implications for Mental Health Professionals*

# CONTEMPORARY PERSPECTIVES ON RATIONAL SUICIDE

*edited by*

**James L. Werth, Jr.**

| USA | Publishing Office: | BRUNNER/MAZEL<br>*A member of the Taylor & Francis Group*<br>325 Chestnut Street<br>Philadelphia, PA 19106<br>Tel: (215) 625-8900<br>Fax: (215) 625-2940 |
|---|---|---|
| | Distribution Center: | BRUNNER/MAZEL<br>*A member of the Taylor & Francis Group*<br>47 Runway Road<br>Levittown, PA 19057<br>Tel: (215) 269-0400<br>Fax: (215) 269-0363 |
| UK | | BRUNNER/MAZEL<br>*A member of the Taylor & Francis Group*<br>1 Gunpowder Square<br>London EC4A 3DE<br>Tel: +44 171 583 0490<br>Fax: +44 171 583 0581 |

**CONTEMPORARY PERSPECTIVES ON RATIONAL SUICIDE**

1 2 3 4 5 6 7 8 9 0

Printed by Braun-Brumfield, Ann Arbor, MI, 1999.
Cover design by Nancy Abbott.

A CIP catalog record for this book is available from the British Library.
⊛ The paper in this publication meets the requirements of the ANSI Standard Z39.48-1984 (Permanence of Paper).

Library of Congress Cataloging-in-Publication Data

Contemporary perspectives on rational suicide / edited by James L. Werth, Jr.
    p.   cm. — (Series in death, dying, and bereavement)
    ISBN 0-87630-936-8 (alk. paper). — ISBN 0-87630-937-6 (pbk. alk. paper)
    1. Suicide.  2. Suicide—Sociological aspects.  3. Suicide—Moral and ethical aspects.  4. Conduct of life.  I. Werth, James L. II. Series.
  RC569.C66   1999
  616.85'8445—DC21
                                                                           98-34142
                                                                                CIP

ISBN  0-87630-936-8 (cloth)
        0-87630-937-6 (paper)

*This book is respectfully dedicated to those
who have suffered needlessly and those
who have attempted to help compassionately.*

# CONTENTS

## Part 1 RELEVANT BACKGROUND ISSUES

### PHILOSOPHERS

### RELIGIOUS LEADERS

## Part 3 SPECIAL POPULATIONS

# CONTRIBUTORS

## Forewords

### Derek Humphry
is president of the Euthanasia Research & Guidance Organization (ERGO!). A former journalist with the *London Sunday Times* and *Los Angeles Times*, he founded the Hemlock Society in 1980 and for 12 years was its executive director. He is the author of five books on the right to die, of which *Jean's Way* and *Final Exit* were bestsellers.

### Rita L. Marker
is an attorney and executive director of the International Anti-Euthanasia Task Force. She has published numerous articles on assisted suicide and euthanasia in medical and legal journals and is the author of *Deadly Compassion: The Death of Ann Humphry and the Truth about Euthanasia.*

## Part 1: Relevant Background Issues

### Philosophers

### Margaret P. Battin
is Professor of Philosophy and Adjunct Professor of Internal Medicine, Division of Medical Ethics, at the University of Utah. She is the author of *Ethical Issues in Suicide* (1982, 1995), *Ethics in the Sanctuary* (1990), and *The Least Worst Death* (1994), and coeditor of *Drug Use in Assisted Suicide and Euthanasia* (1996), as well as editor or coeditor of several other books and author of numerous papers.

### Daniel Callahan
is a philosopher by training and has served as both director and president of The Hastings Center. He is now a Senior Research Associate at the Center; a member of the Institute of Medicine of the National Academy of Sciences; and the author or editor of 32 books, including *The Troubled Dream of Life: In Search of a Peaceful Death.*

### Religious Leaders

### Father Robert Barry
is a Dominican priest and an adjunct associate professor of religious studies at the University of Illinois, Urbana–Champaign. He has published more than 50 articles on

moral and bioethical issues and four books including *Breaking the Thread of Life* on the morality of rational suicide and *Set No Limits* on age-based rationing of medical care.

### Gerald A. Larue

is Adjunct Professor of Gerontology at the University of Southern California and Emeritus Professor of biblical history and archeology at USC's School of Religion. He is President Emeritus of the Hemlock Society, Chairman of the Committee for the Scientific Examination of Religion, a Humanist Laureate, member of the Academy of Humanism, and 1989 Humanist of the Year. His most recent publications include *Geroethics, Playing God: 50 Religion's Views on Your Right to Die*, and *Freethought Across the Centuries*.

## Sociologists

### Steven Stack

is a Professor and Chairperson of the Department of Criminal Justice at Wayne State University. His current projects include the influence of educational attainment on the odds of suicide among African Americans and the structural correlates of suicide among artists.

### Samuel E. Wallace

is Professor of Sociology at the University of Tennessee, Knoxville. His pioneering research on bereavement from suicide, entitled *After Suicide*, was published by Wiley Interscience in 1973. His research and publications also include the areas of human ecology, Latin American studies, deviance, and college teaching.

## Attorneys

### Wesley J. Smith

is an attorney for the International Anti-Euthanasia Task Force and the author of *Forced Exit: The Slippery Slope from Assisted Suicide to Legalized Murder.*

### Kathryn L. Tucker

is director of Legal Affairs with Compassion in Dying and is Of Counsel with the Seattle-based law firm Perkins-Coie. She is an Affiliate Professor of Law at the University of Washington School of Law, teaching on individual liberty in medical decision making. She was lead counsel in both *Washington v. Glucksberg* and *Vacco v. Quill*. She also served as counsel to the sponsors of the 1991 Washington state initiative that sought to legalize aid-in-dying.

## Part 2: Service Providers
## Death/Grief Counselors

### Lois Chapman Dick

is a clinical social worker in private practice in Washington. She is a Certified Death Educator and Grief Counselor. She is a member of the Association for Death Education and Counseling and was the editor of their newsletter *The Forum*. She is also a volunteer member of the King County (Washington) Critical Incident Stress Management team. She produced *In the Midst of Winter*, a film about AIDS that was aired nationally on PBS.

### Richard R. Ellis

is a retired Associate Professor of Applied Psychology, School of Education, New York University. In 1985 he founded the MA program with a specialization in Grief Counseling, and he served as its major professor. A long-time member and former Board Member of the Association for Death Education and Counseling, in 1986 he was appointed the first Chair of its Professional Standards and Ethics Committee. He wrote the organization's Code of Ethics and continues as Chair of the Committee.

## Nurses

### Angela Albright

is a professor and chair of the Undergraduate Nursing Science Department at California State University Dominguez Hills. She has a Ph.D. in counseling psychology and is a master's-prepared clinical nurse specialist in psychiatric mental health nursing. She has completed research on attitudes and knowledge of psychologists and psychiatrists toward suicide. Her interests are in clinical practice with persons with chronic illness and depression, and women's issues.

### Margaret L. Campbell

is an advanced-practice nurse at Detroit Receiving Hospital. She directs the care of patients. Ms. Campbell has published a number of papers related to foregoing life-sustaining therapy. She recently represented the Michigan Nurses Association on the Michigan Commission on Death and Dying, which was charged by the legislature to study and advise about assisted suicide. Ms. Campbell is a member of the Institute of Medicine Committee on Care at the End of Life.

## Physicians

### Robin Bernhoft

is a surgeon in Washington state. He graduated from Harvard and received his MD from Washington University in St. Louis, with a residency at the University of California-San Francisco. After his residency he was a Fellow at the Royal Postgraduate Medical School in London (where he pursued subspecialty training in liver and pancreatic surgery). He was in private practice from 1984-91 before retiring due to a disability. He is an avid writer, speaker, and political activist.

### Richard MacDonald

since his 1993 appointment as Medical Director of The Hemlock Society USA, he researches and writes on medical aspects of physician aid-in-dying and creates dialogue with the medical community. He addresses medical and lay audiences with special emphasis on educating medical students and residents about appropriate care at the end-of-life. He has practiced family medicine in Canada and California for over 40 years, served as Chief of Staff at two hospitals, and chaired a Governing Board.

## Psychiatrists

### Mark J. Goldblatt

is a Clinical Instructor in Psychiatry at Harvard Medical School, and an Attending Psychiatrist at McLean Hospital, Belmont, MA. He has recently co-edited *Essential Papers on Suicide* with J.T. Maltsberger, published by New York University Press.

### Jerome A. Motto

is Professor of Psychiatry, Emeritus, at the University of California, San Francisco, School of Medicine. His career in psychiatric teaching, training, research, practice, and consultation has focused primarily on the recognition, assessment, and management of persons in suicidal states, including the ethical aspects of suicide and suicide prevention. He is currently consultant to the inpatient psychiatric service of San Mateo County General Hospital for patients at risk for suicide.

## Psychologists

### Stephen Jamison

is a social psychologist. He was former president of the Mental Health Association of Marin County, California, and director of Life and Death Consultations in Mill Valley, California. He is an adjunct assistant professor in the Department of Social and Behavioral Sciences at the University of California-San Francisco. He is the author of *Final Acts of Love: Families, Friends, and Assisted Dying* as well as of *Assisted Suicide: A Decision-Making Guide for Health Professionals.*

### Antoon A. Leenaars

is a faculty member of the Department of Clinical and Health Psychology at the University of Leiden, The Netherlands, and is in private practice in Windsor, Canada. He is a past president of both the Canadian Association for Suicide Prevention and the American Association of Suicidology. He has published over 100 articles on suicide-related issues and is Editor-in-Chief of the *Archives of Suicide Research*, the journal of the International Academy for Suicide Research. His most recent book is *Suicide and the Unconscious.*

## Social Workers

### Jay Callahan

is Assistant Professor of Social Work at the University of Illinois at Chicago and has a Ph.D. in social work and psychology from the University of Michigan. He is particularly interested in crisis intervention and suicide prevention and has long been active in the American Association of Suicidology.

### Deborah Cummings

is the Director of Case Management and Social Work at McLaren Regional Medical Center in Flint, Michigan. She is past President of the Michigan Chapter of the National Association of Social Workers and is President of the Michigan Chapter of Social Work Administrators in Health Care. She served on the Michigan Commission on Death and Dying, which made recommendations regarding assisted suicide. She was the original drafter of the NASW policy on Client Self-Determination in End of Life Decisions.

## Death Educators

### David K. Meagher

is a Professor of Health and Nutrition Science and the coordinator of the Thanatology Graduate Study Program at Brooklyn College of the City University of New York. He is the editor of the *Thanatology Newsletter* and serves on the Editorial Board of *The Journal of Loss, Grief, and Care*. He has served as President of the Association of Death Education and Counseling, is an ADEC Certified Death Educator, and has published and lectured on patient's rights and end-of-life issues.

### Judith M. Stillion

is a former President of the Association for Death Education and Counseling and serves on its Board of Directors. A certified death educator, she is Associate Editor of *Death Studies* and has published nearly 100 chapters and articles. The second edition of *Suicide Across the LifeSpan*, coauthored by Eugene McDowell, was published recently. Currently on leave from her position as Professor of Psychology at Western Carolina University, she serves as Associate Vice President for Academic Affairs at the University of North Carolina General Administration.

# Part 3: Special Populations
## Disability-Rights Advocates

### Carol J. Gill

is a psychologist specializing in health and disability. She is Assistant Professor and Director of the Chicago Center for Disability Research in the Department of Disability and Human Development, University of Illinois at Chicago, where she conducts research and directs curriculum development in Disability Studies. Nationally recognized for addressing the complexity of social, cultural, clinical, and policy issues in disability, Dr. Gill identifies proudly as a woman with a disability.

### Karen Hwang

is a research assistant at the Kessler Institute of Rehabilitation, where she is doing research involving mothers with spinal-cord injuries. She received her M.Ed. from Rutgers University in 1995 and is currently working toward her doctorate, also at Rutgers. Her opinion columns have been published in disability-lifestyle magazines, and her piece on assisted suicide was nominated for a "Maggie"—the highest editorial award given by the Western Publisher's Association.

## Gerontologists

### John L. McIntosh

is a Professor of Psychology at Indiana University South Bend. Among numerous publications are five books (three on elderly suicide), book chapters, and journal articles on various topics in suicidology. He serves on the editorial boards of *Suicide and Life-Threatening Behavior, Gerontology and Geriatrics Education*, and *Crisis*. He is a former President of the American Association of Suicidology and recipient of its Shneidman Award for research contributions. He has received both campus and all-university awards for distinguished teaching.

### Erdman B. Palmore

is a Professor Emeritus at the Duke University Center for the Study of Aging. He has published over 100 articles and 17 books, including *Ageism* and *The Facts on Aging Quiz*.

## Survivors

### Patty Rosen

was one of the primary spokespersons throughout Oregon and for the national media in support of Oregon's Death with Dignity ballot measure. Her career in medicine and counseling has varied from developing and implementing programs for a leading medical school to making teaching videos, hosting radio talk shows, and presenting seminars for the medical community and general public. Currently, she lectures, writes, and counsels.

### Adina Wrobleski

was a recognized authority on suicide grief. She wrote about the extra grief problems people have after a suicide. Her specialty was taking complex information and writing about it in clear and uncomplicated language. She wrote two books. She died on April 10, 1997, of brain cancer at the age of 63.

## Conclusion

### Charlotte P. Ross

is Executive Director of the Death with Dignity National Center, was Executive Director of the Suicide Prevention Center of San Mateo County (California) for 22 years, and was President of the Youth Suicide National Center for 5 years. She has been a member of the American Association of Suicidology since its inception, served on the Editorial Board of *Suicide and Life-Threatening Behavior*, was the founding editor of *Newslink*, and has published articles on suicide prevention standards and youth suicide prevention.

# FOREWORD 1   PRO

## *Derek Humphry*

Philosophers can ponder, ethicists can strategize, politicians can compromise, but at the end of the day it is the general public who decides what societal values shall predominate. So it was in Oregon in 1997 when the citizens of that state voted to keep their Death with Dignity Act which permits, under certain conditions, physician-assisted suicide for a competent, terminally ill adult. By a margin of 60% to 40% on Ballot Measure 51, in a turnout of over 1 million electors, Oregonians reaffirmed their 1994 decision (Ballot Measure 16) that they wanted this medical procedure available to them if they were dying.

The Oregon Legislature, prodded by special-interest lobbyists, wanted the citizens to reverse themselves on the 1994 decision, claiming that they were at the time ignorant of the true facts about hastened death. Many citizens took offence at being told they were mistaken and took special pains to repeat their vote. Others changed their vote. Most of the nearly $4 million spent by the campaign to repeal the Act came from Roman Catholic churches and institutions, plus a hefty sum from the Mormons. With all donations and their mainly religious sources reported in the media, an aggrieved response may have been triggered on the part of some voters that they were being dictated to by certain religious forces. Oregonians are noted for their independence in religious matters, and if there is one traditional principle in American life that is most admirable it is freedom of religion, plus freedom from other peoples' religions. It was, incidentally, an entirely postal vote, giving people the opportunity to reflect, and perhaps discuss, their decisions while at home.

The Oregon double vote on precisely the same law is an historic test of public opinion because this is the only place in the world in which the citizenry have been asked to decide on the rightness or wrongness of physician-assisted suicide. All previous changes in existing laws on this subject—in the Netherlands, Australia, and Colombia—were carried out by elected representatives or judges.

Why do I think that the people of Oregon decided that they wanted choice in dying at the end-of-life?

Pain can be a major reason, or fear of pain. Thanks to the clamor in the past decade of the right to die movement, the subject of pain management is now being seriously addressed in America, following the leadership of the British. Millions of dollars are being spent, and many fine and dedicated minds are devoting enormous time and energy to the improved control of terminal suffering. Throughout the 1980s, few listened to us when our movement protested that there was too much unnecessary pain in the modern dying process. It has taken our successes in the ballots and our near-successes (and a lot of noise) in the legislatures, together with reaching the U.S. Supreme Court with two important appeals (both rejected, finally) to force the health professions to take a truly in-depth look at how poorly they care for the dying.

It is commonly accepted that the best place, currently, to die in America is Oregon, precisely because of the 1994 passage of the Death with Dignity Act. All of a sudden, after that first vote, the health professions woke up and started forming task forces and study groups and holding seminars, all to improve the care of the dying. Hospices saw a 20% increase of patients referred to them by doctors, and the use of morphine began to surpass that in any other state in the nation.

Another reason for the Oregon decision is psychic pain, best known to ordinary people—as distinct from academics and physicians—as distress, unhappiness, sadness, and being a burden through their dying process on those whom they love. The sheer strain of being subjected to multiple medical procedures, however skillfully and caringly administered, is a strain on the body and mind. There is also the process of obvious deterioration of a body once healthy and active, a body in which the person once had considerable pride. Prolonged medical care, being continually in and out of hospitals, being jabbed incessantly for laboratory testing purposes, being attached to bits and pieces of equipment, and taking lots of drugs which often have uncomfortable side-effects are what add up to distress.

Observing that they are losing control, being subjected constantly to medical regimens, and having to endure a lifestyle never previously considered can combine to contribute to the unhappiness of terminal patients. Not being able to enjoy the old pasttimes and friendships, no longer being able to walk the dog or weed the garden—whatever it is that makes life tolerable—these are the things that make for sadness. Knowing that life is drawing to a close, being conscious that they must soon say a final goodbye to those whom they love, and giving up hard-worked-for and prized possessions all contribute to the grief, or self-mourning, of the patient.

We hear from strident right-to-life critics that, if we pass laws permitting hastened deaths to be chosen by dying people, those who are a burden, physically or financially, will either be pushed into quick deaths or feel obliged to check out prematurely. This is their "slippery slope" argument.

It is the most natural of human feelings not to want to be a huge physical, emotional, and financial burden on family, and one of the more admirable human feelings, in my opinion. In the right to die movement we tell people who approach us with this problem that, if they look carefully, they will probably find that family is only too pleased and proud to take care of them, and also that it is "payback" time for younger people to look after the older folk facing their ends. But let us be honest and admit that the "burden" question is sometimes a genuine component to be "fed into the hopper" when considering the end. (I am definitely not referring here to persons who are permanently disabled or handicapped in some way. In the Oregon law, and others to follow, such persons could only get assisted death if they were terminally ill, asked for it, and met the conditions.)

All of the above states of mind add up to that factor called "the quality of life." It is not a phrase to which the opponents of assisted dying make much reference. Quality of life is a state that even the most caring and expert physician cannot assess. Neither can the most experienced psychiatrist nor the well-equipped health technician quantify it.

Quality of life is far too intimate, too personal, and too individual for others to be involved in. It is the quintessence of the meaning of life in the human species. It is what makes our lives so varied and interesting, distinct from robots. It is far too glib to pass this factor off as "depression" in the ready parlance that is so fashionable nowadays.

Although nobody more than I welcomes the wonderful research being done into pain, and the saintly work being done by a burgeoning hospice movement, this will never provide the whole answer, the universal solution, as some claim. No matter how superb the quality of terminal care, a small number of patients will want to bring their lives to a faster close. A truly free society will, with certain safeguards, permit that.

One of the great benefits of having a legalized assistance-in-dying procedure in place is that it will give patients great comfort to know that—if their sufferings get completely out of hand—they could ask their doctors to help them to die. It will reduce the number of suicides that are carried out far too soon because the patient fears losing control, worried by the prospect of another stroke or lapsing into a state of unconsciousness or incompetence. It will reduce the number of "mercy killings," those horrific domestic events when one person slays the person they care for most in the world because they overwhelmingly feel that it is their human duty to take charge and relieve the other's suffering. Many of these tragedies result in the perpetrator also killing himself or herself, either out of a wish to die together after a good relationship, or guilt, or—more likely in my view—dread of society's retribution with a prison sentence.

None of these reasons is by itself a justifiable reason to request and receive doctor-assisted dying. A combination of a number of the reasons is.

Lawful assistance in dying is also needed to lift the grossly unfair burden it is currently placing on those brave doctors who are—in cases in which they feel medically and morally justified, even obligated—actively helping their patients to die. Nobody can collect statistics on this syndrome because, although it is a criminal act throughout America, there are only two convictions recorded both in New York State, one in 1996 and one in 1998. Still, nobody dares gather data on the action. It is the secret "crime" of the bedroom, except in the Netherlands, where it has governmental sanction and we are kept aware of the results through extensive research. I estimate that it happens many hundreds of time a year in America. Being asked to independently supply lethal drugs covertly, without the ability to consult other health professionals on the advisability of what they are about to do, is completely unfair to these doctors. Besides assisting suicide being a felony (except, since 1997, in Oregon), although, as I have said, there are only two recorded convictions, doctors also act secretly for fear of becoming the notorious first "test case." Dr. Kevorkian opens himself to criticism for many of his actions, but his openness, courage, and determination are unquestionable and unique in this field.

Physician-assisted suicide must essentially be a team effort. Doctors, nurses, mental health professionals, and social workers should all (if they choose) be involved in a decision whether or not to accelerate the death of a suffering, terminally ill person who requests it. The awesome nature of being party to the ending of a human life is too great for one person to shoulder.

Finally, there is the matter of patient empowerment.

Why do so many people—upwards of 100—go to Dr. Jack Kevorkian to die, and tens of thousands more buy my book *Final Exit* to study how to achieve this themselves if they need to? In perusing some of the lengthier written accounts of the lives of Dr. Kevorkian's clients, it becomes clear that these are "take-charge" persons, willing to avail themselves of the best that modern medicine can offer until it runs out of options and death is beckoning, but not willing to be sacrificed on the altar of the out-of-date ethics of the American Medical Association.

So the answer lies in the area of individual control and choice. The terminally ill person—or in the cases of many of Dr. Kevorkian's clients, the irreversibly ill person—when planning his or her own death at last feels in control of what is happening. It is the concluding action that he or she will do in life. He or she has thought it over and elected to go out this route. This is the way for him or her (but not for everybody) of dignity and of pride. For how we die is the ultimate civil liberty.

# FOREWORD 2

## Rita L. Marker

When I was invited to prepare a foreword for this book, I was asked to address the question, "Is there such a thing as rational suicide?" Put another way, the question could be: "Is there such a thing as a suicide that could be carried out after one has:

1. Reasonably considered current and probable future conditions
2. Considered the impact that such action would have on one's self and others
3. Drawn logical conclusions based on these considerations and
4. Made a reasoned decision?

To answer succinctly and unequivocally, "Yes."

But to leave my response at that one-word statement of the obvious would neglect the important underlying, and far more important, question, "Why are we concentrating on whether suicide itself can be a rational act?"

Are we saying that, because an act is rational, it is good? Further, are we saying because an act is rational, assistance in performing that act should be ethically and legally acceptable?

I believe that those who favor assisted suicide seek to elicit an affirmative response to these questions. Those who have openly acknowledged their support for legalized assisted suicide have made much of focusing on the determination of rationality and often use such determinations as a component in proposals for changes in law or policy.

Criteria for rational suicide have been proposed by a number of ethicists, pundits, and activists. Although there are variations among these proposals, there are basic requirements that are generally set forth. For example, in 1995 this book's editor published a list of conditions that, if met, would indicate that a decision to commit suicide is rational. The conditions were that the person's condition is unremittingly hopeless; the decision was freely made; and the person has engaged in a sound decision-making process that included consultation with others and consideration of the impact of the actions to be taken (Werth & Cobia, 1995, p. 238).

It is both interesting and important to point out that these conditions include a requirement that there be a "hopeless" condition. Similarly, among the criteria found in virtually all proposals for legislation that would permit assisted suicide, there is a reference to a "terminal" or "incurable" condition.

It is, in my opinion, intellectually dishonest to state, on the one hand, that an individual can make a rational decision to commit suicide and, on the other hand, to require that a person must be experiencing hopelessness before the decision could be considered rational. Consider the following two scenarios:

George, a 68-year-old widower, is a retired psychologist who has been diagnosed with a condition that is terminal, according to his doctor and one other physician. George has been told that his predicted life expectancy is about 6 months. George considers his situation over several weeks' time. He has lived a full life. Although he is mildly depressed, his judgment is not impaired. He has discussed his condition and the course of action he is considering with persons whose opinions he values highly. After careful deliberation, he comes to the conclusion that he will end his life.

Georgia, a 68-year-old widow, is a retired psychologist. For several years she has considered her life situation and has often expressed the belief that she wishes to die before reaching what she considers an unacceptable old age. She has lived a full life. Although she is mildly depressed, her judgment is not impaired. She has discussed her decision with persons whose opinions she values highly. After careful deliberation, she comes to the conclusion that she will end her life.

According to most proposed criteria for rational suicide, George's decision would be considered rational but Georgia's would not.

Why?

The sole difference is that George has been diagnosed (or misdiagnosed) with a terminal condition. The judgment that George is acting rationally and that Georgia is not has nothing to do with their logic or reasoning processes. Instead it is a value judgment that one decision is right and the other is wrong.

This points out two crucial points.

The first is that a decision may well be both rational and wrong. (Witness, for example, the obvious consideration, planning, consultation with others, and deliberation that were taken by Timothy McVeigh. Although he was acting rationally and with judgment that was not impaired, his decision and the action based upon it were wrong.)

The second point is that the "hopeless" or "terminal" requirement for rational suicide is based on political considerations—on what society will accept—rather than on what is a rational decision-making process.

Because the underlying purpose of focusing on rational suicide is aimed at building support for assisted suicide, these particular criteria are formulated to make the suicide appear good.

However, as discussed previously, rational and good are not necessarily synonymous. Furthermore, the contemporary debate that is taking place across the country is not about suicide itself. It is about one thing and one thing only: Should laws and public policy be changed to permit *assisted* suicide?

Thus, if what is rational can be automatically and erroneously declared to be good, then suicide itself can be framed as good, rather than tragic. It then follows that assisting in carrying out this good will be seen as acceptable.

Certainly it would be far easier to garner public support for assisting in the suicide of someone who has a terminal illness (George) than for someone who does not wish to face old age (Georgia).

I would hope that the readers of this book, as they weigh the contrasting positions of the authors, will keep in mind the difference between what is a rational decision for an individual and what is good public policy.

Additionally, I would ask that readers bear in mind that there are extremely important considerations that must be taken into account as the debate over assisted suicide continues.

As a starting point for that, I offer the following for consideration: in any advocacy for legalization of assisted suicide, proponents make assurances that assisted suicide would only be a last resort, after an individual has been offered all options and has had the opportunity to discuss options with his or her physician.

Although I believe that, with few exceptions, these assurances are sincere, I ask that readers remain skeptical of such assurances. The assurance that every person, prior to receiving assisted suicide, would be offered all options appears protective. Yet there is a vast difference between an *offer* of something and the *ability to accept that offer*.

This difference was acknowledged at a conference on assisted suicide guidelines conducted at the University of Southern California in November 1997. There, Steve Heilig, director of the Bay Area Network of Ethics Committees (BANEC), spoke about the guidelines that his group has formulated. As with any guidelines dealing with the subject of assisted suicide the BANEC guidelines require physicians to offer palliative care to patients before providing assisted suicide. However, when asked if there was also a requirement that patients be able to afford such care, Heilig said that it was not.

Thus the *offer* of all options is grossly misleading. It creates the illusion that all options would be available to people when, if fact, they would not. In practice, offering unaffordable palliative care to a patient who is in pain and who is poor would be akin to offering a Mercedes to a woman who has to walk 6 miles to work every morning. If assisted suicide were to become an acceptable medical option, the inability to afford needed palliative care could well put pressure on patients to decide that assisted suicide is their only affordable option.

It should be noted that economic and societal pressures play a huge role in decisions we make every day That there are such pressures does not negate our ability to make rational decisions. In fact, a recognition of these pressures and a grasp of the reality is an indication of rational decision making. It could, thus, be considered eminently rational for a person to decide that a lethal dose is the only affordable medical "treatment."

But does the fact that this could be viewed as rational mean that this is the type of public policy we wish to see implemented?

# PREFACE

This book could be viewed almost as if it were a debate between opposing sides of the rational suicide discussion; however, it is not an attempt to put an end to the controversy by allowing each side to present their respective cases and then determining who won the debate. Rather, the intent is to bring together spokespersons from several disciplines who can present their arguments for or against rational suicide as a viable concept and, consequently, a realistic option for some people and then leave the final decision about acceptance or rejection of the concept up to each reader.

Although this point is covered in more detail in Chapter 1, one caveat that must be made clear from the beginning is that this book is about rational suicide and *not* physician-assisted suicide. For now, suffice it to say that rational suicide is a broader concept that may or may not involve assistance by another in its implementation and, consequently, is the more fundamental concern. Furthermore, in the current context we are only examining the possibility of rational suicide for people who may be considered able to make decisions. Thus, we are excluding the unconscious and comatose, the mentally retarded, and young children. Neither individuals who are elderly nor persons with one or more mental illnesses are necessarily excluded from consideration (although chapter authors may choose to define rational suicide in such a way that either or both or these groups are not considered).

When I was doing the literature review for my first book on rational suicide, I found that my search for articles and books on the topic took me on a trip through the philosophical, religious, medical, mental health, and legal domains. During this process I thought to myself that such a complicated, expensive, and exhausting investigation would be a deterrent to cross-fertilization of ideas and hinder comprehensive examinations of the topic. As a result, I decided to compile a sourcebook of current pieces that could serve as a foundation for public and professional discussion and debate about rational suicide (and, indirectly, physician-aid-in-dying).

I then had to decide what disciplines to represent in this reference manual. Some were easy, such as law, medicine, mental health, philosophy, and religion. Upon reflection and the suggestions of others, some of these general fields were broken down and other areas were added so that a final list of 14 was accepted (I tried to include crisis interventionists, but neither Charlotte Anderson, Director of the Crisis Center Division of the American Association of Suicidology, nor I could find any contributors for this section). I also wanted to include the voices of two individuals who had had someone close to them suicide. Of course, there are several fields that could have been included but were not, such as anthropology and epidemiology as well as specific groups of professionals such as coroners and emergency medical technicians. In order to keep this book from becoming too unwieldy, inclusion of these other fields will have to wait for another time.

The next task in the development of this book was finding people who could and would contribute chapters from their disciplines' views. My goal was not to find authors who would represent the general membership of a particular field but, rather, individuals who had given the topic of rational suicide some thought and who could contribute original, thought-provoking pieces from either a supportive or nonsupportive point of view (although I recognize, of course, that for most people this is not an either–or issue but one in which there are many possibilities and "shades of gray" and this continuum of acceptance receives more attention throughout the book).

Because I had just performed an extensive examination of the work on rational suicide I was familiar with the authors who had contributed significantly to the literature, and it was these individuals I sought out. I was pleasantly surprised when my "cold calls" to such eminent writers were responded to warmly and supportively. I think the unique multidisciplinary "pro / con" nature of the book helped to entice a list of chapter authors that reads like a "Who's Who" of writers on rational suicide.

All authors were given very simple guidelines: keep the chapters under a certain number of pages, and write from the perspective of a person in your profession. Thus, for example, only the two philosophers were to include philosophic considerations, and the psychiatrists were to write from the point of view of psychiatric clinicians and not discuss the finer philosophical or religious points about the concept. The authors were not allowed to read the submission of the person who was writing from the opposite viewpoint within their section so the paired chapters will not read like a debate. In fact, depending on the discipline, you may find that some pairs of authors examine very different aspects of the concept and controversy, while others appear to have been dueling paragraph for paragraph.

You will also note that the authors may use very different definitions of rational suicide. However, as editor, I decided that this lack of consistency was preferable to forcing the authors to adopt a set of guidelines they were not comfortable using or with which they did not agree. In addition, allowing each author to either define the concept for herself or himself or to adopt a set of criteria from the literature allowed for the opportunity to see if there is a consensus among these authors about how rational suicide should be defined or, if there is not, whether a potentially acceptable set of criteria could be established that would be satisfactory to the majority of contributors.

It was with great anticipation that I entered into this endeavor, and it is with great pleasure that I present the final version to you. As I have mentioned, the purpose of this book is to advance the state of the debate on rational suicide and not to provide the unequivocal answer about its viability as a concept. If one or more of the chapters lead you to think about the idea differently, to understand the topic more completely, or even to reinforce your prereading convictions then the book will have been a success.

One final note: At the end of the book you should find a page that asks you some questions concerning your beliefs about rational suicide and the impact that reading this book has had on your opinions. I would ask that you make a copy of that page and mail it back to me. Your responses will serve as an unscientific survey about the concept and an evaluation of the book. Thank you in advance for your help.

# ACKNOWLEDGMENTS

I have learned an important lesson in putting this book together: being an editor is infinitely harder than being a sole author. If I had known what I was getting into when I began (about two-and-a-half years before I finished), this book never would have been started; however, thanks to the support, gentle (and at times not-so-gentle) prodding, and interest of several people I turned it in (only a year late). First and foremost, I must thank Bernadette Capelle for her infinite patience, wise counsel, and ability to function in the midst of ambiguity (as I failed to keep her informed about my "progress")—without her I never would have finished. I also want to express my appreciation to Elaine Pirrone, who encouraged me to do this book and polished up my initial proposal.

As much as I tried to work on this project on my own time and with my own resources, my employers deserve a great deal of the credit for the finished manuscript. I was on internship when I began searching for contributors, and the staff at Arizona State University's Counseling and Consultation were interested and supportive. Much of the actual work, including the phone calls, e-mail, draft printing, and so forth, was done while I was a mental health clinician at the University of Arkansas' Counseling and Psychological Services so I can definitely say that without the support of both my immediate supervisor, Jonathan Perry, and the Director of the Health Center, Mary Alice Serafini, this book never would have been completed. The interest of my fellow CAPS staff members (Diane, Pornthip, Connie, Reliford, and Greg—as well as Dot and Gerry) was helpful throughout the long process. I would be remiss if I did not also acknowledge my most recent employers and supervisors, Alan Tomkins and Steve Penrod of the Law/Psychology Program in the Department of Psychology at the University of Nebraska, Lincoln. Their hiring me and encouraging me to continue working on projects related to hastened death, such as this book, ensured that it was only a matter of time before the end was reached.

I must also thank all the contributors for their chapters. Several of them went through multiple drafts as I either made or asked for revisions in order to try to make the chapters as comparable as possible in length and format. Their willingness to contribute their insights and experiences to this book is what will make it such an important sourcebook. I should mention that both Sharon Valente and Peggy Battin were extremely helpful as I was brainstorming about the project and trying to line up contributors.

Finally, I need to mention the people who kept moving me onward, never letting me forget that I had to get the book finished—my family. I do not think I would be exaggerating if I said that every phone conversation with my parents and with my sister and her husband over the past year and a half included my having to explain why I was not done yet and come up with a timeframe for completion. And, last but certainly not least, thanks to my partner, Krista, for reinvigorating me with her interest, excitement, and commitment to the area of hastened death.

**1**

CHAPTER          James L. Werth, Jr.

# Introduction to the Issue of Rational Suicide

Rational suicide as a concept is hotly debated yet often misunderstood. Some view it as an oxymoron because they see suicide as an immoral act, a behavior performed by a mentally ill individual, or a tragedy for the survivors and society. Others consider it acceptable because they see suicide as an extension of a right to die, a behavior that may be the result of careful deliberation of options, or a potentially liberating act for those left behind. Furthermore, just as there are a range of views about suicide itself, and therefore rational suicide, there are many ways that rational suicide has been defined.

This chapter is intended to provide a foundation for the ones that follow by creating a context for the book. Toward this end, the first section differentiates rational suicide from aid-in-dying and, more specifically, physician-assisted suicide. The second section describes some of the presently articulated sets of criteria for rational suicide, in order to show the range of views on the matter. The chapter concludes with an overview of the book's contents.

## ☐ Rational Suicide Versus Aid-in-Dying

The concept of aid-in-dying (whether by physician or significant other) can mean many things, ranging from providing a person with the support, means, or opportunity needed to follow through with a decision to die up to and including administration of the death-dealing action (see, e.g., Annas, 1994). Similarly, it can relate to acts of omission, such as not performing cardiopulmonary resuscitation (or withholding other potentially lifesaving interventions), or acts of commission such as lethal injection (and I would add withdrawing life support). Complicating this discussion even further is the murky issue of intent, as in, "The extra morphine was meant to kill the pain, not the person."

However, regardless of what one means by aid-in-dying, the bottom line is that a decision must have been made to allow, enable, or assist the person to die based on the determination that the person's choice to die is rational (or "reasonable") and therefore legitimate. In other words, it must be the case that before someone (physician, family member, significant other, friend) agrees to help another person die, the helper must believe that the asker's decision is acceptable, justifiable, reasonable, and rational. And just as surely, regardless of who delivers the death-dealing action, the person's decision to die is equivalent to suicide (in that suicide is killing oneself; see Maltsberger, 1994). Clearly, if the person takes action to hasten her or his own death, then that is suicide. However, it could also be considered suicide if a person who is unable, for whatever reason, to take direct action herself or himself asks another to do so instead. This is because the asker has indicated that she or he wants to die, is unable to perform the final act herself or himself, and, *but for* the impediment, would kill herself or himself without needing the assistance of another. At this point it should be noted that some commentators (e.g., Werth & Gordon, 1998) have moved away from the terms *rational suicide* and the associated *assisted suicide* to use other terms such as *hastened death* or *aid-in-dying* to more clearly differentiate what they believe to be two distinct acts (see also, American Psychological Association, 1997). However, the term *rational suicide* is used throughout this book for reasons outlined in this chapter.

Thus, even though these forms of aid-in-dying could be viewed as suicide, making the issue of rational suicide of primary importance, much of the current discussion and debate around the aid-in-dying arena has centered on what has variously been called *physician-assisted suicide, physician aid-in-dying,* or *voluntary euthanasia* (active and passive). This focus on the role of the healthcare provider in the life and death decisions of individuals is natural because the actions of magnetic personalities (e.g., Jack Kevorkian, Timothy Quill), high-profile court decisions (e.g., in Washington and New York and subsequently the U.S. and Florida Supreme Courts), and grassroots public initiatives (e.g., in Oregon and Michigan) have involved, in one way or another, physicians helping (either passively or actively) people die. However, most of the discussion about physician aid-in-dying has failed to address the more fundamental issue of whether or not people can make a rational decision to die (regardless of whether the decision involves taking their own lives or asking for the assistance of another).

This then leads to the heart of the relationship between physician aid-in-dying and rational suicide: the answer to the question of what the proper role of the physician is when a person wants to die does not address the more basic question of whether suicide (or, alternatively, a *decision to hasten death*) can ever be rational. As a result, before one can come to a determination (through the courts, legislatures, or public initiatives) about the appropriateness of physician aid-in-dying one should first determine whether or not a person can make a rational decision to die. The conclusion that a person can rationally determine that hastening death is her or his best option does not answer the question of whether or not such a person should receive aid-in-dying but it lays the necessary foundation to allow for consideration of this possibility and the proper role of the physician; however, the controversy around aid-in-dying (by physician or another person) becomes moot if it is decided that a person cannot make a rational decision to suicide. In short, all assisted deaths (whether or not they are called suicides) should be rational, but not all rational deaths (i.e., rational suicides) are necessarily assisted.

# ☐  Criteria for Rational Suicide

If it is the case that a person's decision to die must be deemed rational before the person herself or himself or another individual can be allowed to follow through with actions that may bring about death, then there must be some acceptable way of assessing the rationality of the decision. However, just as there are differences of opinion about whether or not suicide can ever be rational, there is a similar lack of consensus about what would constitute a rational suicide. Obviously the presence of several different definitions, or sets of criteria, for rational suicide complicates and hinders discussion.

It should be stressed that even people who do not believe there can be rational suicides could still find an acceptable set of criteria for rational suicide but then argue that a person could not, for one reason or another, meet the specified criteria (see, e.g., Siegel, 1986). So, for example, a mental health worker could say that a capacity to form reasoned decisions (legally called *competence*) is a requirement but then argue that a person who is suicidal does not or even cannot have this capacity; or an advocate for older adults or persons with disabilities might say that the choice must be made without coercion from others but point out that societal prejudices preclude free choice by disenfranchised groups.

Therefore, a common set of criteria is important for the discussion of rational suicide not only for those promoting the idea that a decision to hasten death can be rational but also for those who argue that rational suicide is impossible, because without common ground the debate is disjointed and unproductive. To take but one obvious example, the groups for which rational suicide would be considered a viable alternative will have an impact on how much support and opposition (and from where this support and opposition comes) a given set of criteria will have. Thus, if one examines the basic criterion of what conditions would allow for suicide to be seen as a rational alternative to continued life, one sees a range from nothing to life itself. That is, at one extreme are those who say that suicide can never be rational and at the other are those who believe that everyone has a right to suicide. Obviously, the more lenient the conditions for suicide, the more opposition there is to the acceptance of those particular potential criteria, however, without an agreement on which groups are being discussed the different sides will not be able to meaningfully dialogue.

In order to illustrate the different definitions or sets of criteria that have been offered, some are delineated here. Although a thorough review of the literature is beyond the scope of this chapter, a few of the more commonly referenced, more thorough, and more recent sets of criteria are outlined subsequently below (see chapter 5 of Werth [1996b] for more references).

Motto (1972, p. 184) succinctly stated that for a person to be able to "exercise his [or her] right to suicide" he or she must meet these two criteria: "(a) the act must be based on a realistic assessment of his [or her] life situation, and (b) the degree of ambivalence regarding the act must be minimal." In regard to the first, he said that "one limitation I would put on his [or her] right to suicide would be that his [or her] assessment of his [or her] life situation be realistic as *I* see it" (p. 185, emphasis original). He then said that for a suicide to be rational, the person must have decided that suicide is the best option given the aforementioned assessment and given her or his personal "philosophy." About the second criterion, Motto said that if a person presents herself or himself as a client then Motto assumes that the person is ambivalent about the wish to die and therefore intercedes. In later works Motto (e.g., 1994) expanded upon these ideas by mentioning the need to examine the impact on significant others and their involvement in the decision-making process, congruence with spiritual and other values, exploration of alternatives, and the need to rule out the possibility of psychological or social origins of the suicidality.

Battin (1995) proposed that in order for a suicide to be considered rational a person must meet all or most of five criteria. First, the person should have the "ability to reason," which means that the person does not make errors in logic and that she or he can appreciate the consequences of the decision to suicide. Second, for the decision to be rational it must be based upon a "realistic world view"—a view that is consistent with the views of the surrounding culture. Next, the person needs to have adequate (and correct) information. On this point Battin specifically mentions that depression can inhibit information processing, but she also adds that a depressed person is not necessarily irrational. The fourth criterion is that the suicidal act should allow for the "avoidance of [possible] harm" (which would include psychological and physical pain and suffering). Finally, in order for a suicide to be rational, the act should be in "accordance with [the person's] fundamental interests," which could be seen as being related to the person's underlying values.

Diekstra (1986, pp. 14–15) said that for a decision to suicide to be rational it must be made in the presence of "unbearable physical and / or emotional pain" with no hope of improvement, the person should have made the decision of her or his own "free-will," and the desire to die should be "enduring." In addition, the person must not be "mentally disturbed" and the death should not cause "unnecessary or preventable harm" to others (he also listed three other criteria related to helping a person suicide that are beyond the scope of this book).

Even though she was arguing against the possibility of rational suicide, Siegel (1986) articulated one of the more frequently cited definitions. She stated that,

> The defining characteristics of a rational suicide are: (1) the individual possesses a realistic assessment of his [or her] situation, (2) the mental processes leading to his [or her] decision to commit suicide are unimpaired by psychological illness or severe emotional distress, and (3) the motivational basis of his [or her] decision would be understandable to the majority of uninvolved observers from his [or her] community or social group. (p. 407)

Humphry, one of the founders of the Hemlock Society USA, listed the "ethical parameters for autoeuthanasia" (i.e., rational suicide), (Humphry, 1987, p. 336). First, the person should be a "mature adult" who has made a "considered decision," as evidenced by actions such as belonging to a right to die organization or having a living will, and has made a will. The decision to suicide should be based on the presence of "advanced terminal illness" that is causing the person to suffer or a "grave physical handicap" that leads to a quality of life unacceptable to the person; however, the suicidal act should not occur immediately upon finding out about the condition and without seeking appropriate medical help. Further, the treating physician should be informed and consideration given to her or his reaction. Finally, the person should not involve others in the act and should leave a note explaining why suicide was chosen as the best option.

Dunshee (1994), who was President of the Board of Directors of the then-Washington-based organization called Compassion in Dying, outlined the guidelines that a person must meet and abide by if she or he is to be eligible for assistance by this agency. The person must be of "sound mind" (if there is any doubt the person is referred to a mental health professional) and be terminally ill (two physicians expect death reasonably soon, usually within 6 months) with a condition that causes suffering that has created an unacceptably low quality of life. The individual must have sought out alternatives to suicide, especially as these alternatives relate to her or his belief systems, prior to making three requests for assistance that are separated in time. Finally, the person's significant others must have accepted the individual's decision to suicide.

In a bold and unprecedented move, the National Association of Social Workers (NASW, 1994) developed a policy statement on "Client Self-Determination in End-of-Life Decisions" that stated that a social worker could be present at an "assisted suicide" if such a role fits within her or his value system. Although the statement did not explicitly define when a social worker could decide not to interfere with a suicidal act, some criteria are implicit within the document. The person should have a "terminal and irreversible condition, a progressive chronic illness, or chronic intractable pain" (p. 59). Further, "self-determination assumes that the client is mentally competent" (p. 58). Following this assessment, "competent individuals should have the opportunity to make their own choices but only after being informed of all options and consequences" (p. 60). Therefore, the policy stated that

> the appropriate role for social workers is to help [clients] express their thoughts and feelings, to facilitate exploration of alternatives, to provide information to make an informed choice, and to deal with grief and loss issues. . . . [They] should explore and help ameliorate any factors such as pain, depression, a need for medical treatment, and so forth. . . . [They] should act as liaisons with other health care professionals and help the [client] and family communicate concerns and attitudes to the health care team . . . [They] should encourage the involvement of significant others, family, and friends in these decisions. (p. 60)

Instead of relying solely on intuition or clinical experience as others have done, Werth (1996b; Werth & Cobia, 1995) came up with a set of criteria for rational suicide based on two national surveys of psychologists in which participants were asked to provide their definitions of the concept. The written responses were analyzed and a comprehensive set of criteria for rational suicide was formulated that could be used by mental health professionals to determine if a client who is suicidal has made a rational decision to die. Werth (p. 62) stated that a decision to suicide could be viewed as rational provided the following conditions were met:

1. The person considering suicide has an unremitting "hopeless" condition. "Hopeless" conditions include, but are not necessarily limited to, terminal illnesses, severe physical or psychological pain, physically or mentally debilitating or deteriorating conditions, or a quality of life no longer acceptable to the individual.
2. The person makes the decision as a free choice (i.e., is not pressured by others to choose suicide).
3. The person has engaged in a sound decision-making process. This process should include the following:
   a. Consultation with a mental health professional who can make an assessment of mental competence (which would include the absence of treatable major depression);
   b. Nonimpulsive consideration of all alternatives;
   c. Consideration of the congruence of the act with one's personal values;
   d. Consideration of the impact on significant others;
   e. Consultation with objective others (e.g., medical and religious professionals) and with significant others.

It is noteworthy that this list, generated by reviewing the responses of over 400 participants, appears to incorporate most of the points raised by the authors of the other lists of criteria outlined previously in this chapter.

In a follow-up study (reported in Werth, 1996b) Werth found that the majority of respondents (nearly 80%) from a national survey of members of the American Association of Suicidology, members of state mental health ethics committees, and members of the American Psychological Association's Division of Psychology and the Law stated that this list was acceptable as stated or with only minor revisions. The majority of the respondents also stated that a mental health professional who followed these guidelines would not be breaking ethical (85%) or legal (50%) standards of care and, even if the respondent believed a case could be made against the professional, only one person proposed suspension of the person's license; the others mentioned much more mild sanctions such as education or additional supervision. These results suggest that Werth's criteria may provide an acceptable means of assessing the rationality of a decision to suicide. However, the list still needs more research and application by other researchers and practitioners in order to refine and define the individual items further (see Werth & Gordon, 1998, for an expanded set of considerations).

There have been numerous other proposals for criteria, such as in the Oregon Death with Dignity Act (Oregon Right to Die, 1994), the Harvard Model Act (Baron et al., 1996), and the guidelines set forth by the Bay Area Network of Ethics Committees (Heilig, Brody, Marcus, Shavelson, & Sussman, 1997). These roughly parallel the suggestions set forth here.

## ☐   The Role of this Book in the Rational Suicide Debate

The lists of criteria for rational suicide provided in the previous section illustrate that although there may be some agreement on certain points, there currently is not a definitive set of criteria that can serve as a foundation for discussion and debate. One of the secondary purposes of this book is to try to contribute such a set of criteria by reviewing how the chapter authors choose to define the concept within their works. However, the primary purpose of this book is to provide the general and academic public with a sourcebook for dialogue on the topic of rational suicide (and, as noted previously, tangentially the aid-in-dying debate). Toward this end the book is divided into three main parts beginning after this chapter and ending with a summary chapter. In order to not appear biased one way or the other, the sections are divided into paired chapters, and within each pair the chapters appear in alphabetical order (for example, the first section has the "pro" philosopher chapter written by Battin followed by the "con" philosopher chapter written by Callahan; the next pair are the chapters on religion and in this set the "con" chapter by Barry appears first followed by the "pro" chapter authored by Larue; and so forth).

### Relevant Background Issues

There are several theoretical areas that must be discussed to provide a foundation and a context for the more personal accounts that follow. The four fields in this part of the book were selected because of their current and historical relevance to the topic of rational suicide and their concern with the potential impact of an acceptance of the concept.

Philosophers have been debating the rationality of suicide since the times of the ancient Egyptians, Greeks, and Romans. In the present forum, Margaret P. Battin presents her well-known view that suicide can be rational and provides responses to arguments against accepting the concept; Daniel Callahan contends that rational suicide is a philosophically unsound concept for several reasons and offers his unique interpretation of the use of historical arguments for accepting suicide in some cases.

Like philosophy, religion has been at the center of the debate about the rationality of suicide since the beginning and many of the arguments against the idea are based on religious grounds. Robert Barry states that faulty assumptions are a crucial part of the misunderstandings and discussion, and he says that once these misinterpretations are corrected the basis for support of rational suicide disappears. Gerald Larue contends that the religious scriptures do not proscribe suicide, and he adds that many religious arguments against the possibility of rational are based on false assumptions.

Steven Stack, a research sociologist, presents data that he says show that an acceptance of rational suicide is dangerous and could have extremely negative repercussions for our society. In contrast, Samuel Wallace, who has studied the impact of suicide on the significant others of the person who died, argues that rational suicide in and of itself is not hazardous, only a liberalized interpretation of the idea is problematic.

The next pair of chapters was written by attorneys, each of whom has been active with organizations associated with their respective viewpoints. Wesley Smith asserts that the current state of the law and the proper role of the law argue against rational suicide. From the other side, Kathryn Tucker argues that rational suicide is an acceptable act according to her interpretations of the Constitution and relevant case law. At this point it is important to note that these chapters (and all the pro and con chapters of the book) were written prior to the Supreme Court decisions on the two "physician-assisted suicide" cases that came before it, and which were announced in late June 1997 (*Vacco v. Quill* and *Washington v. Glucksberg*) This fact does not invalidate the legal comments made, but this context must be kept in mind when reading.

## Service Providers

This major section includes paired pro and con chapters written from the points of view of various professionals who serve on the front lines with individuals who are suicidal. Depending on the styles of the respective authors, the chapters include a mix of personal experiences, reviews of the literature, and results of research. However, the authors were instructed to write from within their discipline and, as much as possible, not to stray into other areas.

Counselors in the field of death and dying are inevitably faced with people who are near the end of their lives and do not want to die in a particular manner. Lois Chapman Dick speaks from her experience in working with hundreds people who have died and contends that suicide is not necessarily a bad thing for the person who is dying nor for the person's significant others. In contrast, Richard Ellis contends that most counselors do not have the basic background necessary to be involved in these types of discussions and determinations, and he also dismantles the criteria for rational suicide from his perspective as a counselor.

Nursing professor Angela Albright contends that with adequate comfort care, pain medication, and personal contact people do not need to suffer physical pain or degradation and therefore do not need to suicide. Meanwhile, Margaret Campbell, an active-duty hospital nurse, discusses her experiences based on working with individuals who are in pain and otherwise suffering, and also how witnessing these events impacted her beliefs about the possibility that suicide can be rational.

Similarly, the pair of physicians write from their personal experiences but come to different conclusions. Robin Bernhoft discusses his experiences working with dying and suffering individuals but contends that with adequate pain control and care, people do not need to suffer nor lose their dignity. Richard MacDonald likewise speaks of his attempts to alleviate the pain and suffering of his patients through many different techniques, medications, and treatments but, at times, to no avail.

Perhaps more than any other profession, psychiatrists are faced with the reality of suicide. In fact, research has shown that about half of all psychiatrists will have a client die by suicide (Chemtob, Bauer, Hamada, Pelowski, & Muraoka, 1989). Mark Goldblatt uses arguments based both on the role of the unconscious in decision making and on the possibility of biological determinants of behavior to contend that rational suicide is not possible because the factors influencing the decision making are not in conscious awareness. Jerome Motto summarizes 24 points he has gleaned from the literature and decides that rational suicide is a reality.

Although not at as high a risk of having a client suicide as psychiatrists, psychologists also work with clients who are suicidal and therefore face the possibility of working with clients who may have made rational decisions to die (Chemtob et al., 1989). In fact, Werth (1996b) reported that 20% of the respondents in one of his national surveys reported having at least one client who had rationally suicided. Steven Jamison is one such psychologist, and he says that people can rationally suicide, but he also states that there are a number of psychological variables that must be taken into account during the decision making process. Antoon Leenaars discusses several events in the history of psychology to argue that the term "rational" is inappropriate to use in conjunction with suicide.

The con author of the pair of chapters by social workers, Jay Callahan, has been a leading voice against the National Association of Social Workers' policy on "Client Self-determination in End-of-Life Decisions;" the pro author, Deborah Cummings, was instrumental in its development. They present their very different views about social workers' roles in end-of-life decisions, the viability of rational suicide, and the NASW statement.

One group of professionals, death educators, has a special awareness of rational suicide and special responsibility for teaching future professionals about the concept. David Meagher states that the role of death education is to prepare people to deal better with all aspects of death and all alternatives at the end-of-life. Although not disagreeing with this general idea, Judith Stillion says that because of pressure by others to choose suicide and the impact on significant others, suicide is not the best option for a person.

## Special Populations

In discussions of rational suicide attention often is given to the potential impact on vulnerable populations such as the elderly and persons with disabilities. Because of their relevance to the discussion at hand, experts in the areas of disability and rehabilitation and gerontology were invited to contribute their perspectives based on their study of, and experience with, these populations. A third special group, survivors of suicide, which is conspicuously absent from most written discussion of the topics of suicide and rational suicide, was added because of their obvious personal interest in the debate about rational suicide.

The two advocates for persons with disabilities address the potential impact of prejudice and discrimination (i.e., "ableism") on the end-of-life decisions of persons with disabilities. Specifically, Carol Gill argues that because of the very pervasive, negative stereotypes about people with disabilities, there is tremendous societal pressure and coercion for such an individual to "choose" an apparently rational suicide that is actually not as rational as it may initially appear. On the other hand, Karen Hwang says that rational suicide is a possibility for individuals with disabilities just as it is for those without disabilities.

Both of the authors of the pair of chapters on gerontology have written books about suicide and the elderly or ageism and both use their extensive knowledge and experience of older adults to argue for or against rational suicide. John McIntosh states that the issues prompting older adults to suicide can, for the most part, be ameliorated by attending to issues such as loneliness and depression. In contrast, Erdman Palmore argues, that just as ageism can be used as an argument against the idea of rational suicide, it can also be ageist to not allow for older people the possibility of rationally suiciding.

Research has shown that survivors of suicide often have especially difficult grief reactions to the death. The last two authors write about their views of the possibility of rational suicide, given their experience with a suicide by someone close to them. Patti Rosen's daughter was dying of cancer when she asked Patti to help her die; now, several years later, Patti talks about the decision-making process her daughter went through and also shares her own experiences before and after the death. Adina Wrobleski vehemently opposes the idea that a suicide can be rational based on her personal experience, her interactions with hundreds of survivors, and the possibility of depression interfering with any rational decision making by the suicidal person.

## ☐ Conclusion

Death and dying have been taken out of the dark, back wards of hospitals and thrust into the public eye. A convergence of events and factors have brought issues previously ignored and denied by most people into the limelight. With the advent of medical technology capable of keeping people alive longer than ever, even past the point at which they may regain consciousness, there has been an increasing percentage of the general public that has expressed concerns about the process of their dying, the method of their death, and the amount of control they will have over decisions relevant to their lives and deaths.

Although physician aid-in-dying has garnered the majority of the attention in the discussions about the possibility of "death with dignity," in actuality the more fundamental concern is rational suicide. By presenting pro and con points of view from individuals representing several fields, this book provides a comprehensive, contemporary sourcebook for discussion about the topic. In the end, however, the final decision will be made by each individual, for as Maris (1983, p. 224) said, "In the last analysis you will have to decide whether or not suicide is ever rational and, if so, in what circumstances, for whom, and so on. How could it be otherwise?"

Margaret P. Battin

# Can Suicide Be Rational? Yes, Sometimes

To the extent that any of our decisions are rational, decisions about suicide can be rational. Of course, this does not mean that all such decisions are rational or even that most of them are, and indeed many people who suffer suicidal impulses are profoundly disordered, irrational, and tragically disrupted in their thinking. But some choices for suicide can be rational under the same criteria we would use to assess any other act or choice.

Here are five criteria that I think are crucial in determining which suicides may be rational and which are not. I use the term *rational* in two senses, adverbial and substantive; these criteria attempt to capture both. The first three criteria—*ability to reason, realistic world view*, and *adequacy of information*—attempt to answer the question of whether suicide can be chosen in a "rational," unimpaired way, and the other two—*avoidance of harm* and *accordance with fundamental interests*—explore whether suicide can ever be a "rational" thing to do.

## ☐ Criteria for Rational Suicide

### Ability to Reason

For a person to be able to reason implies at least two distinct things: that in moving from the premises from which she begins to the conclusion she reaches, she maintains good logical form (that is, does not make mistakes in logic), and that she can foresee the consequences of the positions she adopted or the actions she plans to undertake (that is, she knows what will probably happen because of what she is doing).

This chapter is loosely based on Chapter 4 of my *Ethical Issues in Suicide*, first published in 1982 and then again in 1995, and again in 1996 under the title *The Death Debate: Ethical Issues in Suicide*, by Prentice-Hall, Inc.

Many persons who attempt or commit suicide do make mistakes in logic. Suicidal thinking often involves both syntactic and semantic fallacies, the most characteristic of which is a confusion between oneself as experienced by oneself and oneself as experienced by others (Shneidman & Farberow, 1957). For example, in thinking that because people who kill themselves get attention, a person who considers suicide in order to get attention is making a simple logical error: the person who now craves attention will not be present to experience it. It may of course be very difficult to foresee with full accuracy the impact of one's suicide on others, but there is one consequence of suicide that can be foreseen with certainty: the individual who commits suicide will be dead.

But this is precisely what a great many people who commit suicide do not accurately foresee; they tend to assume that even after death, they will continue to have experiences, continue to interact with other persons, and continue to play some causal role in the world. This is a frequent error in reasoning by people who commit suicide, including psychotics and children. It is particularly characteristic of so-called dyadic suicide (Shneidman, 1968), where the intention of the individual is to injure, manipulate, insult, or impress someone else, to "get even" with them. It may also be characteristic of many "surcease" suicides, through which a person seeks peace, relief, freedom from pain, and so on: death may be seen as alluring, inviting, liberating, and deep; these visions too assume that the person who commits suicide will nevertheless experience such states. But whether the suicide's aim is the dyadic "I'll make you love me after all" or "I'll make you see how much you need me," or the surcease "I'll get relief at last," these intentions are likely to involve the same basic error in reasoning: assuming that the self who is now contemplating suicide will still be the subject of experiences after the person is dead.

However, although many suicides involve these errors of reasoning, not all do. A person may in fact succeed in "getting even" with someone else even if she no longer exists to appreciate that fact. Similarly, a person seeking surcease may put an end to his pain without experiencing relief from it. For those individuals whose religious or metaphysical beliefs include the possibility of a sentient afterlife, the assumption that suicide results in nonexistence may be challenged, and it is not irrational (although it might be false) to assume that one will have continuing experience or relationships after suicide. Furthermore, some individuals place little or no value on themselves as subjects of experiences or participants in relationships but place great importance on the ways in which they are viewed by others: reputation and honor may be paramount to these individuals, while continuing experience is not. These individuals too rarely confuse the notion that they will be viewed in a certain way after death with the erroneous notion that they will be able to observe or experience this view; such suicides are not irrational in this respect.

It is very easy to grant that some, perhaps even most, suicidal individuals do reason in fallacious ways—the juvenile and psychotic suicides who do not understand that they will be dead, the romantic adults who glamorize death, the get-even revenge seekers who assume that they themselves will continue to exert influence on people who survive them. But although we may readily grant this point, this is not to establish that all persons who commit suicide commit these logical errors. In the absence of any compelling evidence to the contrary, the possibility remains open that some persons do choose suicide in preference to continuing life on the basis of reasoning that is by all usual standards adequate.

Not only are not all suicides irrational on grounds of inadequate ability to reason, but it is in principle possible to discover before a person's suicide whether it is or is not rational in this respect. The trained counselor will be able to elicit and explore a person's reasoning processes (Battin, 1994), but so will family, friends, and associates—if, indeed, they discover that person's plans for suicide in advance. Among the many reasons for not ignoring a person's hints that she is planning to kill herself is the fact that responding to such hints, and discussing a person's plans in advance, in detail, offers one of the best opportunities for exploring whether it is rationally planned on the basis of reasoning that is logically adequate. This still does not mean that such a suicide is the rational thing to do, but adequate reasoning must be part of the picture.

## Realistic World View

A rational decision must also be based upon a realistic view of the world. Many types of suicide are clearly highly irrational in this respect. Most extreme is that of the person with schizophrenia, based on bizarre beliefs about the nature of the world. Yet there are many less severe sorts of irrational reasoning about the world that influence choices about suicide. For example, an individual may have a relatively realistic picture of the world as a whole but fail to have a realistic conception of his own life situation, including his identity, position in the world, and on his particular talents, abilities, and disabilities. Some similar but milder distortions of a realistic worldview are quite common: extremely low self-esteem and the overly inflated ego. As these conditions become increasingly pronounced it is increasingly appropriate to say that decisions made on such bases are irrational.

The notion that rational suicide requires a realistic world view also raises difficulties concerning suicides based on strong religious convictions. To grant that a religious person is "rational," we usually insist only that her beliefs be consonant with her surrounding religious culture, and we do not consider whether the world view of the religious culture as a whole is realistic or not. If a religious person's beliefs include the existence of an afterlife involving continuing sensation, intellect, and heightened spiritual experience, she is not therefore irrational; if on her suicide is undertaken with this afterlife in mind, we cannot therefore label it irrational per se. To be sure, some religious traditions hold that such an afterlife is precluded for those who commit suicide and that such persons can expect the highly negative experience of hell instead, but this is only to argue that suicide is imprudent, not irrational. Similarly, for those whose world view is distorted by low self-esteem or overly inflated ego, those distortions must be fairly pronounced before they will be labeled irrational in ordinary circumstances; so too with respect to suicide. We must assume that some suicides—particularly those involving a coolly realistic view of the world that finds it wanting, in which a person makes a careful assessment of his situation and finds it worse than death, whatever that involves—meet this criterion of realistic world view.

## Adequacy of Information

A rational action is not only performed in accordance with acceptable logical principles and based on a realistic world view, but also is based on adequate information, both about present circumstances and about the future. Many suicides fail to meet this criterion. Inadequate information about present circumstances may involve simple ignorance of some important fact—that help is on the way, that a reprieve has been granted, or that a drug to reverse one's otherwise fatal illness has just been discovered—or it may involve distortion of all information about one's circumstances and environment, present and future (Motto, 1972). Of course, choices cannot count as irrational if they are made in the absence of important relevant information that one has no way of knowing, although they may certainly be irrational if one makes no attempt to obtain information that would be rational to get in the situation or if the information is distorted once it is obtained.

Depression is a factor in a large range of cases involving inadequate information (Brandt, 1975). Some choices are irrational because the person does not adequately process information from outside sources; but information can also be inadequate due to internal psychological factors. A depressed person's view of the range of possibilities for alternative actions may be severely restricted, and the rationality of his judgment thus seriously affected. He sees only the negative possibilities; the positive ones are closed to view. Because of its characteristic effects on the ways in which we store, process, and utilize information, and because of the way in which it affects our preferences, depression may seriously interfere with the rationality of a decision—about suicide or about anything else.

It may seem that if depression is present in all or nearly all suicides, then all or nearly all suicides are irrational. However, not all suicides associated with depression are irrational, even if many or most are. After all, there are some situations in which the narrow view produced by depression cannot be greatly broadened, at least within a realistic world view: the future may in fact be limited and bad, and depression only confirms what a realistic view already shows. Particularly if depression is reactive, a response to negative circumstances and serious losses, it may not be possible to change the circumstances or reverse the losses, and it is not irrational to think things are bad or that the future is likely to be bad also. Of course, a currently depressed person may "adjust" to the situation in the future, but that still does not make her choices, based on current realistic reactions to bad circumstances, irrational. She recognizes that the future will be bad, and makes a choice—a value-based choice—about whether she is willing to undergo the process of coming to adapt to it.

Inadequacy of information about the future also may affect suicide decisions even if depression is not involved. Suicide is often undertaken to avoid future evils: physical or mental suffering, torture, falls from honor, the discovery of misdeeds, bankruptcy, old age, or even boredom. But in the real world it is difficult to be certain exactly what will occur, and one can never be entirely sure that a particular event will happen. Effective suicide means certain death, whereas torture, bankruptcy, or boredom are, at worst, only likely evils. History is full of tales of narrowly missed cataclysms, impossible rescues, stays of execution, and miraculous cures of hopeless disease.

This argument is most pressing in medicine. Few physicians would agree that any particular case is absolutely hopeless; although many conditions are clearly terminal, there are also cases in which patients unpredictably and inexplicably recover. Thus it often is argued that if a feared event, such as death due to cancer, may not occur after all or may not occur very soon, suicide to avoid it would be irrational: completed suicide is certain death, whereas the death due to cancer is only highly likely.

But this does not entail that suicide to avoid future evils that have not yet occurred is irrational in general. Although there may be some chance that a feared and highly likely event will not occur after all, it is not therefore rational to act in accord with such a hope; it is rational to bank on a likely event, not a highly unlikely one. It is true that the terminal patient may survive an extended period of pain and recover entirely, but it is irrational to count on this unless there is some secondary gain from doing so, because the very strong chance is that this will not happen.

It is important to see clearly the consequences of the faulty argument that suicide to avoid future evils is always irrational. If the claim that negative future circumstances are never fully certain is used as an argument against suicide, it may condemn the person to highly likely suffering by encouraging an irrational hope (Flew, 1969). Although pain and suffering are by no means inevitable in terminal illness and can often be avoided with adequate palliative care, there still may be situations in which suffering cannot be avoided. Users of the argument that "there's always hope" as a reason against suicide, although beginning from a premise that is technically true, must accept responsibility for the suffering they cause by fostering unrealistic hopes, as well as credit for the good fortune of those whose remote hopes come true. After all, for every individual who survives to a complete and full life because she was persuaded by the claim "there's always hope" to forego a suicide that she rationally chose when her situation seemed hopeless, many others die in miserable conditions they wished to avoid: the hope did not materialize. Suicide to avoid likely future evils is not irrational as a calculation of future interests; if the likely loss is great enough, to bet against such evils would be folly, to act to avoid them the rational move.

This of course applies only to future evils whose likelihood we can predict with a strong degree of assurance. In fact, many fears, including many medical fears, are based only on the flimsiest evidence, and in these cases suicide to avoid the feared situation would indeed be irrational. But if the future evil is so calamitous that no chance of other positive experience outweighs the risk of suffering it, suicide to avoid it may be rational even if its probability is far from certain: the end stages of some diseases, involving both severe physical suffering and mental symptoms that cannot be effectively treated, may be like this. In such cases, the timing of a suicide can be crucial in whether it counts as rational: early suicides might not be rational, if the future course is less certain and a period of important positive experience possible before the end stage occurs; a later suicide, given more probable information about the final deteriorative stages and a realistic assessment of prospects for pain and symptom control, could well be a rational choice.

Closely related is the issue of whether a person can foresee how he will react to predictable future events (Brandt, 1975). Reactions to past although similar evils may provide some basis for predicting one's own reactions to future evils, although of course your predictions may be warped by depression or strong emotional states, and it still is hard to tell how you will actually react to things you now fear; some future evils turn out to be "not so bad" after all. Just the same, this fact does not make avoidance of future evils theoretically mistaken, any more than it makes it a problem to set positive goals: after all, you cannot always be sure how you will respond to those future states either. What the prospective rational suicide must calculate is just how damaging it will be if things do turn out as he fears and his reaction to them is as negative as he expected, and then consider whether this risk is offset by the possibility of other, better outcomes.

Finally, there is a general sense in which no suicide decision can be adequately informed, because, as philosophers from Epicurus on have pointed out, we can never have knowledge of what death actually is: death is a leap into the "wholly unknown" (Devine, 1979; Rosenbaum, 1986). To claim that suicide is a leap into the wholly unknown is, strictly speaking, correct, except that it seems to suppose that suicide is a leap into *something*—the wholly unknown. Yet each individual will have his or her firm convictions of what is to come after death; just as we do not consider beliefs that are consonant with the beliefs of the individual's cultural group irrational, so we do not count as irrational a choice made with respect to alternatives about which an individual, in concert with her religious group, believes herself fully informed. The general sense in which we are inadequately informed about the nature of death is part of the sense in which we are inadequately informed about the metaphysical character of the universe and about which religious claims, if any, are true. This does not show the suicidal act to be any more inadequately informed, or any less rational, than any of our other important moral choices.

This consideration is particularly important in medical settings in which suicide or assisted suicide is the issue. In trying to develop criteria for whether assisted suicide might be rational in response to a particular terminal illness, at a certain stage of terminal deterioration, or in a certain degree of pain, it is sometimes easy to forget that patients are all different and come with differing background religious and metaphysical beliefs. The rationality or irrationality of their choices regarding suicide is a function not only of whether or not they have adequate information about such things as the nature and probable courses of their diseases or their likely reactions to deprivations and losses, but also of these often widely differing background conceptions of the universe.

## Avoidance of Harm

To be rational, we also assume, an action must accord with the individual's own interests in the protection of his person and body from harm. Self-mutilating people are irrational because they cause themselves harm; suicides may strike us in the same way, because we assume that it is in one's own prudential interests to remain alive. Both physical and psychological harm are crucially important to avoid, but the harms that it is in general rational to avoid can also include a far wider range of social, familial, financial, and other harms.

However, argued Epicurus, death cannot be a harm to the individual who is dead (Martin, 1980). The process of dying painfully or of knowing you are going to die can, of course, constitute a harm, and death can involve harms to one's projects, property, reputation, or other interests. But once you are dead, Epicurus argued, you no longer exist, and therefore you can no longer be harmed. For this reason, provided she selects a painless method of suicide and is not torn by anguish beforehand, the person who commits suicide cannot be said to harm herself, because once the act is completed she no longer exists. On this view, even a hastily planned, irrationally chosen, impulsive suicide, undertaken for wholly inadequate reasons, cannot be a harm to that individual, because that individual is dead.

If so, it could be objected, then it would be no harm to someone else to kill him, at least if it can be done quickly, painlessly, and without warning. But we do think that killing someone is a harm, even if it is done quickly, painlessly, and without warning, because death harms the person whose death it is. Are we wrong? No, it can be replied, since we can understand "harm" not simply in terms of bodily injury or pain but also in terms of deprivation of pleasures, satisfactions, and other goods (Nagel, 1979), or what we call the *praemium vitae*. Killing someone, even though it is done swiftly and painlessly, deprives him of these goods, and because killing him deprives the person of all such goods, it is the greatest possible harm to him. But then, it is argued, suicide must be a harm too—like killing, the greatest harm—because it also deprives a person of all the *praemium vitae*. Consequently, because it is irrational to harm oneself (unless of course some greater good can thereby be attained), it is irrational to commit suicide.

But this view—although widespread—may not be correct. Death seen as a harm because it involves deprivation of the *praemium vitae* is seen as a harm because it involves the deprivation of goods: pleasure, satisfactions, benefits, and so on. But it is not a harm to be deprived of evils: pain, suffering, gnawing fear, abject need. We do not count it irrational if one acts to avoid such harms. But if so, surcease suicides could be rational after all, because they are undertaken to avoid states that are perceived as evils: they serve to avoid bad things, not deprive one of good things, and would be most clearly rational if it would be primarily bad things that would have remained in a person's life.

Clearly, we count most harm-avoiding activities as rational. But this does not tell us whether harm-avoiding suicides, as distinguished from other harm-avoiding activities, can be considered rational. The answer depends in part on whether we consider death or suffering to be the greater evil. If death is the greater evil it is irrational to seek it, even if suffering can thereby be avoided. If, on the other hand, irremediable, relentless suffering is viewed as the worst thing that can befall a human being, then death undertaken to avoid it is not irrational.

Of course, it is not irrational to avoid harm—including pain and suffering—if there is some purpose to be served by undergoing it. Many Catholic writers argue this way against the rationality (and moral permissibility) of suicides to escape suffering or pain: committing suicide would be irrational as well as immoral, because it would evade that suffering, which could serve a profoundly important further purpose. Even within the Catholic tradition, however, some thinkers distinguish between "constructive" and "destructive" pain, or pain that serves some further emotional or spiritual purpose and pain that does not. In practice, of course, it often is hard to distinguish these, but one might be tempted to formulate a kind of rule-of-thumb approximation: the more severe, longer-term and less transitory the pain threatens to be, the more it interferes with mental functioning, and the dimmer the outlook for pain-free recovery, the less likely that enduring the pain can serve some further emotional or spiritual purpose and the more rational an attempt to avoid the pain by suicide. Some Catholic writers would reject this view; but some would hold that if pain approaches what we sometimes call "animal" suffering, there is no spiritual or other benefit to be hoped for by forcing a person to endure it.

Fortunately, enormous progress has been made in the medical control of pain. New drugs and new methods of analgesia are under continuous development, stimulated in recent years by the focus on the harsh realities of dying that is part of the social movement favoring legalization of physician-assisted suicide (Chapman & Gavrin, 1996). But not all suffering is a matter of pain alone. Hospice programs are extremely effective in controlling most physical pain—the usual estimate is that about 95% of cases of pain can be successfully controlled, even in terminal illness—but report less success with other problems like difficulty swallowing and generalized weakness. Furthermore, physical pain is often accompanied by severe emotional pain, and it is not always easy to differentiate the two. But it is important to distinguish between them because our responses to suicide based on avoidance of them are often quite different: we tend to be more accepting of suicide to avoid severe physical pain, more rejecting of suicide to avoid emotional pain.

Most emotional pain, like most physical pain, is transitory or can be treated. The transitoriness of most depression can hardly be emphasized strongly enough, because depression is so widely associated with suicide in contexts other than terminal illness. Yet not all physical pain, emotional pain, or depression can be relieved, and if we do acknowledge that surcease suicide can be rational if such pain serves no further purpose and cannot be relieved, it is still not clear what degree it must reach before suicide to avoid pain is rational. Must it be associated with terminal illness or reach excruciating levels?

The answer may depend on the amount of other experience permitted during pain or during pain-free intervals, and whether this other experience is of intrinsic value. If experience uninfected by pain is no longer possible, the choice of suicide may seem most rational. This answer may appear simplistic, but it has an important practical correlate: it means that our efforts to measure pain itself may focus on the wrong thing. We should not be assessing levels of pain as much as the capacity to experience and enjoy anything else besides pain. If little else is possible, we may be most sympathetic to suicide intended to avoid pain. Here suicide serves to avoid harm to oneself, rather than cause it.

## Accordance with Fundamental Interests

In general we regard an act as rational only if it is in accord with what we might call one's ground-projects or basic interests, which themselves arise from one's most abiding, fundamental values (Williams, 1976). Sometimes these ground-projects or fundamental interests are self-centered, in the sense that they are concerned with the acquisition or arrangement of things for one's own benefit; sometimes they are altruistic and concerned with the benefit of someone or something else. An act that conflicts with the satisfaction of one's ground-projects or fundamental interests and goals is irrational; an act intended to satisfy them is rational, in the sense that it is an attempt to achieve one's own ends. If a person has multiple but conflicting ground-projects, it is rational to try to satisfy the most basic of these. But because suicide ends life and hence precludes the possibility of further action, it may appear to thwart any attempt to satisfy one's ground-projects or fundamental interests and so appears to be irrational in every case.

It is true that you cannot satisfy certain kinds of interests if you are dead. But not all ground-projects require a person's continued existence: your most important project may be altruistic or centered on others or involve the furtherance of some institution or cause; this may continue even if you no longer exist. Of course, being dead precludes your appreciation of the fact that your ground-projects or fundamental interests are being satisfied. But this does not mean that suicide, or causing yourself to become dead, can therefore never be rational; your interests may in fact continue to be satisfied whether you are alive or not. And because your interest was in the success of the ground-project, not in your appreciation of that fact, there is no reason to think that suicide would necessarily run counter to these basic interests. It need not therefore have been irrational, although in many cases it is.

Furthermore, there may be cases in which not your life but your death is required to promote the ground-projects to which you have allegiance. Socrates, facing the hemlock, reasoned that given his fundamental commitment to preserving the laws of Athens, he would thwart those interests if he tried to escape execution, not protect them. Hence he allowed himself to be required to commit suicide: he saw this as the rational consequence of his commitment to the laws. Given the circumstances, suicide was the only effective means of achieving his paramount ends.

But can suicide be rational insofar as it permits satisfaction of basic goals or fundamental interests, even for individuals who do not have commitments to other persons, institutions, causes, or principles? After all, some people's most fundamental interests involve self-understanding, self-revelation, and perhaps self-perfection. But if one's basic ground-projects are self-centered, can suicide ever be rational, if that self will no longer exist? Clearly, in many cases the answer is no. But in some situations suicide may be in itself expressive of that person's deepest personal, moral, or aesthetic convictions and represent a clear refusal to compromise with a flawed world: one thinks of the suicides of protesters during the Nazi period or the Vietnam war, attempts not only to change the course of historical events but to express oneself in protest: I do not wish to live in this kind of world. This is not necessarily depression speaking or the incapacity to adapt to changed, worsened circumstances; it may sometimes be an expression of that person's deepest values and concerns, the ground-project of living a morally decent life in a morally decent world. Paradoxically, it may seem, in some few cases the choice of suicide may further this end by expressing that person's basic, central concerns.

One last issue presents itself concerning the concept of rational suicide. In cases in which suicide is a rational choice, because it prevents harms, accomplishes goals, or expresses what is central to a human being, is it always also rational to choose to remain alive? If suicide is sometimes a rational choice, is it ever *the* rational choice—the only one? Clearly, if strategies other than suicide will equally well prevent harms, accomplish goals, or express a person's deepest convictions, staying alive and using these other strategies will be at least an equally rational choice, and because it preserves life and life's further options, evidently the more rational one. But if other strategies will not succeed, suicide may be the only rational thing to do.

## ☐  Conclusion

Many other choices in life—what work to pursue, whom to marry, what adventures to seek and what dangers to avoid—are sometimes rational, sometimes irrational under the five criteria explored in this chapter. Similarly, suicide can be rational or not, depending on whether it meets these criteria. Although most suicides that are reported as such fail to meet one or more of them, not all suicides do. Suicide can be rationally chosen, if a person reasons clearly, has a realistic view of the world and of his or her own situation in it, and has adequate, undistorted information; and suicide can be a rational thing to do if it avoids harm and is in accord with one's fundamental interests. These cases may be few; but whether they are suicides to avoid pain and suffering in terminal illness, suicides of self-sacrifice for altruistic reasons, or suicides of honor or principle, it is important to respect these difficult but significant human choices.

Daniel Callahan

# Reasons, Rationality, and Ways of Life

A few years ago I was invited to appear on a national television program to respond to a case of a long-planned suicide, a husband and wife in their early eighties, both a bit frail but neither of them suffering nor dying. With me on the program were their twin daughters, each fully supportive of their parents' decision. They spoke, in fact, with pride about their parents' act. It seems that the parents had, many years earlier, decided that when their lives began running downhill because of old age, they would commit suicide—not to relieve suffering, but to avert suffering. They had an image in their minds of what would count as a decent life, and when that life appeared ready to decline, that would be the end for them. That moment came and they committed suicide together.

All of the suicides I had known were of people who had long been troubled and unhappy. Some final burden triggered their suicide but it had been there in potentiality many years before that happened. The suicide of the elderly couple was different, a far more modernized version of a motive for suicide, the purely "rational" suicide. By just about any conventional criteria of those who have argued for such a category, the elderly couple's was a rational suicide. They were educated, highly successful people, well able to reason about life. They did not, so far as I knew, have a history of depression or mental instability, and they had given many years of thought to their decision, one that was fully consistent with their view of the good and goods of life, and with what they took to be their vital interests. All the evidence at hand suggested that they fully understood the consequences of what they had planned to do. Indeed, what their daughters most admired about their parents was the rationality, consistency, and coherence of their decision.

I had two responses to the story I heard, and to the proud daughters. One of them was that, in some obvious and conventional sense of "rational," suicide could be perfectly rational. The other response was a profound sense of dismay and repugnance at the story, how all kinds of unreasonable, undesirable things can be done in the name of rationality. What I was hearing, I decided, was not just a story about "rational" suicide, but a story about what two people considered a good way of life and, with it, a good way of death. I want in this chapter to try to articulate dismay and repugnance despite the rationality of their decision.

I start with the belief—based on my own experience—that if people that suicide can be rational, they usually mean to affirm that it can (even if, strictly speaking, it is possible to distinguish between the rational and the good). They want to use the favorable connotation of "rational" to help carry the moral weight of justifying suicide. I come to this conclusion because, other than riding the coattails of rationality, there seems to me nothing much to be gained by casting the problem of suicide as one of rationality.

Rationality is no sure defense against error, bias, and self-deception. The important arguments and disagreements of philosophers and other intellectuals over the centuries rarely if ever turn on failures of rationality among the disputants. The fact that suicide has for a long time and by many people been held to be irrational, an emotional or mental aberration, does not by itself suffice as a warrant for casting the moral issue as one of rationality—although it helps explain its use tactically. At worst, then, <u>the term *rational* is little more than a red herring, diverting attention from more significant problems about suicide</u>. At best, it might be possible to say that rationality would be a necessary condition of a justifiable suicide, but never a sufficient condition.

I say more about the idea of rationality subsequently, but before I do, I want to introduce the two main questions I explore here. The first is this: ought people to build into their notion of a good (and rational) life a standard proviso that, if life becomes intolerable, suicide ought to be considered one of a number of reasonable options they might pursue? The second question: ought society to psychologically and morally accept suicide as a socially reasonable and acceptable option for those who find their lives intolerable? Needless to say, a legitimation of the rationality of suicide could make it more acceptable for individuals, and this would be reinforced by a more generally favorable social attitude.

At stake in the discussion of "rational" suicide is individual and social legitimation. Rationality, I want to suggest, does not and ought not provide a foundation for that legitimation. I want to show that, if we pursue the idea of rationality far enough, we see that rationality as such tells us nothing of importance about the moral meaning of suicide, but that what counts as a "reasonable" approach to suicide may take us in a more promising direction.

What I have done already is to make a distinction between the "rational" and the "reasonable." This is an important distinction from two perspectives. The first is that rationality is, as such, a formal notion only; that is, it is a way of characterizing the way we reason. The rational can, in that respect, be seen as the opposite of the arational; that is, the rational is orderly and systematic, going from premises to conclusions in a logical fashion or inductively drawing sensible conclusions from varieties of evidence. The well-formed syllogism is the classical paradigm of rationality. The arational can be characterized as an indifference to, or ineptitude about, the logical steps of good reasoning; some reasoning we call "sloppy" as a way of capturing that indifference or ineptitude. The rational can also be counterpoised to the irrational, by which is ordinarily meant the irruption into the reasoning process of feelings, emotions, or biases that distort or preclude orderly reasoning to valid conclusions. I take it that, when it is said by some that suicide cannot be rational, they mean that alien ingredients will always be introduced into the reasoning process, most likely depression or other elements that preclude clear thought.

Even if, however, we agree that a process of reasoning is rational—not falling prey to the arational or the irrational—we may well disagree with the results. We may think an otherwise rational decision is, in actuality, an unreasonable decision despite its apparent and conventional rationality. Why? Because the starting premises were flawed, or because some crucial steps in working with those premises were overlooked farther down the line, or because some relevant considerations were omitted. Mistakes in reasoning, or failure to think of everything that might be relevant, are not ordinarily taken as evidence of a lack or rationality, nor ought they to be.

Philosophers and other intellectuals argue all the time about this or that. Yet it is rarely the case that one side or the other is simply arational or irrational—even if each side believes the other utterly wrong. Instead, the hunt for the flaws in the arguments of the other side most commonly takes the form of looking for faulty premises or spotting subtle errors in reasoning. Typically enough, those accused of fallacious reasoning defend themselves by saying that, in fact, their reasoning is not fallacious but has been misunderstood by the critic; and sometimes that is correct. Usually what is happening is that one side believes the other has a wrong or unreasonable position, and an effort is then made to find the fatal flaw that is responsible for that position. Sometimes, but not often, the flaw will be some bit of sheer irrationality, but more often it will not be. Mistakes in reasoning can be made by otherwise perfectly rational people.

I point out these easily observable phenomena to reiterate the distinction between the rational and the reasonable. I have defined the *rational* as, roughly, a consistency between premises and conclusions. The *reasonable* I define as consisting not only of the rational, but also of the quality of the premises, or other starting points. Justification of those starting points may require defending a way of life or a broad perspective on the world. Precisely because of these demands for justification, there is much room for divergent values and starting points. That is why otherwise rational people can disagree, even when none fall into arationality or irrationality. I fully concede that suicide can be rational in the conventional sense of that term. Criteria for conventional rationality can be set out and easily met. The couple I cited at the beginning of this chapter seem to have met such criteria in deciding upon suicide as a fit way to end their lives.

Most notably, claims of rationality do not depend upon showing that a person's values are good and proper values, only that the person has values and acts or reasons in ways compatible with them. Conventional rationality is, in this sense, what is commonly called *instrumental rationality,* getting straight the relationship between ends and means. If life is miserable, instrumental rationality could well conclude that ending the life will end the misery. That is a correct conclusion: death does solve many problems.

But instrumental rationality is able to justify actions we consider good and reasonable, and those we consider wrong and unreasonable. For those interested in cotton farming before the Civil War, the holding of large numbers of slaves was seen as the only rational way of making such a venture economically viable; and it may well have been. Given Hitler's premises about genetics and inferior peoples (a widespread view in the West during the first half of the 20th century), his murderous campaign against the mentally ill, the retarded, and Jews was perfectly rational. Those same Greek and Roman cultures sometimes commended for their embrace of suicide also accepted the subjugation of women, the keeping of slaves, infanticide, and a number of other practices we now consider simply barbaric. They believed that bodies, including their own, were property, which could be disposed of as they saw fit; so also, given sufficient power, could the bodies of others. Given their premises—the way they understood human life and the value of that life—they were doubtless acting rationally in accepting those practices as in accepting suicide.

I conclude, then, that to describe an act or a set of beliefs as rational is not to say much of importance about it. Our decisions may be rational, but that does not show whether they are good or bad, reasonable or unreasonable. That is why I called rationality a necessary but not a sufficient condition for determining what counts as reasonable. I would add one additional consideration as well, brought out most effectively by the philosopher Alasdair MacIntyre (1988). He argues that ideas of rationality, and criteria for rationality, cannot be separated from particular historical traditions and ways of life. He takes special pains to debunk the Enlightenment myth that

> reason would replace authority and tradition. Rational justification was to appeal to principles undeniable by any rational person and therefore independent of all those social and cultural particularities which the Enlightenment thinkers took to be the mere accidental clothing of reason in particular times and places. (p. 6)

Why did that belief fail? Simply because, MacIntyre argues, "both the thinkers of the Enlightenment and their successors proved unable to agree as to what those principles were which would be found undeniable by all rational persons." (p. 6)

Two observations are pertinent here. One of them is that, when I hear efforts to justify rational suicide, they seem almost always to adopt the Enlightenment assumptions about reason: that there are timeless and placeless standards of rationality applicable to suicide decisions. If this is so, it can only be because the standards are of trivial importance. All rational people seem to agree that (p) and (−p) are contradictory and cannot be held at the same time; but that is one of the few matters upon which rational people everywhere agree. The other observation is that, if we are meaningfully to talk about suicide and reason, we must talk about traditions and ways of life to determine the reasonableness of suicide. It is not enough to show that some suicides, perhaps many, are rational. That does not take us very far.

Asking whether suicide is a reasonable course to adopt if life has become miserable is of course a far more complex matter than determining whether it can be rational. I will try to get at this matter by returning now to the two questions I posed at the beginning of this essay: should individuals build into their conception of a good life the belief that suicide is a rational and reasonable solution to the problem of a miserable outcome to that life? Should society legitimate suicide to the point that it is a socially acceptable way for people to deal with the most grave misfortunes of life? Both of these questions, I believe, force us to find and locate suicide within an existing or possible tradition and a way of life that seems plausible and justifiable. The answer to both questions, I argue, should be no.

I want to get into the two questions by steps. The first step is to ask just why it is that most societies have either condemned suicide or taken the view that it represents some kind of emotional or mental breakdown in the person who commits suicide. It seems utterly unhelpful to note that many religions have strictures against suicide and thereby classify opposition to suicide as religious. The more interesting issue is why quite diverse religions and societies have taken that position.

I offer a hypothesis, one that seems to me a good moral argument. The general repugnance most societies, and religions, have to suicide stems from the perception that it represents a profound failure to cope with life. But it is a social and not just individual failure: it breaks the solidarity that people should have in the face of the evils and tragedies of life. Almost all lives will have to face the death of loved ones,

.in and suffering of illness, occupational failures and reverses, family misery,
-in the most extreme cases—wars, massacres, persecution, and unleashed sav-
.ry. Life at its worst offers us many reasons to be rid of it, and most people will at
some time in their lives think of suicide as a tempting escape, definitive and final.

Why do most people not give in to that temptation? Perhaps, as is sometimes
alleged, it is a fear of the act of suicide, or superstition, or an unwillingness to take
one's rational conclusions to their final stage. However, I suspect it is because we
have been socially tutored that, despite pain, suffering, and tragedy, life ought to go
on, and that we owe it to each other not to despair in the face of evil and misfortune.
We are implicitly asked by our fellow human beings to give witness to the possibility
of human endurance and the need to transcend evil by bearing it in our own lives.
We need the help of other people in coping with what life throws our way, and one
of the most fundamental goods that others can give us is the example of their lives
in enduring pain and misery. If others can do it, so can I. And if I cannot do it, I will
thereby be failing in my duty to others, failing to give them the kind of help that
they, by simply enduring, have given me. One reason why we typically feel a sense
of loss and pity when someone commits suicide is because we guess that the person
has not only chosen to leave life, but also to leave the human community in a way
that does some harm to those of us who remain: the harm of someone who could not
find out how to maintain solidarity with us in the presence of pain and suffering.

For all of the evident advantages of suicide, most otherwise rational people do not
choose it as a way of managing their lives and their sorrows. No doubt there is a
powerful drive for life, a desire just to stay alive, that is operating here. It probably
has deep biological roots, a way of coping with the various threats to life, whether
social or biological. The uniqueness of human beings among other creatures is that
they can contemplate, and carry out, fantasies about being dead and thus being rid
of their burdens. Yet comparatively few act on those fantasies. Most interestingly as
well, the pain, suffering, tragedies, and disappointments of life are not good predictors
of who will attempt or actually commit suicide. Most people are able to tolerate the
evils of life without committing suicide: even the severely handicapped, on the one
hand, and those imprisoned in inhuman concentration camps, on the other, rarely
commit suicide. They just do not take that way out even if a terrible ending awaits
them. Most people who are dying, even if they are undergoing great pain, do not
request much less pursue suicide.

Human misery, in brief, seems a poor predictor of suicide—even though, in the
narrow sense of rationality, it offers a clean escape. For that matter, one feature of
rationality even in the narrow sense is that rational behavior is predictable behavior.
We generally know, about ourselves and other human beings, how we will act in
common situations: we will put on the brakes at red lights, not go around safety
fences on high cliffs, seek food when we are hungry, and so on. Although we might
predict that most suffering people will give some thought to suicide, we can also
predict that most of them will not make that choice. Does that seem intuitively sensible
to us, or counterintuitive? The only good predictor of who will commit suicide seems
to be those who had an earlier history of depression. Is that just an accident? Although
the fact of an earlier history of depression in the overwhelming majority of those who
commit suicide hardly precludes the possibility of rational suicide, it does tell us that,
for most people without a history of mental illness, suicide is not the way in which
they will cope with their misery. What is there that singles out the believer, and
practitioner, of rational suicide from the rest of us? More courage? Less tolerance for
pain and suffering? I have not the faintest idea of the correct answer to this question,

but my guess is that they formulated a different way of looking at life from the rest of us and then acted on it. In MacIntyre's (1988) terms they acted with a particular tradition of values and ideas of the good and a particular tradition of rationality.

The question before us is whether we want to embrace that tradition in our society, not necessarily to make it the only or dominant tradition but at least to make it acceptable and honorable for those who choose to live by it. Is it, that is, a reasonable tradition, which can be justified as surely rational but just as surely and more importantly a prudent and persuasive way of acting in the face of pain and suffering? Now there is not, so far as I can see, any public and articulated tradition of suicide as a way of life in our society. There does, however, seem to be a kind of prototradition, part of the ethos of a liberal society, that some people apply to suicide. That tradition holds that competent individuals may make whatever moral choices they want, including suicide, if there is no demonstrable harm to others. A reasonable choice in this tradition is one that is compatible with a person's values and self-perceived interests, *whatever* they might be. At the least, the choice should be rational (internally coherent and consistent), but at most it will qualify as reasonable if the person has thought long and hard about it and can offer, to himself or herself, some defensible justification. It is not the job of society, in this tradition, to determine what counts as a reasonable way of life, or defensible premises for committing suicide.

I believe that this tradition is simply wrong (not irrational), unconscionably thin, and relativistic. It is not enough to put forward an individualistic, formalistic kind of response, and then to say that suicide is reasonable if it is compatible with a person's values and self-perceived interests. That repeats the ultimate failing of those criteria for "rational" suicide that rest, in a wholly circular manner, on the premise that an act is acceptably rational if consistent with the actor's self-perceived interests. That just takes us back to the trivial sense of rationality, that of interior consistency and coherence. In this case, to determine whether suicide is a reasonable act must be to determine whether it is *actually* in people's interest—because they can be mistaken to think it is—and whether it is *actually* in the interest of society to see it legitimated as a reasonable option for those who choose it.

The only good way to get at the question of what is really in our interest is to ask ourselves whether we want to be the kind of people who believe suicide to be reasonable and to live in the kind of society that thinks it is? I argue that no one should want to become that kind of person, and that no one should want to live in such a society. At the same time, we should be willing to understand and empathize with those who, not as a way of life but as a desperate and singular act, commit suicide in the face of severe travail. We should all be able to understand why that can happen, but we should no less be able to understand why we do not want to legitimate such acts as a standard part of our way of life.

In light of the problem of suicide, how might I go about deciding what kind of person I ought to be, and whether I ought to let myself become the kind of person for whom suicide is a legitimate option? I would want to begin by trying to determine how I should evaluate the pain and suffering that might come into my life. If I choose to be the kind of person who simply tolerates no severe suffering that might be remotely avoidable, then suicide will look attractive. If I also believe that I ought to be the kind of person who can control life as far as is possible, accepting nothing that is not self-chosen, then suicide will look even more attractive. If I believe that it ought to be me, and not my society, that determines what counts as intolerable suffering, then suicide will have gained a few more points in my eyes. Finally, if I can persuade myself that suicide is truly a private act, of no consequence to those around me (assuming I have discharged any formal obligations I might have to them before committing suicide), then my own case for suicide will have been nicely made.

But I might choose to be another kind of person. I could perceive that a good part of life requires bearing pain and suffering and that, although it may never be good in itself, the price of trying to evade it at every turn can be a high one, limiting my possibilities for flourishing and fulfillment. A life based on the negative value of the avoidance of suffering would seem a thin and defensive kind of life. But stop. In the case of rational and reasonable suicide, are we not talking mainly about undue or excessive or meaningless suffering, not the ordinary suffering that comes with living a life? Not necessarily, for if we want to leave it to individuals to determine what counts as excessive or meaningless—that is, to have no substantive standards at all—we open the door to judging even ordinary suffering as unacceptable. The elderly couple I cited at the beginning of this article—who saw the downward trajectory of aging as itself unacceptable—show that this is not just a theoretical possibility. The step from a desire to be relieved of suffering to the averting of suffering is a short one.

I have hypothesized in this chapter that one of the reasons why most societies have refused to legitimate suicide as a routine way to relieve suffering is because of the need for solidarity in the face of suffering. We somehow ought to show each other that we can bear what life throws in our path in order that we each may better bear it. I need the witness of my neighbor that pain can be borne just as she or he needs the same witness on my part. If we are essentially social creatures, not simply isolated moral monads, then our life with other people will affect the way we look at life: we will learn from them just as they will learn from us. Suicide is, in that respect, not a private act at all: families have to live with its aftermath, even as do those who merely collect the bodies of those who have committed suicide. We are models for each other's lives, even if we think we are not. A society that legitimated suicide as a way of life would be creating a wholly different set of models: those who choose to reject the older tradition of solidarity in favor of a more contemporary tradition of self-determination and the evasion of suffering.

Actually, I think our present situation, in which suicide has not been legitimated as a reasonable way of coping with suffering, but in which individual suicides are rarely condemned, is a good one. We have reached a tolerable balance between a resistance to suicide as a way of life and routine death, and its acceptance on rare occasions as the sad, desperate act of someone stretched beyond his or her limits. We feel pity and sorrow and sometimes perplexity at such a death and we hesitate to pass moral judgment. That seems to me a good balance. But the pressure now is to disturb that balance, to see the moral status of suicide elevated, attitudes toward suffering and the sharing of suffering altered, and the idea of rational suicide used to imply that, if the minimal test of rationality can be established, then the case for suicide has de facto been made. It has, however, not been thereby made. I have offered here only the most cursory sketch of another way of thinking about suicide, by trying to goad people to think about how they *ought* to live their own lives (not just what their "interests" are); and by getting society to ask what kind of a community it wants to be.

Father Robert Barry

# The Catholic Condemnation of Rational Suicide

In this chapter, I wish to briefly review the approach of the Roman Catholic Church to suicide. It appears that rational suicide is following abortion as a mainstay of post-modern and post-Christian society and is swiftly becoming a permanent fixture of contemporary liberal, secular culture. That Catholicism will oppose this vigorously is seen in the recent papal encyclical *Evangelium Vitae* (Pope John Paul II, 1995). This is one of the harshest papal encyclicals written in the 20th century, matched only by the 1937 anti-Nazi message of Pope Pius XI (1937) *Mit Brennender Sorge*. Condemning contemporary hostility to life in apocalyptic terms, *Evangelium Vitae*'s final section compares our 20th century assault on innocent human life to the dragon of the Book of Revelation (Rev 12:4) who seeks to devour every helpless child.

One must begin any study of suicide by defining it, and I believe the following definition of suicide is acceptable to the Catholic perspective:

A suicide is a deliberate and voluntary performance or omission, done with adequate free-dom and knowledge, that aims at the destruction of one's life. It is a planned, chosen, intended, and consented action to bring death as either a means or an end in itself. It is a choice made where death is reasonably expected to result from the specified performance or omission in common circumstances and situations. (Barry, 1994a, p. 201)

## ☐ Biblical Teachings on Suicide

Some (e.g., Battin, 1995) claim that the condemnation of suicide in the Scriptures is either unclear or absent, but a close reading cannot support this view. Judeo-Christian Scriptures censure or approve of actions in many different ways, sometimes by explicit

All Biblical references are taken from the *New Jerusalem Bible*. (1965). New York: Doubleday.

legalistic condemnations, and at other times by recounting actions or deeds that are held up by the Judeo-Christian community for denunciation. Moral judgments were often shown by the kind of relation created by the action between the agent and God or one's neighbor.

There are two perspectives on suicide in the Old Testament. On the one hand, suicide was condemned in various ways by the Biblical writers, such as that of Ahitophel (2 Sam 17); on the other hand, some reflexively lethal acts were not censured because they were commanded or permitted by God, such as Samson's (Jgs 13). Samson's self-sacrifice illustrated his unswerving devotion to God. Later Judaism was more tolerant of heroic suicide in defense of the faith, as was illustrated by the story of Razis the high priest (2 Mc 14). Nicanor the Greek sought to destroy Judaism and thought the capture of one as noble as Razis would demoralize the Jews. Razis was determined to frustrate this, and rather than suffering capture, he tried to impale himself on his sword but missed the stroke and then threw himself from a tower. Not yet dead, he tore out his entrails and threw them among the soldiers (2 Mc 14:42). All of these actions were but a sign of his unwavering fidelity to the Mosaic Law and hatred for those who persecuted the Jews.

Generally, Judaism condemned suicide, and this is seen in those cases in which someone was tempted to suicide but denied permission to do it by God. The Book of Jonah is the best example of this, and it is strikingly similar to the Elijah cycle (1 Kgs 19). Jonah was like others in the Old Testament who wished for death—Moses (Nm 11:14), Tobit (Tb 3:6), and Job (Jb 6:9; 7:15)—but Yahweh would not grant their wishes and he either questioned the rightness of their motives or gave them encouragement, aid, or revelations to help them in their troubles. Jonah was a reluctant prophet called to preach repentance to Ninevah at a time when the Israelites detested them (McGowan, 1968). Rather than heeding Yahweh's call to preach repentance, Jonah boarded a ship headed in the opposite direction, and when he was in danger of drowning, a giant fish was sent by Yahweh to save his life. When he finally made it to Ninevah and preached a message of repentance, the Ninevites bitterly disappointed him by repenting. Jonah went outside the city and sulked under a vine (Jon 4:9) hoping that the Ninevites would be punished, and he asked Yahweh for death. This episode is strikingly similar to that of Elijah who brooded under his broom tree and asked for death because Israel would not repent (1 Kgs 19:4). Elijah sulked because of infidelity of the people and the king, but Jonah because Yahweh was merciful to Israel's enemies and did not punish them. Jonah fled the Lord, but Elijah sought him in the wind, earthquake, and fire, and because Jonah asked for death for narrow-minded and selfish reasons, he was not given the comfort of revelations from Yahweh as was Elijah but was challenged with questions from God. From the perspective of the morality of suicide, Yahweh did not grant permission for suicide for any reason, neither for the altruistic reasons of Elijah or Moses nor the selfish reasons of Jonah. He did not want to bring death to the Ninevites, Elijah, or Jonah but wanted all of them to live. He would even show this desire to give life to all by using nature to save them, for the crows fed Elijah and the whale saved Jonah.

An identical approach to suicide is found in the story of Tobit and Sarah. The aim of this story was to reassert the validity of faith and virtue at a time at which God had apparently abandoned his people (Dumm, 1968). Both Tobit and Sarah suffered deeply from the misfortune of the world, for Tobit was mysteriously blinded and Sarah became the victim of the cruel sport of heartless women who reminded her of her failure as a mother (Tb 3:9–10). Disconsolate at their cruelty, Sarah went to her room intending to hang herself but instead offered a prayer to God and Yahweh did not allow her to die (Tb 3:10–16).

Many suicides in the Old Testament were performed by those who were utterly alienated from God such as Saul and Ahithophel, and these were condemned. Saul violated his divine consecration and was punished for this by rebellion in his kingdom. Saul was specifically anointed by Yahweh to be the great king and unifier of the Chosen People, but he betrayed his mission by falling into sorcery, idolatry, and witchcraft (1 Sm 28). For this, he slowly became entangled in the snares of sin, infidelity, and death until he was so deeply enmeshed that he could not escape, and the depths of his involvement were confirmed by his self-killing. Ahithophel was a member of David's council, but he advised Absolom to take possession of David's harem, which was a treasonable act. Then he recommended that he himself pursue David and kill David (2 Sm 17:23), and when this plan failed he hanged himself (2 Sm 17:28).

The suicide of Judas Iscariot illustrates the New Testament's critical view of this act, for he committed suicide in imitation of Ahithophel and apparently was Ahithophel's New Testament counterpart. By suiciding prior to the death of Jesus, Judas ironically proclaimed him to be in the line of the Davidic kingship, just as the suicide of Ahithophel ironically proclaimed the kingship of David (McKenzie, 1965). Judas was called to the apostolic ministry by Jesus, but he rejected this call and betrayed Jesus (Mt 10:4; Mk 3:19; Lk 6:16). And the Christian tradition has long held that he was the only one certainly excluded from the kingdom because he did not repent of his suicide (Jn 6:71; Brown, 1970). His betrayal and suicide gave new emphasis to the utter gravity of his abandonment of his apostolic call (Cross, 1970).

A good example of the New Testament rejection of suicide is seen in the episode reported in Acts of the Apostles in which Paul attempted to stop the jailer of Philippi from killing himself when Paul and Silas were freed from prison by an earthquake:

> Late that night Paul and Silas were praying and singing God's praises while the other prisoners listened. Suddenly there was an earthquake that shook the prison to its foundations. All the doors flew open and the chains fell from all the prisoners. When the goaler woke and saw the doors wide open he drew his sword and was about to commit suicide, presuming that the prisoners had escaped. But Paul shouted at the top of his voice, "Don't do yourself any harm, we are all here."
>
> The goaler called for lights, then rushed in, threw himself trembling at the feet of Paul and Silas, and escorted them out, saying, "Sirs, what must I do to be saved?" They told him, "Become a believer in the Lord Jesus, and you will be saved, and your household too." Then they preached the word of the Lord to him and to all his family. (Acts 16: 25–34)

This passage clearly shows the emptiness of claims that the Bible does not condemn suicide or is unclear in its rejection of it. In a situation in which some might justify suicide, the leading Christian apostle vigorously denounces it and instead calls for faith. This scene is important for Christian teaching on suicide because it shows that the Apostolic verdict was clearly against suicide.

# ☐ Catholic Moral Arguments Against Suicide

It is not possible in this short space to recount the entire Catholic teaching on rational suicide, but its traditional teachings are well stated in the writings of St. Augustine and St. Thomas Aquinas. In *The City of God*, St. Augustine argued that Christians do not commit suicide in any circumstance and that Christians have no authority to self-execute. Augustine's (1972a) beliefs here are quite clear: suicide is wrong because it is deliberate killing of the innocent.

> For it is clear that if no one has a private right to kill even a guilty man (and no law allows this), then certainly anyone who kills himself is a murderer, and is the more guilty in killing himself the more innocent he is of the charge on which he has condemned himself to death. (p. 27)

He denied that it was legitimate to kill oneself for any reason, even to escape sin, which for Augustine (1972b) was the most compelling reason possible:

> It is significant that in the sacred canonical books there can nowhere be found any injunction or permission to commit suicide either to ensure immortality or to escape any evil. In fact we must understand it to be forbidden by the law "You shall not kill," particularly as there is no addition of "your neighbor" as in the prohibition of false witness, "You shall not bear false witness *against your neighbor*." But that does not mean that a man who gives false witness against himself is exempt from guilt, since the rule about loving one's neighbor begins with oneself, seeing that the Scripture says "You shall love your neighbor as yourself." (pp. 31–32)

In contrast to Augustine, Aquinas argued against suicide because it was contrary to nature and the virtues. According to Aquinas, the aim of Christian life was to grow in both the cardinal and theological virtues and develop our powers to act in accord with them. He presented some new arguments against suicide and he held that it was not only against love, but also against fortitude, prudence, temperance, hope and faith, our obligations in justice to the community and God, and ultimately our natural inclination to life. Suicide is contrary to fortitude because the suicidal person does what is evil in a situation in which doing what is right and good is difficult (Aquinas, 1947c). The demands of fortitude differ from case to case, but one who deliberately kills another innocent person because of fear violates this virtue. Less proximately, suicide is contrary to prudence and temperance. It violates prudence because it is not a morally good means to a morally legitimate end (deliberately destroying innocent human life is *not* morally good) (Aquinas, 1947c). And often, individuals kill themselves by letting emotions of self-pity get the best of them, and they violate temperance, which requires us to not let disorderly emotional states lead us into sin. Suicide was against hope that gave individuals the motivation to seek to do what was truly good, especially in difficult circumstances (Aquinas, 1947b). In a suicidal action, one reacts to stress, threats, and demands so violently that one destroys innocent life to escape, and the virtue of hope prohibits allowing even desperation or despair to justify acts of self-destruction. For Aquinas, suicide also compromised the virtue of faith because faith is a part of charity and suicide is contrary to this virtue (Aquinas, 1947a). Suicide violated justice because deliberately destroying innocent human life is not an act that is properly due it (Aquinas, 1947c).

## ☐ The Contemporary Development of the Roman Catholic Teaching Against Suicide

Relatively new arguments have emerged in contemporary Catholic teachings against suicide. In comparison with arguments on behalf of the morality of suicide, Catholic arguments have been much more open to modern developments in philosophy, psychology, theology, and morality than have those of suicide advocates (Sacred Congregation for the Doctrine of the Faith, 1981). And in response to the horrors of 20th century genocide as seen in two World Wars, racial "cleansing," and the international abortion and contraception movements, Catholic teachings have vigorously affirmed the transcendence of human life while suicide advocates have continued to ascribe only a limited and utilitarian value to it (McCormick, 1981; Pope Pius XI, 1930).

Modern Catholic teachings hold that suicide violates not so much the dignity of human life as its sanctity, and this new view owes a great deal to the classical *imago Dei* doctrine as its foundation, which held that man was created in the image of God and this is the source of the sanctity, value, and dignity of human life (Pope Pius XI, 1930). Because of the *imago Dei*, genuine sanctity is attributed to human nature and a sacred zone surrounding human life forbidding deliberate killing of the innocent had to be recognized (Barry, 1994b). This argument has proved to be quite persuasive in the 20th century because of the profound disrespect and even scorn or hatred shown toward human life in this astonishingly murderous century.

The second new element in Catholic teachings against suicide asserts that self-killing should not be endorsed because it is not a genuinely rational action, as it is driven by the obscure psychological forces of passion, guilt, fear, revenge, self-hatred, and despair, which overwhelm reason (Barry, 1994a). More than claiming that suicide is an act contrary to the virtues and implicitly an act resulting from a gross character defect, as Aquinas did, contemporary Catholic arguments against suicide now stress that it is a capitulation to these dark and eminently mysterious powers and should not be regarded as rational (Pope John Paul II, 1995). The 20th century is remarkable for its advances in understanding of human psychology, and far better than in any previous century we comprehend the intense pressures that often drive actions and how we need to master these forces to achieve psychological wholeness. The Catholic argument that suicide is irrational because it flows from these destructive and illogical compulsions is quite powerful because we are a century that has only recently awakened to the presence and the potency of these drives (Grisez, 1980). Catholic teachings have shown a greater openness to the advances of suicidology than have suicide advocates, and Catholicism has endorsed the view that suicide is evidently irrational in almost every instance because of the psychological forces that drive people to it; on the other hand, suicide advocates (e.g., Wickett, 1989) have in large part ignored this almost universally endorsed view.

Contemporary Catholic arguments against suicide have also been quite responsive to modern trends and developments. In the high middle ages, the Catholic Church held for the speculative and theoretical possibility that capital punishment could be justly and fairly imposed, and it simply declared that the state had the moral right to visit a sentence of death on some individuals for certain capital crimes (Welty, 1963). But this teaching has been substantially qualified in this century because it has become clearer that this sentence could not be imposed in a fair and nondiscriminatory manner (United States Catholic Bishops, 1980). Similarly, contemporary Catholicism views suicide as uncontrollable and, unlike suicide advocates, Catholic teachings now hold that liberal suicide laws cannot control suicide in practice and protect the innocent from it. This was the hard lesson not yet fully learned from the Romantics, Dadaists, Nazis, and contemporary Dutch who attempted to institute suicide programs that degenerated into uncontrollable suicide epidemics (Barry, 1994a). And just as many now protest capital punishment because it cannot be administered with adequate protection for the innocent or with sufficient controls against bias, so also suicide programs cannot be instituted with sufficient controls or protection for the innocent. This has been ignored by contemporary suicide advocates, who claim that their proposals contain measures to control suicidal practices and protect the innocent.

Finally, contemporary Catholic teachings about the administration of analgesia and medical care hold that it is morally legitimate to offer adequate analgesia to patients in deep and unremitting pain so that they are spared profound and intractable pain, even if this would shorten their lives (Barry & Maher, 1990). Rather than making suicide more necessary now than in previous decades, advances in therapy, health-care, pastoral care and analgesia have abolished many of the justifications suicide advocates invoke to warrant self-killing. Pieter Admiraal (1987), the leading contemporary proponent of rational suicide in Holland, even admitted that pain is not a sufficient reason for choosing suicide any more. The only reason that suicide advocates can invoke to justify suicide is loss of dignity, but Catholic theology counters this by arguing for a dignity and value in all forms of human suffering.

# ☐ Conclusion

Werth and Cobia reported that nearly 80% of respondents from a small sample of the members of the American Association of Suicidology believed that suicide could be rational in some situations and presumably justifiable (reported in Werth, 1996b). And Werth (1996b) has argued that a suicide could be rational if a patient's situation is hopeless but the person is not in a clinical state of depression; however, this is an oxymoron. If a person declares his or her situation hopeless, someone can fairly ask how he or she can not be in a state of depression, and it might well be that Werth's class of rational suicides is empty. From the Catholic perspective, this suggests that many contemporary mental health professionals have a rather low opinion of their capabilities to help these suicidal people through their crises and despair.

Catholicism looks at the plight of Jesus on the Cross and declares that if that situation was not one which could have been pronounced hopeless and destructive of one's dignity, nothing could be so declared, and yet it did not consider suicide for him morally justifiable. To those professionals who believe that a client's situation is truly hopeless and without any redeeming qualities, Catholicism would simply ask that these professionals refer these clients to those pastors, ministers, and priests who have confidence and faith in the cross to save and redeem. Catholicism believes that Jesus confronted the most undignified and cruelest situation possible and did not believe it warranted self-extermination and this should apply to all of us as well.

August Comte (1876) claimed that the eternal glory of Roman Catholicism was that it has always condemned rational suicide. Whether one considers this to be a glorious moment for Roman Catholicism or not is a matter of personal judgment, but his claim is accurate, for in comparison to the other major religions of the world, Catholicism is one of the few that has aggressively refused to condone suicide.

# 5

CHAPTER  Gerald A. Larue

# Is Rational Suicide Rational?

Mr. X is a successful 58-year-old businessman in a city of nearly 1 million inhabitants. He is a respected member of the Mayor's Advisory Board, a deacon in his church, and a member of the city's Arts Council. He is a generous supporter of organizations including a center for battered women, an outreach center for juveniles in trouble, an alcoholic rehabilitation center, and a shelter for indigents.

He has been happily married for 25 years. His wife, his son who is graduating from college, and his two teenaged daughters, are proud of who he is and what he represents. He is an ideal husband and father.

The local newspaper has decided to publish a "profile" on him, and in doing the preinterview research an aggressive young reporter has uncovered a part of Mr. X's past that is unsavory, marked with dishonesty, selling government military secrets, and brutality that may have included murder. To conceal his past, Mr. X had changed his name and had moved to a different part of the nation.

During the interview, the reporter confronts Mr. X with this information and with the data that support the findings. There is no way that Mr. X can deny the charges and he tells the reporter that long ago he had changed and left his early life behind but if this material is published he will be ruined—financially, socially and, he is sure, even in the eyes of his family. If the story goes to print he will commit suicide. The story is published and Mr. X commits suicide. (This outline is a fabrication, but rests, in part, on an actual case.) Rational or irrational suicide? Who decides?

Recently, in a survey of some 200 practicing psychologists, 81% said that they believed in the idea of rational suicide and spelled out the circumstances under which they believed the profession should allow suicide (Werth & Cobia, 1995). Their criteria include:

1. The patient has an unremitting hopeless condition.
2. The patient makes the decision as a free choice and is not pressured by others.
3. The person has followed a sound decision-making process, including

- Seeing a mental health professional qualified to assess psychological competence
- Considering all alternatives

- Weighing whether the act is consistent with one's personal values
- Taking into account the impact of suicide on family and friends
- Talking with objective others, such as clergy or medical professionals, and significant others

Mr. X is clearly in an impossible situation. His life will be virtually destroyed by the newspaper story. So dark and heinous is his past that he knows that his friends will turn from him, that criminal charges could be pressed, and that his family will be crushed. To Mr. X, the story constitutes a social death sentence and he has no intention of suffering through it. His choice to die is of his own free will. No one pressures him. Many times he thought about the possibility of his past becoming known and made public and he had determined that his death would be best for all concerned. Much earlier, as his career began to blossom, he entered into therapy and although he did not reveal the whole story he shared enough to let the therapist know that should he ever be confronted publicly with his past he would either simply disappear again or commit suicide. At that time there was no immediate threat of suicide and the therapist had no need to have Mr. X confined for observation. The therapist expressed understanding of the dilemma, suggested that should that dark time come there might be other solutions, but did not challenge the reasonableness of Mr. X's thinking. Mr. X was a clear-thinking, competent individual.

Mr. X had considered the impact of his suicide on family and friends. They would be shocked, horrified, and repulsed. Perhaps they would understand that suicide was, in the mind of Mr. X, the only honorable way out. His family was not involved in his past; they never knew about this dark side of his premarital life. He was sure that they would receive compassionate support from friends, their pastor, and the church members. They would not be isolated or ignored. They were mature individuals who, although confused about this hidden side of a man they loved, would recover and their lives would go on. His investments, plus an insurance policy on which the time clause concerning suicide had long ago run out, would leave his family financially secure. Over the months and years his story would fade into the outdated news files and he would be forgotten.

Not every person will accept Mr. X's suicide as rational even though his behavior can be assessed as such according to the criteria set forth by psychologists. Society has developed other ways of looking at suicide—largely out of fear and for self-protection. Suicide can be interpreted as a threat to the community in that it can be seen as symbolizing a religious and philosophical crisis in society. The concept of rational suicide challenges and rejects accepted societal values that have been undergirded by theology, philosophy, and communal behavior. Self-killing raises questions about the meaning and value of life and about the significance of living by demonstrating that, for the suicidal person, basic norms have lost their effectiveness and tabooed behavior has become acceptable. Years ago, when movie star George Sanders committed suicide, it was popularly reported in the media that he did so because he was "bored" with life. His act challenged the notion that life can be interesting, continually creative, and worthwhile. Suicide, therefore, presents individuals with choices between continuing existence and nonexistence. It removes the individual from the fate of dying "naturally" of old age or for a cause or by illness or accident. The person is in control and chooses the moment and method of death.

Societal uneasiness with self-killing is apparent in the common assessment of suicide as the act of a coward or of the mentally disturbed (which would imply that the act is never rational) or of someone too weak to cope with life. On a more personal and deeper level, such labels may reflect a concern that a suicide might encourage others to appraise the validity and relative importance of their occupation, thinking, and lifestyle. In general, lives are governed by routines. We tend to follow similar patterns day after day after day. Routines are most acceptable when they are thoughtless routines. Evaluation of personal living patterns can be devastating. Further, if one considers the brevity of personal existence within the continuum of time and the insignificance or trivial nature of most human activity and behavior within the context of the lives of the billions of people who have lived and who now live on the earth, the meaning of personal existence can be dwarfed and reduced to nothingness. Suicide by a relative or friend or by a Mr. X or a George Sanders can permit disturbing awareness of the littleness of human life to surface and suggest that living may not be the greatest good nor death the greatest evil.

Mr. X's suicide may be condemned by theologians. Statements such as "only God gives life and only God should take life" or "our lives are on loan from God and only God should determine when the loan is to be paid back" are faith statements based on unproved and unprovable theological conjectures or beliefs. Arguments suggesting that there is some value in suffering can be contested. Obviously, suffering in others can call forth empathetic feelings and provoke compassionate responses. Perhaps, the suffering person may be given new insight into the preciousness of health and of life as well as an awareness of how other sufferers may feel. Most rational persons would choose happiness and nonsuffering over suffering no matter what merits may be claimed by theologians. The suggestion made by some Christian groups that somehow present-day irremediable human physical and mental agony can be interpreted as a means of sharing in Christ's suffering is grounded in theology, not in the reality of pain and agony. To even hint that there may be merit in limiting pain-killing medication to make such a theological identification appears to rate religious beliefs above human pain and suffering. The Rev. Charles Meyer, chaplain and assistant vice-president for Patient Services at St. David's Hospital in Austin, Texas commented that,

> Suffering may be physical, but . . . it may also be psychological or spiritual for the patient and the family, including indignity incompatible and inconsistent with the way the person lived. Suicide / assisted suicide / hastening death may then be seen as the kindest way to relieve suffering—the most loving thing to do for all involved. Arguments decrying such action because "suffering is redemptive" have no understanding either of redemption or of the type of prolonged death possible in our health-care system. (Larue, 1996, p. 163)

There can be no questioning the fact that in the minds of many clear-thinking persons some kinds of suffering, and extreme suffering in particular, can be viewed as meaningless and purposeless.

Suicide has been accepted without comment or condemnation in the religions of many ancient societies. For example, the detailed study by Drodge and Tabor (1992) demonstrated that the 2,000- to 3,000-year-old Jewish and Christian scriptures have absolutely nothing to say about the rightness or wrongness of suicide. It is only when theologians read in their expanded interpretations that a commandment such as "thou shalt not kill" (which, properly translated, reads "thou shalt not commit homicide") can be used as a biblical precept outlawing self-killing. Dr. Hassan Hathout (1996), an Islamic scholar, has interpreted Surah 4:29 of the Qur'an as a prohibition against suicide; on the other hand, in a footnote to the verse, 'Abdullah Yusef 'Ali (1994) claims that the verse deals with violence against "our own brethren," not with self-killing (p. 183). In other religions, we find similar modern interpretative patterns of ancient texts that are supposed to have been produced by divine authority—despite what may be seen as inconsistencies. For example, Raju (1974) noted, "In Hinduism, Buddhism, and Jainism, death through starvation was permitted for various reasons, although suicide itself was condemned. Fasting and starvation were forms of self-purification" (p. 19). Thus ceremonial suicide or what might be called religious suicide is endorsed; nonreligious suicide is forbidden. What a theological convolution!

In our Western culture, despite the lack of condemnation in the Bible, the Christian church moved away from the recognition of suicide as an acceptable way to end life. In volume 1 of *The City of God*, St. Augustine (1994), a fifth century writer, condemned suicide as a crime and a sinful act violating the biblical commandment "thou shalt not kill" (Chapters XVI, XVII, XX, XXI, XXV). During the 13th century, St. Thomas Aquinas in *Summa Theologica* (1975) argued that suicide is a mortal sin; contrary to natural law; damaging to the human community; and representative of human usurpation of divine privilege for decisions about life and death which, he claimed, belong to God alone (II, ii, question 64). These attitudes have become the heritage of the Christian church and in particular the Roman Catholic Church and, subsequently, of society in general.

Traditionally, Roman Catholic communities refused suicide victims the funeral rites of the church or burial in ground that had been consecrated by the sprinkling of holy water and the incanting of "In the Name of the Father, the Son and the Holy Spirit" (Cleary, 1986, p. 266). In some rural communities, I have seen in Roman Catholic cemeteries plots of unconsecrated earth in which those who died without the blessings of the church were buried. These graves, often untended and overgrown with weeds, became stark commentaries on religious beliefs and served as warnings to those who would violate religious taboos. Today, many Catholic priests do not refuse the rites of the church nor burial in Roman Catholic cemeteries to victims of suicide (Cleary, 1986). There can be no question that Durkheim's 1897 sociological study, *Le Suicide* (republished, 1951), together with more recent analyses of causes of suicide, has enabled clergy and laity to appreciate the social forces and the complex pressures of existence within the confusion of modern society that can distort individual perspectives and disorient persons. On the basis of such reasoning, it becomes impossible to fix responsibility or blame or guilt solely upon the suicide victim; some blame, perhaps most blame, must rest on society in general. Protestant and Jewish clergy also tend to treat the issue of suicide with compassion and understanding; but the more conservative the theological stance, the greater the difficulty associated with rites and burials. None of these religions condone suicide as a way of dealing with life's pressures, but condemnation is reserved. Muslims believe that those who take their own lives will not be permitted to enter the Muslim paradise.

Despite the negative connotations, suicide has been accepted by some thinkers as rational. In his brief essay, "On Suicide," David Hume (1963), the great 18th century Scottish philosopher, could find no valid legal, moral, or religious arguments against suicide. On the contrary, he argued that suicide could be viewed as consistent with the best interests of society and with moral and religious concepts (pp. 585–596). The existentialist philosopher Albert Camus (1955) proposed that suicide was a way of settling the issue of the absurdity of life (pp. 3–8). The 1973 Humanist Manifesto, formulated by the American Humanist Association, contained a forthright statement endorsing an individual's right to suicide:

> To enhance freedom and dignity the individual must experience a full range of civil liberties in all societies. This includes freedom of speech and the press, political democracy, the legal right of opposition to governmental policies, fair judicial process, religious liberty, freedom

of association, and artistic, scientific and cultural freedom. It also includes a recognition of an individual's right to death with dignity, euthanasia, and the right to suicide. (p. 6)

Ethical Culture, a noncreedal religion without fixed, unchangeable or dogmatic doctrinal positions, entertains no requirement that members either believe or not believe in a deity. Most members of this religion would tend to accept the statement produced by the American Humanist Association. Indeed, when the Association published "A Plea For Beneficent Euthanasia (1974)," two Leaders (Ethical Culture "clergy") together with 10 other clergy persons (representing Methodist, Episcopal, Congregational, Unitarian, Baptist, United Church of Christ, and Judaic congregations) were signers of the document (Kohl, 1975, pp. 233–238). In Ethical Culture Societies, each member is encouraged to take responsibility for making ethical choices in whatever situations come to him or to her during a lifetime. The choices made are expected to be rational and humanistic, self-nurturing, and nurture-giving.

Some Ethical Societies have attempted to formulate a statement that embodies their beliefs and ethical commitments. For example, the Los Angeles Ethical Society (of which I am the Leader) defines itself in the following statement:

> Ethical Culture is a humanistic religious and educational movement inspired by the ideal that the supreme aim of human life is working to create a more humane society. Our faith is in the capacity and responsibility of human beings to act in their personal relationships and in the larger community to help create a better world. Our commitment is to the worth and dignity of the individual and to the treatment of each human being so as to bring out the best in him or her. Members join together in ethical societies to assist each other in developing ethical ideas and ideals, to celebrate life's joys and to support one another through life's crises, to work together to improve our world and the world of our children. (Surtshin, *Ethical Times*, p.4)

This statement suggests that although ethical behavior and choices are primarily personal and individual, they are always made with respect to the well-being, rights, and freedoms of others.

Because, in Ethical Culture, there are no deontological (rule) ethics or acceptance of absolutes or commandments (divinely or otherwise given) to outlaw suicide, and no theology of guilt and threat of divine punishment to thwart suicide, members tend to evaluate self-killing in terms of Fletcher's situation ethics. Situation ethics calls for the examination of each individual situation in and of itself. In place of legalistic ethical guidelines, situation ethics calls upon the individual to act according to a basic principle which is, according to Fletcher, *agape*—the New Testament term for love—which is to be distinguished from *eros* or erotic love and *philos* or friendship (Fletcher, 1942). In a nontheological setting, Fletcher would substitute *summum bonum* or the greatest good. The choice of action or the determination of what is a right or proper action is, therefore, guided by the particular setting in which an individual finds himself or herself. In a similar situation another individual might choose to act differently. The right to choose implies that the instrument of decision making is reason, not adherence to a set of prescribed regulations. The action is directed towards what is perceived to be the greatest good for the individual and, perhaps, society.

Thus, Ethical Culture members, familiar with the usual theological and societal arguments against suicide, would judge the act according to situation ethics. They might suggest that the argument that suicide robs society of potential strength and input may contain some truth but may not be true in all cases. Ethical Culturists would recognize that a terminally ill cancer-ridden person who, in unremitting pain, chooses suicide may not only serve his or her own best interests but relieve family, friends, and society of the futility of trying to ease suffering or of seeking desperately to find some kind of meaning in a life that has severely diminished quality.

There can be no denying that some self-killing is not rational. Nonrational suicides are committed during periods of deep depression and despair when feelings of low self-esteem or loneliness or abandonment that could ordinarily be treated with counseling or medications seem to be without surcease. These suicides do not employ the rational patterns discussed here; they reflect the way an emotionally disturbed individual sees the world at a given moment in time.

The higher rate of suicide among the elderly (Stillion, McDowell, & May, 1989, p. 159) has raised the question as to whether or not elder suicides could be labeled rational. Primary causes of elder suicide include social isolation and loneliness, boredom, depression, the feeling of being useless and without purpose, financial hardships, loss of friends and loved ones and the desire to avoid being a "burden" to others. Each of these causes could be remedied by counseling, financial aid, and social involvement. Other elders, those who have contracted terminal illness and are in pain or severely incapacitated, find their present life patterns unbearable and hence may reasonably choose to "die with dignity" by taking their own lives.

The fears that many elderly experience when they contemplate the loss of physical and mental capacities were dramatically demonstrated in the case of Janet Adkins (Larue, 1992, p. 246). Adkins, a 54-year-old woman who had worked with Alzheimer's patients, was fully aware of what her doctor's diagnosis of Alzheimer's disease portended for her. After consulting with her family, her pastor (Unitarian), and others who were close to her, Adkins decided to end her life while she was still mentally competent. On June 4, 1990, by pushing the plunger on Jack Kevorkian's suicide machine, Janet Adkins enabled thiopental sodium to enter her bloodstream through an intravenous line inserted in her arm. In 25 seconds she was unconscious and the lethal dose of potassium chloride that followed resulted in a painless death within 6 minutes. Although Kevorkian assisted in the suicide, the decision of Adkins to take her own life and the act of pushing the plunger was, without question, a rational, voluntary act of suicide or self-killing. She exercised her right and her ability to choose whether to live and suffer mental and physical decline from the disease or to end her life before the disease rendered her incapable of making decisions. There is no indication that she has become a role model for the elderly, but her suicide symbolizes the kind of reasoning required by the psychologists mentioned at the beginning of this chapter to be recognized as rational. It is important to note that although for many old age may be a time for "dissatisfaction, despair and disgust," for others it "can be a period of increased life satisfaction and ego integration" (Stillion, et al., 1989, p. 163).

From the point of view of the religion of Ethical Culture what is most important is what should be central to all persons in a democratic society—namely, the freedom to choose. If adherents of some religious organizations reject rational suicide on the basis of theology or supernaturalism, that is their privilege. However, their choice does not support an argument that all suicides are to be viewed as irrational. Nor should their particular theology be used to condemn rational suicide. So far as Ethical Culture is concerned, each individual has the right to exercise free choice—and, we would hope, rational choice—concerning his or her own life and death. For humanistic religions, like Ethical Culture, there can be no question that some suicides deserve to be recognized as rational choices between living and dying.

CHAPTER

Steven Stack

# The Influence of Rational Suicide on Nonrational Suicide: A Sociological Analysis of Attitudes

Sociological analysis is not designed to make value judgements on various social problems. As a science, it can, however, illustrate whether certain premises in public debate are empirically tenable. For example, in the debate over the death penalty, there is often the issue of whether or not capital punishment is an effective deterrent to homicide. This premise can be tested empirically (e.g., Stack, 1987).

Sociological work on rational suicide has been largely restricted to attitudes (e.g., Anderson & Caddell, 1993; Cohen, Fihn, & Boyko, 1994; Huber, Cox, & Edelen, 1992; Leinbach, 1993; Sawyer & Sobol, 1987; Vigeland, 1991). Much of this work is largely descriptive, providing an assessment of how much groups such as physicians, survivors of euthanasia, and the general public support rational suicide and euthanasia. Some try to explain the variation in such beliefs.

Herein the term *rational suicide* refers to a class of suicides that receive some cultural support given the special circumstances motivating the suicide. Although a clear line cannot be drawn between rational and nonrational suicides, it is assumed that the greater the cultural support for a class of suicides (e.g., suicides in the case of terminal illness) the greater the presumed rationality of the suicides. A class of suicides that receive little cultural support, such as suicides in which the victim was simply "tired of living" in the United States (Stack & Wasserman, 1995), is assumed to be largely nonrational in character. Euthanasia is seen as the deliberate putting to death of a person who is suffering from an incurable disease. This may, or may not, be a case of rational suicide depending on other circumstances.

A key limitation of the work on attitudes toward rational suicide is that it neglects the consequences of such support on other attitudes and behaviors. It is unclear, for example, whether support of rational suicide is associated with support of suicide in

**41**

general, or what we might call nonrational suicide. Further, it is not clear to what extent attitudes toward suicide contribute to actual risk of attempted or completed suicide.

The present chapter contributes to the debate on rational suicide by addressing the first neglected issue. The focus is on this question: does support of rational suicide contribute to support of suicide in general?

This issue has some practical implications for the debate on rational suicide. If the answer is yes, it would seem that the promotion of a culture supportive of rational suicide would decrease the value of life not just for groups such as the terminally ill, but for groups not physically ill at all. If so, the promotion of rational suicide may have what sociologists term latent functions or unintended consequences. These unintended consequences, if any, need to be taken into account in the debate on rational suicide. If cultural support for rational suicide has the unintended consequence of promoting large numbers of nonrational suicides as well as the desired rational suicides, this, it would seem, would weaken the case for rational suicide.

## ☐  The Significance of Culture in Sociological Analysis

Culture, or a set of attitudes, beliefs, and values, is one of the fundamental parts of a sociological analysis of the social order (e.g., Johnson, 1992). One of the dominant explanations of deviant behavior, such as suicide, has been cultural. Learning theory, an explanation centered on learning cultural attitudes favorable to the commission of deviant acts, has emerged as one of the key explanations of deviant behavior (e.g., Warr & Stafford, 1991; see review in Akers, 1994). Simply put, learning theory posits that the acquisition of positive attitudes toward a behavior such as suicide will tend to increase the risk of that behavior. In other words, ideas may lead to actions. Akers's (1994) book-length review of the empirical literature concludes that there is more support for learning theory than any of the other major explanations of criminal behavior. Persons who adhere to attitudes supportive of criminal behavior such as believing it is exciting, that their victims "deserve" to be victimized, and so forth are indeed more likely to engage in actual criminal acts. In many scientific studies procriminal attitudes are the single most important factor contributing to juvenile delinquency (e.g., Matsueda & Heimer, 1987).

Unfortunately, there has been little work on the link between cultural approval of suicide and actual suicide risk. One reason for this is that unlike juvenile delinquents, who are available for interviews after the commission of crimes, suicide victims are not available for interviews after their suicides. Suicidologists have had to develop other means for assessing the link between attitudes and behavior.

The key answer to this dilemma has been to study suicide at the level of social groups. In particular, the attitudes of groups at high risk of suicide (e.g., the divorced, males) are compared with the attitudes of groups at low risk of suicide (e.g., the married, females). If attitudes supportive of suicide lead to suicides, then it seems plausible that groups with high suicide rates should also be high in degree of attitudes supportive of suicide. A series of studies has tended to find that this is the case (e.g., Sawyer & Sobel, 1987; Stack & Wasserman, 1995; Stack, Wasserman, & Kposowa, 1994). For example, the married tend to be more disapproving of suicide than the divorced. In turn, the married have a much lower suicide rate than the divorced. Ideas, then, lead to actions. To date, the weight of the evidence suggests that cultural support for suicide is probably causally linked to actual suicide rates. As such, the study of attitudes toward suicide can be legitimated as worthwhile in its own right.

The present chapter is restricted to an analysis of attitudes on rational suicide and how they relate to attitudes on the cultural acceptability of suicide in general. It performs the first empirical test of the notion that persons with a higher approval of rational suicide tend to have a more generalized approval of suicide—nonrational suicide—as well.

## ☐ Methodology

The data employed in this report are from the 1990–1993 World Values Surveys (World Values Study Group, 1994). Complete data were available for 40,109 persons in a total of 35 nations. A list of the nations is provided in Table 1. The surveys were conducted on representative national samples of the adult population in each of the 35 nations. A further description of the research methodology is available in World Values Study Group (1994).

Definitions of rational suicide have followed a number of patterns (Diekstra, 1986; Humphry, 1987; see review in Werth & Cobia, 1995). A recurrent pattern has been the notion that it may be rational for a person to suicide if that person is faced with a terminal illness (Werth & Cobia, 1995).

Herein support for rational suicide is measured as support for the ending of one's life in the case of being incurably sick. This is the only dimension that is measurable in the world values surveys. A person's support for rational suicide was measured on a scale from 1 to 10, 1 being the case in which the respondent believed that ending one's life when incurably sick is never justified. The other extreme value of 10 refers to the attitude that to do so is always justified.

A person's support for nonrational suicide is measured as the degree of her or his approval of suicide in general. This is also measured on a 10-point scale, with 1 meaning that suicide is never justified and 10 that suicide can always be justified.

It is important to disentangle support of rational suicide from factors that are associated with it. For example, public support for suicide tends to be higher among males than females, lower among churchgoers, and lower among the married (e.g., Stack & Wasserman, 1995). If we do not control for these effects, the impact of attitudes referring to rational suicide on attitudes toward nonrational suicide may be exaggerated. That is, the influence of factors such as gender, church attendance, and marriage may "load on" the variable of attitudes toward rational suicide. This may make the influence of that variable artificially too large. Therefore, I controlled for the influence of the following variables using standard statistical techniques (ordinary least-squares regression analysis) as used in previous research (e.g., Stack et al., 1994): gender, church attendance, marital status, age, satisfaction with financial status, education level, and parental status (details on the coding of these variables are available upon request).

## ☐ Findings

The average score of each nation on support for rational suicide is given in Table 1. For all nations combined, the average score is 4.11. Hence, nations falling below 4.11

**TABLE 1.   Public Opinion in Support of Rational Suicide in 35 Nations**

| Nation | Average Public Support Scores for Rational Suicide |
|---|---|
| Austria | 3.76 |
| Argentina | 2.72 |
| Belgium | 4.92 |
| Brazil | 2.66 |
| Britain | 4.67 |
| Bulgaria | 3.60 |
| Canada | 4.98 |
| Chile | 2.70 |
| China | 6.82 |
| Denmark | 5.60 |
| East Germany | 3.97 |
| Finland | 6.14 |
| France | 5.22 |
| Hungary | 4.37 |
| Iceland | 4.67 |
| India | 3.31 |
| Ireland | 2.57 |
| Italy | 3.80 |
| Japan | 5.46 |
| Latvia | 4.06 |
| Mexico | 3.99 |
| Netherlands | 5.98 |
| Nigeria | 3.28 |
| Northern Ireland | 3.40 |
| Norway | 4.24 |
| Poland | 2.39 |
| Portugal | 3.11 |
| Romania | 3.57 |
| Russia | 3.70 |
| Slovenia | 4.06 |
| Spain | 4.23 |
| Sweden | 5.07 |
| Turkey | 3.23 |
| USA | 4.17 |
| West Germany | 4.10 |
| **All nations** | **4.11** |

Note:   range: 1 = no support, 10 = high support. Source: 35 National Surveys, 1990–93 World Values Surveys.

such as Argentina, Chile, Ireland, Italy, and Poland are considered to be relatively low in cultural support for rational suicide. In contrast, nations with scores above 4.11 include China, Denmark, Japan, the Netherlands, and Sweden. This latter group of nations is assumed to be relatively high in cultural support for rational suicide.

The principle concern of the present chapter is to what extent, if any, are nations with strong cultural support for rational suicide also marked by strong cultural support for suicide in general? A series of multivariate statistical analyses were performed to answer this question. Only the basic findings are discussed in this report. Readers interested in the details of the statistical analysis can contact the author for the relevant statistical tables.

First, the survey evidence from all 35 nations was pooled into the same analysis. The variation among nations in national approval of rational suicide, documented in Table 1, was controlled using an appropriate statistical technique in which 34 variables were entered, one for each of n−1 nations (see Stack, 1996 for a further discussion of this technique). In this analysis of all 35 nations taken together, support for rational suicide was found to be strongly predictive of support for nonrational suicide. A unit increase score on the 10-point scale of support for rational suicide was associated with an increase of 0.26 units in support for nonrational suicide.

It is possible that in some isolated nations support for rational suicide would not be linked to support for nonrational suicide. Therefore, a statistical test was done for each of the 35 nations taken separately.

The highlights of these 35 analyses are given in Table 2. An intuitively appealing statistic from these analyses is the simple regression coefficient. This tells the reader how many units of change in attitudes toward nonrational suicide are brought about by a 1-unit change in attitudes supporting rational suicide. Both attitudes are measured on a 10-unit scale.

For example, the first row presents the results from Austria. As the support for rational suicide increases by 1 unit (say from a score of 3 to a score of 4), the approval of suicide in general increases by 0.33 units. This may not seem like a dramatic increase to some readers; however, it is statistically significant or greater than we would expect by chance. Further, in an analysis of other standard statistical coefficients (beta coefficients), attitudes toward rational suicide were found to be the factor most closely associated with the variance in support of suicide in general. For example, it was 17 times more important than age and 5 times more important than gender in explaining attitudes supportive of suicide in general in France.

The amount that attitudes toward rational suicide influence attitudes toward nonrational suicide varies somewhat from nation to nation. The smallest degree of change is in China, where a 1-unit increase in attitudes toward rational suicide brings only a 0.08 increase in the score in support of nonrational suicide. The largest coefficient is for the Netherlands. There, a 1-unit increase in support for rational suicide brings a 0.53-unit increase in support for suicide in general.

An inspection of the appropriate standardized regression coefficients, which are statistics used to measure the relative importance of each factor in the equation, determined that attitudes toward rational suicide was the single most important correlate of attitudes toward suicide in general in 34 nations. The one exception was China. In China two factors were more important: age and satisfaction with household finances.

To summarize the main findings of the analyses: the greater the support of rational suicide, the greater the support for nonrational suicide; this relationship was significant in all 35 nations; and in 34 of 35 nations attitudes toward rational suicide was the most important determinant of attitudes toward suicide in general (of eight correlates).

# ☐  Conclusion

Little is known about the extent to which support for rational suicide lends itself to support for suicide in general. Given that Western cultures tend to strongly support the value of life, cultural attitudes that devalue life are assumed to also be devalued.

**TABLE 2.   Change in Support for Nonrational Suicide Associated with Change in Support for Rational Suicide**

| Nation | Effect on Support for Nonrational Suicide of a One-Unit Change in Support for Rational Suicide (change in score) |
|---|---|
| Austria | 0.33 |
| Argentina | 0.14 |
| Belgium | 0.28 |
| Brazil | 0.13 |
| Britain | 0.33 |
| Bulgaria | 0.28 |
| Canada | 0.25 |
| Chile | 0.20 |
| China | 0.08 |
| Denmark | 0.21 |
| East Germany | 0.23 |
| Finland | 0.32 |
| France | 0.32 |
| Hungary | 0.36 |
| Iceland | 0.15 |
| India | 0.14 |
| Ireland | 0.30 |
| Italy | 0.31 |
| Japan | 0.29 |
| Lativia | 0.15 |
| Mexico | 0.37 |
| Netherlands | 0.53 |
| Nigeria | 0.15 |
| Northern Ireland | 0.24 |
| Norway | 0.32 |
| Poland | 0.35 |
| Portugal | 0.08 |
| Romania | 0.25 |
| Russia | 0.18 |
| Solvenia | 0.32 |
| Spain | 0.30 |
| Sweden | 0.31 |
| Turkey | 0.44 |
| USA | 0.28 |
| West Germany | 0.28 |
| **All nations** | **0.26** |

The present chapter offers the first systematic evidence that support for rational suicide is significantly associated with support for suicide in general. Basically, the greater the support for rational suicide, the greater the support for suicide in general.

Part of what I found from the 35 national surveys, then, is that advocacy of rational suicide is associated with advocacy of nonrational suicide. Further, support for rational suicide is the most important determinant for support of nonrational suicide. Hence, any advocates of rational suicide who argue that support of rational suicide is not associated with support of suicide in general are probably incorrect. Support for one form of suicide is associated with support of the other form.

A remaining issue is to what extent support for suicide actually leads to suicidal behavior. In particular, do nations high in cultural support of suicide actually have higher suicide rates? Although it is beyond the scope of the present analysis to systematically investigate this issue, it has been addressed elsewhere. I found (Stack, 1996) that the level of cultural support for suicide in a nation was significantly associated with actual suicide rates in a sample of 35 nations. Further, cultural support for suicide was typically the strongest contributing factor to national female suicide rates and the second most important determinant of national male suicide rates. This evidence suggests that cultural support for nonrational suicide is associated with actual suicidal behavior or actions. In turn, the present chapter finds that support for nonrational suicide is related to support for rational suicide. Putting these two propositions together, we have the notion that support for rational suicide would be expected to be associated with higher suicide rates.

Some caution should be exercised, however, in interpreting these results. They are based on what sociologists call *cross-sectional data,* or data at one point in time. I have matched attitudes on rational suicide with attitudes on nonrational suicide around 1990. The latter, in turn, were matched with suicide rates circa 1990 in my other work (Stack, 1996). It is not clear if changes over time in suicide attitudes would produce changes in attitudes toward nonrational suicide over time.

Recent research results cast some doubt on the influence of some aspects of culture on suicide. Elsewhere it was determined that changes in legal rulings on rational suicide in the Netherlands were not significantly related to changes in Dutch suicide rates (Zalman & Stack, 1996). The changes that apparently encouraged the spread of physician-assisted suicide in the Netherlands were closely associated with other changes in Dutch society such as a substantial increase in family breakdown as indexed by the divorce rate. Hence, change in attitudes toward rational suicide may simply be part of a much larger cultural complex of attitudes and behavior. Once indicators of this greater cultural nexus, such as the divorce rate, are controlled, the link between attitudes toward rational suicide and suicide may be greatly weakened. That is, for example, attitudes favoring rational suicide and the incidence of suicide may both be related to a third factor such as divorce. A trend toward family breakdown may, for example, cause both an increase in attitudes favoring rational suicide and an actual increase in suicide. Further work is needed in this area. However, adequate data are not yet available from a major scientific study on a variety of nations.

In summary, previous sociological work has neglected the influence, if any, of norms favoring rational suicide on cultural support of suicide in general. The present study explores this issue and does so with data from a large number of nations. In all cases, cultural support for rational suicide has a significant effect on cultural support of suicide in general. Cultural support of rational suicide then, may, inadvertently increase actual suicidal behavior by giving more legitimacy to the phenomenon of suicidal behavior.

## CHAPTER 7

Samuel E. Wallace

# The Moral Imperative to Suicide

Suicide is in keeping with the highest ideals of life; it is a rational act to maintain quality of life; it is the expression of devotion to the family and community. Finally, suicide is the fundamental right of every adult individual, just as the U.S. courts have recently ruled. To suicide is often not only idealistic and dutiful, frequently it is also a moral imperative. Under circumstances that I elaborate in this chapter, not to suicide would be reprehensible.

The truth of the foregoing is evident in the deaths we call heroic when Christians, Jews, Moslems, Buddhists, and Pagans die enthusiastically in witness to their beliefs. Today's religious tolerance lessens but does not eliminate those believers who die in service to their gods. History is replete with a long list of hero–martyrs for the state, a list that includes every nation's military and civilian agents.

The moral imperative to suicide is also celebrated in the deaths of those we might call the secular moral: those whose values stem not from religion or the state but from the purely "moral." The classic (U.S.) Western shoot-out involves no less than the imperative to die voluntarily rather than accept dishonored or demeaned life. The fact that the hero typically lives in the classic Hollywood ending rewards him for the sacrifice he was willing to make. Against all odds he lives but he was prepared to die.

Many contend that the deaths of disciples of Christ, Mohammed, and Buddha, and the other heroic deaths just described, are not suicide. By definition, circumscription, interpretation, signification, intention, and semantics, many writers restrict the word *suicide* to "a selfish event," one "unconcerned with the welfare of the species" (Shneidman, 1985, p. 38). Battin (1995) lists five criteria necessary for "rational suicide" that rule out most suicide. Graber (1981, p. 60) argues that suicide is irrational unless it can truly be said that the person is better off dead, as if the person committing suicide thought about no one else or nothing as abstract as an ideal.

In the mainstream of our American culture today suicide has been condemned as vainglorious (Aquinas, 1990), irrational (Gonsalves, 1990), irresponsible (Maris, 1982a), sinful (Aquinas, in Donnelly, 1990), selfish (Shneidman, 1985), murderous

(Freud, 1933), "an impoverished self-transformation" (Maris, 1982a, p. 11), a sure sign of mental illness (Szasz, 1976), meaningless (Margolis, 1978), immature, ignorant, a violation of the social contract, against God, and even a denial of the basic instinct of self-preservation (see Mayo's excellent review, 1983.)

The number of grounds on which suicide has been denounced is exceeded only by the passion with which it has been condemned. Because torture, death, and other punishments cannot be inflicted on the person who commits suicide, the person's body has been left unburied, staked through the heart, scattered, thrown to the dogs, and desecrated in even more hideous manners. Unable to punish the person sufficiently even with the foregoing, the church and the state have seized his or her estate, turned his or her family into homeless beggars, and banished his or her name from respectable society.

Although our punishment of the person who commits suicide today is less physical, it remains quite brutal socially. As many researchers have observed, myself (Wallace, 1973) among them, the spouses and families of the suicide victims are shunned, cut off from respectable society, and isolated. Suicide seems to be condemned with special passion by suicidologists. Certainly one of the founders of this new specialty, after an entire lifetime studying suicide, insisted that it is "a selfish act" (Shneidman, 1985, p. 38). Such passionate denunciation by those so familiar with suicide is especially noteworthy since greater knowledge through research typically ameliorates conventional disapproval.

The passion provoked by suicide suggests the accuracy of Ernest Becker's brilliant analysis in *The Denial of Death*. Becker (1973, p. 15) argues that "the fear of death is natural and is present in everyone, that it is the basic fear that influences all others, a fear from which no one is immune." Becker prefers to call the fear of death "terror . . . in order to convey how all consuming it is when we look it full in the face" (p. 15). Becker continues, "[T]here will never be anything wholly secular about human fear. [An individual's] terror is always 'holy terror'—which is a strikingly apt phrase. Terror always refers to the ultimates of life and death" (p. 150). Becker also argues that "[C]onsciousness of death is the primary repression, not sexuality" (p. 96). "[Humans are] the only animal who can often willingly embrace the deep sleep of death, even while knowing that it means oblivion" ( p. 116).

Becker's analysis certainly offers a powerful explanation for the passion with which suicide is condemned. If the "consciousness of death is the primary repression," how threatening must be the willful acceptance of death! To choose to die, "even while knowing that it means oblivion," must create "holy terror"—an anxiety so great that its source must be censured in the strongest terms possible. Without the explanation by Becker, one would not think that a decision to die would cause such a passionate outcry.

Although the accuracy of Becker's theory may be disputed, the emotion provoked by suicide cannot be. Beyond doubt also is the fact that thousands, even tens of thousands, continue to commit suicide every year. No matter how strong the exhortation against suicide has been, many continue to take their own lives. Are *all* these people mentally ill? Demented? Would-be gods? Selfish egos devoid of true feelings for family? Given all of the objections that have been raised against suicide, is it nevertheless possible that one suicide was justifiable?

The first point to note is that we can choose death both directly and indirectly, by jumping from the bridge as well as by refusing that which could possibly save or prolong our life: an experimental medical procedure or a very expensive one; change from a lifestyle of having unprotected sex or ingesting excessive drugs; confession to whatever our torturer wants. The traditional definition of suicide, that is, the one used by Durkheim in his famous study (1951), encompasses both the direct and the indirect, including the deaths of heros and martyrs. Christians need to be reminded that in the first four centuries after Christ, tens of thousands of Christians, among them almost every one of the original disciples, chose death rather than recanting their beliefs. To martyr was to witness; their day of death became their birthday in heaven. Bowensock (1995, p. 63) argues that throughout their persecution by the Romans, Christians not only understood suicide as an honorable course in defense of one's own ideals but displayed considerable enthusiasm for such martyrdom. Christian belief in such witness continues to the present in the thousands who are killed defending such ideals as liberation theology, social justice, and freedom of religion. "Blessed Are the Persecuted," Lesbaupin (1975, p. 88) states, citing scripture for validation: "We suffer with him that we may also be glorified with him" (Romans 8:17); "Who loves life loses it, and who loses his life for my love keeps it for life eternal" (John 12:25).

The other observation I need to make about the definition of suicide is the same one I made in my 1973 publication *After Suicide*. Virtually every one of the approximately 500 empirical studies of suicide in the past 200 years has documented the many different types of suicide. Given its diversity, no one can reasonably contend that all suicide has any single universal characteristic. All suicide is neither abhorrent nor not; insane or not; selfish or not; rational or not; justifiable or not. Martin (1980, p. 50) observes that "moralists . . . find most suicides to be such horrible crimes that . . . they prefer to deny that [praiseworthy] acts are called suicide." For these and other reasons I do not use definitions to present my case for the justifiability of suicide. I am content to contend that some suicide is justifiable.

I argue that just as everyone has an inalienable right to "life, liberty, and the pursuit of happiness," so everyone has an inalienable right to die. Such rights cannot and shall not be abridged. Just as no other person, including those who presume to speak for God or the State, may dictate the proper terms of one's life as an adult, so none may legitimately impose the manner of one's death. Note that those who would prohibit suicide do so typically on elitist grounds, that they know better than the person who would commit suicide what is best for him or her. Examples are often helpful, and so I would like to further our discussion by describing the death of my father. His death was not by suicide, yet it was willful. It was my first intimate encounter with death.

I was in my final term of residence for my doctorate when my older brother, Bill, called me in Minneapolis. "Dad's in the hospital and it looks like this is it," he began in the direct manner our father had taught us. "He may hang on for a while but if you want to visit with him while he's fully conscious you'd better come now." Bill and I went on to discuss the several earlier times our father had been pronounced "dead" but had recovered, and we compared them to this one. Bill quickly convinced me, as he had our other six siblings, so I began my preparations to leave that weekend for Kansas City, Missouri.

We gathered at the same home in which we had all spent most of our lives. Everyone was now together for the first time in years, and it was a warm although sad homecoming. A schedule of shifts had already been created to make sure Dad had 24-hour care. Never one to display emotion, Dad acknowledged the occasion of our gathering with an extra long embrace for his girls and a prolonged handshake for us boys. No effort was made to deny what was coming, nor did we speak openly of it with Dad: to do so was simply not his way.

It was on my shift, about an hour before the first light in the eastern sky, when Death first came for my father. He struggled, said something unintelligible to me, and then woke to look up at me. "Tell them I'm going," he said before going back to sleep. Without haste or hesitation, all gathered at the hospital following my call. We went into his room, forming a large circle with Mom on the inside next to Dad. Shortly his eyes opened, circled the faces gathered around, and then he raised his right arm as a kind of last gesture; but he only got it halfway up before it and he fell deep into the bed. Someone on the hospital staff who had apparently been waiting outside came into the room, took Dad's pulse, nodded yes, and left. Bill asked me to give a prayer.

Instead of a prayer, I wanted to applaud, to say: "Well done, Dad. You lived life on your own terms including ending it with your family gathered around. Would that everyone could have such a death! Well done, John." That is what I wanted to say. Dad was always a vigorous man, one for whom coming home from his work at the newspaper, where he was an old-fashioned word processor called a linotype operator, simply meant starting another kind of work. Work, work, work, that is what he truly enjoyed—almost as much as he did his kids—and the former after all was just another way to pursue the latter; kids do take a lot of work. Knowing all this I wanted to say to and for my father: "Well done also in rejecting continuance with less than what you have always been. Just as you dominated your life, so you dominated the circumstances of your death. Well done, indeed." Such were my prayers but at the time of my father's death they remained silent because I knew they were not conventional, not what I was supposed to say. (I finally shared them at our family reunion in 1994; my brother Bill told me that he had felt the same way.)

I have described my father's deathbed scene to picture firmly that classic of so many lives and of so much art and literature. With it in mind, I can now meaningfully ask: can such a scene, so familiar in the past, be reenacted today? Hypothetically I could ask: could my father have such a death today? Or to keep it personal, what must I do today to die as my father did, should I be so fortunate?

At the first approach of death "someone" would need to lock the hospital door. Without what can only be accurately called a restraining order, one drafted by agents of the State and approved by one of its judges, hospital staff would push family aside and insist on continuing essential life processes. Without at least a Living Will or better yet a Durable Power of Attorney (Humphry, 1991a), medical intervention would simply be routine. The difference between when my father died in 1959 and today is that medical technology can now prolong "life" beyond what it could then. My father died as he did because he had reached the limits of medical technology then (at least for ordinary or common folk). Today that limit is much different.

Medical technology has so pushed the limit that even the definitions of life and death have changed. It is not necessary to describe these changes, as they are well known. What I wish to point out is that today we have a postmodern medical technology and a Dark Ages mentality about it. Let me illustrate this by continuing to use my father's death as an example.

Medical technology now makes my father's kind of death impossible without active intervention. Unless the patient stipulates in advance, in writing, and in judicially approved form that such intervention is not desired, it *will* take place. Because it is technologically possible, we allow such intervention to occur as a matter of routine. As we thus actively intervene in the process of dying, we argue that human intervention, including by the dying, is somehow wrong—morally, spiritually, religiously, and more. Some say for humans to intervene is to "play God," ignoring the humans behind the machines whose intervention is assumed *not* to be "playing God."

I choose my father's death purposely in part to narrow the scope of our inquiry. He was 69 years old and had lived those 69 years very fully. I remind the reader of that so as not to allow any shift of the argument to the younger, those less blessed, and so forth. In cases such as his, intervention must be seen not only as a decision to act, whether to prolong or terminate, but also as an interruption in a dying process. To extend the length of dying is to intervene no less than to refuse to extend it. Secondly, in my example, the process involved is dying. For my father and those whose deaths are like his, the dying process has become paramount; when we intervene we merely prolong it.

Perhaps the acceptance of death, willful death under circumstances like my father's, should not be called suicide at all. Suicide is ordinarily seen as the interruption of a living process; for those of whom I speak, suicide is the intervention in a dying process.

By whatever name it is called, certainly my father's death had little in common with the deaths I began to study the next year. I was then living in the traditional Latin culture of Puerto Rico. I had decided that I wanted to try to find out why so many Puerto Ricans were so violent. I simply could not understand why they killed not just anyone but their best friends and closest family members. How could they hack one another into pieces, usually over something as trivial as a domino game?

What I learned from that research that is relevant to my topic now is that some people commit suicide by obliging another to kill them. To cite just one example among many, a man went into a bar, obviously after a very bad day for him. To no one in particular, he started cursing, conjuring up the demons of his day to smite. From the furthest corner came another to his face who screamed, "You can't insult me like that!" Surprised at first, he doing the cursing now welcomed an actual object for his heretofore generalized wrath. When he was then assaulted, I had to ponder who was the real victim. As I researched the phenomenon called *victim precipitated homicide*, I found that Stephen Crane (1898a,b) had already described it in "The Board Wacker," Von Hentig (1948) had named it "victim precipitation," and Nagel (1963) had introduced it into the mainstream of criminology. Individuals do commit suicide by having someone murder them.

Seven years later I was part of a research team at the Harvard Medical School, Laboratory of Community Psychiatry, studying bereavement. Robert S. Weiss was studying grief when death was expected, as is the case with cancer patients' families. I proposed a study of bereavement from suicide. Suicide, I had come to understand, was far from a solitary act. Not only did some suicide by provoking murder, but some symbolically committed homicide by their suicide. That is, their suicide was, as Freud put it, "murder in 180 degrees." That research taught me that some suicide is indeed an effort to kill another.

It is these three decades of research on death that I wish to bring to the reader's attention before returning to the topic of the justifiability of suicide. The lesson of the first decade leads me to condemn suicide when done by provoking another to murder. The lesson of my second decade of research impels me to condemn suicide that seeks to symbolically kill another. Having condemned those types of suicide, under what circumstances is suicide justifiable? I believe that suicide is justifiable in defense of one's ideals, one's beliefs, one's values.

It was in defense of such ideals that the early Christians accepted martyrdom rather than recant. It was in defense of his faith that Archbishop Romero forfeited his life in San Salvador in 1982. Defense of one's ideals remains the justification for willful death among emergency workers, among law-enforcement officers, among the military, among firefighters, and among other servants of the public. Emergency personnel endanger their lives and willfully give them that we might live. They defend those ideals more than they value their own lives. Although death is not desired, they are absolutely convinced it is better than the alternative of abandoning their ideals.

Such death is heroic, not just justifiable but praiseworthy, because it is in defense of one's ideals. As such it parallels the thousands of other deaths whose heroism is more private. Neither the public firefighter nor the private citizen who also accepts death prefers it. Rather, both accept death as a necessary corollary to the ideals they embrace. For the firefighter it is duty to those in danger; to the same person off work it is duty to self. Allow me to illustrate with reference to an unpublished research participant of mine, whom I will call Samuel Henry.

Sam Henry's entire life had been spent on or in the close vicinity of a small river. He was on that river from his earliest memories through every one of his life's most significant events. He met a young lass on the river and courted her on it. After marriage and the birth of their only child he built a house on that river and all three continued to live on it.

In later years, after their daughter had married and moved out, after 40 years of a marriage devoted to each other, he had what they called a "stroke." Afterwards, he could no longer devote himself to his wife, his daughter and her husband, the work at the mill, or even to his boat. He could not tie his own shoes, feed himself, or even tell his wife what he wanted to eat. After a year of trying various therapies to no avail, he went down to that river he loved and shot himself. The ideal he thus defended was the person he would be; had been for so long. He did not prefer death but accepted it rather than continue a living death. Sam Henry's death was heroic; it was accepted in defense of ideals. It is not something anyone should condemn.

In a society with less need than ours to deny death, some of the disapproval and certainly much of the violence of willful death would be eliminated. It is extremely unfortunate that our anxieties about death are so strong that we cannot permit persons like Samuel Henry to die peacefully. We deprive them of all nonviolent ways to die and then are revolted by the violence they use.

Perhaps, finally, we have reached the real question that should guide our inquiry: how can *we* be prepared to accept another's decision to die? In pursuing the answer to that query, perhaps we shall find in that old enemy a friend. To make suicide legal, acceptable, ethical—okay in all possible ways, as Maslow (1968), Fletcher (1981), and others have argued—depends on us: the person will do it anyway, following the age-old moral imperative to suicide.

Such a change in public attitudes toward death including by suicide is now underway. Continuing to be influenced by elite moralists including those of the church, the public continues to condemn all manner of death, especially that by suicide. Undeniably, such attitudes must be taken into account because they wound the family and friends of the suicide so deeply.

Continuing to follow the highest ideals not only in their decisions but also in other's reactions to their decisions, some suicide in ways not ordinarily recognized as suicide. That is, they end their lives by the willful accident that will spare their loved ones the public rejection that would follow a suicide. Clearly, until we cease our wholly unrealistic denial of death we will be unable to deal with it, especially in its many faces, and especially when one of us willfully accepts death as a moral imperative.

## 8
### CHAPTER

Wesley J. Smith

# "Rational Suicide" As the New Jim Crow

"It was a rational suicide," said Joe Cruzan's friend, Dr. Ronald Cranford, after Cruzan hanged himself. "He was never going to get better" (Gianelli, 1996, p. 10).

So, what terrible disease did Joe Cruzan have that would somehow make his self destruction "rational?" Cancer? AIDS perhaps? Lou Gehrig's disease? No. Joe was not physically ill. He was deeply depressed, probably due to the 1990 death of his daughter Nancy Cruzan, who died by intentional dehydration after her parents obtained court approval to cut off her feeding tube-supplied food and fluids, because she was disabled by severe brain damage. Indeed, according to another friend, Nancy's death had become, for Joe, a "wound that would not close" (Gianelli, 1996, p. 10).

When Mary Erisman first heard that her mother, Isabel Correa, wanted to die with the assistance of Jack Kevorkian, she was appalled. Isabel was not terminal. She was disabled due to a spinal cord condition that caused paraplegia, a curling of her hands, and painful neuropathy. But rather than being a rallying point in the family to protect Isabel's life, Mary's resistance to her mother's suicide appears to have been seen as cause for *Mary*, not Isabel, to get counseling. Mary was soon made to see that her resistance to her mother's self-destruction was somehow, in Mary's words, "meeting my own selfish needs" rather than protecting her despairing mother's life. With Mary finally willing to abide by Isabel's desire for "rational suicide," her mother flew to Michigan and became Kevorkian's 40th known assisted suicide (DeHaven, 1996).

The tragic suicides of Joe Cruzan and Isabel Correa are examples of the kinds of conditions that a number of mental health professionals and euthanasia advocates believe should entitle a person to a so-called "right to die." Under this new and radical theory of law, not only should the state give its official sanction to the concept of "rational suicide" (throughout this chapter, the term "rational suicide" is in quotes to indicate my disagreement with the concept), but as a consequence, it must grant a legal right to doctors (or others) to facilitate such "rational" deaths. In other words, despairing and suffering people should have the legal right to be killed by doctors (euthanasia) or have their suicides assisted by them (physician-assisted suicide).

# ☐ Suicide, "Rational Suicide," Hopeless Illness, and the Law

It has often been said that the United States is a nation of laws, not of people. This important truth reflects one of our country's greatest strengths; that the vitality of our freedom and the continuing morality of our culture do not depend on men and women, who by definition are here today and gone tomorrow, but rather and in large measure on the rule of law.

Law serves many vital purposes. It seeks to maximize individual freedom; at the same time, it protects the community and individuals from conduct that society deems destructive, a concept our Founders called "ordered liberty." Law, by legalizing or prohibiting conduct, also expresses the overarching values of the society and serves as a powerful statement of our culture's ideals. For example, in passing civil rights laws, society not only protects traditionally oppressed populations but also strongly communicates our fundamental belief in the inherent equality of all men and women. Seen in this light, law is the great through-line of society; it governs conduct, communicates who "we" are, provides a link with the traditions of the past, and helps to create our values, our ethics, our hopes, and our dreams.

This latter aspect of law is especially relevant in the ongoing societal debate about whether the idea of "rational suicide" should be seen not only as a theoretical sociological and psychological concept but also as a legal right. Accepting "rational suicide" in law is a new and radical idea. Up until now, the primary purpose of organized society, as reflected in law, was to protect the lives of all citizens—including people who, for whatever reason, are self-destructive. This underlying ethic was once so strongly expressed that suicide itself was deemed a criminal act. That changed, appropriately, as mental health professionals convinced lawmakers that suicide was not a crime but, rather, a cry for help. As a consequence, suicide and attempted suicide were decriminalized—not because the state had abandoned its interest in protecting the lives of self-destructive people— but precisely because we understood that there are better and more effective ways for the state to perform this vital function.

Thus, the decriminalization of suicide did not establish a "right" to kill oneself. Rather, the law became more nuanced and balanced in its approach to protecting the lives of suicidal people. For example, the police are still required to prevent suicide if they are able. People who attempt to kill themselves can be detained for observation, and if they are deemed beyond a reasonable doubt to be a significant threat to themselves, they can be hospitalized until the crisis passes. (Many once-suicidal people, who are glad to be alive today, would be dead had not society cared enough to protect them from themselves during their time of despair.)

At the same time, all states prohibit euthanasia and most states likewise prohibit assisted suicide as criminal acts. The public-policy purpose behind these criminal statutes is to reduce the danger that dying and ill people will be exploited or coerced into an early death, and to protect overall society from the harm that would occur in public attitudes and mores should killing of people who are dying, sick, or disabled become routine and unremarkable.

This well-established public policy is under concerted attack at all levels by euthanasia advocates and others, who want the state to pick and choose which citizens' lives it will and will not protect. Rather than being a universal obligation of the state, they seek to create a legal category of persons whose lives are not to be protected—people like Joe Cruzan and Isabel Correa—whose deaths these advocates consider "rational" and thus a matter of legal right, meaning that they would be entitled to active assistance in dying through physician-assisted suicide or euthanasia, if that is their desire.

Who would be entitled to "rational suicide?" Those whose self-destructions are seen by social engineers, euthanasia advocates, and some mental health professionals as appropriate, because of "hopeless illness," a concept recently defined, based on a survey of psychotherapists, as "terminal illnesses, [maladies causing] severe physical and or psychological pain, physically or mentally debilitating and/or deteriorating conditions, [and] circumstances where [the] quality of life [is] no longer acceptable to the individual" (Werth & Cobia, 1995, p. 238).

"Hopeless illness" and similar terms—such as "incurable illness" and "desperate illness," which are used to describe people's suicides as "rational"—are cleverly designed to fool the listener or reader into believing that the reference is narrowly drawn. But if one pays close attention to what is actually described in the definition, it can be seen that the term would apply to death on demand for anyone with more than a transitory death wish. For example, a condition causing "severe physical or psychological pain" could be virtually any illness, injury, or emotional malady, from incontinence to chronic migraine headaches, from clinical depression to diabetes, from arthritis to cancer. Moreover, *any* person who wants to commit suicide does so because he or she perceives that "life is no longer acceptable"; otherwise, they would not want to die.

## ☐ "Rational Suicide" as a Form of Oppression

Advocates of legal recognition of "rational suicide" believe that they are maximizing individual liberty. But what they actually are doing, even if they do not mean to, is creating a new form of oppression.

At its core, all oppression is based on a division of human beings into different categories, some of whom receive special rights and privileges or greater protection than others do, because of a false belief that some humans are somehow better than other humans. Oppression has been predicated upon differences of race, gender, sexual orientation, national origin, religion, tribe, age, and other categories that have served the purposes of oppressors, now perhaps including state of health or happiness. Oppression is especially insidious if formalized into law. The Jim Crow statutes in the Old South, which legalized discrimination based on race, are illustrative. They not only gave African Americans short legal shrift, but they actively promoted a racist and oppressive culture by giving the states' imprimatur to bigotry, thereby encouraging and legitimizing the overt, extralegal racism that was then common in Southern society. Thus, the very laws that required segregated schools were essential ingredients in creating the oppressive climate that permitted and even encouraged lynchings, even though technically such vigilante murders were against the law.

So too would it be if the state created a legal right to "rational suicide." Although the laws' wording would be couched in words of compassion and liberty, language, such as "separate but equal," does not always mean what it says. By making "rational suicide" a legally recognized and enforceable right, the underlying message would be for the state to proclaim that all human lives are not of equal inherent worth, that some of us (the healthy, able-bodied, and relatively happy) are worth protecting, even from self-destruction, but others of us (the "hopelessly ill") are people whose lives are of such little use that their deaths are best for all concerned. The impact of this legalized *healthism* would be no different from the consequences that flowed from institutionalizing racism in the law—it would create a new category for culling humans into privileged and oppressed classes, thereby influencing cultural outlook as well as impacting upon the state's legal obligations towards its citizens. In other words, "rational suicides" would not only be permitted but actively encouraged—just as the societal message behind Jim Crow laws promoted overt and covert racism.

This disturbing truth is evident when comparing the underlying values expressed in court cases that have found laws prohibiting physician-assisted suicide unconstitutional and those that have ruled that laws against physician-assisted suicide are proper and in keeping with the state's duty to protect the lives of all of its citizens. (Space permits only the comparson of two of such cases: *People v. Kevorkian* [1994], which ruled that Michigan's law criminalizing assisted suicide was constitutional, and *Compassion in Dying v. Washington* [1996], which ruled that the state of Washington's similar law was not.)

It is safe to assume that everyone reading these words knows who Jack Kevorkian is and what he does. Generally, the media describe Kevorkian as aiding "terminally ill" people to die. This is not true. As of this writing, approximately 28% of Kevorkian's known victims were "terminally ill", that is, the person would be expected to die naturally within several months. Many were disabled, including 20% who had multiple sclerosis and Isabel Correa, disabled by a nonterminal spinal cord condition. At least three had no organic disease at all, according to autopsy results. (These three were Marjorie Wantz, who complained of severe pelvic pain; Rebecca Badger, who believed falsely that she had multiple sclerosis; and Judith Curren, an obese woman [269 pounds] who had been diagnosed with chronic fatigue syndrome and other nonterminal autoimmune conditions, none of which could be detected on autopsy.) Thus, it is accurate to say that Kevorkian is "practicing" the kind of "medicine" that those who promote a legal right to "rational suicide" for the "hopelessly ill" intend to make legitimate and lawful.

Early in his campaign, Kevorkian was arrested for facilitating suicides, after which he attacked the law against assisted suicide in the Michigan courts as unconstitutional. His case ultimately reached the Michigan Supreme Court, which ruled not only that the Michigan law (which has since lapsed) was proper under the United States Constitution, but that, even absent a specific statute banning assisted suicide, such activity is a common law crime in Michigan. (The U.S. Supreme Court subsequently allowed the ruling to stand when it refused to review the case.)

Of particular interest here, the Michigan Supreme Court, in its 5–2 decision, found that the law prohibiting assisted suicide promotes the ideal that all human lives are of equal inherent worth and thus are equally entitled to the state's protection. For example, in a footnote the court wrote:

> Society's respect for the value of every human life, without reference to its condition, the cornerstone of American law, is inconsistent with a State's recognition of a legal right to . . . assisted suicide, or . . . voluntary euthanasia. . . . Recognition of the dignity of human life demands resistance, rather than concession, to the real or imagined death wishes of those who are afflicted with pain, depression, a sense of personal worthlessness or a sense of burdensomeness to others. A humane society provides support of every kind, including moral support, to those who are burdened in order that they may live. (*People v. Kevorkian*, 447 Mich 436, 437; 527 N.w.zd 714, 729 [Mich., Dec 13, 1994], citation omitted).

In other words, people are people are people, and the state's interest is in preserving life, not promoting or facilitating death.

This humane approach accurately expresses the purposes behind the traditional Western ethic embodied in law: to protect and value all human life. But protecting and valuing all human life is just what proponents of creating a legal right to "rational suicide" hope to destroy. They see laws that protect the lives of "hopelessly ill" people not as recognizing the dignity and intrinsic value of their lives but rather as paternalistic, intrusive, and akin to state despotism.

This skewed view was at work in *Compassion in Dying v. Washington* (1996) which, in a ruling of 8–3, the Ninth Circuit Court of Appeals directly contradicted the reasoning and values expressed by the Michigan Supreme Court (although the case is not controlling in Michigan). Rather than protecting life, according to the majority of the Ninth Circuit, laws prohibiting assisted suicide "force" people to stay alive. The state may engage in this totalitarianism against the young and healthy because "forcing a robust individual to continue living does not, at least absent extraordinary circumstances, subject him to 'pain . . . and suffering that is too intimate and personal for the state to insist on'" (*Compassion in Dying v. Washington*, 1996). (This nihilistic value system was also evident in the oral arguments made by the attorney for Compassion in Dying, Kathryn Tucker, who asserted that there "is no viable life" in a "patient in a terminal condition.")

If the Ninth Circuit's reasoning prevails, it will not be long before the "hopeless illness" category replaces the terminal illness category set forth in the decision as the criteria for exercising the new legal right to physician-assisted suicide (or euthanasia), removing from the protection of the state the lives of tens of millions of its citizens. Indeed, the *Compassion in Dying* case is quite specific on the point. As the quotes from the decision cited here demonstrate, it is not "only" the terminally ill who would have the right to be killed but also:

The disabled:

> While we recognize the legitimacy of these concerns, however, we also recognize that seriously impaired individuals will, along with nonimpaired individuals, be the beneficiaries of the liberty interest asserted here—and that if they are not afforded the option to control their own fate, they like many others will be compelled against their will, to endure protracted suffering. (p. 825)

People worried about money considerations and being a burden:

> While state regulations can help ensure that patients do not make uninformed, or ill-considered decisions, we are reluctant to say that, in a society in which the costs of protracted health care can be so exorbitant, it is improper for competent, terminally ill adults to take the economic welfare of their families and loved ones into consideration. (p. 826)

People who want to die because they receive inadequate access to health care:

> One of the prime arguments [in favor of laws prohibiting assisted suicide] is that the statute is necessary to protect the poor and minorities from exploitation. . . . In fact, . . . there is far more reason to raise the opposite concern: the concern that the poor and the minorities, who have historically received the least adequate health care, will not be afforded a fair opportunity to obtain the medical assistance [with suicide] to which they are entitled. (p. 825)

People (including children) who cannot decide for themselves due to legal incompetence:

We should make it clear that a decision of a duly appointed surrogate decision maker, is for all legal purposes the decision of the patient himself. (p. 832, n. 120)

The *Kevorkian* and *Compassion* cases precisely illustrate the starkly opposing value systems competing for public acceptance in the ongoing political and legal struggles over whether the law can appropriately recognize a right to "rational suicide." The issue presented is stark: do we continue to adhere to the traditional Western ethic that sees it as the state's vital duty to protect the lives of all of its citizens through its laws and public policies, or do we eschew such protection from those deemed to have "nonviable lives," abandoning them to self-destruction in the name of liberty and compassion and "not forcing" the suffering among us to stay alive? In order to adequately answer this question, two more issues need to be looked at: can vulnerable populations be protected from exploitation, coercion, and abuse if a right to self-destruct is enacted into law, and is recognizing a right to "rational suicide" necessary to alleviate the suffering of "hopelessly ill" people?

## ☐  Protective Guidelines Do not Protect

Proponents of a right to "rational suicide" assure that laws permitting physician-assisted suicide or euthanasia would be tempered with "protective guidelines" to prevent abuse. Of course they ignore the fact that such guidelines already exist in the form of an absolute prohibition. They claim that the prohibition does not hold and that physician-assisted suicide should thus be "brought out of the darkness and into the light" through legal regulation. But this assertion would no more prevent killings in excess of the vaunted guideline regulations than raising the speed limit to 70 mph has prevented speeding. In other words, it simply will not work. Indeed, violations of guidelines are likely to increase, because the state's smiling countenance on some killings legitimizes the death act itself.

This is exactly what has already happened in the Netherlands, which in 1973 legally made euthanasia available by promising not to prosecute doctors who kill patients so long as certain protective guidelines are followed. (Technically physician-assisted suicide and euthanasia remain crimes in the Netherlands.) These protective guidelines, similar to many proposed by those who wish to create a legal right to a "rational suicide," have been enacted into Dutch statutory law, including that (Gomez, 1991, p. 32):

> The request must be made entirely of the patient's own free will and not under pressure from others.
> The patient must have a lasting longing for death. In other words, the request must be made repeatedly over a period of time.
> The patient must be experiencing unbearable suffering.
> There must be no reasonable alternatives to euthanasia.
> Doctors must consult with at least one colleague who has faced the question of euthanasia before.
> Only a doctor can euthanize a patient.
> The euthanasia must be reported to the coroner, with a case history and a statement that the guidelines have been followed.

In actual practice, these guidelines offer precious little protection for the weak, vulnerable, and despairing, nor have they effectively inhibited doctors from euthanizing patients who fall outside their parameters. Rather, the quasilegalization of "rational suicide" has created a value system and a culture that widely views killing patients as a proper form of "treatment." This has led to widespread violations of the guidelines, such as euthanasia or physician-assisted suicide of people who were not near the end of their lives, some of whom were not even suffering from physical symptoms at the times of their deaths, including documented cases of the deaths of an asymptomatic HIV patient (WGBH-tv, 1993); a young woman who feared that her anorexia, then in remission, would return (WGBH-tv, 1993); and a woman with skin cancer because she was upset by the scars on her face (O'Keefe, 1995), all without legal consequence.

As the types of patients killed by doctors have steadily expanded, so have the permissible killing categories under the protective guidelines. For example, babies born with birth defects can now be legally euthanized based on quality of life determinations. Similarly, people who are depressed with no underlying physical illness or injury are also eligible, thanks to a 1993 Dutch Supreme Court case approving the physician-assisted suicide of a woman named Hilly Bosscher. Hilly wanted to kill herself because her children had died over the course of several years and because her marriage had been dissolved due to years of abuse. A Dutch psychiatrist named Chabot assisted his "patient's" suicide after meeting with her only four times over a 5 week period—without any attempt to treat her—based on his assertion that "persistently suicidal patients, are . . . terminal" and that their condition can constitute "an incurable disease" (i.e., a "hopeless illness") ("CQ Interview," 1995, p. 243). The Dutch Supreme Court, building on previous euthanasia cases that liberalized the practice, blessed Dr. Chabot's prescription for ending his patient's suffering by helping to end the patient, ruling that there was no difference for purposes of the law regulating physician-facilitated death between physical and emotional suffering.

This shocking case is absolutely consistent with how a legal right to "rational suicide" based on "hopeless illness" would ultimately be applied in this country. Recall that the definition of "hopeless illness," cited earlier, includes maladies causing "severe psychological pain" that are "mentally debilitating" under "circumstances where [the] quality of life [is] no longer acceptable to the individual" (Werth & Cobia, 1995, p. 238). This is how it was for Hilly (and for Joe Cruzan). Thus, her assisted suicide, using this country's euthanasia jargon, was "rational." That dedicated treatment by mental health professionals and caring community outreach might have saved her life seems never to have entered her "doctor's" mind. This assisted "rational suicide" was then, in actuality, an abandonment of Hilly actively encouraged by Dutch law.

That is not all. Under Dutch euthanasia guidelines, involuntary euthanasia is not supposed to happen. But, it does—and how! According to a study sponsored by the Dutch Government known as the Remmelink Report (1991, volume I, p. 13), in 1990, 1,040 people died from involuntary euthanasia, lethal injections given without request or consent, an amount equivalent to three deaths every single day. (If the same percentage of patients were involuntarily killed by doctors in the United States, it would amount to 16,000 such deaths per year.) Of these involuntary euthanasia cases, 14% were fully competent to make their own medical decisions but were killed without request or consent anyway (volume II, p. 49, table 6.4). Moreover, 72% of the people killed without their consent had never given any indication that they would want their lives terminated (volume II, p. 50, table 6.6). An additional 4,941 patients were killed by intentional overdose of pain medication without request or consent, not for the purpose of palliating pain but to end the patient's life (volume II, p. 58, table 7.2), a figure that would amount to approximately 78,000 people each year using United States demographics.

The Dutch experience teaches us that once the state abandons the protection of some of its citizens based on healthist notions that some lives are not worth living, the desire to die becomes paramount, not whether it is right or wrong to accommodate the desire—a protection the vaunted guidelines are supposed to provide. At the same time, paradoxically, once society grants doctors a license to kill based on a legal recognition of "rational" self-destruction, they come to see themselves as having the right to choose whose lives should end—regardless of whether the patient expressed a desire for "rational suicide."

Thus, guidelines do not protect. Rather, they merely legitimize killing by doctors and assure falsely that all is under control. Not only do guidelines not protect, but studies show that in this country, the legalization of euthanasia and physician-assisted suicide would lead to the victimization of traditionally oppressed groups. This truth was specifically noted by the New York State Task Force on Life and the Law (1994), appointed by former governor Mario Cuomo to investigate whether physician-assisted suicide and euthanasia should be legalized. After more than a year of intensive study, the committee's recommendation was a unanimous and unequivocal no, in part because euthanasia and physician-assisted suicide would be practiced through the "prism of social inequality and bias that characterizes the delivery of services in all segments of our society, including health care" (p. xiii). In other words, racism, ageism, sexism, bigotry against disabled people, and issues of class and socioeconomic status would all materially impact upon killing decisions. Moreover, as the Report noted,

> In light of the pervasive failure of our health care system to treat pain and diagnose and treat depression, legalizing assisted suicide and euthanasia would be profoundly dangerous for many individuals who are ill and vulnerable. The risks would be most severe for those who are elderly, poor, socially disadvantaged, or without access to good medical care. (p. ix)

## ☐ A Better Way

If a legally recognized "rational suicide" is not the answer, what is? It certainly is not the status quo. At present, too many suffering and despairing people are abandoned to their misery because of unwise public policies that inhibit, rather than promote, appropriate and compassionate care (a partial cause for the demands to legalize physician-assisted suicide and euthanasia). Here is where truly beneficial legal reform can make a tremendous difference in the lives of suicidal people, improving individual lives and validating the value system behind the law that every life matters.

First, rather than create a "right to die," we must establish a right to receive medical care and treatment. This right to adequate health care should include access to expert palliation (pain- and symptom-control) services. Currently up to 50% of cancer patients receive inadequate pain control, as do many AIDS patients and other people with chronic and terminal conditions. But, as the New York State Task Force (1994) noted, once suffering people receive adequate pain control and treatment for depression, the desire for "rational suicide" disappears in almost every case.

Second, we need to rescind laws that interfere with doctors' ability to control their patients' pain. For example, many states now require triplicate prescriptions for narcotic agents, a very cumbersome process that discourages many doctors from fulfilling their professional responsibilities. Moreover, in our zeal to win the "war on drugs," some physicians report harassment by law enforcement and regulators if they aggressively treat their patients' pain. As a consequence, suffering patients become innocent victims of society's desire to prevent drug abuse. Surely, we can inhibit drug abuse without depriving people of desperately needed medication to control their suffering.

Third, public policy, as expressed through law, needs to send the loud and clear message that we expect doctors to treat pain aggressively and take their patients' suffering as seriously as they do the conditions that cause suffering. Mandatory education on pain and symptom control should be required as a condition of initial and continuing licensure. (Medical schools traditionally give short shrift to the subject.) Failure to aggressively palliate pain should be considered a failure of professional responsibility, leading to the possibility of civil malpractice suits and regulatory penalties. Physicians who are not adept at controlling serious pain should be required to refer patients to a pain control specialist, and health insurance companies must be prevented from financially punishing doctors who do.

If these tasks were accomplished, the message sent by the law would be to value the lives of all citizens, not just the young, the healthy, and the vital.

## ☐ Conclusion

In which direction do we wish to take society? Do we really want the law to give society's imprimatur of approval to "rational suicide?" Do we want physicians to be legally permitted to abandon their despairing and suffering patients to death because of their inability or unwillingness to truly help the patient overcome difficulty? Indeed, do we want medical professionals to be able to suggest self-killing to patients with difficult cases (or financial problems) as just another "treatment option?" If so, the law should recognize the existence of "rational suicide." However, if we want to improve access to healthcare and the quality of medical services that are rendered, if we want to value and honor the importance of each of us, we should reject "rational suicide" and instead focus on the many opportunities mentioned and unmentioned in this chapter to improve the medical system and the delivery of truly compassionate caregiving.

To abandon or to care for; that is the question. Choose the former and embrace a new form of legal oppression and state-sanctioned abandonment. Choose the latter, and the whole idea of "rational suicide" can be thrown on the junk pile where it belongs.

## 9
CHAPTER

Kathryn L. Tucker

# Physician-Assisted Dying: A Constitutionally Protected Form of "Rational Suicide"

A majority of states, including Washington and New York, have statutes that prohibit assisting suicide (see *Compassion in Dying v. Washington*, 79 F.3d 790, [9th Cir., 1996] [en banc], rev'd sub. nom., *Washington v. Glucksberg*, 117 S.Ct. 2258 [1997]). These statutes are understood to prohibit physicians from assisting their mentally competent, terminally ill patients to hasten death. The assisted-suicide statutes in Washington and New York were recently challenged in federal court under the Fourteenth Amendment to the United States Constitution (*Id., Quill v. Vacco*, 80 F.3d 716 [2d Cir., 1996], rev'd *Vacco v. Quill*, 117 S.Ct. 2293 [1997]). The Fourteenth Amendment provides, in pertinent part: "[N]or shall any State deprive any person of life, liberty, or property, without due process of law; nor deny to any person within its jurisdiction the equal protection of the laws."

The patients and physicians bringing these cases maintain that the U.S. Constitution protects the right of a mentally competent, terminally ill person to choose to hasten his or her death in a manner that is sure to result in death, is nonviolent, and preserves dignity by self-administering drugs prescribed by a doctor for that purpose. They argue that the Fourteenth Amendment protects the individual decision to hasten death with physician-prescribed medication and that statutes prohibiting physician-assisted suicide deny equal protection, guaranteed by the Fourteenth Amendment, to competent, terminally ill adults who are not on life support.

The substance and status of this legal reform effort are discussed in this chapter. Given the broader discussion in this book regarding "rational suicide," it is important to appreciate that the kind of "suicide" at issue in these lawsuits is much more limited than many supporters of "rational suicide" would endorse. These cases are limited to mentally competent patients in the final phase of terminal illness who wish to hasten death by self-administering medications prescribed by their doctor for that purpose. The limited scope of the suits is intentional, as the constitutional interests of the patients and doctors on the one hand and the State on the other vary considerably if any of the limiting factors are altered.

# ☐ Summary of the Constitutional Challenge

## The Fourteenth Amendment Protects Individual Liberty

The United States Supreme Court has consistently recognized that the Fourteenth Amendment's protection of liberty extends to important personal decisions that individuals make about their lives and how they will live them (e.g., *Cruzan v. Director, Missouri Department of Health*, 497 U.S. 261, 1990 [refusing unwanted medical treatment]; *Griswold v. Connecticut*, 381 U.S. 479, 1965 [contraception]; *Loving v. Virginia*, 388 U.S. 1, 1967 [marriage]; *Pierce v. Society of Sisters*, 268 U.S. 510, 1925 [child rearing and education]; *Prince v. Massachusetts*, 321 U.S. 158, 1944 [family relationships]; and *Skinner v. Oklahoma*, 316 U.S. 535, 1942 [procreation]). For example, in *Planned Parenthood v. Casey* (112 S.Ct. 2791, 2805 [1992]), the Court stated, "It is a promise of the Constitution that there is a realm of personal liberty which the government may not enter." The challenged statutes, which make aiding suicide a criminal act, prevent mentally competent, dying citizens from choosing to shorten the period of suffering before death by self-administering drugs prescribed for the purpose of hastening death. The state thus intrudes into and controls a profoundly and uniquely personal decision, one that is properly reserved to the individual, to be made in consultation with his or her doctor. These statutes thereby abridge the liberty guaranteed by the Fourteenth Amendment.

## The Fourteenth Amendment Guarantees Equal Protection

The challenged laws do not seek to punish suicide, or attempted suicide. In addition, citizens have the right to refuse, or direct the withdrawal of, life-sustaining treatment with the intent to hasten death. This right has been based on a common law right to be free of unwanted bodily invasions (see *Union Pacific Railroad Co. v. Botsford*, 141 U.S. 250, 1891) as well as a state or federal constitutional right of privacy or liberty (see *In re Colyer*, 99 Wn.2d 114, 1983; *In re Grant*, 109 Wn.2d 545, 1987; *In re Quinlan*, 70 NJ. 10, 335 A.2d 647, 1976). Physicians who comply with such requests are immune from prosecution under the challenged statutes (see the Washington Natural Death Act, RCW 70. 122.100, 1979). Some terminally ill patients, thus, are able to choose to hasten their inevitable deaths with medical assistance. This distinction between a dying patient whose condition involves life-sustaining treatment and one whose condition does not violates the Equal Protection Clause of the Fourteenth Amendment.

# ☐ The Challenge to Washington's Assisted Suicide Statute

In *Compassion in Dying v. Washington* (79 F.3d 790, 9th Cir., 1996), Washington's assisted suicide law (RCW 9A.36.060) was challenged. It should be noted that the plaintiffs did not challenge the entire statute, only the "or aids" provision as quoted here. This statute is virtually identical to similar laws in New York and many other states:

1. A person is guilty of promoting a suicide attempt when he knowingly causes or aids another person to attempt suicide.
2. Promoting a suicide is a class C felony.

The plaintiffs in the *Glucksberg* case included terminally ill patients, physicians who treat terminally ill patients and Compassion in Dying, a nonprofit patients' rights, services, and advocacy organization based in Seattle, Washington. Compassion in Dying provides information, counseling, and assistance to mentally competent, terminally ill adult patients considering hastening their deaths. The patient plaintiffs suffered from cancer, AIDS, and emphysema and desired to obtain prescription drugs to hasten death. All of the patient plaintiffs died within several months after the case was filed.

The State of Washington defended its statute primarily on grounds that the state has interests in preventing suicide and preserving life.

Plaintiffs argued that the state's reported interests do not outweigh a competent dying patient's interests in hastening impending death. A general state interest in preventing suicide has no application to a fully competent, dying adult. Such an individual is not cutting short a viable life for reasons stemming from mental illness or instability. Rather, this individual is at the end-of-life because of the progress of terminal disease, is cutting short a period of intolerable suffering, and is fully mentally competent. The state's interest in preserving life is substantially diminished if a patient is in the final phase of terminal illness. Thus, mental competency and terminal phase are "bright lines" in the lawsuits, with significant import to the constitutional balancing that must be conducted.

On May 3, 1994, the District Court declared the Washington law unconstitutional, concluding that a competent, terminally ill adult has a constitutionally-protected right to hasten death with physician assistance (*Compassion in Dying*, 850 F.Supp. 1454, 1462 [1994]). Although the court found that the interests of a state may justify regulating this activity, a total prohibition of this activity was held to place an undue burden on the exercise of a constitutionally protected liberty interest (*Id.* at 1465). The court held that the Washington law also violates the Equal Protection Clause because it impermissibly treats similarly situated groups of terminally ill patients differently (*Id.* at 1467). In overturning the Washington statute, the court stated:

> The liberty interest protected by the Fourteenth Amendment is the freedom to make choices according to one's individual conscience about those matters which are essential to personal autonomy and basic human dignity. There is no more profoundly personal decision, nor one which is closer to the heart of personal liberty, than the choice which a terminally ill person makes to end his or her suffering and hasten an inevitable death. From a constitutional perspective, the court does not believe that a distinction can be drawn between refusing life-sustaining medical treatment and physician-assisted suicide by an uncoerced, mentally competent, terminally ill adult. (*Id.* at 1461)

On appeal, a three-judge panel of the United States Court of Appeals for the Ninth Circuit voted 2–1 to reverse the District Court decision (*Compassion in Dying*, 49 F.3d 586, 1995).

Plaintiffs successfully petitioned for a rehearing by a larger number of Ninth Circuit judges, a procedure known as "rehearing en banc," and this panel became the largest to hear any case involving constitutional aspects of end-of-life decisions.

On March 6, 1996, in a landmark 8–3 decision the Ninth Circuit affirmed the District Court decision, holding that "there is a constitutionally-protected liberty interest in determining the time and manner of one's own death," and that Washington's statute prohibiting physician assistance in the form of drugs prescribed to mentally competent, terminally ill adults who wish to hasten death violates the Fourteenth Amendment (*Compassion in Dying v. Washington*, 79 F.3d at 193-94).

In an exhaustive opinion, the Ninth Circuit held:

A competent terminally ill adult, having lived nearly the full measure of his life, has a strong liberty interest in choosing a dignified and humane death rather than being reduced at the end of his existence to a childlike state of helplessness, diapered, sedated, incontinent. How a person dies not only determines the nature of the final period of his existence, but in many cases, the enduring memories held by those who love him. . . .

In this case, by permitting the *individual* to exercise the right to *choose* we are following the constitutional mandate to take such decisions out of the hands of the government, both state and federal, and to put them where they rightly belong, in the hands of the people. We are allowing individuals to make the decisions that so profoundly affect their very existence—and precluding the state from intruding excessively into that critical realm. The Constitution and the courts stand as a bulwark between individual freedom and arbitrary and intrusive governmental power. Under our constitutional system, neither the state nor the majority of the people in a state can impose its will upon the individual in a matter so highly "central to personal dignity and autonomy." Those who believe strongly that death must come without physician assistance are free to follow that creed, be they doctors or patients. They are not free, however, to force their views, their religious convictions, or their philosophies on all the other members of a democratic society, and to compel those whose values differ with theirs to die painful, protracted, and agonizing deaths. (*Id.* at 813–14, 839; emphasis original; citation omitted).

Importantly, the Ninth Circuit recognized that the loved ones of the dying patient may be present at the hastened death so that the patient need not be alone (*Id.* at 838, footnote 140).

The Ninth Circuit recognized that state laws regulating physician-assisted dying "are both necessary and desirable to ensure against errors and abuse, and to protect legitimate state interests" (*Id.* at 832–33). For examples of proposed procedural safeguards, see Oregon's Death with Dignity Act (ORS 127.800 et. seq., 1994); Baron and colleagues (1996); and Quill, Cassell, and Meier (1992). Regulation of physician-assisted suicide, however, may not impose an undue burden on the protected liberty interest (*Compassion in Dying*, 79 F.3d at 835, 1996; citing *Planned Parenthood v. Casey*, 112 S.Ct. at 2828, 1992).

The State of Washington successfully petitioned for review of the en banc decision by the United States Supreme Court.

On June 26, 1997, in a unanimous decision, the Supreme Court reversed the Ninth Circuit en banc decision, holding that "the asserted 'right' to assistance in committing suicide is not a fundamental liberty interest protected by the Due Process Clause" and that Washington's ban on assisted suicide is "at least reasonably related" to "important and legitimate" government interests. (*Washington v. Glucksberg*, 117 S.Ct 2258, 2271, [1997]; citation omitted).

The Court began its analysis by articulating the question to be answered in general form: "[W]hether the 'liberty' specially protected by the Due Process Clause includes a right to commit suicide which itself includes a right to assistance in doing so." (*Id.* at 2269). The Court next inquired whether this asserted right has any place in "our

Nation's history, legal traditions, and practices." (*Id.* at 2262). Finally, the Court concluded:

> The history of the law's treatment of assisted suicide in this country has been and continues to be one of the rejection of nearly all efforts to permit it. That being the case, our decisions lead us to conclude that the asserted "right" to assistance in committing suicide is not a fundamental liberty interest protected by the Due Process Clause. The Constitution also requires, however, that Washington's assisted-suicide ban be rationally related to legitimate government interests. This requirement is unquestionably met here.... First, Washington has an "unqualified interest in the preservation of human life." . . . [L]egal physician-assisted suicide could make it more difficult for the State to protect depressed or mentally ill persons, or those who are suffering from untreated pain, from suicidal impulses. The State also has an interest in protecting the integrity and ethics of the medical profession.... Next, the State has an interest in protecting vulnerable groups—including the poor, the elderly, and disabled persons—from abuse, neglect, and mistakes.... Finally, the State may fear that permitting assisted suicide will start it down the path to voluntary and perhaps even involuntary euthanasia.... [These] are unquestionably important and legitimate [State interests], and Washington's ban on assisted suicide is at least reasonably related to their promotion and protection. (*Id.* at 2271–75; citations omitted).

Although the Court's decision in *Glucksberg* was unanimous, five Justices wrote or joined concurring opinions that limited the scope of the majority's ruling and carefully reserved issues for future cases. For example, Justice O'Connor explicitly stated that the Court did not reach the "narrower question whether a mentally competent person who is experiencing great suffering has a constitutionally cognizable interest in controlling the circumstances of his or her imminent death." (*Id.* at 2303). Additionally, Justice Breyer stated that on the narrower, more difficult question, there was "greater support" in "our legal tradition" for a "right to die with dignity." (*Id.* at 2311). These comments, and others, suggest that the federal constitutional protection of the choice at issue remains open to future developments.

## ☐ The Challenge to New York's Assisted Suicide Statute

Shortly after the challenge to Washington's assisted suicide statute was filed, a virtually identical case, *Quill v. Vacco* (870 F.Supp 78 [S.D.NY 1994], *rev'd*, 80 F.3d 716 [2d Cir. 1996]), was filed in the United States District Court for the Southern District of New York challenging New York's assisted suicide laws.

The *Quill* plaintiffs included terminally ill patients suffering from cancer and AIDS, and physicians who treat terminally ill patients. All of the patient plaintiffs died within several months after the case was filed.

The State of New York defended its statutes on grounds similar to those raised by the State of Washington, primarily state interests in presenting suicide and preserving life.

On December 15, 1994, the constitutionality of the New York assisted suicide law was upheld by the District Court. Plaintiffs then appealed to the United States Court of Appeals for the Second Circuit.

On April 2, 1996, the Second Circuit ruled unanimously that the New York law prohibiting physician-assisted suicide violates the Equal Protection Clause of the Fourteenth Amendment because it "does not treat equally all competent persons who are in the final stages of fatal illness and wish to hasten their deaths," and distinctions made with respect to such persons "do not further any legitimate state purpose" (*Quill v. Vacco*, 80 F.3d 716, 2d Cir., 1996). The *Quill* court found (*Id.* at 727):

> Indeed, there is nothing "natural" about causing death by means other than the original illness or its complications. The withdrawal of nutrition brings on death by starvation, the withdrawal of hydration brings on death by dehydration, and the withdrawal of ventilation brings about respiratory failure. By ordering the discontinuance of these artificial life-sustaining processes or refusing to accept them in the first place, a patient hastens his death by means that are not natural in any sense. It certainly cannot be said that the death that immediately ensues is the natural result of the progression of the disease or condition from which the patient suffers. . . .
>
> Moreover, the writing of a prescription to hasten death, after consultation with a patient, involves a far less active role for the physician than is required in bringing about death through asphyxiation, starvation and / or dehydration. Withdrawal of life support requires physicians or those acting at their direction physically to remove equipment and, often, to administer palliative drugs which may themselves contribute to death. The ending of life by these means is nothing more nor less than assisted suicide. It simply cannot be said that those mentally competent, terminally ill persons who seek to hasten death but whose treatment does not include life support are treated equally (*Id.* at 729).

The *Quill* court declined to find that there is a constitutionally protected liberty interest at stake in light of what it defined as an "admonition" given by the Supreme Court in *Bowers v. Hardwick* (478 U.S. 186, 194; 1996), disfavoring expansion of protected liberty interests (*Quill v. Vacco*, 80 F.3d at 716; 1996). Soon after the *Quill* decision was issued, a United States Supreme Court decision relating to gay rights was decided in a way that suggests that *Bowers* may be of little precedential import (*Romer v. Evans*, 1996 U.S. LEXIS 3245).

In answer to the argument that the state has an interest in preserving the life of all of its citizens at all times and under all circumstances, the court wrote:

> But what interest can the state possibly have in requiring the prolongation of a life that is all but ended? Surely, the state's interest lessens as the potential for life diminishes. And what business is it of the state to require the continuation of agony when the result is imminent and inevitable? What concern prompts the state to interfere with a mentally competent patient's "right to define [his or her] own concept of existence, of meaning, of the universe, and of the mystery of human life," when the patient seeks to have drugs prescribed to end life during the final stages of a terminal illness? The greatly reduced interest of the state in preserving life compels the answer to these questions: "None." (*Quill v. Vacco*, 80 F.3d at 729-730; citations omitted).

One member of the court filed a concurring opinion expressing his view that both liberty and equal protection grounds supported striking the challenged law but advocating a "constitutional remand" to allow the legislature an opportunity to reconsider the issue and redraft legislation (*Id.* at 738–743.)

The State of New York successfully petitioned for review of the Second Circuit's decision.

On June 26, 1997, in a unanimous decision, the U.S. Supreme Court reversed the Second Circuit's decision, holding that New York's ban on physician-assisted suicide does not violate the Equal Protection Clause of the Fourteenth Amendment because "the distinction between assisting suicide and withdrawing life-sustaining treatment . . . is both important and logical; it is certainly rational." (*Vacco v. Quill*, 117 S.Ct. 2293, 2298; 1997). The Court found:

The distinction [between assisting suicide and withdrawing life-sustaining treatment] comports with fundamental legal principles of causation and intent. First, when a patient refuses life-sustaining medical treatment, he dies from an underlying fatal disease or pathology; but if a patient ingests lethal medication prescribed by a physician, he is killed by that medication. . . . Furthermore, a physician who withdraws, or honors a patient's refusal to begin life-sustaining medical treatment purposefully intends, or may so intend, only to respect his patient's wishes. . . . A doctor who assists a suicide, however, "must, necessarily and indubitably, intend primarily that the patient be made dead." Similarly, a patient who commits suicide with a doctor's aid necessarily has the specific intent to end his or her own life, while a patient who refuses or discontinues treatment might not. (*Id.* at 2298–99; citations omitted)

In *Quill*, as in *Glucksberg*, the concurring opinions limit the majority's holding. Justice O'Connor, for instance, has this to say about the Court's finding in *Quill*:

Our holding today in *Vacco v. Quill* that the Equal Protection Clause is not violated by New York's classification, just like our holding in *Washington v. Glucksberg* that the Washington statute is not invalid on its face, does not forclose the possibility that some applications of the New York statute may impose an intolerable intrusion on the patient's freedom. There remains room for vigorous debate about the outcome of particular cases that are not necessarily resolved by the opinions announced today. How such cases may be decided will depend on their specific facts. (*Id.* at 2310).

Such comments suggest that the legal theories explored at the beginning of this chapter may be successfully employed in the future to establish Federal constitutional protection for physician-assisted suicide in cases of terminal illness.

# ☐ Conclusion

While the U.S. Supreme Court recently upheld laws that criminalize physician-assisted suicide, it did not definitively reject recognition of a right under the Federal Constitution to choose to hasten inevitable death with physician assistance, leaving open the possibility that the Court will extend federal Constitutional protection in the future. It can be anticipated that the strong majority of the population favoring freedom of choice on this matter (see, e.g., Stewart, 1997, pp. 6–7, concluding that "the American public strongly supports allowing a doctor to assist a terminally ill, suffering patient end his or her life . . . support is in the 69% to 75% range") will press for legislative reform. It can also be anticipated that challenges to assisted-suicide prohibitions based on state constitutional provisions, which are often more protective than the federal Constitution, may be made.

PART

2

# SERVICE PROVIDERS

**CHAPTER**    Lois Chapman Dick

# Rational Suicide: Life and Death Your Way

Can suicide ever be considered rational? What is the definition of rational? According to *Webster's New Collegiate Dictionary* (1981, p. 951), the word rational has several meanings: (1) having reason or understanding; (2) relating to, based on, or agreeable to reason; (3) reasonable. *Webster's New World Thesaurus* (1974, p. 364) has a long list of synonyms for rational, including stable, calm, cool, deliberate, discerning, discriminating, level-headed, collected, logical, knowing, sensible, and wise. Suicide is defined in the *Dictionary* as "the act or an instance of taking one's own life voluntarily and intentionally especially by a person of years of discretion and of sound mind" (p. 1156). The *Thesaurus* (p. 437) lists synonyms of suicide: self-murder, self-destruction, and Hara-Kiri. Hara-Kiri is suicide by disembowelment practiced by the Japanese samurai or formally decreed by a court in lieu of the death penalty. The definitions and synonyms of rational and suicide seem somewhat contradictory to me. Perhaps this is an indication of why *rational* suicide is questioned.

Well, here I am at 60 years of age and what do I want for my future? What I want is to live as long as I can at the level of living that I like. My darling Nathan, who died in January of 1995, and I had agreed that if either of us got a terminal illness that we would not *make* each other live forever. We both strongly believed in the right to leave this planet on our own time schedule. Fortunately, he died quickly of a heart attack / stroke while in his van as he was coming back from shopping. No one was hurt when he died and he went quickly. That's the way he wanted to die. Not that I wanted him to go, but at least he did not suffer for years with an illness.

I have more than just the academic knowledge of death, stress, trauma and suicide. I have been held at gunpoint twice and knifepoint twice and been in five fires and two plane crashes. And, over the years both professionally and personally, I have been with almost 400 people as they were dying. I have also spent time with their loved ones after these people died. Some of them committed suicide, but these suicides were with the "permission" of the family because of the fact that the individuals were getting close to the end of their lives and were in terrible pain. I have had this privilege owing to my work in hospitals; to volunteer work with emergency-services personnel, the police, and the military; and to producing my film *In the Midst of Winter*. *In the Midst of Winter* is about living, loving, and loss because of AIDS and many of those we interviewed were nearing death while in horrendous pain.

I am a certified death educator and grief counselor and I go around the country doing training about death, dying, and grief. Every once in a while someone will ask my about my credentials. I tell them my college degrees and work experience. I also mention that I am a death educator. As I sometimes say, there are two things we generally do not talk about in this culture: sex and death. And at least one of them is inevitable.

## ☐  The Old Person's Friend

These days we make it harder and harder to die. Years ago we used to call pneumonia the "old person's friend." My understanding of this phrase is that when elderly people who could not live life the way they wanted to anymore contracted pneumonia there was no cure and so they died—something they wanted to do but did not feel they should do by committing suicide.

Many elderly people whom I have met over the years do not enjoy their prolonged lives in a nursing home or a hospital intensive care unit. They are getting attentive medical care, but they hate their inability to *live* life *their* way. They are immobile. Their minds do not work the way they used to, and this complicates personal communication with those they need and those they love. They cannot go out and dance or dine. They can not even decorate their Christmas trees. What used to make life lovable has been taken away from them by their aging or disability. We are supposed to live as long as we can, even at the cost of losing our enjoyment of living and our ability to give what we consider proper love to others.

I have a neighbor down the street who is probably in his late 80s or early 90s who was raised in the southern part of the United States, so he has a drawl. He saw me working in my yard and came over and said, "Hey, Lois! Somethin' just happened that's gonna make you laugh like crazy." I said, "Tell me about it."

> Well honey, I just went for my annual medical check-up and my doctor asked me what I was eatin' these days. I told him I was having my bacon and eggs and toast almost every morning unless I had pancakes with maple syrup. I was eating my beef steak and pork chops frequently. And I was havin' a beer at least once a day. You know what he said to me? He told me that I shouldn't eat and drink that stuff as often as I do, it wasn't healthy. I was committing dietary suicide. I told him he was a donkey. I should eat and drink differently? Why? So I could die in perfect health?

We both laughed and hugged each other. He is still taking the responsibility for his living and perhaps his dying. I do not see him as suicidal. Perhaps his style of living is a form of rational suicide. Then again, it may just be the way he *enjoys* living.

There was a client of mine a number of years ago who said to me, "Lois, why can't I just die? I am so sick. My doctor says I don't have much longer." I responded, "Just do what you need to do for you and those you love. Have you talked to them about your wanting to die?" He looked at me with a frown on his face and then said, "Well, of course not, I don't want to hurt them." I looked at him gently and then said, "No, you won't hurt them if you talk about your wanting to die. You will only help them by giving them 'permission' to let you go." He smiled and seemed more relaxed. I waited a few more minutes and then said, "What are you thinking?" He replied,

> I was thinking about my Dad who died years ago. He was 98 years old and in terrible pain from his physical problems and he didn't feel like he *should* die. He was worried about us kids. My Mom wouldn't talk to us about his death. Boy, I sure wished she had because both myself and my sister wanted to let Dad die. We knew he loved us and was afraid to leave us. He was concerned that we would feel that he had abandoned us.

Another patient once said to me, "Lois, what can I say to my family about my dying and how I want my life to be all over?" I looked at her and then said, "Merely talk openly with them about what you want. Tell them it is okay for them to ask you questions about what you *and* they want, given your death coming in the future." She said, "You mean I can actually talk to them about my death?" I told her that the best thing she could do for them was to talk about her need to die—to get an end to her pain and suffering.

Several years ago I got a call from a family who said that their 18-year-old-son, who had been diagnosed with cancer at age 13, was now approaching the end of his life. They felt he should come and talk to me about what he was experiencing. When he walked slowly into my office I could see clearly that he was miserable, both physically and emotionally. I asked him what he was experiencing. He did not say anything for several moments and then he told me that he just wanted to die. He had enough of his pain and lack of ability to do all the things he used to do. "I wish I could go somewhere and just take a lot of pills and die. But, I don't feel comfortable doing that because it might hurt my Mom and Dad." I asked him if he had spoken directly with his parents about his wish and he replied that he had not. I suggested he do so as soon as possible. He then said, "Okay, ask them to join us here." I asked his parents, who were sitting in my living room (my office is in my home) to join us. He looked at them and said, "Mom and Dad I'm sorry, but I just want to die. I hurt and hate the fact that I can't do any of the things I like doing anymore. Would you mind just letting me go?" Both of his parents started to cry. They said that they thought they understood some of what he might be going through. They would not demand that he live any longer than he wanted to. He said, "Thank you, Mom and Dad. You know I love you." He stopped taking his chemotherapy and radiation and died 2 months later. His parents grieved his death, but they also said that they were glad they "let him go when he wanted to go."

Recently I went to the home of a client. She had been diagnosed with cancer and received a great deal of treatment, treatment she said she hated. She would not go back for more treatment even if her physician had suggested it. At that time she felt that she would not live more than several months longer. I suggested to her that she have a video made of herself talking to her two children and others about whom she cared. The video would be available to them immediately after she died and also in the years to come. In the film she spoke of both the good times and the bad times in her life. She looked directly at the camera as she was lying on her sofa in pain and told her children how much they have meant to her over the years. She died one week later.

She and her husband were divorced years ago, but they became loving and caring friends. Sometimes we cannot live with each other, but we can become loving friends. He was always there for her. In fact they were living together so that she could have the care she needed. What an example for their children! Yes, she wanted to die. She did not commit suicide, but I could certainly understand her wanting to do so. And I suspect that her ex-husband might have gone along with it too, and even helped her if she needed assistance.

## □ Compassion in Dying

There are others who feel as I do. One of them is Dr. Ralph Mero, who was the Executive Director of a volunteer group in Washington called Compassion in Dying. It was organized in 1993 to provide information, counseling, emotional support, and personal presence at the time of death to terminally ill patients considering hastening their deaths. Dr. Mero defines rational suicide as death hastened by the use of medication prescribed by a licensed physician as contrasted with death accomplished by violent means (personal communication, July 1993). He feels that it is critical to distinguish between typical acts of suicide and the desire to hasten death by patients in the end stage of terminal illness. He believes that the person with a terminal illness seeking death is not depressed but is exhausted by the prolonged process of dying and deterioration. I totally agree with him.

I believe that many with terminal illness also feel that they are creating pain for those they love, not to mention sometimes very high expenses because of prolonged medical or nursing care. We need more compassion for the dying. We need to share more of their suffering by talking more with them about what we suspect they are going through and telling them to be open and direct with us about what they are experiencing, informing them that they do not have to "protect" us. They need to be honest with us. This is what I call the "judicious application of guilt." They then feel that they are not being "selfish" in their wish to die but are actually helping those they love.

Through the years I have seen that, all too often, the death of a doctor's patient is viewed as a mistake. Doctors are supposed to heal people or keep them alive no matter what the cost or pain to them and their loved ones. This may have a negative impact on the physician–patient relationship. More and more of us are siding with an individual's right to die. The U.S. Supreme Court decision in the case of Nancy Cruzan (*Cruzan v. Director, Missouri Department of Health*, 1990) acknowledged this as well, although in doing so it essentially ignored the physician–patient relationship, and left each state to pass its own laws regarding implementation of any such procedure. How is this impasse among the patient, the physician, and the law (written law, religion, and custom) to be resolved?

I have a wonderful physician and friend in Washington. His name is John Ball and he is an endocrinologist. In 1990 he wrote an article entitled "The Proscribed Prescription," at my request for *The Forum*, the newsletter of the Association for Death Education and Counseling. One of the points he emphasized was the following:

> We are a nation founded on individual freedom. The first order of responsibility is that each of us deal with our own mortality. We should make a living will stating our wishes and / or obtain a durable power of attorney for health care matters. I think drivers' licenses, along with a space for organ donation, should have another space indicating that you have a living will on file. It's ironic that one might not be able to produce such a document, just when one needs it most. (Ball, 1990, pp. 1, 12)

Later I asked him how he felt about rational suicide. He responded:

Thirty years ago in a huge city hospital, [I] scampered down three flights of stairs to retrieve [my] third admission of the day from the accident floor. She was small and very dry and [feverish] and old . . . and crumpled under the blankets. After an hour or so of intravenous fluids she opened her eyes and stopped moaning. [I] took her hand, introduced [myself] and told her she had pneumonia but would recover. She moved her lips in response but no sound seemed to come out. [I] indicated by sign and voice that [I] couldn't hear her. Twice, she motioned [me] closer, until she cupped [my] ear with her hand and held it near her lips. Her voice and the intensity of her gaze pierced [my] brain simultaneously. "Let me die, you son-of-a-bitch," she said. Of course, [I] didn't. She died anyway. She never spoke again. (personal communication, August 1995)

Over the next three decades Dr. Ball said he listened better and heard more. For example, there was Debbie, an artist and dog trainer who lived life to the utmost in an effort to stay ahead of the cystic fibrosis and bacteria that were destroying her lungs. The last time she and Dr. Ball met she said, "Don't let me die in pain and don't let me die alone." He did not. Dr. Ball feels that as a physician his role as another person considers ending her or his life is to be there, to listen, to be compassionate, and to speak little, but to review all things. In his words:

As an individual, my deeply personal vision of life has been that of an oarsman on a river. While subject to currents, rapids, sweepers and tides, I'm free to row my boat as I will. Whatever my destination on the river, I would want my hands on the oars. And someone to be there.

Dr. Ball always thinks of his patients and their needs first. *He listens to them and hears them.* He will give them warnings about the consequences of their possible behavior healthwise, but he also allows them to make the choices. All too often patients do not state up front what they want. They just, literally, hand over their bodies to the doctor and say the equivalent of "fix me" instead of making their own decisions known.

## ☐ Death with Dignity

Death with dignity: do we still believe in this concept? It used to mean death without pain; without fear; and without physical, mental, or spiritual degradation. There are times when this happens naturally. At other times it means withdrawing artificial life support to allow natural death to occur. And, in some instances, it is the intentional self-determined choice of the dying patient who is convinced that the continuation of life is not worth the deterioration of his or her physical and emotional well-being.

The saddest situations I have seen over the years as a counselor and consultant are when the parents of young children are diagnosed with potentially terminal illness. The parents almost always feel that they have to remain living as long as possible for their children. Yes, family is important, but what is the cost that these parents must pay in terms of pain and extended treatment that may not even be beneficial? I have had clients who, when they were children, watched as their parents died painfully. Their parents felt that they had to extend their lives to take care of their children. Almost all of my clients, when they were adults, have talked about their feelings of guilt. They have said that they felt they were responsible for making "mommy" or "daddy" suffer.

When they come to me for counseling as adults they talk of how helpless they felt as children and how their ill parents did not even talk to them about what they, the parents, were going through physically and emotionally. The parents were not trying to be cruel. They felt they were protecting their children from what they, the parents, were experiencing. You may remember when you were a child and walked into a room in which a parent with a problem was sitting. You could probably see or sense his or her difficulty. I believe that we need to share more with our children about life *and* death. If we do, they will feel they are more helpful to us and grow up with a better sense of what life is all about.

When is death better than life? I recall hearing that many prisoners of war during World War II preferred to die rather than act in ways that they considered beneath them or inhumane. Self-respect was more important to them than merely existing. When we are facing our own deaths are we sometimes "at war" with those around us—people who insist that we continue to live?

There is another group of individuals who may, at times, rather die than live—people with disabilities. Sixteen years ago when I was a social worker in a hospital a teenager named Brad was brought into the emergency room. He had been playing baseball and dived head first into home plate to score a home run. The cost was that he broke his spinal cord and almost died. Since that day he has been paralyzed from the neck down.

How many of you know what it might be like to be in his situation? He has to have 24-hour nursing-care assistance at a cost of about $250,000 per year. He cannot feed himself, he cannot sit up on his own, go to the bathroom alone, or even pet his dog. He has said to me on many occasions, "People don't see me. They just see my wheelchair."

One of his complaints has been that he could not even kill himself if he wanted to because of his disability. He has, at times, felt that he does not have a life worth living, so why should he continue to exist? He is totally wheelchair bound when he is out of bed; he operates the wheelchair by moving his chin on an extended knob. He therefore has little access to many of the ways of committing suicide.

There is a international organization of which I am a member called the Association for Death Education and Counseling. It is composed of several thousand people who are involved with death education and grief counseling. Membership is diverse and includes nurses, doctors, educators, firefighters, police officers, counselors, hospice workers, funeral directors, and others who are in one way or another involved in death, dying, and grieving. One of our members is a woman named Jinny Tesik. She lives in Washington and was on the Advisory Committee for Compassion in Dying. She feels that there is justification for rational suicide based on her personal experiences with her stepmother and father (personal communication, July 1993):

In 1986 I took an indefinite leave of absence from my position on a Seattle Hospice Team to help my father care for his terminally ill wife, my stepmother of 36 years. She died slowly and stoically from lung cancer.

Unable to live alone, due to his own battle with emphysema, Dad returned to Seattle and lived with me for the last 2 years of his life. Before he agreed to move up here, he told me that he would never allow his disease to control him the way his wife's lung cancer had controlled her. He intended to take his life while he still had his dignity, his self-respect, and above all, control of his life. He made me promise that I would honor his choice as we had honored his wife's choices.

The emphysema progressed to the point that Dad was tethered to 30 feet of oxygen tubing. Breathing became more and more difficult. Eating became a problem because food interfered with his breathing.

Jinny accepted her father's decision to commit suicide by taking an overdose of medication.

> When I think of my Dad's death I feel great compassion and love. I feel the dignity of a man who chose to die as he chose to live—his way. No matter how wonderful a hospice is or how advanced science and pain control are, there will always be people who will still choose to be in control of their deaths. We owe it to them and to their loved ones to support them in compassionate dying. For those who choose their own death in their own time let it be peaceful, loving, and legal, not shattered by violence and crime.

## ☐ Conclusion

I have never helped anyone commit suicide. However, over the years I have had a number of pets. When they were old and in excruciating pain they would look up at me and appear to be asking me to help them leave this planet. We went to the veterinarian and I had them "put down" as I held them in my arms. Then I took them to my home and buried them in my backyard with a personal ceremony and tears. They gave me unconditional love and I wanted to give them freedom from pain.

In the United States we allow abortion, although as I write this chapter there are questions about how late in a pregnancy it can be performed. Abortion is the ending of life for certain children by actions of people other than the children. If we can allow this legally, then how can we *not* allow rational suicide—the ending of life for some adults? The adults I am talking about are rational in the sense that they have sought medical or psychological help for their illness or pain and their physicians or counselors have acknowledged that there is no cure for their illness or pain and they are *not* mentally impaired. Yes, I believe that there can be *rational suicide*. I also believe strongly in the words on a sweatshirt that I frequently wear: *GO FOR IT! Life is not a dress rehearsal.*

Richard R. Ellis

# Counselors and Rational Suicide: Voices from the Opposition

*Truth is rarely pure, and never simple.*
(Oscar Wilde, *The Importance of Being Earnest,* 1895).

The existence of this book clearly demonstrates that rational suicide is an issue of many facets, some which challenge conventional wisdom. Wilde had it right. As we shall see, one operational definition of rational suicide requires that the one who assesses the mental competence of the person considering suicide should be a mental health professional. This could include counselors. This chapter takes issue with the notion that we can speak of counselors as if that title confers the professional competency to make the required assessment on all who claim it.

As an educator and trainer of Master's-degree and doctoral students in counseling and counseling psychology since 1966, and as the founder and coordinator of the New York University M.A. program in grief counseling since 1984, I try to prepare students for working with the general population, terminally ill patients and their loved ones, and survivors of loss. This preparation includes their study and discussion of suicide. I also maintain a small private practice; most but not all of my practice is in grief counseling. In this chapter I present a voice in opposition to counselors who consider rational suicide an option for some people.

## ☐ Definitions of Suicide

Death by suicide is a completed escape from pain via a lethally intended act. Anguish, disturbance, or perturbation nurture the suicidal person's need to escape. The basic pain is psychological, but physical pain can be a major contributor promoting the suicidal person's escape to nonbeing. The suicidal person can employ his or her own hand or invite the hand of another to commit the lethal act (Shneidman, 1985, 1996).

The desire to escape from pain (Shneidman, 1996) is the motivating force, the driving engine of suicide. Psychological pain is always present in the mind of the suicidal person. Shneidman refers to it as *psychache*, which derives from thwarted or distorted psychological needs (p. 6). Physical pain is not centrally involved in most suicide (Shneidman, 1996). Not included in the definition presented here are the religious and cultural suicide traditions of *suttee* in India, *seppuku* (more recently, *hara kiri*) in Japan, and certain martyrs of Islam. The present definition also excludes those definitions having a prequalifying adjective, such as *attempted* or *para-*. The definition accompanies those which espouse and promote suicide prevention.

## ☐ Definitions of Rational Suicide

Rational suicide is a concept that stands as the antithesis of the above definition. Basically, rational suicide is a choice for self-cessation that is made in consultation with appropriate others and free from psychological illness or severe emotional distress. Siegel's (1986) description of rational suicide includes the lack of psychological illness or severe emotional distress and adds the presence of a realistic assessment of the situation, and the objective understanding of the community or group.

Werth (1996b) provides a useful description of rational suicide. Without providing a conceptual definition, he offers an operational definition derived from empirical research (Werth, 1994; Werth & Cobia, 1995; Werth & Liddle, 1994) in the form of criteria for rational suicide (Werth, 1996b). Briefly they are (partly paraphrased):

1. The person considering suicide has an unremitting "hopeless" condition, including terminal illnesses, severe physical and/or psychological pain, physically or mentally debilitating and/or deteriorating conditions, or quality of life no longer acceptable to the individual.
2. The person makes the decision as a choice free of pressures from others to suicide.
3. The person has engaged in a sound decision-making process that included:

   a. Consultation with a mental health professional capable of assessing mental competence and the absence of treatable major depression;
   b. Nonimpulsive consideration of all alternatives;
   c. Consideration of the congruence of the act with one's personal values;
   d. Consideration of the impact on significant others;
   e. Consultation with objective others (e.g., medical and religious professionals) and with significant others. (p. 62)

Clearly item 3a directly relates to the counselor, a member of the community of mental health professionals. It is the mental health professional who is expected to assess the mental competence of the person considering suicide. I submit that only some counselors, not all, are equipped by virtue of their training and experience to make that assessment.

## ☐ Counselors

Who are the counselors? As a group they comprise a variety of subgroups. We may categorize them by extent or level of training and education, by population served, by the setting in which the counseling occurs, or by techniques applied. The title of *counselor* can be and is claimed by those who simply choose a descriptive adjective to precede it, such as financial, beauty, investment, and so forth. Usually these individuals possess specific information, sometimes knowledge, about their chosen topic but have had little or no formal training or education to prepare them to counsel. In most cases the title *advisor* would be more accurate than that of counselor. Throughout history the individual who believed he or she needed help in resolving an issue turned to a friend, neighbor, or elder. Byrne (1995) refers to the help that these persons who were not formally trained offered as *traditional counseling*. Perhaps on a higher level of help is that which Alcoholics Anonymous and Narcotics Anonymous offer (Brown & Srebalus, 1996). Ex-alcoholics or ex-addicts provide counseling to abusers. These nonprofessional counselors (or perhaps more accurately, technicians) have no formal training or education. Their expertise comes from their life experiences.

Each of us probably knows of someone who, without benefit of formal preparation to be a counselor, has an excellent understanding of human behavior and interpersonal relationships, has remarkable intuition about other people, has a deep sense of caring for others, and listens. Similar individuals can and do render in many instances as high a quality of service as professional counselors. The length of their therapeutic arms does not, however, stretch out infinitely. They usually are limited in their understanding of, for example, the potential effects of transference and countertransference, the differences between treatable and nontreatable depressions, what constitutes adequate assessment of mental competence, and, often, the difference between advising and counseling.

> In contrast, the professional counselor, regardless of the field [in which the counselor specializes], is well educated and trained in that field and devotes full time to it. The professional psychological counselor is not only well prepared but also educated and trained in interpersonal relationships. (Byrne, 1995, p. 3)

Within the topic of rational suicide a critical issue is the preparation of counselors who do or will work with a person considering suicide. By definition (Werth, 1996b) these counselors are required to be expert in the area of clinical assessment and able to work with a person who has an unremitting "hopeless" condition, a terminal illness, severe pain, or an other debilitating or deteriorating condition. Very few individuals who can be categorized into any of the subgroups of counselors mentioned here have sufficient and appropriate training for this work.

No one knows for certain how many counselors there are who are not formally trained; most professional counselors in the United States are trained at the Master's or post-Master's (not including doctoral) levels. The next largest group is trained at the doctoral or postdoctoral level.

## Master's Level Counselors

Minimum preparation for a professional counselor is successful completion of a Master's degree in counseling. Most Master's level programs resemble each other, but the range of emphases and depths of experiences for the students may vary widely, particularly from state to state. To establish standards of preparation, in 1981 the American Counseling Association (ACA), representing most counselors, established the independent Council for Accreditation of Counseling and Related Educational Programs (CACREP). Accreditation in the United States is a voluntary process that nongovernmental units perform. As of January 1996, programs in 109 institutions of higher education have CACREP accreditation. Of those programs, 251 are at the Master's level and 34 are at the doctoral level (Armstrong, 1996). In 1993 a report stated that only 15% to 20% of the 360 to 500 (depending on how one counts them) counselor-preparation programs in the United States have accreditation (Weinrach & Thomas, 1993).

Currently one of the largest constituent groups within the ACA is the American Mental Health Counselors Association (AMHCA). Among its priorities is licensure (Brown & Srebalus, 1996). AMHCA efforts have been productive: as of June 4, 1998, the legislative bodies of 45 states and the District of Columbia had enacted licensing regulations of professional counselors (AMHCA, 1998). The programs include eight core curriculum areas, require comprehensive attention to assessment via additional course work and assessment practica, and require several hundred more hours of clinical instruction and internship. Neither AMHCA nor CACREP standards require preparation for work with dying, grieving, or suicidal persons.

My reading of several existing, Master's level CACREP-accredited programs finds the content of the appraisal area usually, but not in all cases, to be an introductory survey. In some programs a course in measurement and evaluation is the appraisal experience. In both instances there is no quarrel with the content presented. Appraisal, however, is not the equivalent of assessment. On the other hand, my reading of programs in mental health counseling found required courses and some type of practicum in assessment. It would seem that counselors in these programs could be competent in assessing the mental competence of the person considering suicide.

## Doctoral-Level Counselors

Doctoral-level programs, usually approved by the state, generally are extensions of the programs in the previous subsection. The counseling world includes programs to prepare counseling psychologists. The American Psychological Association (APA) represents a large majority of psychologists. The APA Committee on Accreditation has been accrediting programs in counseling psychology since 1953; by 1993 it had accredited 65 programs (Hollis & Wantz, 1993).

A cornerstone of these and related programs is the year-long course in clinical assessment. Usually there are also in-depth courses in projective and other assessment techniques. Of all programs in counseling, the psychologically-based doctoral programs are most likely to prepare competent practitioners in the art and science of clinical assessment. Neither the states nor APA standards require preparation for work with dying, grieving, or suicidal persons.

# ☐   Codes of Ethics and Rational Suicide—Competence

A key element in the professional identity of a profession and its constituent members is its code of ethics. "Ethics are the rules or standards governing the conduct of a person or members of a profession" (Soukhanov, 1992, p. 630).

Each of the more established behavioral scientist groups has a code of ethics. Members are expected to abide by and to uphold the code. Nonmembers who provide professional services typical of those who are members are judged by the same standards as are the members; this is especially true in our courts of law.

I submit that a large number of the generic mental health community professionals may be in danger of breaching both the ACA and the APA codes of ethics in the area of professional competence. The current APA *Ethical Principles of Psychologists and Code of Conduct* (1992) states, "Psychologists provide services, teach, and conduct research only within the boundaries of their competence, based on their education, training, supervised experience, or appropriate professional experience" (p. 4). The current ACA *Code of Ethics and Standards of Practice* (1995) states under Section C: Professional Responsibility, "Counselors practice only within the boundaries of their competence, based on their education, training, supervised experience, state and national professional credentials, and appropriate professional experience" (p. 7).

Well-intentioned, empathic, caring, compassionate counselors may slip into the abyss known as "beyond one's competence." When clients raise the possibility of ending their pain by ending their being, what happens if these well-intentioned counselors have no training in assessing the mental competencies of the clients? To quote Pope and Vasquez (1991):

> Although the omniscient, omnipotent, and error-free clinician is a myth, therapists and counselors have an ethical and legal responsibility to offer clients a basic and adequate competence. . . . Given the encouragement of clients who may hold exaggerated beliefs about our talents, it may be difficult for us to acknowledge that we simply are not competent to intervene in a particular situation. (pp. 51–52)

The temptation is great. Counselors want to trust their intuition, but in these situations the *Code of Ethics* calls for us to be professional and observe the caveat. Only those counselors trained in assessment can make the evaluation, and then they use their intuition to aid their educated interpretations of the data.

## ☐ Credentialing Individual Counselors

Although CACREP accredits programs, another arm of ACA is the National Board for Certified Counselors, which sets standards and certifies individuals. It is the largest counselor-certifying body; it has now certified over 20,000 counselors. "Certification is a nonstatutory process provided by a governmental body, agency, or association which, upon the individual meeting specified standards, awards the individual a specific title" (Forest & Stone, 1991, p. 13).

Other organizations offer similar certifications. One example is the Association for Death Education and Counseling (ADEC), an international professional organization with a membership of over 2,200 professionals from over 20 different related occupations, including counselors and psychologists. ADEC established a National Certification Review Board in 1981 to set standards for certification at several levels in death education and grief counseling. Currently certification includes Professional Death Educator, Associate in Bereavement Support and Education, Professional Grief Counselor, and Professional Grief Therapist. ADEC's professional certifications require the individual to have successfully completed at least a Master's-degree in a program related to the specific certification title. I noted previously that the great majority of related Master's-level programs do not include clinical assessment. It would be appropriate for an ADEC-certified professional to make a clinical assessment only if that professional had successfully completed the requisite training and supervised experience in clinical assessment.

Note that it is common practice for some providers of short-term education on courses and workshops to award certificates of achievement. These certificates should not be confused with the certification discussed here. Certificates of achievement recognize the participation of individuals in those experiences. In addition to providing recognition they can be useful as evidence of continuing education.

More restrictive than certification, licensure grants to individuals who meet specific standards the legal right to practice a specific profession; as such, licensure determines who can practice that profession (Bradley, 1995; Shimberg, 1981). Licensing is a state function. Most states license counseling psychologists and other psychologists.

## ☐ What the Suicidal Person Presents

After addressing who the counselors are and what they have to offer their clients, it is appropriate to look at the potentially suicidal person. The view here is essentially that of Edwin Shneidman, who is preeminent in the field of suicide and of suicide prevention.

Shneidman (1985) has studied hundreds of individuals who have suicided and who were about to suicide. Although each suicide is idiosyncratic, he has identified 10 characteristics of suicidal acts. The first two seem to be situational:

1. *The common stimulus is unendurable psychological pain.* "Reduce the level of suffering, often just a little bit, and the individual will choose to live" (p. 124).
2. *The common stressor is frustrated psychological needs.*" The clinical rule is: address the frustrated needs and the suicide will not occur" (p. 126).

The second two are conative (striving):

3. *The common purpose is to seek a solution.* Suicide is not a random act. Its logic is inexorable.
4. *The common goal is cessation of consciousness.* It is less a moving toward death and more a moving away from consciousness of unendurable pain. "What the person needs is the advocacy of a good person, a champion, an ombudsman who will intervene by speaking to others, making arrangements with others" (p. 131).

The next two are affective:

5. *The common emotion is hopelessness-helplessness.* The person readily capitulates and can do nothing; no one can help.
6. *The common internal attitude is ambivalence.* The person can jump off the bridge and scream for rescue (p. 135).

The next one is cognitive:

7. *The common cognitive state is constriction.* The range of choices has narrowed to two. Shneidman contends that the path to those two followed courses of illogical reasoning.

The next two are relational:

8. *The common interpersonal act is communication of intention.* Clues are there in about 80% of suicides. Ambivalence is at work.
9. *The common action is egression.* It is an escape from distress, permanently (p. 145).

The 10th and final is:

10. *The common consistency is with lifelong coping patterns.* How the individual has handled stress, upset, pain, and so forth over the history of that individual is a strong predictor of whether that person will suicide. "That is our main handle on individual prevention" (p. 149).

My overall understanding of these 10 characteristics is that suicide is, by Shneidman's definition, irrational. In the arena of suicide the counselor will not be dealing with rational suicide. Instead the counselor will be called upon to combat the irrationality, to identify the fallacious reasoning, the inconsistencies. The counselor may not remove the searing pain but can work to ease the suffering; even with a little easing the suicide may be averted. Some of the frustrated needs may be met with the counselor's aid. (For a challenge to Shneidman's interpretation of the above ten characteristics, see Werth [1996a].)

Of course effective counselor interventions are not as simple as these suggestions may imply. Working as a counselor in the arena of suicide requires training, courage, and intelligence. It is difficult. However, if the alternative to working toward suicide prevention is agreeing with the person's intention to suicide, where does that leave us? "Suicide is not a treatment" (Foley, 1996a, p. 1).

# ☐ Pain

The previous section, in part, addresses psychological pain. An important precipitant of psychological distress is physical pain (Foley, 1995). Uncontrolled pain is a factor for the person considering suicide; persistent pain impedes the person's ability to utilize support from family and others (Foley, 1995). Similar to Shneidman's belief that physical pain is not central to most suicide, Foley finds no correlation between suicidal ideation and pain intensity or relief. For example, suicidal ideation in AIDS patients with pain probably relates more to an ongoing mood disturbance than to experienced pain intensity.

Counselors need to be aware of the dangers in overidentifying with clients in pain and of the possibility of the intrusion of transference and countertransference issues. Foley (1995) reminds us that "there is significant confusion between compassion and competence. Suffering is defined as 'unrelievable'" (p. 175). Rational suicide may not be the only compassionate response.

People are driven to want death if their pain produces psychological and existential suffering. "The presence of depression and other pain-induced mental illnesses raises grave doubts about whether requests for assisted death are rational" (Nelson, 1995).

Nelson (1995) believes that the medical community does have the techniques for effective response to pain and depression. The New York State Task Force on Life and the Law (1994) found a serious gap between what medicine can achieve in the control of pain and suffering "and the palliative care routinely provided to most patients" (p. 35); even though the effective treatments are available, too often patients do not receive them. Reasons for this situation include lack of professional training, knowledge, and attention to pain assessment; unfounded fears of causing addiction; and the practices of pharmacies. Further, more attention has been given to acute pain and cancer pain than to chronic pain; medical research, training, and practice also have neglected chronic pain.

Of particular interest to counselors is the Task Force recommendation that an interdisciplinary approach to pain and symptom management of both chronic and acute conditions be the norm. This approach seeks input from the patient and family members. Cassell (1995) reports that since their student days physicians have heard that the basis for most diagnoses are the patient's symptoms; however, physicians favor objective tests and measurements over the taking of patient history. He finds some physicians moving away from interest only in the disease and toward interest in the subjective state of the patient. "We want now to relieve the pain, suffering, hopelessness, loneliness, despondency, grief, and other subjective accompaniments to serious illness, even when we cannot influence the disease" (p. 187). He concludes that if pain is treated better, suicide is not necessary. Writing about terminal illness, Quill (1995) says that the standard of care for the dying is comfort.

## ☐ Codes of Ethics and Rational Suicide—Prevention

The current codes of ethics of the ACA (1995) and the APA (1992) do not directly address either prevention of suicide or rational suicide. The ACA *Code of Ethics*, Section B, says, "The general requirement that counselors keep information confidential does not apply when disclosure is required to prevent clear and imminent danger to the client or others . . ." (p. 5). The APA *Ethical Principles*, Section 5.05, says, "Psychologists disclose confidential information without the consent of the individual only as mandated by law, or where permitted by law for a valid purpose, such as . . . to protect the patient or client or others from harm" (p. 10). In the past some have interpreted these statements as requiring prevention of suicide. Rational suicide now is a challenge to that interpretation. APA Principle D (Respect for People's Rights and Dignity, p. 3) affirms self-determination as a right.

## ☐ Conclusion

This chapter addresses counselors and rational suicide by echoing the voices from the opposition. I have limited my choices to issues of which I would like all counselors to have an awareness regardless of their current or future positions. Issues about medical treatment of pain and the delivery or nondelivery of that treatment impinge on the work of counselors who work with terminally ill patients and their families. The issues are limited in number and focus but do, I believe, cut to the core of counseling practice.

Consider Werth's (1996b) definition of rational suicide. Item 1 refers to "an unremitting 'hopeless' condition, including terminal illnesses," and so forth. It is not clear whether this condition is physical, or psychological, or both. Use of the term "hopeless" clouds the issue more. Hopeless is a state of mind; terminal is a physical state. Even for the dying person there always are levels of hope, each dependent upon the day's reality. Perhaps the lowest level of hope is to be kept as comfortable as possible. There is no need to be hopeless. Dying is not dead. Counselors can support the dying person's hopes.

Item 3 requires the person to have "engaged in a sound decision-making process that included. . . . [c]onsultation with a mental health professional capable of assessing mental competence and the absence of treatable mental depression." This is a large, important issue for counselors. The soundness of the decision is debatable. If we equate soundness with rationality, and if we follow Shneidman's thinking, the person choosing suicide is not capable of making a rational decision. The counselor may, however, intervene in ways that may alter the person's decision. Item 3a poses great potential danger. Counselors are part of the generic mental health profession. Despite the large number of counselors, only some of them have competence in clinical assessment. Thus, one cannot assume that "counselors" can make the required assessment.

The relevant codes of ethics of both ACA and APA (and there are other similar codes) clearly stress the necessity for counselors to confine their practice to the limits set by their levels of training. Unethical behavior is not condoned, and ignorance is no excuse. The point of limited practice is amplified by additional sections of the codes that prohibit counselors from falsely advertising, implying, or otherwise promoting themselves as having competence beyond their training.

The ACA and APA codes directly address neither suicide prevention nor rational suicide. To my ear the language of the totality of both codes is now more tolerant than earlier codes of potential possibilities that would include suicide. Perhaps the dialogue has begun among members of both organizations.

I recently checked the content of the four major counseling journals, between 1993 and 1996. There was only one article on rational suicide (Rogers & Britton, 1994). I relate that information to my knowing that there exists only one Master's level program with a specialization in grief counseling; it is the one I founded at New York University several years ago. Only one? This is a sad commentary on our profession.

The number of papers presented at ACA and APA annual conferences on suicide, death, dying, and grieving may be counted on only a few fingers. It seems that the counseling profession has yet to value substantially work in the venues of dying, death, and grieving. The American public is yet a few steps further behind the profession; this may be collective wisdom at work. Probably sooner than most of us expect, the idea of rational suicide will strongly challenge older wisdom.

I ask counselors to learn as much as possible about the issues and positions that form the dialogue about rational suicide. While they are learning I keep thinking (in paraphrases) about something else Oscar Wilde wrote: for every complex problem there is simple, direct solution—and it is wrong.

# 12

CHAPTER        Angela Albright

# Nursing: Against Suicide

"Death with dignity," "maintaining autonomy," and "quality of life" are concepts that have made their way into nursing's professional literature and into the jargon of the workplace. Nursing has traditions that advocate all of these. In recent times, these concepts have been used as arguments for the right of patients who, faced with incurable illness and accompanying physical and mental discomfort, decide that death is better than living.

Compelling arguments can make suicide seem like a rational act and complicity with it a compassionate one. However, nursing experience informs us that patients expressing the wish to die are often, in fact, seeking to be relieved of physical or emotional pain, or to no longer be burdensome to others. To be compliant with suicidal wishes may suggest agreement with suicidal patients that their lives are no longer meaningful, or acknowledgment that the burden they impose is too great. Compliance implies that there is nothing left for the nurse to offer the patient and nothing left for the patient to offer to anyone. It seems that the feeling of having nothing left could *not* be validated with the kind of certainty that would allow nurses to comply, to join in the despair. I suggest that nurses cannot be life-affirming and at the same time in collusion with a suicidal plan.

Nursing's origins as well as its modern practice are based on an ethic of care that reflects a value placed on the sanctity of life. Within this framework, nurses assist patients to function at their highest possible level of health. That is, rather than being cure-oriented, nurses focus on coping with illness, minimizing the effects of illness, and assisting the individual to reach whatever level of health is realistically possible. This would include providing a terminally or seemingly hopelessly ill patient with comfort, hope for quality of what life is left, and assistance in living well until death. As a patient moves toward the end-of-life, there are inevitable days of setbacks, discouragement, wondering if the struggle is worth it. However, most patients do not progress to the point of actually requesting death (Siegel, 1986). With the minority that do, nurses must very carefully consider what responsibilities they hold.

## ☐  Nursing's Responsibilities

The code of ethics of the profession is clear that preservation of dignity, autonomy, and privacy and assistance toward relief of suffering are the responsibilities of each nurse (American Nurses' Association [ANA], 1985). It also specifically states that nurses should not interfere with patients' rights to make choices about their treatment, including the right to refuse treatment. This, however, is not the same as endorsing nursing actions that would enable a patient to actively pursue death. The nurse must be willing to stay with the patient and discover what, exactly, has led the patient to that statement, and to plan interventions to alleviate the conditions that would compel a patient to wish for death. The ANA has published a position statement that details nursing's concerns about assisted suicide (ANA, 1994b). A task force on the Nurse's Role in End-of-Life Decisions continues to seek input into these issues in order to consider all points of view.

It has been argued that some patients really do not have more options, and therefore suicide prevention measures should not be taken (Humphry, 1991a). Such a conclusion would likely find acceptance in a culture that generally is not exposed to great hardship and suffering and tends to avoid unpleasantness and search for a "quick fix." As the notion of rational suicide becomes more popular in society at large, nursing as a profession has held firm against supporting assisted suicide (ANA, 1994) and must continue to examine critically its values about any kind of suicide-enabling actions. It is also imperative that each nurse individually examine his or her own attitudes and values.

If the argument for being able to choose to die is that it is a more dignified choice than lingering, what does that say about those who do choose to live until a "natural" death occurs? Is a suicide necessarily a dignified death? If it truly is an act of last resort, can it really be considered a choice? If it is carried out with the sanction of friends, family, and nurses and healthcare providers, is it felt as an obligation carried out in order to relieve others? What are the psychological consequences for suicide survivors? These are serious questions that are not typically addressed by arguments for the support of rational suicide. The nursing code certainly does support patient dignity, autonomy, and individuality (ANA, 1995). What is yet to be made clear is just how suicide necessarily is an autonomous and dignified choice, an expression of individuality.

It is somehow assumed that if a suicide is "rational," it is also dignified, or at least more dignified than death would be otherwise. The term "rational suicide" is considered by many professionals to be an oxymoron. Boldt (1989), for example, argues that:

> it is illogical to advocate, as some have done, for the right to suicide, on grounds that it promotes human dignity. Does a dead [person] experience dignity? Suicide may offer an *escape from* the *indignity* of an unendurable or degrading life; but, where is the dignity in suicide? Human dignity is rooted in a good life, a sense of community, a positive sense of self-worth, and so on. We promote human dignity when we provide these life conditions; not by guaranteeing the right to suicide. (pp. 6–7, emphasis original)

Patients with terminal illnesses are often dealing with various indignities such as dressing changes on recalcitrant and weeping wounds and an inability to do basic self-care functions such as urination and defecation. Nurses and immediate caregivers are frequently invading personal space, necessarily touching and viewing what are normally considered private body parts. Different patients suffer more than others with this breach of privacy. Some agonize more than others over alterations in body image as they mourn their healthy, intact bodies.

The wish to die is different from a wish to no longer suffer indignity or to prevent an "undignified" death. The nurse is in a primary role to provide or restore dignity in living. Nurses are indeed privileged to encounter patients in potentially epiphanous moments and experiences. Nurses are present when dire diagnoses are delivered, when it becomes clear that medical treatments have failed, when patients are struggling to come to terms with their finiteness, when they are thinking about what is left to be done, when they are letting go, and when they are attempting to finish their life's stories. Suicides are often correlated with illness-related events such as exacerbation of symptoms, poorly managed pain, or advancing disease (Breitbart, 1993; Massie, Gagnon, & Holland, 1994; Valente & Saunders, 1994). Persons with AIDS may also be depressed and at risk for suicide in the face of the loss of close friends (Valente & Saunders, 1994). These patients in particular might also be facing great discrimination as they feel blamed for causing their own illness. Nurses can be a powerful force in providing an environment of respect for the gravity of these events, in setting a tone of positive regard, and in providing the emotional support needed to pursue end-of-life tasks. Even if family and friends falter in support, nurses are in a prime position to fill in between the lines, to be constant, and to share the faith to the end.

In a more concrete way, nurses extend dignity by simply being understanding of needs of bodily privacy, and by being respectful of the person during ministrations. There are countless ways that caregivers can and do create indignity with lack of sensitivity in regard to personal space and bodily handling. There are at least an equal number of simple ways such failures can be minimized and respect for the individual communicated while nursing tasks are completed. Holding a respectful attitude that conveys that the person is more to the nurse than just another assignment goes a long way to mitigate the effects of bodily and personal-space invasion.

Empathic failures are inevitable, even among the most aware, the most emotionally present nurses. However, striving for high levels of empathic regard, respectfulness, and genuineness in nursing care is and should be nursing's focus. Nurses and patients, within their relationship, experience their humanness, their worth to one another. It may very well be that the relationship with a nurse or nurses will be significant in verifying the goodness of life. Energy spent in advocating for rational suicide may be energy channeled away from extending to patients the best nursing and nurses have to offer in practice, and in research.

# ☐ Physical Suffering

There is no doubt that patients with illnesses such as cancer or AIDS may experience excruciating and unrelenting levels of pain. Pain is often cited as one of the justifications for a rational suicide. This is a difficult area in which to generalize; patients differ greatly in pain perception and pain tolerance. In relatively recent times, partially spurred by the hospice and palliative care movement, much more has been learned about pain, its emotional aspects, its mechanisms, and its relief (Foley, 1991). Studies have shown that most patients in intractable pain are undermedicated or are not treated with all the available and appropriate interventions (Blolund, 1985a, Heilig,

1988). Smith (1993) points out that there are many ethical issues raised in the treatment of cancer pain that include the travesty of inadequate treatment, the need for adequate education for professionals, and the lack of agreement on adequate morphine doses. There is a very significant relationship between requests to die and the inability to get relief (Brietbart, 1993; Massie et al., 1994). Chapman (1993) has described pain not only as sensory information but also as having an emotional aspect that:

> interrupts ongoing goal-directed activities, disturbs normal biorhythms . . . and compels expression through facial grimace, altered posture, diminished activity, guarding behaviors, and verbal complaint. . . . The expression recruits support from the social environment. . . . The emotional aspect, therefore, determines the suffering that accompanies pain. (p. 83)

Because of the magnitude of the impact pain has on all aspects of living, pain management should be a very high priority. It is indeed the obligation of every nurse who works with terminally ill persons to be knowledgeable in state-of-the-art pain control and to advocate that such pain control be available to their patients in hospice programs, acute in-patient settings, and home healthcare. With proper assessment and intervention, pain levels should be brought under manageable control. Nurses must take responsibility to consult with specialists in pain management and to learn state-of-the-art interventions that are both physiological and psychological. Pain, or the anguish that accompanies it, should never be a cause of a person's wish to die.

## ☐ Impairments in Mental Status

Many patients with debilitating illnesses fear the effects of loss of cognitive abilities. Valente and Saunders (1994) have described how mental-status changes in persons with AIDS can influence suicidal thoughts. They point out that changes in mental status that accompany illnesses are preventable or treatable through alleviation of contributing factors and simple interventions such as helping patients keep oriented. A lapse in mental status should not be viewed as an end that justifies wanting to die.

### Depression

Major indicators for depression such as anorexia, malaise, poor concentration, and sleep disruption could easily be attributed to medical illnesses (Cassem, 1995). Indeed, medical illness may mask a depression that is treatable. To address the issue of missed mood-disorder diagnoses, the *Diagnostic and Statistical Manual of Mental Disorders,* 4th edition (American Psychiatric Association, 1994), has offered a category of mood disorder that is "[d]ue to a general medical condition." This is of great importance because of the powerful impact that treatment of a major depression can have. Nurses working with the chronically and terminally ill need to be very skilled in recognizing depression and facilitating both pharmacologic and psychosocial interventions. Suicidal thinking is likely to be reduced if the feelings of hopelessness, worthlessness, and bleakness that are hallmarks of depression lift.

Preillness coping styles and availability of support systems also must be considered when assessing the depressed patient who is feeling hopeless. Hedge (1991) reminds us that there are some little-understood but potentially powerful relationships between mood and immune system functioning. Such relationships need to be considered when strategizing about interventions.

It is argued that seriously ill patients might be depressed because of their multiple losses and their impairment; in other words, their depression is "appropriate" or "understandable" (Stephany, 1993). However, merely because a depressed mood is understandable does not mean it is permanent or will not respond to intervention, or that relief can only be obtained through death (Cassem, 1995). Surely a dying person is understandably sad; indeed the nurse must encourage the sharing of that sadness. It is in the outward expression of this sadness, hopelessness, fear, and or rage that a person learns more about himself or herself, about what his or her life is and has been, and about what is important to him or her. It is a grave mistake to assume that suicide is the only viable option because the depression appears to be appropriate.

## Fear of Burden

Another source of mental anguish is the fear of being a burden to friends, loved ones, and even to caregivers. Patients feel subtle communications that the caregivers are low on patience, that loved ones are anxious about money, and that their family members are indeed tired due to the tasks of attending to an ill person in addition to their regular responsibilities. In today's managed care environment, which emphasizes cost control, patients may accurately perceive that they are viewed as a cost burden. Patients may realize that they are expected to die sooner than later. It might be that it is the nurse who is the patient's last source of encouragement and hope. Hope, of course, not that the patient will return to health but that each day of the patient's life will have some meaning; that his or her personhood will be acknowledged.

It is hoped that, among the discomfort and indignities that might abound, there will survive some small joy, some passion sparked, if nothing other than the immense satisfaction that comes from being connected with another person; that in at least some small way, for maybe a moment, the fact of being alive is good. Nurses are often present with patients in their worst moments, when the darkest of thoughts prevail, when all seems lost. A connection during these times might be at a nonverbal yet knowing level. As Benner (1984) has pointed out, some of the most important moments in nursing are wordless ones. Nurses testify that they learn much about living from their dying patients; dying patients find they learn about living when faced with the reality of death. Most patients do not seek suicide (Siegel, 1986). The fact that many continue to find living the better choice should tell us something. Death may result in no more pain or suffering, worrying, or feeling burdened; however, it does not necessarily offer anything else or the opportunity to have one more moment of life that is well lived.

It is assumed that if quality of life is low, then death is the only alternative. What one believes about what happens after death may influence a choice about suicide. Because that is a matter of faith and belief, it behooves each nurse to examine how his or her own values might influence a response to a person who has expressed a wish to die. Regardless of one's personal beliefs, yet in full awareness of them, it is essential for nurses to be willing to explore with patients what their thoughts and feelings are that underlie the wish to die.

A criticism of those who reject the notion of rational suicide is that they maintain a paternalistic attitude of suicide prevention that avoids dealing with death anxiety. However, the nurse who squarely faces a patient who is expressing the wish to die and asks to be told all about that wish is not avoiding the issue at all. It is indeed the telling of the story, the feeling of being heard, that affirms one's self, and diminishes loneliness and isolation and feelings of hopelessness and futileness. The power of connection, the fact that feeling heard and understood feels good should never be underestimated (Rogers, 1951). The nurse, hearing the patient's perceptions, misperceptions, anxieties, fears, and pain, has many data with which to work in terms of planning interventions that are likely to diminish the feelings that have compelled a patient to express the wish to die.

# ☐  Conclusion

Nursing is committed to caring. I have argued that caring does not mean a paternal beneficence that would preclude honoring autonomy or denying a death with dignity. What caring requires is practicing nursing at its very best; utilizing research and experience to provide suicidal patients with relief from the suffering that has brought them to such thoughts. Barriers to adequate care must be identified and addressed, particularly in today's climate of cost containment (Coyle, 1992). To advocate for rational suicide may support patients' beliefs that their worth has ended, that they are discardable, that their life no longer has meaning. It seems far better, and within the ethic of care, to value each moment of a patient's life and to put efforts into facilitating quality of life until the point of death.

Margaret L. Campbell

# A Nursing Position that Supports Rational Suicide

On first inspection, the issue of rational suicide may not seem highly relevant for nursing consideration, because nurses are generally not patients' first-level providers of healthcare. However, advanced practice nurses in many states have prescriptive authority as primary practitioners and may be faced with this issue directly in the context of a primary nurse–patient relationship. Nurses without prescriptive authority may also encounter this issue as they collaborate with other caregivers, notably physicians, to deliver direct care.

In this chapter, grounds for a nursing position to support rational suicide are offered, including a response to the "nonnecessity with adequate palliative care" argument. The basis for a supportive nursing position comes from the *American Nurses Association* (ANA) *Code for Nurses* (1985), the *Nursing Social Policy Statement* (ANA 1995), testimony provided to the Michigan Commission on Death and Dying (1994), clinical and personal experience, and relevant empirical evidence.

## ☐ Definitions

The following definitions and concepts are used to frame this argument.

*Aid-in-dying* refers to providing a person who intends to commit rational suicide with the means to do so, which may include assistance with administration. Aid-in-dying is not restricted to physicians but may be provided by other caregivers or by significant others.

A *rational suicide* is one that meets the following criteria, adapted from Werth (1996b) (see also Chapter 1):

1. The person considering suicide has a "hopeless" condition, including, but not limited to, terminal illness, pain, physically or mentally debilitating or deteriorating conditions, and a quality of life no longer acceptable to the individual.

2. The person makes the decision as a free choice.
3. The person has engaged in a sound decision-making process, which includes:

   a. Consultation with a mental health professional if there is concern about decision-making capacity;
   b. Nonimpulsive consideration of all alternatives;
   c. Consideration of the impact on significant others.

4. Suicide is the alternative of last resort.

*Palliative care* refers to a focus on symptom control and psychoemotional support of patients and significant others. Palliative care may include foregoing life-sustaining therapy, which is the noninitiation (withholding) and discontinuation (withdrawing) of interventions that support life and in some cases prolong dying (President's Commission, 1983a). Decisions to abstain from life-sustaining therapy are distinct from decisions to hasten dying, such as through rational suicide, because in foregoing therapy an anticipated death is allowed to occur, but in rational suicide the death is made to happen because of an intervention. In one case death is expected, in the other death is guaranteed (President's Commission, 1983a).

*Suffering* refers to a level of distress brought about by an actual or perceived threat to the integrity or continued existence of the whole person. Suffering may occur in the presence or absence of pain and other symptoms. Suffering is unique to each individual (Cassell, 1991).

## ☐  Code for Nurses and Policy Statements

The ANA is the professional organization for nurses. The ANA is responsive to issues of relevance to nurses and their clients through its organizational units and state nurses' associations. A nursing response to an issue is grounded in the organization's *Social Policy Statement* (ANA, 1995) and the *Code for Nurses* (ANA, 1985). The *Social Policy Statement* is a document that is used as a framework for understanding nursing's relationship with society and our obligation to the clients we serve. According to the *Social Policy Statement*, "Society grants the professions authority over functions vital to itself and permits them considerable autonomy in the conduct of their affairs. In return, the professions are expected to act responsibly, always mindful of the public trust" (p. 3). The *Code for Nurses* states, "Nursing encompasses the protection, promotion and restoration of health; the prevention of illness; and the alleviation of suffering in the care of clients, including, individuals, families, groups, and communities" (p. i). The *Code* also states, "Since clients themselves are the primary decision makers in matters concerning their own health, treatment and well-being, the goal of nursing actions is to support and enhance the client's responsibility and self-determination to the greatest extent possible" (p. i).

The principle of respect for persons underlies the *Code for Nurses*. This principle compels nurses to be responsive to patients' needs for care at the end-of-life through measures directed at alleviating suffering. Suicide may be a rational alternative for some individuals. Nursing's contract with society underlies the *Social Policy Statement* (ANA, 1995). Society may seek a nursing commitment to support rational suicide. Each of these documents may provide a basis for supporting rational suicide.

An ANA Task Force on the Nurse's Role in End-of-Life Decisions developed organizational positions about assisted suicide and active euthanasia that were adopted by the organization in December 1994. These positions were based on the following statement from the *Code:* "[T]he nurse does not act deliberately to terminate the life of any person" (ANA, 1985, p. 3). The assisted-suicide position states:

> Nurses, individually and collectively, have an obligation to provide comprehensive and compassionate end-of-life care which includes the promotion of comfort and the relief of pain, and at times, foregoing life-sustaining treatments. The ANA believes that the nurse should not participate in assisted suicide. Such an act is in violation of the Code for Nurses and the ethical traditions of the profession. (ANA, 1994a, p. 1)

The ANA rationale for these positions (1994a,b) is developed along two themes: professional integrity and a social contract based on trust, and the potential for negative professional and societal consequences and abuses. Although the ANA acknowledges the profession's profound commitment to the patient's right to self-determination, the organization believes that there are limits to this commitment, specifically in participating in a suicide. Furthermore, the ANA takes the position that killing another human being is in contradiction to the Hippocratic tradition to "do no harm."

## ☐ Arguments Supporting Regulated Rational Suicide

In my view, the most compelling reason to favor rational suicide is that there are persons with intractable suffering for whom there are no satisfactory options, and these individuals can make a rational choice to hasten death. The person who is suffering is the only one who can define the suffering and make a determination about its bearability and acceptability. A rational request for suicide must be responded to in a timely, humane, comprehensive, and holistic manner.

My professional experience suggests that suffering may be sufficiently reduced or eliminated for nearly all patients, leading to the conclusion that suicide is a solution for very few persons. Adequate palliative care, such as through a hospice program, should be the end-of-life standard for all who are dying. Suicide is not a replacement for palliative care but could be an alternative for those few patients who cannot achieve satisfactory relief from suffering.

There are limited data about the effectiveness of palliative care. The few studies that have been reported suggest that between 15% and 35% of patients dying in hospice programs have unrelieved pain or suffering (Kasting, 1994). Opponents of rational suicide do not have a response for those patients who cannot be helped with palliative care. If we embrace the idea that alleviation of suffering is a nursing imperative, then we must have an alternative for those who can achieve relief in no other manner.

Some opponents of rational and assisted suicide offer a "terminal sedation" alternative for patients with intractable suffering (Byock, 1993; Truog & Berde, 1993; Truog, Berde, Mitchell, & Grier, 1992). In these circumstances, the patient's suffering can only be reduced through large doses of analgesics, sedatives, and barbiturates that produce a state of "suspended animation." That is, the person is alive and presumably comfortable but in a state of drug-induced anesthesia, hypnosis, or unconsciousness. These patients require round-the-clock attention to needs such as hygiene, warmth, positioning, and secretion clearance, and measures directed at ensuring privacy, respect, and meeting the grief needs of the family. In this state, patients are no longer able to interact with their environment, nor engage in life-closure tasks. They merely exist as the biological process of dying follows its course. Patients may perceive no benefit from this response to their suffering, because they merely exist for several more days but are unable to profit from that additional time. The limited or nonexistent benefit, from the patient's perspective, from this condition warrants consideration for suicide and aid-in-dying. In fact, the same agents used to achieve this "terminal sedation" are the agents of choice for suicide. The only apparent difference between terminal sedation and suicide and aid-in-dying is in the dosage of the agent used and the amount of time after drug administration before the patient dies.

Another limitation to palliative or hospice care as the standard response to suffering is that there are some conditions that can produce suffering for which there are no palliative care interventions or therapies to withhold or withdraw. The Michigan Commission on Death and Dying (1994) was convened by the state legislature to develop and submit recommendations regarding legislation concerning the voluntary self-termination of life. The Commission heard public testimony on the issue of assisted suicide at each of its meetings and through statewide public hearings. A compelling case was offered to this Commission for consideration by a young woman destined to develop Huntington's disease. This 30-year-old woman related to the committee her observations about the deaths, from Huntington's, of her mother, brother, and uncle. She described their physical and mental deterioration. This disease, although predictable through genetic markers, currently has no cure. Treatment is palliative and sometimes requires restraints and heavy sedation to control the associated psychosis.

This woman stated her acceptance of her genetic fate, and her love of life. She identified a need to live fully during her remaining time before the disease manifests, but she went on to indicate her need to be able to choose suicide (with assistance) before the inevitable psychosis eliminates her abilities to be self-determinative.

Like Janet Adkins, the first client of Jack Kevorkian, some view the predicted course of dementing and debilitating diseases as undesirable life experiences. In these types of illnesses there are no specific life-prolonging interventions to withhold or withdraw. Suicide remains an option for these people; however, many fear that they will "botch the job" and endure even more suffering as a result. I believe it is a rational decision for a capable person to choose to avoid these progressive illnesses, after considering all the alternatives to improve care and ensure respectful treatment.

I favor regulated rational suicide and aid-in-dying for an additional reason. I do not believe there should be an arbitrary limit imposed on a person's right to self-determination. In other types of patient choices, for example to choose or refuse therapy, the decision is supported based on the adequacy of the patient's capacity to make a rational decision. The object of the decision has less relevance than the capacity of the decision maker to process information and make a rational judgement. Yet there is a different standard when the object of the decision is suicide. I believe it is unjust to hold these patients to a different decision-making standard.

The law presumes that all persons are competent to make decisions if they have the ability to communicate choices, understand relevant information, appreciate the situation and its consequences, and manipulate information rationally (Applebaum & Grisso, 1988). This standard treats competence as an issue of fact that is independent of the actual treatment choice (Markson, Kern, Annas, & Glantz, 1994).

The current standard about patient decision making permits refusal of life-sustaining therapies even if the illness or injury has the potential for reversibility. Patients may refuse treatment even if the expected outcome of the choice is death. This standard is based on patient autonomy and capacity to make an informed decision. Yet patients with no therapies to withhold or withdraw, who make a rational choice to have their deaths hastened, have a limit placed on their autonomy. I suggest that this is an arbitrary limit without sufficient justification.

## ☐ Social Policy Concerns

It is feared that acceptance of rational suicide has the potential for serious societal consequences and abuses (Brock, 1992, Byock, 1991; Callahan, 1992). These abuses are most likely to occur in the case of vulnerable persons, such as the elderly, poor, and disabled.

Regulating rational suicide may actually minimize the risk to vulnerable persons. Even in the face of statutory bans, there is evidence of covert aid-in-dying by physicians in the United States (Meier, 1994), including the highly publicized and problematic activities of Jack Kevorkian. Legalized aid-in-dying would seek to ensure that it is used as an alternative of last resort, only in response to durable, voluntary requests from competent patients (Miller et al., 1994).

The Michigan Nurses Association (MNA) took a position on assisted suicide in 1994 while I represented them on the Michigan Commission on Death and Dying. The MNA position preceded the one adopted by the ANA. The MNA was represented on the Commission by me and an alternate member. We recommended the MNA's organizational position after extensive study of the issue.

The MNA took a position favoring assisted suicide as an alternative of last resort for competent persons whose suffering cannot be relieved or satisfactorily reduced with alternative strategies (MNA, 1994). Furthermore, a number of safeguards should be legislated to prevent abuse, such as consultations with medical, mental health, independent-living, and palliative care specialists, and public reporting and oversight.

The MNA believes that this position is consistent with nursing's commitment to patient self-determination and to alleviating suffering. Although the *Code for Nurses* takes a position that killing is always wrong, I believe that view is too narrow and is not consistent with the values of some members of society and the profession.

In summary, the ANA has taken a position opposing a nurse's participation in suicide or euthanasia, but the ANA position does not address the concept of rationality with regard to suicide. Although I am supportive of the organization, I offer a different position for individual consideration. I believe that it is wrong to neglect the request for support from those few persons who have no other alternative and who have made a rational decision about suicide.

**CHAPTER**

Robin Bernhoft

# Are Compassionate Care and Suicide Mutually Exclusive?

"Marge" was 49 and terrified when I saw her in the Emergency Room for rectal bleeding. She had a superficial tumor in her anal canal, from which I took a biopsy. I explained gently that I would like her to come to my office the next day, and that if the "lump" was anything at all, it could almost certainly be cured without further surgery.

Marge did not come in. We phoned her, left messages, and sent registered letters but heard nothing for almost a year. She was in Europe, paying a monstrous quack $300 a day for vitamin enemas. When the cancer obstructed her bowels, someone did an "operation" not described in the surgical books, and then left her wounds to fester until her money ran out, after which she was ignored by doctors, nurses, and kitchen staff alike.

When she finally came to me, her pelvis was full of cancer. Infection drained from the places in which she had been inexplicably slashed by her European "surgeon." We controlled her symptoms and made her colostomy (bowel-drainage site) clean and effective, and she did reasonably well, in her own opinion, but the widespread, infected cancer killed her not long after. She died alert and comfortable, but needlessly, as the cure rate for her tumor with proper treatment is over 99%.

Why did she go to a charlatan in Europe? Marge is not the first to do such a thing. I have seen other patients' curable cancer rapidly, expensively, and tragically made incurable by greedy and unscrupulous quacks. Why do people like Marge desert our healthcare system—which almost magically cures so many—to answer tabloid ads for unknown practitioners in foreign countries? I believe the fault is chiefly ours. We have created a medical environment that not only drives people to foreign impostors, it also drives many who stay here to despair and thoughts of suicide. In my opinion, much of the current interest in "rational suicide" stems from the Kafka-esque failings of our medical delivery system—aspects that can and must be changed. Until we do so, it strikes me as inhumane to consider legalizing "rational suicide."

I approach the issue of "rational suicide" as a surgeon whose subspecialty is liver and pancreatic surgery, as the younger brother of a man whose spine and ribs were destroyed by cancer, as the father of a disabled child, and as a doctor with a deep concern for social justice who considers that human dignity demands good quality care. "Rational suicide" is not strictly a medical issue, but medical conditions can lead to suicidal thinking. A doctor who wishes to advise a patient on suicide must not only address his or her medical problems but also consider values far broader than the technical details of therapy.

I do not consider "rational suicide" a religious issue. My analysis is not based on religious assumptions. I will not offer criteria that would make "rational suicide" acceptable. To do so begs the entire question, just as defining "rational incest" might beg that question. Instead, I explore practical circumstances within American medicine that cause the criteria of Werth and Cobia (1995), Battin (1995), or Motto (1972) either to create insurmountable problems or to break down completely.

American healthcare is often technically excellent, but our style of delivery drives many to despair. This creates much of the current interest in "rational suicide." Cultural trends contribute, of course, as does journalistic fascination with the antics of Humphry and Kevorkian, but our ability to dehumanize so many of our patients is the chief factor making "rational suicide" a salable commodity. In that sense, "rational suicide" may be considered, at least in part, an iatrogenic (doctor-caused) disease.

Many people find the American medical environment extremely alienating. Go to any busy cancer or AIDS center and talk to people in the waiting rooms. Many patients are angry—and not just at their disease. They are also mad at their doctors. They are enraged that they have to wait so long to be seen, that their doctor never explains anything to them or talks down to them.

They often feel less than human. Diagnostic procedures hurt and are seldom clearly explained. Caregivers treat them more like malpractice risks or damaged organs than like suffering fellow humans. Disability or cosmetic disfigurement may drive them into seclusion. They may be involuntarily isolated from friends and family, for example, by bone-marrow transplantation. They do not know what is happening to them from day to day. They are afraid of the future, not knowing what to expect, whether to fear or to hope. They cannot get answers to their most basic, anxiety-ridden questions.

To say patients are alienated is to understate the case. Many feel as if their worlds are coming to an end. They live in a reality they loathe, thrust against their will into a world in which hope seems embodied in procedures or chemicals that they have never heard of and cannot pronounce—their only allies busy physicians who often treat them with the warmth of an IRS agent. Typically, they are given brief, bewildering explanations (which we doctors rather optimistically call "informed consent") and forms to sign and then are sent through endless corridors to cold rooms where they undergo painful, often humiliating diagnostic procedures on hard tables at the hands of doctors whom they have never met and who often do not talk to them. The results of these tests will determine their destiny and are usually known to radiologist and clinician within minutes. They often are not shared with the patient for days.

Therapy can be as unpleasant as diagnosis. Painful operations are frequently done without adequate attention to postoperative pain control (Hill, 1995). Lengthy courses of radiation or chemotherapy may be necessary, often delivered in sterile chrome-and-glass surroundings. Many patients understand little of what is going on, seldom or never communicating clearly with doctors or nurses (President's Commission, 1982). Despite all this, surprisingly few patients opt for vitamin enemas by the Mediterranean sea.

Patients who stay in the system often develop complications they do not understand. They phone for relief, waiting for ages on hold for the receptionist to tell them that the doctor will call back. The doctor does call, at 10 PM, obviously exhausted, and phones in a prescription that cannot be filled until morning. Next day, the patient finds the pills "don't work." Perhaps they were prescribed incorrectly (i.e., wrong pills, small doses, too infrequently) because the doctor (as is more often the case than not) does not know how to treat pain (Elliott et al., 1995). The instructions on the bottle may be unclear, or the patient may not be able to read well enough to follow them, as happens perhaps 60% of the time (Williams et al., 1995). Demoralized by substandard palliative care, the patient gives up and phones the local "right to die" society.

Pain medicine almost always works if the right drug is given often enough in appropriate doses (Twycross, 1994). Comfort can almost always be achieved without mental confusion or sleepiness. Unfortunately, pain often persists because the wrong drug is given, or because too little of the right drug is given too infrequently. Conversely, many patients are "drugged" by too much of the right drug, too often.

Either problem—excess or insufficiency—can be quickly remedied by a physician or nurse fully trained in pain control. Unfortunately, most physicians and nurses in this country lack such training, so more often than not the patient suffers unnecessarily (Portenoy, 1989; World Health Organization, 1990). It is not surprising that patients become fed up with "doctoring." Given these common deficiencies in care, the fact that so few actually request suicide suggests strongly that most gravely ill people treasure the time they have, however little some doctors may respect its quality (O'Brien et al., 1995). Abundant evidence shows that if pain, depression, and abandonment are addressed, suicidal ideation ceases, and virtually all—even the overwhelmingly ill—regain their desire to live (Foley, 1991). My brother, for example, lived for over 6 months paralyzed with multiple spine and rib fractures from his bone marrow cancer. Because his Mayo Clinic physicians knew how to keep him comfortable *and* mentally clear, Larry used his time in helping his survivors do the inescapable "work of grieving" described by Kübler-Ross (1969) and others. He and we considered it time of uniquely high quality.

Regrettably, my brother's experience is not typical. Many well-intentioned physicians (Elliot et al., 1995) and nurses (Brunier, Carson, & Harrison, 1995; McCaffery & Ferrell, 1995) have not been trained to palliate. Proper drug administration is widely misunderstood (World Health Organization, 1990), even by specialists (Portenoy, 1989). Irrational fears of narcotics (Hill, 1990) are common: for example, fear of addiction, or of the so-called double effect—inadvertent death resulting from comfort care—so often cited by prosuicide physicians as a reason supporting legalization. In reality, because morphine has such a wide therapeutic index (the margin of safety between an effective dose and a fatal dose), inadvertent death is very rarely an issue for a competent physician. This is not new information (Jaffe, 1970).

Treatable depression is commonly ignored or taken as situational and appropriate (Conwell & Caine, 1991). Whereas British doctors and nurses have been broadly trained in this area for over 20 years, palliative medicine has only recently become a recognized specialty in the United States, with few practitioners. Palliative care addresses not only pain and depression, and the various physical complications of disease (and of its treatment), but also the social, spiritual and psychological aspects of life included in an holistic approach. Done properly, palliative care makes suicide "irrelevant" (Foley, 1991; Stoddard, 1978).

Certain features of our medical culture oppose the adoption of these broad principles of palliative care. American physicians are generally taught in medical school to maintain "professional distance" between self and patient. No doubt some distance is a good thing, for clear thinking is needed in crisis. Excessive psychic distance, however, should be condemned, for it makes the doctor seem cold and uncaring and interferes with effective communication, predisposing many patients to alienation, despair, and thoughts of suicide.

Further, we doctors tend to judge ourselves on our achievements. That is what drives us to work so hard. Unfortunately, we judge others the same way, which can interfere with equitable patient care. My son, for example, who has Down's syndrome (at age 10 he can only read a few hundred words) suffered a brief lung problem at birth. During his week in the intensive-care unit, one of his doctors suggested we cut off his food and water. In her opinion, Andrew was not sufficiently human to deserve the care he received. Such prejudicial attitudes towards persons with disabilities are both common (President's Commission, 1983b) and sanctioned by law (*Doe v Bloomington Hospital,* 1983). This being true, it seems axiomatic that many doctors find suicide by disabled people more "rational" than suicide by the whole and prosperous.

Similarly, racial bias is neither unknown in medicine nor irrelevant to this discussion. Numerous studies show that African American men *with* health insurance are much less likely to be offered needed treatment for heart disease than white men with insurance (Giles, Anda, Casper, Escobedo, & Taylor, 1995). This disparity is worst in the Southeast but exists in every state, applying also to Hispanics, but not to Asians (Carlisle, Leake, & Shapiro, 1995). In the 1970s, many involuntary postpartum sterilizations of Latina mothers were carried out at Los Angeles County Hospital (Velez, 1979). Permits were done in English, but the patients, who spoke and read only Spanish, had no idea what they were agreeing to. This policy was ended by court order.

It seems inevitable that legal suicide would be "chosen" more often by racial minorities and by the differently abled for two reasons: first, bias would lead many doctors both to take their suicidal desires at face value and to ration care away from such patients, thereby increasing the number of suicide requests; second, even without bias, the medically underserved would lack access to first-class palliative care and would therefore be more likely to "choose" death for lack of the comfort measures available to the medically affluent.

No "choice" rhetoric will obviate these injustices, nor provide workable safeguards. Not only are many patients both functionally illiterate (Williams et al., 1995) and unable to understand their doctors' explanations (President's Commission, 1982, vol. II, p.12), it is clear that their "choices" are heavily influenced by their physicians. Those who would argue that patients control the situation should contemplate the assessment by the President's Commission of the medical professional's ability to manipulate informed consent:

> Blatant coercion may be of so little concern in professional-patient relations because, as physicians so often proclaim, it is so easy for health professionals to elicit a desired decision through more subtle means . . . patients will, if they trust their doctor, accede to almost any request he [or she] cares to make . . . [since he or she has] an ability to package and present the facts in a way that leaves the patient no real choice. (President's Commission, 1982, vol. I, pp. 66–67; see also President's Commission, 1983b, vol. I, p. 28, vol. II, p. 260)

Doctors who wish to manipulate consent can do so, even in the patient's native tongue.

American doctors tend to carry a military paradigm into clinical work. We "fight" cancer, we seek to "conquer" disease. When we "win," we feel good about ourselves. When we fail, we feel uneasy, perhaps a little depressed. We often see the unfortunate patient for whom we "can no longer do anything"—anything, at least, that we doctors value, such as cure—as a reminder of our professional limitations. We may even see the dying patient as a traitor who has "gone over to the enemy." Mere palliation strikes us as beneath our dignity, a thinly veiled failure—something that matters only to the patient. Hence our ongoing reluctance to adopt innovations that have been commonplace in Britain since the 1970s. Also, palliative care pays poorly, is time-consuming, and is emotionally exhausting. These realities help account for the dismal results and poor doctor–patient communication reported by the SUPPORT Principal Investigators (1995). Such results compare very poorly with palliation in good English or American hospices.

Unfortunately, expansion of palliative care runs against the trend of healthcare funding. Hospice-style care (usually administered at home) is easily the most cost-effective way of dealing with terminal illness, but it has never been adequately funded. Medicare, Medicaid, and local fundraisers have been the chief mainstays of support; private insurance has ignored hospice, or covered it sporadically. The current move toward managed care aggravates this neglect. Despite clear evidence of its cost-effectiveness, first-rate palliative care is becoming less available as health-insurance companies shunt funds away from existing hospice programs. Many hospices have had to cut services, even though they were inadequate to meet existing demand, let alone the demand that would exist if patients were to become aware of their services, and if their services were freely available, as is generally the case in England.

Managed care also pressures physicians, through "economic credentialing," to provide as little care as they can get away with. This has already led doctors to refer patients with treatable cancer to hospice without telling them their cancer is treatable, for palliation is cheaper than aggressive care (Dr. Laurel Herbst, Hospice of San Diego, personal communication, 1994). Increasingly, doctors will be forced to choose between giving their patients high-quality care and keeping their jobs. Even well-meaning doctors will find themselves forced to ration care away from those who complain the least, those least capable of fighting back, and those whose neglect induces the least guilt. Logical candidates for denial of care are the terminally ill, the disabled, the medically underserved, and racial minorities. Certainly, the vigorous competition of managed-care companies for Medicare business suggests that they plan aggressive rationing of care of the elderly (Ebert, 1995). Economic pressures will make patient suicide seem increasingly "rational" to physicians who wish to keep their jobs, or maintain current levels of income.

The criteria suggested for instituting "rational suicide" are intensely subjective, giving immense power to the physician advising the patient. Given that most doctors are not trained to treat pain and depression, nor adept in communicating with patients, legalized "rational suicide" would open a Pandora's box of injustices. None of the proposed criteria for "rational suicide" takes into account the realities I have described. Motto (1972), for example, has no requirement for fully informed consent regarding medical options (assuming that some medical problem is the inciting cause of the suicidal wish), nor for establishing the competency of those offering medical advice. Motto's approach generates major quality-control problems. His only criteria are that the "act must be based on a realistic assessment of [the patient's] life situation, and . . . the degree of ambivalence regarding the act must be minimal" (p. 184). He adds that the assessment must be "realistic as *I* see it" (p. 185, emphasis original). To paraphrase Humpty Dumpty, "when I say 'realistic,' it means exactly what I want it to mean, no more and no less." Motto seems blissfully unaware that many people will commit suicide unnecessarily to relieve correctable pain or depression, because many well-intentioned physicians are unaware that such problems are correctable; to such physicians, substandard care and the resultant desire to die will both seem "reasonable."

Battin (1995) does address the need for adequate (and correct) information, without specifying how that goal is to be reached in the current environment, but adds that the decision must be based on a "realistic world view"—a view "consistent with the views of the surrounding culture." The former goal is unattainably utopian, while the latter conjures up panels of Disney scriptwriters adjudicating difficult cases. One wonders what Battin would propose for those whose views differ from the surrounding culture.

Werth and Cobia (1995) and others add various criteria that from my perspective ignore the alienation and hopelessness generated by the potentially correctable features of our medical culture. In 1996, we are able to relieve virtually all pain and most depression, have many ways to address the various forms of abandonment, and have ample clinical experience that suicide is seldom desired if such needs are met. It seems to me astonishing that we should be improving access to suicide, when we could be correcting those aspects of our medical system that push people toward despair. It would almost seem there is a subconscious institutional urge to get rid of suffering people rather than take the effort to address their needs. Perhaps such an urge, if it exists, might be driven by financial or demographic considerations—for example, the large numbers of "baby boomers" nearing retirement and infirmity, and the relatively small numbers of subsequent generations who will be called upon to pay their medical bills.

Subconscious urges aside, the various "safeguards" are mostly rhetorical. For example, to offer as a safeguard the rule that a dying patient must not be pressured to choose suicide seems to me both disingenuous and unenforceable: disingenuous because it sounds reassuring, yet ignores both the multivalence of the human will and the subtlety of emotional pressure; unenforceable, because such pressure is usually too subtle to be visible to outsiders. ("Don't worry about your healthcare costs, mother, little Jimmy doesn't really need to go to college.")

"Rational suicide," whether physician-based or not, would most likely require some medical involvement, probably certification of appropriateness. This would involve review of the mental state of the person for whom suicide is proposed, and also of the adequacy of informed consent. Because many doctors are untrained in the diagnosis and treatment of pain and depression, unable to communicate meaningful informed consent even in their areas of technical competence, subject to bias (conscious or unconscious) against the disabled and people of color, and under increasing pressure to ration care, it would seem that legalizing any form of "rational suicide" in the present environment would generate much more grief and injustice than it could alleviate.

Furthermore, medical authorization of suicide gives too much power to physicians, just as euthanasia does. The Dutch experience with euthanasia (Fenigsen, 1991; "Medische beslissingen," 1991) suggests that such power can corrupt even the most humane medical community (Gomez, 1991). It would seem that physicians are too fallible, too human to make "rational" suicide workable.

# ☐ Conclusion

"Rational suicide" is a crucial watershed for medicine. It creates a dichotomy: are we to begin taking suicide requests more or less at face value (worrying, perhaps, about emotional authenticity), even though we can usually correct the factors that produce them and thereby restore the will to live (Foley, 1991)? Or shall we restructure our medical culture to correct its many problems? Obviously, moving to "rational suicide" will be easier, demanding less of us as a profession; it will also silence those patients who implicitly demand we change our ways. But change is not impossible, and early efforts to do so are encouraging (Elliott et al., 1995; Washington State Medical Association, 1992).

In the long run, Margaret Mead's (1963) warning about the implications of any physician-based suicide system may come to fruition: not only in the destruction of doctor–patient trust that she described, but also in the overall cheapening of human life, debasement of culture, and destruction of the concept of inalienable rights (Spitzer, Bernhoft, & deBlasi, 1998). We tend, already, to limit full membership in the human family to those who look or achieve as we think they should. Legitimizing suicide will aggravate this process and narrow our understanding of human personhood even further (Fenigsen, 1995; Humphry, 1991a, pp. 58–62). As Fenigsen points out, acceptance of death as a valid therapeutic option (whether administered, or merely approved, by physicians) will not expand medicine; in Holland, at least, it is replacing medicine.

Richard MacDonald

# Physician-Assisted Rational Suicide

Addressing the topic of rational suicide from the point of view of a family physician with over 40 years experience in practice, I have the advantage of having seen medicine change from a relatively nonscientific, office-based profession to its current technology-dominated style in medical centers with the possibility of extending life in even the most dire clinical situations. Penicillin had just been discovered when my class entered premedical studies. Most of the current capabilities such as advanced cardiopulmonary resuscitation, and ventilator and pharmacological support were years away. As a result, those of us in primary care who were in practice before the medicalization of dying may have a more pragmatic approach to terminally ill patients than more recently trained physicians, who appear to have been taught that death is the enemy that must be fought to the bitter end.

In the 1950s, aware that our capabilities to delay dying were limited, the death of a patient was not our personal failure. With this understanding, we focused on comfort and other aspects of patient care that now seem less considered since the development of much of the technology currently available. If a patient had only a short time to live, the alternatives available were explained to the patient and family. In most cases there were few options. Home would most frequently be the preferable setting for the final weeks of life, to facilitate having loved ones near the patient for the obvious benefits that such companionship provides, as opposed to the sterile and less compassionate surroundings in a medical facility. With this approach the attending physician was able to offer comfort care with necessary pain medication and sedatives to keep the patient as comfortable as possible. Rarely would there be any questions raised about the possibility that the physician had overprescribed medication or had helped the patient to die prematurely. Perhaps we were assisting "rational suicide."

This background may explain my belief that suicide in those with incurable disease may be a reasonable approach to a difficult decision that must be made by the patient, hopefully with prior full disclosure of the options available. Accepting the possibility that a patient might contemplate suicide because of unacceptable pain or insufferable indignities, permitting him or her to discuss feelings regarding what options to consider may avert or delay that action. If a physician is open to such discussion, the patient may opt to handle the final weeks or months, supported by family and friends, with medication controlling pain or discomfort. My experience has been that most terminally ill patients who discuss suicide openly with me do not find it necessary to seek that final solution.

Those of us who have been working for legalization of rational suicide, aided by a physician, if necessary, feel that that approach would be preferable to the informal manner in which such requests have been handled in the past. Guidelines could be established to avoid the abuses feared by some. These precautionary regulations would include the requirement that the patient be mentally competent when making his or her request for medication to end life. There must be verification, by more than one physician, that the disease is incurable and that the patient is likely to die within 6 months. Psychological factors must have been considered and coexisting depression, if felt to be present, treated. The patient must be free of coercion by other parties, but with open discussion with family members and any spiritual advisor encouraged by the physicians. Adequate pain control must have been made available, so that pain would not be the primary reason for seeking suicide as a means to hasten death. Also, the patient must be in control of the process, with written advance directives for a proxy to have power of attorney if the patient becomes incapable of making decisions.

# ☐  Terminology

Consideration of this subject makes it necessary to think about terminology. Suicide, as it was usually defined during my years of practice, indicated that someone with an unwell mind but a probably healthy body decided to stop his or her emotional misery by ending living, usually in a traumatic manner. Therefore, this was considered irrational. In contrast, rational suicide is when a patient with an unwell body, but a competent mind, has decided to stop all suffering by ending dying, in a nontraumatic way, an act that many would consider a victory for reason. Let me give an example that may illustrate the difference. One of my patients suffered a severe depression over the severance of a relationship with a married man. She attempted suicide with a drug overdose and was found by her son, close to death. At the emergency department, we were able to intubate her just as she suffered a cardiopulmonary arrest, and she was successfully resuscitated, although in a coma for 3 days. She improved with appropriate antidepressant medication and psychiatric counseling. After about 10 years of apparently happier relationships, she was diagnosed with a malignancy of the pancreas, with a prognosis of approximately 6 months to live. Her last few weeks had such reduced quality of life that she expressed her wish to have medication to shorten the time of dying. This was a rational suicide wish, in my opinion, and the patient was provided with medication to control pain as well as sedatives, with which she ended her life when she felt there was no value remaining.

Most dictionaries define *rational* as that which has reasoning or understanding and is, therefore, reasonable. Unfortunately, because of the emotions that surface when life and death are discussed by those with differing points of view, reason sometimes disappears in the debate. If a dying patient with no further acceptable options of treatment makes an informed and competent decision to discontinue futile treatments, indicating a wish to stop living, I believe that this may be accepted as reasonable. To many who consider this to be rational, the term *suicide* is not appropriate for one seeking release from a life that has lost any semblance of quality. We feel that *self-deliverance* is more appropriate and that one who seeks assistance in dying should be able to do so, within some legal limits, rather than being subject to the continuing social stigma attached to suicide. If one feels, as I do, that death is preferable to prolonging dying for a patient with no semblance of "life" remaining, then it seems evident that, to be a truly *rational* act, there must be assistance available from a physician. In this way, the possibility of failed attempts will be minimized, and the patient and his or her loved ones benefit by having death occur in the most peaceful, comfortable manner possible. Therefore, it is my contention that this subject cannot be separated from the current debate on "physician-assisted suicide."

# ☐  Background Issues in the Ongoing Debate

In the past few years, with my involvement in debates and presentations about end-of-life decisions, I have found considerable change in both public and professional attitudes about physician-assisted death, with many now in favor. For family doctors who, like I, have been practicing medicine for three or more decades, this debate is necessary because of remarkable advances making it possible to extend the process of "natural" dying for months or years. These inventions were created to intervene appropriately in acute illness and trauma, to be used for a limited period of time, following which the patient would return to a life with quality that was acceptable to him or her. Unfortunately, there has been inappropriate use of these capabilities in chronic disease and with dying patients, with futile treatments in those suffering in the later stages of malignant disease with no hope of returning to any quality existence. The use of ventilators in such patients, and in those in a permanent vegetative state, is now common. Prior to the early 1970s, I recall no technology of this type.

With this medicalization of dying, there has been a change in the usual location of death, which, in the early years of my practice was most often the patient's home. Now, over 80% of patients die in medical facilities, which is in marked contrast to the 25% to 40% of 40 or 50 years ago (Wanzer et al., 1989). With this ever-increasing ability to extend living, or delay dying, there has evolved the demand of patients to regain some control over where, when and how death occurs. This has been a natural extension of advocates encouraging more involvement of the patient in making all medical decisions, rather than the continuance of the usual paternalistic pattern that has existed in the doctor-patient relationship.

An example of futile use of available technology is seen in an extensive study that took place in two phases, financed by a grant from the Robert Wood Johnson Foundation, and was designed to improve care for those with serious illness (SUPPORT Principal Investigators, 1995). The first investigation revealed "substantial shortcomings in care" for the patients. In a large percentage of cases, the physicians did not know, or failed to follow, the wishes of the patients as to the application of life-supporting technology. In almost half of the recorded cases, pain was a persisting complaint in the final days or weeks of life. The second phase indicated no improvement in these deficiencies, in spite of attempted interventions. The results confirmed what most of us in primary care medicine should have known and reinforced what those of us in "right to die" organizations were striving to emphasize as areas of needed change in medical care for the terminally ill. The conclusions emphasized the need for society as a whole to rethink the approach to end-of-life decision making. Besides the less than desirable conditions of dying caused by inappropriate use of technology, it was evident that the financial cost was inordinately high for poor results. This study defined for many in medicine, as well as for society, that it is time to reexamine what we do *to* those with serious, potentially life-ending, illnesses, rather than *for* them. Many of our efforts merely prolong the time of dying, when we might assist some to end their lives in a reasonably comfortable way, by finding the least difficult way of rational suicide.

That many patients have been kept alive for months or years of poor-quality existence, by use of ventilators and other technology, despite their expressed wishes or written advance directives, should give physicians pause in their relentless battle against the perceived enemy, death. It appears to me that many lay people have a more rational view of the life process than do their physicians. I have found little, if any, required study of end-of-life care in most medical schools. A survey of primary-care residency programs in the United States revealed that less than 8% required a rotation that included hospice care (Plumb & Segraves, 1992). Medical textbooks have details of treatment options for every imaginable disease, even those of such rare occurrence that most students will never encounter a single case during their years of practicing medicine. However, little or nothing is written regarding what we, the attending physicians, can offer if all our treatment options are exhausted and our patients are considered terminal. It is time that this situation was remedied, with required courses on adequate pain management, hospice care, bereavement, and end-of-life decisions being added to the curricula. It appears that this problem of inappropriate care for the terminally ill may be so deeply ingrained in the thinking of the majority who practice in the high-tech medical centers that any changes necessary to offer even a modicum of dignity and comfort to the dying will have to come from some force outside of medicine. The grassroots movement associated with "death with dignity" may prove to be the center of that change. When members of organizations that are part of that movement speak of rational suicide, it appears that they mean they wish to have more control over treatment decisions made near the end-of-life. When there is talk of the right to die, what is really being sought is the right *to be permitted* to die, with some choice about the time and location of dying.

The rational choice of death, in the terminally ill, ends dying in someone with such a poor quality of life that he or she has decided that death is preferable to continued suffering and indignity. Therefore it is reasonably assumed that the decision to end one's life in such a situation is made in one's best self-interest. It is my belief that those who choose to help a terminally ill person to end the dying process are also acting in the best interest of that patient, in keeping with established ethical guidelines. If a patient has decided that such an action is beneficent to him or her, any who aid the patient in accomplishing that which he or she has chosen as a course of action are acting compassionately, with no maleficence.

Oregon voters passed the Death With Dignity Act in 1994 (Oregon Right to Die, 1994), permitting those with definable terminal illness the option of requesting a prescription from a physician that could be taken if they chose to end a life with what they felt to be an unacceptable quality of living. Clearly, because the patient would take medication with the intent of ending his or her life, this act legalized rational suicide. The continuing debate on these issues has had some salutary benefits in the way of more attention being paid to pain management in the terminally ill, and expanded teaching on end-of-life care in the medical school at Oregon Health Sciences University (Lee & Tolle, 1996). Referrals to hospice have increased and comfort-care programs have been instituted at many hospitals. It is my belief that these options and rational suicide, with physician assistance, for those few patients for whom even the best terminal care does not suffice to give relief, should be included in the continuum of care taught to students and residents who may enter a practice that includes treating terminal illness. It is likely that, given improved terminal care and the opportunity to discuss the choices available to them, those with incurable illness will be less likely to select suicide as the best way to conclude their life. However, assistance in such cases is more frequent than was commonly believed. Timothy Quill's 1993 book, *Death and Dignity*, relates his assistance in helping a patient to die as peacefully as possible. In personal contacts, many physicians revealed that they aided patients in ending the dying process. I have helped several of my patients, with no hope of recovery, to die when I concurred with them that ending life in circumstances of intolerable pain and or indignities was indeed rational. My experience, in this regard, includes removing a tube from the trachea, or windpipe, of a 75-year-old, who had inoperable cancer of lymph nodes in the chest that were compressing her trachea. This was prior to the time of ventilators, and there was no possibility of further treatment, or of any improvement. Consultants in this case, well-qualified in oncology and surgery, would not agree to discontinue the artificial breathing tube, in spite of the obvious futility of the situation. Because she was mentally competent and in an agonizing situation, her wish to die appeared entirely rational to me, a conclusion shared by her family. She pleaded with me, by demonstrating with her hands, and trying to voice her wish, to have the tube removed. She died in my arms within minutes, with the nurse in attendance thanking me for bringing relief and peace to this lady.

## ☐ The Future

Although the conclusion of this debate is unclear, it will not disappear. As our aged population continues to increase, with longevity aided by healthier lifestyles and medical developments, there will be an increasing number of people who will be living productive lives into their eighth and ninth decades. As a result, it is likely that more and more deaths will result from degenerative diseases such as cancer. With that scenario, the frequency of requests for assistance in shortening the time of dying might well increase. Thus, the quality-of-life issue will become even more important than the quantity of life. I agree with Howard Brody (1992), a respected physician and ethicist, who declared that:

> Medicine produces a good death when it uses life-prolonging interventions as long as they produce a reasonable quality of life and a reasonable level of function (defined in the terms of the patient's own goals) and when it then employs the highest quality of hospice-style (or palliative-style) terminal care. (p. 1885)

To use these technologies to prolong dying is inappropriate and often contrary to the wishes expressed by the patient and family. Such an approach, using futile investigations and treatment, can lead to a "bad death."

What has been heard, many times over, at meetings of right to die groups, such as the Hemlock Society USA, are examples of what most patients fear. That is, overtreatment in the terminal stages of a disease that has already been identified as one without hope of recovery. If there is no reasonable possibility of returning the patient to some meaningful quality of life, then further death-delaying medical interventions should not be entertained. What is needed is compassion and caring exhibited by an honest declaration of the hopelessness of the situation, and the reassurance that the physician will not abandon the patient in this most difficult final stage of dying. Although we may tell the patient that "there is nothing more that we can do to stop the illness from taking your life," there is much caring, as opposed to treatment, that can and must be offered to the patient and his or her loved ones. As Brody (1992) succinctly stated, "walking away, denying that medicine can do anything to help the patient's plight, is an immoral abrogation of medical power" (p. 1886). It is my belief that if a physician has religious, ethical, or other beliefs that prevent discussion of a dying patient's request for aid-in-dying, there is an obligation, by medical ethical principles, to ensure that the patient is referred for the best that is available in palliative care. Ignoring this obligation is abandonment, in my opinion. Failing to discuss the possibility of achieving what the patient would call a "good death," by a planned, rational suicide, or to refer to someone who can help the patient in facing the inevitable is against ethical and moral principles of beneficence and autonomy.

Further, I believe that physicians, who control access to pain medications, have two duties when treating patients with conditions that cause pain and suffering: first, to end already occurring pain by prescribing adequate and appropriate analgesia; and second, not to cause further harm, in the way of pain and suffering, by ordering futile investigations and treatments with no hope of returning the patient to a quality of life acceptable to him or her. Some who oppose rational suicide in the terminally ill insist that any and all pain symptoms can be controlled. This is incorrect. Some pain in terminal disease, such as spread of cancer to many bones, or increasing pressure inside the skull, from enlarging tumors, cannot be adequately alleviated. In these few patients, for whom even the best of palliative care is insufficient, I wonder how any could deny that ending life may be the best alternative. Some of these patients can be assisted by the principle of double effect (by which death is hastened with increasing dosages of analgesics and sedatives, but with the expressed intent being to control symptoms), accepted as appropriate by many in medicine, including those with religious beliefs opposed to suicide. This may be reasonable if the side effects of treatment can be well controlled but may mean that the patient is so sedated as to be unconscious and unable to interact with loved ones. All intravenous and stomach tube feedings should be discontinued if family and medical caregivers have agreed on this approach to shorten the time of dying. Because of the failure of some medical centers and physicians to allow patients to die, it has been necessary for those wishing that right to seek even more control over the medical decisions taking place when death is near. In this way, rational suicide has included the demand for aid-in-dying if it appears that the patient is to suffer a prolonged time of dying with inadequate control of the symptoms and indignities that are making for a poor quality of life in whatever time remains.

Ending one's own life remains a very difficult decision. However, when faced with the manner of dying frequently observed in our medical facilities, with tubes emanating from each bodily orifice, and mechanical support systems noisily functioning 24 hours a day, is it not reasonable that some would choose, in advance, to refuse such an end? Suicide in someone with the prospect of having a medicalized death, in a coldly dispassionate hospital room, might easily be determined by a reasonable person to be a most rational decision. A survey reported in *Suicide and Life-Threatening Behavior* (Werth & Cobia, 1995) found that, of 200 practicing psychologists questioned, 81% said that they believed in the idea of rational suicide.

The current practice of medicine has many obligations. An article in the *Hastings Center Report* eloquently states the relationship between physician and patient (Miller & Brody, 1995): "The generic duty of fidelity contains two component duties: the duty not to abuse the trust on which a therapeutic physician–patient relationship depends, and the duty not to abandon patients" (p. 11). The authors also say, "We believe that most, if not all, legitimate medical practices can be encompassed by three goals: healing, promoting health, and helping patients achieve a peaceful and dignified death" (p. 11). In the practice of family medicine, these goals have been honored for many decades. I believe those of us privileged to be entrusted with the care of patients must continue to care for them, regardless of incurable disease.

## ☐ Conclusion

What is most apparent to me, in reading many books and articles related to this subject, is that individual, personal beliefs play a very major role in the decisions that patients might make regarding discontinuing treatments or seeking an end to the suffering that they are experiencing. These beliefs also are most important in the approach that any physician might offer to his or her patients. Although I strongly favor the principle of autonomy, I understand and accept that each patient and each physician has the right to a personal point of view. Some patients may wish to have "everything done" to remain alive. However, if a patient wishes to have all treatment discontinued and adequate pain medication to relieve suffering, in spite of it shortening life, but the physician believes that he or she must do everything to preserve life no matter how intolerable the suffering may be, that physician is incorrect in imposing personally held beliefs on the patient. The subject of death and dying has been one that our society, including the medical profession, has failed to address in a reasonable manner. Death not only ends life; it also ends the dying process, which for some may be a very prolonged ordeal, made even lengthier by the technology available in America. Ending the painful, dehumanizing process of dying for one with a terminal illness should be considered rational and does not deserve to be compartmentalized into the category of suicide, this term more properly being reserved for those with depressive illness. I, for one, shall continue to support the concept of rational suicide, with the continuum of care including physician aid in this endeavor, when requested by a competent, terminally ill adult.

CHAPTER

Mark J. Goldblatt

# Rational Suicide: A Psychiatrist Against

*Rational suicide* is a term that implies that people may at times make a judicious decision to end their lives. This chapter is written from the perspective of a psychiatrist and questions the circumstances under which such a situation may occur. It is difficult to envision such clear-cut circumstances, free from the entanglements of ordinary life.

The debate over rational suicide highlights two opposing concepts: on the one hand is the right of each individual to autonomy. This includes the ability to act as one wishes, within acceptable societal norms, to end one's life. Of course, this should happen at an appropriate time, following careful consideration of issues relating to quality of life, and fears of intolerable degradation or pain associated with terminal illness. On the other hand, we are faced with the neuropsychological influences that affect all of us and limit self-awareness, to some extent. As a result, intellectual responses are intertwined with emotional reactions. Can it be possible to make a rational decision to end one's own life? Or is the issue of ending one's life too emotionally laden, too interwoven (possibly biologically ingrained) into our concepts of who we are, and what we are? This chapter examines the difficulties involved in coming to an autonomous decision to end one's life. Can such a choice truly be free from the influence of a biological brain under neurochemical stress, or an emotive mind responding to conscious and unconscious influences? What about pressures from external forces such as society and loved ones?

Psychiatrists are physicians who deal with mental illnesses and the emotional suffering that results from diseases of the mind, the brain, and the body. In one area of study, neurobiology has begun to open up the intricate workings of the brain. In another sector, psychodynamic research has focused on the psychological impact of an individual's development and the effect of interpersonal relationships. Psychiatrists have considerable exposure to suicidal patients and may be especially well placed to participate in the debate over rational suicide.

The difficulties associated with making a rational decision about suicide may be separated into three categories. The first relates to the field of neurobiology. Evidence has accumulated over the past few decades about the powerful role of neurotransmitters in the treatment and pathogenesis of the major mental illnesses. As is discussed in this chapter, increased understanding of the neurobiology of depression and other mental illnesses has improved treatment of these conditions. As mental illness is present in nearly all cases of suicide, treatment of the underlying disorder can greatly diminish the extent of suicidal behaviors in patients considering ending their lives. The concept of rational suicide must account for those who are acting under the influence of a brain illness, such as depression, that can easily distort one's view of the present and hopelessness about the future.

The second area that clouds rational decision making is the emotional upheaval confronting anyone facing the end-of-life. The threat of unbearable pain or the progressive loss of independence adds to the psychic upheaval. Some may respond with profound feelings of despair. Others may be aware of feelings of guilt, shame, or rage. Some people may desire suicide in order to avoid such destabilizing feelings. Unconscious motivations may also lead to dangerous suicidal actions.

Third, we must consider the influence of other people on any individual's decision to commit suicide. Everyone is affected by important figures, such as family and friends, in making a decision to live or die. Individuals who are considering rational suicide will undoubtedly be influenced in some ways by their loved ones. In addition, there is the pervasive influence of society and the messages conveyed about the value of life. This danger of manipulation is increased with the involvement of unscrupulous family members or exploitative agents who stand to gain from this death.

In this chapter I consider the manifest appeal for rational suicide and then discuss the biological substrate of psychiatric illness that is associated with suicide, as well as intrapsychic forces and interpersonal influences as they relate to decisions about suicide.

## ☐ The Appeal of Rational Suicide

Rational suicide may appeal to diverse groups: those fighting for their own right to die autonomously and without pain in the face of overwhelming disease; individuals who have nursed a loved one through great terminal suffering; and physicians who daily face dying patients who are incurable and in pain. From such standpoints it is easy to see the appeal of rational suicide. Everyone would want to be able to end one's life at the right time, to exert control over the final days and limit any pain and suffering.

These concerns may be assuaged by addressing the two factors of greatest manifest distress: pain management and fear of abandonment. Adequate analgesia already exists to cover almost all levels of pain. Reassurance that the treating physician will listen to the patient and has the capacity and willingness to provide the appropriate analgesia can alleviate this concern. The fear of being left to die, alone and uncared for, is another pressure for rational suicide. Through word and action physicians can find ways to reassure patients that they will not be abandoned by their caregivers as their health and functioning deteriorates.

The arguments appealing for rational suicide are remote from direct patient care. Hendin (1993) writes that the discussion over euthanasia has been dominated "by philosophers and non-psychiatric physicians who are often uninformed about the psychological and psychiatric dimensions" of suicide (p. 1903). He stresses the need to understand the psychological frame of mind of someone considering suicide:

For suicidally depressed individuals, control over whether they live or die provides the illusion of control of many of life's existential anxieties including those over dying. The relief provided many depressed patients by the decision to die misleads physicians unfamiliar with suicide into thinking that assisted suicide is the proper course of action. (p. 1903)

Physicians unfamiliar with suicidal patients may miss the diagnosis of a treatable depression in those patients who long for death.

## ☐ Psychiatric Illness

One of the most important contributors to any suicide is the effect of mental illness. In almost all cases of people who suicide (close to 95% in most large studies) there is an associated psychiatric diagnosis (Barraclough, Bunch, Nelson, & Sainsbury, 1974; Dorpat & Ripley, 1960; Robins, Murphy, Wilkenson, Gassner, & Kayes, 1959). The most common diagnosis that is associated with suicide is an affective disorder. Major depression is found in approximately 40% to 70% of these cases. Alcoholism is associated with about 20% to 30% of suicides. Other illnesses that appear commonly among those who complete suicides are schizophrenia, panic disorder, and substance abuse.

Patients suffering from major depression respond favorably to antidepressant medication, psychotherapy, or electroconvulsive therapy. If treated appropriately, almost all patients will recover from the depressive episode, usually with the disappearance of their suicidal ideation. Suicidality seems to be inextricably bound with the illness itself, part of the hopelessness and anguish that accompanies the depressive suffering.

In patients afflicted with severe medical illnesses, there may be some difficulties in making the diagnosis of a comorbid major depressive episode. This is a result of the overlap of medical and depressive symptoms. For example, loss of appetite and energy are diagnostic criteria for depression. These symptoms are commonly found in medically ill patients, either as a result of the illness or as a side effect of treatment. Some authors recommend that clinicians still count these symptoms toward a *DSM IV* (American Psychiatric Association, 1994) diagnosis of major depression to protect against the risk of underdiagnosis and undertreatment of depression (Cohen-Cole, Brown, & McDaniel, 1993).

Major depressive episodes are common in medical populations and frequently underdiagnosed and undertreated (McDaniel, Musselman, Porter, Reed, & Nemeroff, 1995). Although research is limited, two separate studies have showed that cancer patients with depression showed a significant treatment response to antidepressant treatment. These patients had an improvement in depressive symptoms and quality of life when treated with an antidepressant (Costa, Mogos, & Toma, 1985; Evans, McCartney, & Haggerty, 1988). This supports the belief that even in the seriously medically ill, depression is generally responsive to pharmacological treatment or psychotherapy. Although making the diagnosis of depression in terminal illness may be complicated, treatment of the underlying depressive component is often successful in relieving psychological suffering and may even be helpful in prolonging survival time and improving physical health in the medically ill. The resolution of depression is usually helpful in dissipating suicidal pressure.

There is a growing body of research connecting chronic pain and depression. Diener, van Schayck, and Kastrup (1995, p. 348) note that 15% to 90% of patients with depression complain of chronic pain. Their review of the literature showed that "between 5% and 87% of patients with chronic pain exhibit symptoms of depression" (p.

349). The relationship between chronic pain and depression may influence the choice of analgesia, because antidepressants may function as analgesics in certain cases. The precise mechanism of action is unclear, and more research is needed to clarify diagnostic criteria and treatment protocols for those who are suicidal and in great pain.

Another illness that plays a prominent role in completed suicides is alcoholism. Alcohol abuse is commonly implicated in suicide even when other diagnoses are present. Alcohol abuse increases the risk for suicidal behavior for both alcoholic and nonalcoholic populations; abuse is associated with approximately 50% of all suicides (Robins, et al., 1984). As mentioned previously, other diagnoses that are associated with an increased risk of suicide are schizophrenia, substance abuse, and panic disorder. All these conditions are responsive to psychiatric interventions.

The suicide literature documents the association between mental illness and suicide. Brown, Henteleff, Barakat, and Rowe (1986) suggest that this is also the case among the terminally ill. In other words, it would appear that suicide in patients who are severely medically ill is strongly associated with comorbid psychiatric diagnoses. Hendin and Klerman (1993, p. 143) note that although some patients with terminal illness may express suicidal thoughts, this is usually as a result of a transient depression or severe pain, and "the overwhelming majority of terminally ill patients fight for life to the end."

It seems that the threat of an overwhelming illness, and all that it represents, is more likely to provoke suicidal thoughts than the effects of the debilitating illness itself. This is borne out by studies that have shown increased suicidality among those who mistakenly believed they had cancer than among those who actually had the disease (Conwell, Caine, & Olsen, 1990). Similarly, suicide preoccupation is greater in those awaiting the results of HIV antibody testing than in those who knew they were HIV-positive (Perry, 1990).

More research is needed for a better understanding of the risk factors involved in suicide among the medically ill. We know that suicide is not caused by one single factor. Not all who have a terminal illness wish to kill themselves, and not all who suffer from major depression are suicidal. Several other factors probably contribute significantly to the suicidal act. The effects of loneliness, social support systems, personality traits, and psychobiology are certainly important. Depression is frequently undiagnosed in the medically ill population and consequently remains undertreated. This may contribute to increased rates of suicidal ideation in some who are terminally ill.

# ☐ Psychodynamics of Suicide

Psychodynamic explanations for suicide are sought because the *DSM-IV* diagnosis (American Psychiatric Association, 1994) alone does not give us enough information about suicidal behavior. For example, although major depression is a diagnosis that is associated with increased risk of suicide, not all depressed patients become suicidal. Of those patients who are thinking of committing suicide, not all go on to attempt suicide, and not all attempts at suicide lead to death. A better understanding of the patient's state of mind is necessary to improve our understanding of what might lead him or her to suicide.

Hendin (1991) organizes the psychological aspects of suicide into the "conscious (cognitive) and unconscious meanings given to death by the suicidal patient" (p.

1150). Some examples of psychodynamic forces in suicidal patients include intolerable affects of anguish, hopelessness, rage, and guilt. In addition, unconscious fantasies of revenge, rebirth, abandonment and self-punishment often feature prominently in suicidal states. These psychodynamic factors invariably act forcefully in the minds of suicidal patients whether they are suffering from a severe medical illness or not.

Particular psychodynamic themes appear to be especially dominant in patients who are confronted by life-threatening medical illnesses. In such instances issues of control are notably pressing. Fears of dependency surface associated with the threatened loss of status, functioning, or loved ones. These fears may mobilize suicidal plans in certain individuals, as a way of avoiding the difficult emotions that arise. One might say, "I cannot live like this. I need to be in control of my body. I want to be able to take my life when I feel the time is right." This may reflect an underlying fear; "No one will be there to help me when the illness becomes more than I can stand. I will be left alone to suffer without help or caring."

Through treatment with a therapist who is knowledgeable about suicide and empathically attuned, these fears can be made conscious, openly discussed, and appropriately addressed. Uninformed caregivers may mistake the patient's apparent calming down and acceptance of death as a sign that the decision to suicide is correct. However, many patients appear more at ease as a result of the decision to kill themselves. "It is coping with the uncertainties of life and death that agitate and depress them" (Hendin & Klerman, 1993, p. 144).

Maltsberger and Buie (1980) have described some of the powerful unconscious forces that are involved in suicide. They stress the fantasies involved in suicidal thoughts, in particular revenge wishes (e.g., how guilty and sad the mourners will feel after the person dies), as well as fantasies of punishment and wish for riddance (a killing off of a scornful inner presence in patients lacking a sense of integration of the self). They also note the frequency of fantasies about escape and rebirth. All these occur prominently in patients experiencing the ravages of physical illness.

In trying to arrive at the genesis of such suicidal ideation, Maltsberger and Buie (1980) offer a hypothesis about the effects of inadequate early childhood soothing. Receiving appropriate comforting in early childhood is necessary to enable one to endure aloneness and feelings of helplessness. Lack of feeling comforted as a young child is implicated as a cause of later suicidal feelings. Inadequate self-integration is another contributing factor. If such a person (lacking in self-integration and ill-prepared for facing aloneness because of inadequate early comforting) is faced with the loss of physical or intellectual powers, suicidal ideation may emerge. The authors speculate that such dynamics may be at work in "rational suicide"—"carried out to avoid the anticipated ravages of incurable illness" (p. 71).

Empathic listening (psychotherapy) is often very helpful in uncovering the underlying feelings and helping patients bear the unbearable. The unconscious suicidogenic forces most often fade in the presence of a comforting doctor, or friendly listener, able to support a patient as he or she explores these painful psychological areas. Clarification and reality testing of fantasies of death and the imagined effects it would have on the patient or those around reduce self-destructive drives and help the patient deal with the fearful realities of coming to the end-of-life.

## ☐ External Influence

The third significant force that affects suicidality is the influence from the outside. This includes communications from important close object ties (family and friends), as well as groups of people and society as a whole. No one is psychologically isolated from the effects of these currents. Perceptions, based in reality or fantasy, can exert a great influence on patients' decisions to end their own lives.

Patients react to what they sense from relatives. This communication may be in words, or in action. At times, the message may be conveyed through inaction or abandonment. For example, relatives who feel anger or hostility as a result of their helplessness in the face of the patient's decline may find themselves unable to tolerate the sight of their loved one suffering, or the emptiness it creates in their own lives. If the patient perceives this struggle in his or her family, it may fuel his or her own feelings of guilt and dread of being an encumbrance. Suicide serves as an escape from fears of being an intolerable burden to the survivors. This becomes even more pronounced if issues of money are involved. Patients who are burdened with severe guilt may wish to hasten their deaths to protect their families from high medical bills, which may be real or imagined. With terminally ill patients, open and honest discussion between patient and family may alleviate these fears and promote a more forthright exchange of views, leading to a closer bond during this time of farewell. Suicidal feelings are likely to resolve if there is no longer a need to flee from intolerable guilt.

Another significant factor relates to the physicians themselves who unstintingly work to save their suffering patients. Well-intentioned caregivers who are blinded by their own need to provide what they believe to be the right treatment may miss a diagnosis of depression in a terminally ill patient and as a result may go along with the patient's wish to die. These admirable doctors work under very difficult conditions, often with very little support for the psychological trauma such chronic loss of life can produce. Sometimes, when facing patients with little hope of cure, and after having seen similar patients die painful deaths, these caregivers may become "infected" by their patients' hopelessness and support their wish for death. By maintaining her own sense of self the physician is able to remember the effectiveness of various treatments and of the caring that she personally brings to the situation. This combats the sense of helplessness and provides comfort to the patient who may have given up hope.

Phillips (1974) has described the powerful influence of suggestibility for those susceptible to suicide. He documented the rise in subsequent suicides following the publication of suicide stories in the press. This rise was proportional to the amount of publicity the suicide received. Patients who are at risk for suicide are influenced by hearing about others' suicides, especially if the romantic aspects are reported with little attention to the devastation and suffering that accompanies death.

Societies, in general, communicate powerful messages about who is good and deserves life and who does not. In a society in which "rational suicide" is a way of life, there is a great risk that some sectors of society will experience undue pressure to kill themselves under certain conditions. The potential for abuse is a powerful incentive to be extremely cautious in legislating this issue.

# ☐ Conclusion

There are three major reasons why it is difficult to embrace the notion of rational suicide, attractive as it may seem on first pass. First is the robust association of mental illness with suicide. Depression, which is most often associated with suicide, is quite responsive to treatment, as are the other mental illnesses that invariably accompany suicidality. Following improvement in the psychiatric condition, suicidal ideation usually resolves. The second reason is the power of the intrapsychic forces that are associated with suicide. In particular, intolerable affects of rage, guilt, and hopelessness contribute to suicidality. Fantasies of revenge, sleep, or rebirth are common. Psychotherapy is a successful method of treatment that explores these ideas in the context of a safe relationship and leads to reality testing and a more realistic approach to difficult and painful situations. The third reason is the influence of external relationships, the effect of the society as a whole.

Rational suicide is therefore less a form of being rational and more an expression of a wish to die based on conscious or unconscious motivations. There is great need for further research into the last phases of life and in particular those who wish to die by their own hand, or with their physician's assistance, when faced with a life-threatening illness. This is an area that is sadly neglected in the teaching at our medical schools and in our hospitals. Physicians and other healthcare providers need to be actively involved in this dialogue. Suicide experts are important contributors to this discussion, bringing with them experience and commitment. Psychiatrists enter the arena on behalf of our patients, teaching that mental illness is a disorder that can be diagnosed and treated, not banished with the prejudice and fear that has marked historical attitudes. Legislation may be part of the approach to this difficult conflict, but legislation must take into account the complex issues discussed here that influence suicidal people.

# 17
CHAPTER

Jerome A. Motto

# A Psychiatric Perspective on Rational Suicide: 24 Points of View

Any form of self-destructive behavior has traditionally been regarded as pathological, and it was with this preconception that in 1956 I began to study the problem of suicide in psychiatric patients. It was clear from the outset that the issue of suicide and suicide prevention extended far beyond the usual boundaries of clinical psychiatry and psychology, raising questions of medical care, philosophy, ethics, sociology, theology, law, and anthropology. Especially striking was the contrast between value systems in diverse cultures, in subcultures, and in individuals. The initial simplistic model equating suicidal ideas with psychopathology gradually faded in spite of my clinging tenaciously to an intuitive belief that physical survival is a primary motivating force in normal living organisms. Attentive listening finally led me to recognize another reality, specifically, for certain persons, that psychological survival—that is, their perception of themselves and their value system—can take precedence over physical survival. Under certain circumstances, such persons may decide to end their life if the only available alternative *for them* is unremitting agony that resists all pharmacological and psychosocial means of relief.

As the pressure to recognize the concept of rational suicide has increased to the level of state ballot initiatives, debate in the professional community has kept pace, with experienced and knowledgeable clinicians well represented on both sides. A number of observations have emerged from this debate, of which the most important, in my opinion, follow as the focus of this discussion. Although stated somewhat dogmatically, there is room for argument with each point.

## ☐ Points of View

1. Everything can be found in clinical practice, thus any point of view can be illustrated by a clinical example. Although useful for clarification, it must be kept in

mind that single cases tend to have very limited generalizability. This is based on the realization that every person is unique. Every family is unique. Every culture and subculture is unique. What is valid for a given person in a given family and culture may not be valid for another person.

2. The question of whether persons of sound mind should be permitted, under specific conditions (e.g., terminal illness), to end their lives, or to be assisted in doing so, is not a scientific question but a matter of social philosophy. There are thus no "right" or "wrong" positions, only different ways of seeing the problem. Only if one were to insist that suicidal intent is inherently pathological would this philosophical framework not hold.

3. It is difficult to separate the concept of rational suicide from the question of assisted suicide. Unless the former is accepted, the latter cannot be considered. The issue seems to present a unique legal situation as the only instance in which it has been illegal to assist another person to carry out a legal act.

4. There is ample evidence that assisted suicide takes place every day, whether it involves providing a lethal amount of medication by prescription, responding to a request by increasing the rate of flow of an intravenous pain medication, or otherwise facilitating a suicidal act. The basic question posed to society is whether this should continue as a covert procedure or in the open, properly documented, with protection from abuse and from legal liability.

5. The high level of energy infusing the issue of rational suicide does not come from psychiatrists, other physicians, ethicists, the Hemlock Society, or churches. It comes rather from patients and those close to them. The torture endured by families who perceive a loved one as helpless and in agony will continue to generate extreme pressure on healthcare personnel, especially in that small proportion of cases in which palliative measures short of a semi-anesthetized state are inadequate. Hearing the person groan with each expiration, or hearing them repeatedly plead, to "*Please* let me go," can create almost unbearable feelings in family members. It is understandable that the families of those Dr. Jack Kevorkian has assisted in suicide apparently regard him as a heroic figure, and surveys carried out in Michigan indicate that a large majority of the people in that state approve of his efforts (*San Francisco Chronicle*, 1995).

6. The realization has gradually emerged that rational suicide may have benefits that go beyond relief of suffering or assertion of autonomy. A planned death has been found in some instances to unite families in a profound way, by providing opportunity for leave taking and for reconciliation with alienated members. This can serve not only to ease the process for the patient but to forestall the lifelong burden of guilt and regret experienced so often by surviving family members. Such a process is much more difficult with the uncertain timing of a natural death.

7. The concept of *assisting* a person in a rational suicide received considerable impetus in the 1980s from the Hemlock Society and its director, Derek Humphry. Daring to openly champion the option of a "humane and dignified death," this group gave international visibility to the issue, using a "terminal illness" model. Although they encountered resistance, there was also evidence of widespread support for responding to the wishes of persons whose remaining life could be measured in hours, days, or weeks. The focus was reconceptualized into a more acceptable image, changing from "assisted suicide" to "aid-in-dying" or "self-deliverance." This provided the clear advantage of advocating *helping* the natural process rather than *interfering* with it.

During the 1980s the growing problem of AIDS gave impetus to the idea of a self-determined death, the most important elements of which were that: people contemplating ending their lives were not necessarily near death but were often in the prime of life and still functioning at a high level, and that the focus switched from the "terminal illness" to the "while I'm still in charge" model. The latter had been advanced in the 1960s and 1970s by the elderly who were burdened by chronic, deteriorating, and progressively disabling illness, but it did not command a prominent place in the national awareness. The AIDS community was unique in that so many of its members repeatedly had observed the natural course of the disease and resolved to avoid an experience that they perceived as humiliating and degrading. The shift away from the "terminal illness" model, however, creates new concerns about the potential abuse of the concept of rational suicide. Both models are now debated, at times with insufficient clarity as to which is being addressed.

8. The question of physician participation in the process of rational suicide, whether as a psychiatrist or a nonpsychiatric physician, has precipitated much discussion about the violation of medical traditions. If we consider the most important traditions of medicine to be the preservation of life and the relief of suffering, we must ask what guidelines we have if these two values are in conflict, so that addressing one forces us to violate the other. Which value has precedence is not always clear, and such a conflict forces each physician to draw on his or her own philosophy of life—and death—for resolution.

9. Persuasive arguments have been advanced, especially by those who provide hospice services, that the optimal end-of-life experience is with the provision of "comfort care," including adequate pain control, management of distressing physical symptoms (e.g. nausea, difficulty breathing), and appropriate emotional support for both patient and family until a natural death occurs. It seems clear, however, that these goals are not always achievable at an acceptable price. The eminent Dutch psychiatrist and pioneering suicide prevention worker, Nico Speijer, wrote in his suicide note that his pain was controlled only by a dose that turned him into a kind of zombie (Diekstra, 1992, p. 71). *For him,* comfort care was intolerable. For others, the presence of persistent diarrhea, having to labor for every breath, or becoming unable to speak or recognize family members can be similarly intolerable and can produce emotional pain just as excruciating as unbearable physical pain. For those who are able to accept such experiences and to comply with the limitations of medical management of terminal conditions, hospice-type care can be a Godsend to dying patients and their families. The issue of rational suicide only arises if such care cannot be accepted by the person.

10. For some individuals, being assured the option of a quick, sure, painless, and dignified demise can dramatically reduce the suicidal impulse. A distinguished oncologist reported that after finally acquiescing to a patient's persistent requests for enough sleeping pills to carry out a suicide, he found to his surprise that the pills were not used. The patient is quoted: "The great thing was, once I knew I could do it, life became valuable again. I was back in charge" (White, 1971, p. 4). Preliminary observations suggest that approximately one third of persons who meet commonly accepted criteria of eligibility for support of rational suicide will continue to delay taking that step until a natural death intervenes (unpublished report).

11. Assuring that a suicidal impulse is not a manifestation of depression or other emotional disorder is critical and at times difficult, even for an experienced clinician. At least one psychiatric assessment should address this, a point overlooked thus far in drafting state initiatives for a "humane and dignified death" that permit physician assistance. In many cases the correct diagnostic category is adjustment disorder with depressed mood, but the vagaries of intermixed physical and emotional symptoms (e.g. despondency, fatigue, eating disturbance, sleeping disturbance, poor concentration, altered motor activity, thoughts of death) complicate the diagnostic task. It is

common practice in consultation-liaison psychiatry to overtreat, that is, in uncertain cases to give antidepressant medications and psychosocial support in order to assure that a treatable depression is not overlooked.

Diagnosis continues to depend to a large degree on intuitive judgment, in spite of the simplicity of the current *Diagnostic and Statistical Manual* (Amerian Psychiatric Association, 1994). Clinical instruments (e.g., the Beck Depression Inventory) are not routinely used because of questions regarding validity but deserve consideration in a protocol evaluating the question of rational suicide. There is room for much disagreement among experienced clinicians as to the proportion of persons at significant risk for suicide who would qualify for "no psychiatric diagnosis." In a meticulous retrospective diagnostic study of 134 suicides, one research team found that 6% of its sample had no psychiatric disorder discernible at the time of suicide (Robins, 1980). This seems a very conservative number that could serve as a starting point for discussion. Diagnostic imprecision seems likely to persist as a potential area of controversy.

12. Attempts to define rational take different forms, but criteria tend to cluster around six elements: (1) The person has a clear sensorium. This implies that any cognitive deficit present (e.g., a decrement of short-term memory) does not interfere with perception or reasoning. (2) The person's decision is based on a thorough understanding and a realistic assessment of all the available and pertinent facts. A clear state of mind is not enough. "Realistic," for want of a better definition, is what appears realistic to the knowledgeable clinician. (3) All feasible alternatives have been carefully considered, including simply temporizing, with the knowledge that a person's outlook can be shifted by time alone. (4) No external coercion is present. (5) The idea of suicide is not produced or intensified by psychopathology, such as depression, psychosis, delirium, or a panic state. (6) The person is assessed as capable of forming reasoned judgment. The legal status "competent" is not determined by healthcare personnel.

13. Considering the monetary cost of end-of-life care may sound crass, but in some situations it can be a driving force that is powerful and realistic. Persons who have worked hard all their adult lives in order to assure that their surviving families will have economic security can find it impossible to sacrifice that goal in order to purchase a few more weeks or months of severely compromised life in an intensive-care unit.

14. Fear that subtle (even unconscious) or overt family pressure could lead to a request for assisted suicide is a reasonable concern. It is incumbent on the psychiatrist and other caretakers to explore this possibility carefully and assure that no external coercive influence dictates decision-making.

15. A self-inflicted death carried out covertly can be undignified in the extreme, especially if it occurs in an isolated setting and no provision is made to notify others out of fear that intervention would occur. We must acknowledge that denying the validity of the concept of rational suicide not only fails to prevent its occurrence but can create painful situations for the person and the family as well. This is most clear to the deputy from the Medical Examiner's office, who removes the body from the suicide site. Percy Bridgeman, the 1946 Nobel Laureate in physics, expressed this simply in his suicide note: "It isn't decent for society to make a man do this for himself" (deFord, 1963, p. 10).

16. Fear of a "slippery slope" is often heard. If suicide is considered acceptable for the terminally ill, who is next? The chronically but not terminally ill? The elderly infirm? The severely retarded or disabled? Such concerns are reasonable, especially if we reach back to resurrect ghosts from the Nazi period in Germany, although few would accept any similarity of our own social system to that regime.

It may be useful to consider our experience with the only other intentional death incorporated into our society, that of capital punishment. Society's fear of inappropriate application of this procedure has led to so much equivocation that it has seen very infrequent implementation, preceded by years of protracted reconsideration. Does this suggest that a similar social resistance to accept a legal means of ending a life would be experienced in the case of rational suicide? Would our acute awareness of the danger of extending the scope of a socially sanctioned suicide provide us with as much protection as we need?

17. Even if the slippery slope did not materialize, there would always be danger of abuse of a system sanctioning voluntary termination of life. The potential for abuse is evident, yet the same can be said for *any* beneficial program. If forewarned is forearmed, the challenge is to devise a set of controls that assure that this potential is reduced to a minimum.

18. A point frequently raised suggests that accepting the concept of rational suicide will diminish our society's traditional reverence for life. Bypassing such questions as what constitutes life or the importance of quality of life, it may be argued that the opposite is true. We would not permit an object of reverence to exist in a form that is humiliating or degrading. If we accept that our national flag is an object of reverence, it has been pointed out that when the flag becomes so tattered and torn that its dignity is compromised, we express our reverence by burning it. Personal dignity is a very individual matter, and for some people it can only be maintained by exercising the same option in regard to their own lives.

19. There is a wide gap between moral philosophy and the bedside. Sound theoretical arguments can melt away in the intensity of an individual's need to preserve a sense of personal integrity. General ethical guidelines are accepted as necessary and valuable in psychiatry, but respect for the uniqueness of each person forces us to recognize exceptions. History provides a precedent in the esteem accorded martyrdom, with the clear implication that some human values can take precedence over life itself.

20. Organized psychiatry has been slow to confront the issue of rational suicide directly. The Group for the Advancement of Psychiatry held a symposium in 1973 on "The Right to Die: Decision and Decision Makers," but it offered no recommendations from it. The American Psychiatric Association arranged a scientific debate at its 1984 annual meeting on the question, "Is suicide always a psychopathological event?" but declined to publish the arguments and has never taken a formal position on the question. Although never directly disputing the concept of rational suicide, the official stance has focused on its relationship to the issue of physician-assisted suicide, stating unequivocally that "it is inappropriate for physicians to participate—in any procedure that would purposely cause the death of a patient" (Psychiatric News, May 20, 1994, p. 30).

On an individual basis, however, acceptance of a role for physician assistance of rational suicide is readily found among psychiatrists, as it appears to be in 55% to 60% of physicians in general (Bachman et al., 1996; Lee et al., 1996). In spite of this, the danger of "psychiatric invalidation" has been noted, in which a patient's request to die can be nullified by a psychiatric diagnosis influenced more by the needs of traditional medicine than the status of the patient (Yarnell & Battin, 1988, p. 602). There is little evidence that the wide gap between organized psychiatry and individual psychiatrists will be significantly reduced in the near future.

21. There are vast differences, both practically and philosophically, among "physician-assisted suicide," "physician-assisted death," "voluntary euthanasia," "involuntary euthanasia," and "nonvoluntary euthanasia." Only physician-assisted suicide

and voluntary euthanasia involve the concept of rational suicide, the former implying that persons desire to and are capable of ending their life if given assistance (e.g., a lethal amount of medication), the latter that they are unable to take an active role. Physician-assisted death means that life was shortened by aggressive medication for pain or other symptoms. Involuntary euthanasia implies that death was not desired by the patient (a situation unique to Nazi Germany). Nonvoluntary euthanasia refers to life-terminating acts without explicit and persistent request, such as in irreversible vegetative states or deterioration so rapid that the patient is comatose before end-of-life decisions can be discussed. These categories are important to keep in mind, as discussions of rational suicide sometimes fail to differentiate clearly between suicide, euthanasia, and degrees of voluntariness.

In physician-assisted suicide an important distinction is also made between "active" and "passive" assistance. A physician prepared to prescribe a 30-day supply of sleeping medication or antidepressant may not be willing to administer an equally lethal amount of medication intravenously or to assist the patient to take it orally.

22. It is of interest that our legal and ethical standards will allow a person to refuse food and water, leading to an agonizing death in a few weeks from starvation and dehydration, but will not sanction the intravenous injection of a sedative, resulting in a quiet death in 5 minutes. One might say the former allows for a change of mind while the latter does not, which is reassuring to society, but for a determined and suffering patient that distinction provides little comfort.

23. It seems certain that the pressure on society to provide for a self-determined and dignified death will continue to increase, especially with the progressive aging of our population, the persistence of AIDS as an endemic disease, and annual deaths from cancer numbering over half a million. If that pressure is not relieved by a socially sanctioned and regulated procedure, we might anticipate the growth of a covert network of responders, as has already developed in some parts of the AIDS community. The idea that a decision to suicide cannot be made rationally would receive relatively little attention in such an underground system. That the book *Final Exit* (Humphry, 1991) quickly rose to the top of a best-seller list in 1991 and remained there for weeks seems to indicate that the general population is anticipating such a development more keenly than is our healthcare system.

24. In spite of some distinguished voices to the contrary, the world of psychiatry has moved beyond the question of whether rational suicide is a valid concept, to the practical world of how to respond to the day-to-day problems the concept creates. This transition is very actively in progress, with the most visible developments taking place in the courtroom and in state initiatives under the banners of "right to die" and "humane and dignified death."

There is so much energy involved, with patients and families on one side, and medical–social–legal tradition on the other, that the final outcome is not at all clear. It seems likely that we will finally emerge with some variant of the solution forged in the Netherlands after many years of struggle. Specifically that social sanction of a rational suicide will be conditional, with specific provisions to protect against inappropriate or abusive application of life-ending procedures (Huyse & van Tilburg, 1993). The best interests of the individual must come first, with concern for the family and for the needs of an ethical society respected as well. Some measure of societal accommodation seems inevitable. It is just a matter of time and social readiness.

# ☐ Historical Note

Sigmund Freud, the symbol of dynamic psychiatry during the past century, is said to have "died as he had lived—a realist" (Jones, 1957, p. 246). His last days dramatize much of the current social and professional ferment regarding rational suicide. Cancer of the jaw had progressed to the point at which he could no longer interact with family and friends. He had refused pain medication because "I prefer to think in torment than not to be able to think clearly" (p. 245). In September 1939 he reminded his physician of the latter's promise to help him end his life when it became unbearable, saying, "It is only torture now and it has no longer any sense." He was given morphine, sank into a peaceful sleep, and died the next day (p. 246). This sequence has, to my knowledge, never been questioned as to psychopathology or ethical behavior.

A similar view of death that mirrors Freud's final days has been vividly expressed in poetry (Young, 1968, p. 240):

> Let me die, working.
> Still tackling plans unfinished, tasks undone!
> Clean to its end, swift may my race be run.
> No laggard steps, no faltering, no shirking;
>     Let me die, working!
>
> Let me die, thinking.
> Let me fare forth still with an open mind,
> Fresh secrets to unfold, new truths to find,
> My soul undimmed, alert, no question blinking;
>     Let me die, thinking!
>
> Let me die, giving.
> The substance of life for life's enriching;
> Time, things, and self on heaven converging,
> No selfish thought, loving, redeeming, living;
>     Let me die, giving!

# ☐ Conclusion

This discussion presents a "pro" position only in the sense that it maintains that suicide can be a rational act. Personal and social philosophy, religious beliefs, or simply emotional and intellectual analysis may lead some to characterize such an act as a distortion of values, immoral, undesirable, or simply wrong, but it cannot be dismissed as not real.

A psychiatrist may shrink from the awful responsibility of forming life and death decisions on the strength of intuitive judgement. We want clear rules, a sense of scientific discipline, and some assurance that we are doing the right (ethical) thing. Yet if we relinquish trust in our ability to determine ethical action based on each unique set of circumstances, we give up the basic value from which ethical action springs: freedom of thought and judgment. In considering the issue of rational suicide, it is part of our task as psychiatrists and physicians to heed the dictates of a humane and caring spirit, and to trust its influence on our judgment.

Stephen Jamison

# Psychology and Rational Suicide: The Special Case of Assisted Dying

Until recently, the traditional psychological view has held that *rational suicide* is an oxymoron, in that suicide implies irrationality and is nearly always motivated by the presence of depression, unbearable psychological pain, feelings of desperation and hopelessness, or some unspecified emotional illness (Shneidman, 1992; Winokur & Black, 1992). The implication is that no unimpaired person ever rationally chooses death, including one who is terminally or incurably ill experiencing intractable physiological suffering (Brown, Henteleff, Barakat, & Rowe, 1986; Conwell & Caine, 1991; Koening, 1993).

A similar position has been adopted by various medical associations and other groups as an argument against legalizing physician-assisted suicide, claiming that depression is frequently overlooked in cases of terminal illness, and that humane medical response, palliative care, and use of antidepressant medication can virtually eliminate the desire to die (Foley, 1996; Society for Health and Human Values Task Force On Physician-Assisted Suicide, 1995).

Although there is much truth in this statement, recent case studies of assisted suicide—or assisted dying—counter this general view by showing that there can be substantial differences between suicide and assisted dying among those with terminal conditions with intractable and irreversible suffering (S. Jamison, 1995; Shavelson, 1995). In many instances, these self-determined deaths are nonimpulsive and follow exploration of alternatives and a lengthy process of decision making involving significant others.

Although there is no guarantee that every suicide or assisted suicide by a terminally ill person is rational or is not accompanied by depression, the traditional view is open to several criticisms. I'll discuss some of these in this chapter. First, not only does the traditional view fail to account for the special health-related circumstances of those with terminal conditions, it also ignores the impact of cultural and social changes on attitudes towards suicide in these cases. Second, it does not recognize the often shared involvement of significant others and physicians in the suicide process. And third, it is based on biased research samples of known suicides, ignoring the great majority of assisted deaths that are officially documented as due to natural causes.

To illustrate my argument, I partly draw from both my published (S. Jamison, 1995, 1996, 1997; see also Cotten, 1993) and unpublished research on assisted suicide—in order to examine the effects of experience with hastened death I interviewed 160 people who participated in 140 deaths of people close to them (see S. Jamison, 1995, for an overview of the methodology). After critiquing the traditional model, I set forth some brief guidelines to assess rationality.

## ☐ The Dynamic View of Rational Suicide

Those who support the view that suicide is irrational, and that no unimpaired person rationally chooses death over life, often ignore the facts that certain behaviors are considered more rational in some cultures than others; attitudes about the rationality of certain behaviors can be subject to change over time even within the same culture; and public attention given to these changing attitudes may influence ways in which individuals perceive their own physiological states, the range of personal decisions that are available to them, and the selection of such behaviors. I would argue that suicide and assisted suicide of those with terminal conditions constitute such behaviors.

In Euro-American tradition suicide has long been considered taboo and subject to religious and legal censure. However, suicide in the case of terminal illness has also been influenced by cultural and social changes, shifting authority of religious sanctions in matters of personal choice, and transformations in commonly held interpretations of personal human experience and reasonable action. As a result, all human action, even suicide by the terminally ill, must be seen as subject to contemporary cultural and experiential influences. Psychological models of rational behavior would be wise to take these influences into account.

Questions concerning the rationality of suicide need to be understood in light of several key factors that have impinged upon the strength of formerly dominant cultural and religious traditions in matters of personal choice and behavior. These may include changes in medical practice and ethics and the prevalent causes of death over the past several decades, legal rulings for more than 20 years that favor individual autonomy and choice in regard to medical intervention and end-of-life decisions, and increased public sentiment supporting the legal availability of physician-assisted suicide. The latter is also evidenced in, and affected by media attention to the topic of assisted suicide and recent successes in terms of the Oregon assisted-suicide initiative as well as in two high-profile U.S. Circuit and Supreme Court cases.

Any discussion of the rationality of suicide would do well to begin by taking into account the changing nature of the modern death experience. To ignore this factor would be a mistake, as the prevalent causes of death over the past several decades have shifted from acute conditions with a short dying process—often over a period of hours, days, or weeks—to chronic illnesses with more long-term dying processes. AIDS, many cancers, and incurable degenerative neurological illnesses fit this scenario. Advances in medicine and technology, public health, antibiotics, and emergency care for acute conditions mean that most of us now live long enough to die from degenerative causes. Moreover, some of these conditions consist of physiological suffering with patients reporting intractable pain and lessened quality of life.

Similarly, this transformation in the death experience over the past several decades also has been affected by changes in medical practice geared towards prolonging the end-of-life. These include advances in the technology of diagnosis, pharmacology, and treatment, and increased use of procedures for sustaining life. After its beginning in the 1950s we saw the rise of what Jonsen (1986) has termed the "age of rescue," in which medicine began following a perceived imperative to utilize all available technology to save "identifiable lives." The result is that many of us have witnessed prolonged deaths of significant others, often with an intolerable level of suffering, after a variety of invasive procedures and extensive treatments we perceived to be of little curative value.

As a result, since the 1970s, we also have seen increased attention being paid to the concept of patient autonomy, both in medical ethics and in court decisions concerning the rights of patients at the end-of-life. This has resulted in widescale changes in law allowing for use of advance directives for end-of-life decisions in such documents as living wills, directives to physicians, and durable powers of attorney for health care, in which patients can specify, in advance, the withholding or withdrawing of life-sustaining procedures under certain conditions.

These factors have influenced both public and medical opinion as to the choice of physician aid-in-dying by the terminally ill. Public opinion surveys have found that the overwhelming majority of those surveyed believe that physicians should be able to help terminally ill patients to die. Also, recent physician surveys have found that patient requests for aid-in-dying are common and that "secret" provision of such assistance occurs regularly. In the state of Washington, for example, a survey of physicians found that 12% had received one or more explicit requests for assistance in suicide in the previous year (Back, Wallace, Starks, & Pearlman, 1996). Of these patients, 24% were provided the means to die. And in San Francisco, a survey of physicians treating AIDS patients found that 53% had granted at least one patient's request for assisted suicide—nearly double the percentage in a survey of a similar group of physicians 4 years earlier (Abrams et. al., 1996). Further, recent surveys have found large numbers of nurses also participating (Asch, 1996; Kuhse and Singer, 1993). This research provides strong support for the idea that health professionals' behaviors supporting assisted suicide have been strongly affected by cultural factors combined with their own experiences with dying patients.

Although opinion and behavior surveys provide no guarantee that suicide is rational in any particular case, they do suggest the extent of change at a cultural level toward what is and is not rational to consider, discuss, and select as an appropriate behavior. I would argue that these changes have moved the decision to end one's life out of the realm solely of those with emotional conditions who express suicidal ideation into the general population of the dying. In this way, we must consider that suicide—and assisted suicide—by the terminally ill is increasingly being viewed by the dying themselves, as well as their significant others, their physicians, and the courts as reasonable and socially acceptable solutions to the intolerable conditions of a terminal illness.

These attitudinal changes do not occur in an experiential vacuum. Many with terminal conditions whom I have interviewed described the perception of their own experience as "intolerable" based on comparisons of their own condition with other deaths they historically witnessed. This can be seen in statements such as "Dad's death was easy compared to this," and "a lot of my friends didn't have what I've got." As a result, many strongly opposed the term "suicide" and preferred expressions such as "self-deliverance," "self-determination," "assisted dying," and "ultimate liberty," linking talk of such action to descriptions of their own physiological conditions, irreversible suffering, and vanishing quality of life. In other cases explanations of their leanings toward assisted suicide were closely connected to their perceptions of intolerable deaths they witnessed of partners, family members, or friends who died from conditions similar to their own. Statements such as "I could never go through that," "I won't wait that long," "I could never suffer that much," and "I can only take a little more as it is" were frequently juxtaposed with these stories of less-than-peaceful death. These stories of other deaths gone wrong also influenced their perception of medical care and available alternatives. They used these narratives to reinforce their position in regard to assisted dying. These narratives, which quite often described "inadequate pain relief," "side effects of medications," "failure of hospice," and "lack of concern" by physicians, supported their distrust of a natural death under medical care.

Although distrust of available models of care and fear of an intolerable death obviously were present in many explanations of preference for assisted suicide, this does not mean that distrust and fear always lead to irrational behavior. Opponents of the rational suicide model, by reliance on a 19th-century view of human behavior and death, conveniently seem to ignore more than half a century of change in cultural attitudes, medical practice, law and ethics, and hands-on human experience with the dying process.

Another factor to be considered in support of the rationality of some assisted suicides is the effect of historical assisted deaths within a family or social group which both a patient and significant others may view as a positive model. Among participants in assisted deaths whom I interviewed, I found this to be especially true where the deceased had suffered from AIDS. However, it also was apparent in a number of cases where individuals had suffered from breast or prostate cancer and were members of either self-help support groups or more informal social circles of patients. In some of these cases it was apparent that the presence of other positively defined models of death paved the way for their own ultimate actions.

In this regard, for some the consideration of suicide as an appropriate choice may well be made partly on the basis of what already is acceptable within one's social group. One cannot merely claim that all suicide is irrational if social factors may play a role in the decision process.

Opponents of the rational suicide model often rely on a built-in bias favoring life of any form over death, regardless of the amount of physical suffering a person may be experiencing. This assumes that a rational person values life equally at all times and under all conditions. It ignores the possibility that some who are dying may have a distinct set of values by which they view life as worth living only so long as they can maintain a sense of control, and some self-defined minimum level of quality of life and personhood. Opponents of rational suicide instead suggest that there is no minimum quality of life, ignoring that each of us may have different perceptions of suffering and a different minimum acceptable level of quality of life and may vary in how connected he or she is to the continuation of physical life. As one interviewee told me, "I don't want to die, but it's not an option; it's going to happen anyway. All I can do is decide when enough is enough."

# ☐ The Concerted Nature of Many Suicides Among the Terminally Ill

The opposition model implies that the decision to die is made alone or after one-sided discussions that are likely to be cries for help. The implication is that these suicides occur in isolation. In the case of the terminally ill, however, decisions to die are often made only after participation of significant others and physicians in the decision and planning process (S. Jamison, 1995, 1996). Moreover, such deaths are frequently of a concerted and "assisted" nature, with significant others not only aware of the decision but active participants in the suicide itself.

In my interviews with participants in 140 assisted suicides, for example, it became clear that, in nearly all cases, death followed discussions on a number of topics, including the decision to die, the feelings of—and effects on—significant others, the degree of suffering, quality-of-life issues, treatment options, final timing, and the desire to avoid precipitous, impulsive action. In terms of the final topics, in only a small number of cases (6 out of 140) did initial notification of desire, all discussions, and suicide occur within a 1-week period. Substantially more time usually was involved, ranging upwards to two years among those with AIDS or cancers with remission. In 85 of my 140 cases, suicides were postponed at least once even after these individuals secured what they believed were the means to end their lives.

If such cases of suicide are irrational, this implies a serious inability on the part of significant others, physicians, and, in some cases, mental health professionals to assess the presence of depression or other disorders that may influence a patient's decision. In fact, in 47 of the 140 assisted deaths I studied, physicians knowingly provided the perceived means for patients to end their own lives. If these assisted suicides were not rational, then these physicians either were negligent in not preventing these deaths or were themselves less than rational for participating. The same can be said for significant others who participated in all 140 cases.

I have witnessed the "public" nature of potentially-assisted suicide in discussions within groups I have facilitated for the terminally ill and also in meetings I have held with the dying and their significant others. Opponents might suggest that such discussions are but opportunities for the dying to share and validate their suicidal ideation. Instead, I have witnessed groups serving as forums in which all concerns are discussed, including quality of life issues, possible treatment approaches, alternatives, practical tools for daily living, and ideas for achieving resolution with others on relationship issues. I would argue that discussions between the dying and their significant others present a potential to discuss all of these concerns as well as issues related to financial and emotional burdening. They also provide the opportunity to better understand the perspective of the other, to identify possible coercion by either party, and to attain relational closure. In addition, in many instances I found talk about assisted dying quickly turned into discussion on how to improve quality of care and streamline the delivery of information, complaints, and services within the home.

Instead of seeing in such talk a cry for help, the presence of suicidal ideation, and evidence of depression and irrational decision-making processes, I would argue that such talk by the dying can bear important fruit in terms of improved caregiving, quality of life, and personal relationships.

# ☐ The Problem with Suicide Studies

Opponents of rational suicide often point to studies associating nearly all suicides with depression or other emotional conditions (Barry, 1994a; Marzuk, 1994). The problem with such studies, however, is that data are usually derived from official suicide statistics of cases in which there is clear evidence that deaths are self-intentioned or in which suspicions of a suicide are "validated" through psychological autopsies, medical records, and interviews with significant others. Other studies rely on reports of requests for aid-in-dying by patients in institutional settings.

As a result, studies linking the majority of suicides by the terminally ill with depression are unsubstantiated, as they are based on samples that are biased because they fail to take into account secret suicides and assisted suicides that are officially documented as being due to natural causes. In my own study, for example, 125 of 140 assisted suicides were recorded as deaths from natural causes, and in 41 cases the deaths were signed off as such by the physicians who knowingly provided patients the means to die. Only 15 cases were officially documented as being due to suicide, and in more than half of these cases they were listed as such only because participating survivors felt uneasy convincing physicians or authorities that these deaths were from natural causes. If the population of my own study is in any way comparable to those in the general population who engage in assisted suicide, then nearly 90% of assisted suicides among the terminally ill never make their way into suicide statistics. As a result, it is inappropriate to apply concepts like "depression" and "irrationality" derived from one small sample to explain behavior in a larger, clinically unknown population.

In addition, it is likely that the majority of the dying who engage in assisted suicide are rarely seen by mental health professionals. For example, in only 12 of the 140 cases I studied were significant others aware that the deceased had received any form of counseling during the 2 years prior to their deaths. Moreover, in only 4 cases were patients ever considered "at risk" for suicidal behavior, and in all of these instances this "at-risk" designation had resulted from a failed attempt to suicide that was discovered in progress at some earlier time during the dying process. Two of these failures were the result of not so-lethal prescriptions that were provided for this purpose by the patients' physicians.

Finally, studies linking depression to terminally ill patients' talk about suicide and their requests to staff for aid-in-dying are similarly problematic. First, these studies usually depend on staff-generated reports of suicidal ideation in terminally ill patients within institutional settings or requests from patients for aid-in-dying (see, e.g., Foley, 1991). The problem is that staff members may report only cases involving patients who they feel are "at risk" and who exhibit obvious signs of suicidal ideation. That is, these studies imply that all talk is reported and ignore the likelihood that less emotionally laden talk is not reported. Also, these studies do not account for the vast number of requests for assisted suicide that are made daily in the privacy of physician-patient relationships, but which go unreported in any verbal or written manner.

# ☐ Guidelines For Assessing Rationality

The rational nature of suicide cannot necessarily be determined solely by any one factor, such as a person's disease status, prognosis, or level of suffering. Such factors, although critically important, are not enough in themselves to suggest that an intentional act to end one's life is or is not understandable and rational. I believe that we need to look at several factors (see Heilig & Jamison, 1996; S. Jamison, 1995, 1997). The ultimate list might include:

1. The person's physical condition, presence of a terminal or incurable illness, and amount of intolerable, irreversible physiological suffering experienced.
2. The person's understanding and response to his or her condition, diagnosis, and prognosis, including efforts to obtain a confirming medical opinion, and to discuss with his or her physician unresolved symptoms and discomfort, quality of life concerns, and treatment options and alternatives.
3. The person's treatment response to the conditions experienced, including efforts made to explore available treatment options and alternatives.
4. The person's response to any emotional concerns, including efforts to discuss these with both his or her physician and significant others and to explore the possibility of counseling and treatment
5. The person's mental health treatment history, including prior diagnoses for depression and other conditions, response to treatment recommendations, and evidence of suicidal ideation both before and following the terminal diagnosis and onset of intractable suffering
6. The person's expressed motives for assisted suicide, consideration of social factors, quality of life concerns, and future fears that may be influencing the decision, as well as efforts made to explore possible solutions.
7. The person's expressed values and the congruence of her or his motives for assisted suicide with these values.
8. The person's willingness to discuss with significant others preferences and motives for suicide and to provide others opportunities for communicating their concerns and for discussing and reconciling personal issues.
9. The person's plans for suicide and efforts made to respect emotional needs of significant others and to minimize the possible negative effects on others through selection of the means to die, provision of warnings, absence of efforts to coerce unwanted involvement of others in the death, and attempts to prevent accidental discovery by those who might be adversely affected

## ☐ Conclusion

Given cultural, social, and attitudinal changes toward assisted suicide, the involvement of others in the suicide decision process, and possible bias in research samples, I would argue that there is much to support the idea of rational suicide in many cases of terminal illness. This does not mean, however, that all or even most suicides within this population are rational. Possibilities of depression and other emotional conditions exist, as do social factors that might influence perceptions of quality of life and intolerable suffering. Much more research is needed in this area. Although I oppose the hard-line traditional view that all suicide is irrational, we cannot simply argue away or ignore the possibility of irrationality in specific cases. As a result, I believe that clinical exploration by therapists of a range of these topical categories can be useful in assessing if a client's decision to die might well be a rational act.

# 19
## CHAPTER

Antoon A. Leenaars

# Rational Suicide: A Psychological Perspective

The concept of the right to die is one of the most controversial and elusive issues facing suicidology around the world today. The concept is complex, with many sub-controversies. The single question raised here and in this whole book is: "Is suicide rational?" (Or alternatively stated, "Can suicide ever be rational?") Polls and research (American Association of Suicidology, 1996; Domino & Leenaars, 1995; Special Senate Committee on Euthanasia and Assisted Suicide, 1995) have indicated growing support for the right to die in the United States, Canada, and elsewhere. A persistent question that has been raised, however, is whether people have a sufficient understanding of what they are considering. This observation is even broader because people lack in their understanding of suicide itself.

People are perplexed, bewildered, confused, and even overwhelmed when they are confronted with suicide, including the suicide of a terminally ill person. People do not understand suicide very well. The purpose of this chapter is to define suicide and to address only the question about rational suicide. The *Oxford English Dictionary*, the arbiter of the English language, defines *rational* as "of or based on reasoning or reason." Reason is "the intellectual faculty by which conclusions are drawn from premises." This is the working definition in this chapter. The chapter attempts to provide a psychological perspective on the question. These thoughts are not meant to be exhaustive nor encompassing. They are presented only to raise some questions and to offer a few directions about this one aspect of the right to die debate.

One meaningful pathway to the question is history. From my view (Leenaars & Diekstra, 1995), any understanding in suicidology should be ultimately based on past discussions on the questions. I do this by highlighting three events: a debate about rational suicide between David Lester and myself (Lester & Leenaars, 1996); a debate about intervention between Edwin Shneidman and Thomas Szasz (1972); and reflection on the death of Sigmund Freud. I do not mean to suggest that these are the only historical events relevant to the debate, rather they are the ones that are familiar to me.

# ☐  Is Rational Suicide Rational?

In 1993, David Lester and I debated on the topic of "The Ethics of Suicide and Suicide Prevention." The debate was a keynote address at the conference of the Association of Death Education and Counseling in Memphis, Tennessee. One issue discussed was, "Is suicide rational?"

Lester, a well-respected and prolific researcher, argued that there are two ways to address the issue (Beauchamp & Childress, 1979). One uses absolutes such as "thou shall not kill." The other uses autonomy. Simply stated, autonomous individuals have a right to behave in any noncriminal way they choose. The first leads to positions of opposition, whereas the autonomy view is utilitarian. Lester argued for the utilitarian position, implying that the other is wrong. The conclusion simply follows that suicide is rational. The individual has a right to kill himself or herself.

Next, Lester stated that there are two separate questions in the quest to determine whether suicide is rational? First, "Is the reasoning of a suicidal person logical?" Lester argued that granted the premises of the suicidal person, the reasoning in most cases is logical. There is no logical error; thus, suicide is rational. The second question concerns the rationality of the premises. Although a therapist may label some premises as irrational (Ellis, 1973; Lester, 1993), the therapist's beliefs are equally unproven. The patient, however, is considered irrational until proven rational. Why is the therapist correct? Lester concluded, thus, that the majority of suicidal people do reason logically. Suicide is rational.

My response argued that the a priori question is "why do people kill themselves?" or more accurately "why did that individual commit suicide?" People are perplexed about this question. The suicidal person who takes his or her own life may, at the moment of decision, be the least aware of the essence of the answer. I argued as follows.

Suicide is a multidimensional malaise (Leenaars, 1996; Shneidman, 1985). I do not agree with those who point to an external stress as the cause of suicide. I also do not agree that the cause is only pain. I tend to place the emphasis on the multideterminant nature of suicide. Suicide is *intrapsychic*. It is not simply the stress or even the pain, but the person's inability to cope with the event or pain. The goal of any scheme about human personality, such as personology (Murray, 1938), is one that makes an individual an individual. The scheme should be the study of the whole organism, not only the stress or pain. People do not simply commit suicide because of pain, but because it is unbearable; they are mentally constricted; they cannot cope; and much more.

In addition, from a psychological view, suicide is not only intrapsychic, it is also *interpersonal*. Individuals are interwoven. We live in a world. I disagree with those who point only to some intrapsychic aspects such as anger turned inward or primitive narcissism. Suicide occurs between people (or relationships to some ideal). Metaphorically speaking, suicide is an intrapsychic drama on an interpersonal stage.

With this metaphor in mind, suicide can be clinically understood from at least the concepts described in the following sections (Leenaars, 1988, 1989a, 1989b, 1996):

## Intrapsychic Concepts

*Unbearable Psychological Pain*    The common stimulus in suicide is unendurable psychological pain (Shneidman, 1985). The enemy of life is pain, a *psychache* (Shneidman,

1985; 1993). Although, as Menninger (1938) noted, other motives (elements, wishes) are evident, the person primarily wants to flee from pain experienced in a bottomless catastrophe. The person may feel any number of emotions, such as feeling boxed in, rejected, deprived, forlorn, distressed, and especially hopeless and helpless. The suicide, as Murray (1967) stated, is functional because it abolishes painful tension for the individual. It provides relief from intolerable suffering.

*Cognitive Constriction*    The common cognitive state in suicide is mental constriction (i.e., rigidity in thinking, narrowing of focus, tunnel vision) (Shneidman, 1985). The person is figuratively "intoxicated" or "drugged" by the constriction, exhibiting at the moment before his or her death only permutations and combinations of a trauma (e.g., business failure, political scandal, poor health, rejection by a spouse). In the face of the painful trauma, a possible solution becomes *the* solution. Is one then rational?

*Indirect Expressions*    Complications, ambivalence, redirected aggression, unconscious implications, and related indirect expressions (or phenomena) are often evident in suicide. The suicidal person at the moment of the death is ambivalent. The person experiences humility, submission, devotion, subordination, flagellation, and sometimes even masochism. Yet, there is much more. What the person is conscious of is only a fragment of the suicidal mind (Freud, 1917/1974). There are more reasons to the act than the suicidal person is consciously—rationally—aware of when making the final decision (Freud, 1917/1974; Leenaars, 1988).

*Inability to Adjust*    People with all types of problems, pain, losses, and so forth are at risk for suicide. Depressive disorders, manic-depressive disorders, anxiety disorders, schizophrenic disorders, panic disorders, borderline disorders, and psychopathic disorders have been related to some suicides (Sullivan, 1962, 1964; Leenaars, 1988). Depression may well be the most frequent disorder; however, suicidal people more frequently experience unbearable pain, not depression. Indeed, suicidal people see themselves as unable to adjust. Their states of mind are incompatible with accurate discernment of what is going on—and that is not rational. Considering themselves too weak to overcome difficulties, they do not survive life's difficulties.

*Ego*    The ego with its enormous complexity (Murray, 1938) is an essential factor in the suicidal scenario. The *Oxford English Dictionary* defines *ego* as "the part of the mind that reacts to reality and has a sense of individuality." Ego strength is a protective factor against suicide. Suicidal people, however, frequently exhibit a relative weakness in their capacity to develop constructive tendencies and to overcome their personal difficulties (Zilboorg, 1936). The person's ego has likely been weakened by a steady toll of traumatic life events. This implies that a history of traumatic disruptions—*pain*—placed the person at risk for suicide. A weakened ego correlates positively with suicide risk.

## Interpersonal Concepts

*Interpersonal Relations*    The suicidal person has problems in establishing or maintaining relationships (object relations). There frequently is a disturbed, unbearable interpersonal situation. A calamity prevails. Suicide appears to be related to an unsatisfied or thwarted attachment need, although other needs, often more intrapsychic, may be equally evident (e.g., control, achievement, autonomy, honor). Suicide is committed because of frustrated or unfulfilled needs, needs that are often frustrated interpersonally.

*Rejection—Aggression*    The rejection–aggression hypothesis was first documented by Stekel in the famous 1910 meeting of the Psychoanalytic Society in Freud's home in Vienna (Friedman, 1910/1967). Loss is central to suicide; it is, in fact, often a rejection that is experienced as an abandonment. It is an unbearable narcissistic injury. This injury is part of a traumatic event that leads to pain and, in some, to self-directed aggression (Shneidman and Farberow, 1957). The person is deeply ambivalent and, within the context of this ambivalence, suicide may become the turning back upon oneself of murderous impulses (wishes, needs)—it may be murder in the 180th degree (Shneidman, 1985).

*Identification—Egression*    Freud (1917/1974, 1920/1974, 1921/1974) hypothesized that intense identification with a lost or rejecting person or, as Zilboorg (1936) showed, with any lost ideal (e.g., health, youth, employment, freedom), is crucial in understanding the suicidal person. Identification is defined as an attachment (bond), based upon an important emotional tie with another person (object) (Freud, 1920/1974) or any ideal. If this emotional need is not met, the suicidal person experiences a deep pain (discomfort) and wants to egress, that is, to exit, to get away—to be dead.

## Endnote

In concluding, although the above observations are only one point of view, these elements common to suicide, I believe, have utility in understanding suicide. They at least highlight that suicide is not only due to external stress, pain, or even reasoning. The issues of absolutes or autonomy are philosophical, although they have a place in understanding human behavior (see Battin, 1994). Whether premises are rational or not misses the point. To provide only philosophical speculations on the topic without considering the psychological reality of the malaise is wrong. The question should be, "What is suicide?" and understanding suicide leads us to conclude that suicide is not rational. It is simply not a rational choice. The common consistency in suicide is, in fact, with lifelong adjustment patterns (Shneidman, 1985), not a logical choice about loss, health, employment, or whatever. Suicidal people have experienced a steady toll of painful life events that have undermined their ability to reason.

In the debate with Lester, I concluded by asking, "Are these suicidal people rational?" At the moment of taking his or her life the suicidal person is figuratively intoxicated with unbearable pain, overpowering emotions, and constricted logic. The pain is unbearable. There has been loss. Is anyone at such moment capable of making an informed or "rational" choice?

Indeed, when is any human behavior simply rational? The issue of rational suicide should be eliminated from the debate about the right to die. "Rational" is a construction. No mind is simply rational. These are constructions of Kant, Hegel, and others. Indeed, there are always elements of emotion, conflict, pain, and more in one's mind. Whether behavior is just rational or not is a misdirection. These were the discussions in my philosophy classes, not in my psychology office. The suicidal mind is not rational. The debate of rational versus not rational is misleading. The sooner we leave behind that question, the sooner we can address the real issues in the right to die debate.

# ☐ Is Intervention Moral?

A related and embedded question in the debate about "Is suicide rational?," "Is suicide intervention moral?" In my debate with Lester in Memphis, he argued that intervention is not moral if the person wishes to die; rather, it is controlling and paternalistic. The right to refuse intervention is implied by those that who espouse that suicide is rational. If suicide is rational, no one should intervene. Let us again address the question from a vantage point of history. In 1972, Edwin Shneidman met Thomas Szasz in a debate. The issue that they discussed was, "Is suicide intervention moral?" The debate on the ethics of suicide prevention was held in San Francisco at the University of California.

Shneidman, the father of suicide prevention in North America, argued eloquently in favor of suicide prevention. Szasz (1976, 1986) is well known for his unorthodox beliefs: mental illness is a myth and suicide is a civil right.

Shneidman argued that intervention is needed. He insisted that the therapist-patient relationship should include a sense of responsibility for a life at risk; and that suicide ideation and attempts are expressions of pain, unbearable mental pain, and thus treatable. Shneidman made the now obvious point that, if a patient talks about suicide, it suggests that he or she is ambivalent. He or she may feel hopeless, yet he or she is ambivalent, ambivalent about life and death. A suicidal person who is ambivalent can often be dissuaded. A change, an altered plan, a reduction in the level of perturbation, or so forth is often sufficient to reduce the pain. It should be the psychotherapist's duty to help a person recognize this fact, and guide him or her on the side of life. Szasz, on the other hand, argued that suicide should not primarily be seen from the point of view of pain, ambivalence, and so forth; rather, it should be seen as a civil right. Suicide is in accordance with the principles of civil law. He went on to note that the therapist–patient relationship ought to be a contract between equals. Unless it is explicit in the contract that the therapist will intervene on behalf of the patient, the therapist is not obligated to act and indeed should not do so. For Shneidman, it is the healer's duty to intervene; Szasz considers any treatment that is not specifically contracted for to be unethical. For Shneidman, if a person is suicidal, he or she is simply not in his or her best state of mind. It is the healer's duty to discuss alternatives. For Szasz, uncontracted intervention is a violation of a civil right. Although Shneidman's view has the potential for meddling, the "error" is on the side of life. It is on the side of preventing an unnecessary death. The consequences of Szasz's noninterference, if fatal, are irreversible (Shneidman & Szasz, 1972; West, 1993). In *The New England Journal of Medicine*, Shneidman (1992) summarized his views as follows:

> In human beings pain is ubiquitous, but suffering is optional, within the constraints of a person's personality.... Physicians and other health professionals need the courage and wisdom to work on a person's suffering at a phenomenological level and to explore such questions as "How do you hurt" and "How may I help you." They should then do whatever

is necessary, using a wide variety of legitimate tactics . . . to reduce that person's self-destructive impulses. (p. 890)

My position is akin to Shneidman's: the suicidal mind is often treatable (Leenaars, Maltsberger, & Neimeyer, 1994). We have a right to intervene and that is not controlling nor paternalistic.

Lester, Szasz, and others argue about the right to die (e.g., rational suicide) from a pure theoretical–ethical stance, going as far as to state that, even if one does not believe in the view personally, the issues should be seen only from a logical view. Practical consideration is seen in this view as irrelevant. Kevorkian (1988) goes even further, stating that we should go ahead assisting suicide without discussion of the issues. No debate is necessary. He states that "all of these [issues] have been well debated in the past, and there is nothing new to learn" (p. 2). I disagree with Lester, Szasz, and Kevorkian. We need to talk about these real-life issues. The discussion will have to be ongoing, not an end statement. The "practical" is people. The practical is the issue. We should begin with the practical—the lives of people.

Ethicists and all suicidologists need to be accountable. These are not merely theoretical, ethical, suicidological issues. No person kills himself or herself because of a theoretical argument. They do not kill themselves because of premises. They do not kill themselves because it is their civil right. They kill themselves because of pain, mental constriction, and so forth. This is the suicidal mind. These are not only philosophical issues. We have to, in fact, be responsible for our statements (and in Kevorkian's case, his actions)—to our suicidal people.

## ☐  What Is A Suicide?

For those familiar with the right to die debate, the case of Sigmund Freud is well known (see Leenaars, 1993; Litman, 1967). Freud is a dramatic example in the issues at hand because his work in psychology is so influential. Freud's death has been called a suicide. Yet was his death really a suicide? That should, in fact, be the first question in the debate: "What is a suicide?" The question is not, "Is suicide rational?" but, "What is a suicide and what is not?" Freud killed himself. Was it, as he stated, because of his terminal illness? Or was it because he had been severely depressed at the time? He had been overwhelmed by World War II and had notable problems in his adjustment to moving to England. Freud left Vienna in 1938, when Hitler took over Austria. Those years were onerous for him not only because of the war, but because, since 1923, he had suffered from cancer of the mouth and jaw. The cancer had progressed to a degenerative stage; indeed, the smell was so bad that even his faithful dog refused to be in the same room with him. The pain was unbearable for him. In an aside, in "Moses and Monotheism" (1939 / 1974, p. 132), Freud himself says "[D]o not call me a pessimist." He died by his own wish on September 26, 1939, at the age of 83 years. Was Freud's suicide due only to his terminal illness? Does Freud's suicide, and by implication those of other terminally ill people, differ in essence from other suicides? That should be a key question in the right to die debate.

To add a further thought for consideration about Freud, suicide has a history. It is easy to see that Freud was in unbearable pain, mentally constricted, depressed, forlorn over the loss of his attachment to Vienna, and so forth. Yet there is more. Freud had made a previous suicidal threat. Years before his suicide, he made an overt threat during his engagement to his wife-to-be, Martha Bernays (Leenaars, 1993; Litman, 1967). According to Jones (1957), Freud had decided to kill himself if he lost Martha. In a letter to Martha, Freud wrote, "I have long since resolved on a decision, the thought of which is in no way painful, in the event of losing you. That we should lose each other by parting is quite out of the question. You would have to become a different person, and of myself, I am quite sure. You have no idea how fond I am of you, and hope I shall never have to show it" (Jones, 1957). Freud was quite attached to Martha and, as his history showed, to other ideals (e.g., Vienna, health).

Can Freud's suicide be best accounted for by pain, cognitive constriction, indirect expressions, or identification–egression? Or were there other processes occurring? The question is simply: Is Freud's death best described as a suicide? Or would it be more appropriate to call it "dignified death?" Those questions are the practical. Those questions are much more important than, "Is suicide rational?" and these are not merely semantics. Rational is, as Lester stated, logical thought. However, as we have learned, suicide is not rational. Rational and suicide are paradoxical. "Rational suicide" is an oxymoron. Suicide is never only intellectual. In fact, Freud himself did not see his death as rational but as a means to ease the pain of his cancer.

Ultimately, despite Lester, Szasz, and others, the issue is the practical. We need studies of the deaths of the terminally ill and suicides of those who are not terminally ill; however, to date, there has been little empirical research.

Once we address these questions, then we can address the question of means of death: refusal, withdrawal, euthanasia, assisted suicide. We can examine the role of palliative care. We can examine approaches in the Netherlands and other countries. We can address other questions: for example, is our society willing to provide for the humane needs of the terminally ill, and so forth. However, all this is possible once we stop asking the question, "Is suicide rational?" That is, in fact, to use a common metaphor, a red herring in the debate. Ultimately, the question is, "What is suicide?"

# ☐ Conclusion

There are fundamental questions that people need to address in the debate on the right to die. "Is suicidal rational?" is not one of them. Once we leave behind that question, we can address the issues directly. My position is one of "con" on the question in this book because it is the wrong question. No behavior is simply rational. The suicidal mind is not rational.

# 20
CHAPTER

Jay Callahan

# Rational Suicide: Destructive to the Common Good

Social work is an extremely broad and diverse profession and brings a wide variety of perspectives to the controversy on rational suicide. However, social work also stands for a distinct set of values and principals. I believe two particular social work values are central to a discussion of rational suicide and provide a unique social work perspective: self-determination and individual rights.

Social work, more than any other discipline, has historically emphasized the right of self-determination. The National Association of Social Workers (NASW) *Code of Ethics* (1990), for example, states that "the social worker should make every effort to foster maximum self-determination on the part of clients" (p. 5). The logical extension of self-determination is the perception that suicide, at least in some situations, is rational, and the approval of self-destruction as an exercise of one's right of self-determination. However, I believe that the concept of self-determination has been applied in a simplistic and inappropriate fashion in many instances, and should not always be the highest value.

The second perspective is one of individual rights. Social work has a rich tradition in supporting individuals against economic, social, and political oppression and injustice. This is a valuable and important tradition and should not be disregarded lightly. However, I believe that social work has gone so far in protecting individual rights that the rights of groups, and of society as a whole—the concept of the common good—has been inappropriately and dangerously ignored.

A needed balance may be found by focusing on "individual well–being in a social context" (NASW, 1996). This social work tradition is embodied in the person-in-environment perspective and the ecological approach (Germain, 1994). These perspectives emphasize the need to pay attention to both the individual and the environment. A person can only be understood in a social context. This contextualized view is one perspective that sets social work apart from most other disciplines. However, despite lip service given to the person-in-environment perspective, social work has tended to champion the rights of the individual over the rights of society as a whole, and rational suicide is seen as an individual right. I believe, however, that a balanced view of the individual and society leads us to a different conclusion: that even in the rare cases in which suicide may be "rational," it nonetheless should still not be supported. Such an elevation of rights of the individual over those of society as a whole has significant destructive consequences for the common good.

I attempt in this chapter to demonstrate that most suicides are not rational, and that therefore the right of self-determination should not be extended to these cases. Also, even in the rare cases in which a potential suicide may be rational, I believe that the principle of self-determination, although important, should be secondary to the good of society as a whole.

## ☐ NASW Policy on End-of-Life Decisions

In 1993 the NASW Delegate Assembly passed a policy entitled "Client Self-Determination in End-of-Life Decisions" (NASW, 1994). This policy suggests that social workers should maximize the self-determination of their clients, including supporting and being present at an act of assisted suicide. According to this policy, a social worker should never supply the means for an assisted death but may be present if his or her presence is helpful to the client and is consistent with the values of the social worker. Although assisted suicide is not the same as rational suicide, most advocates of assisted suicide believe that a significant proportion of these suicides are rational.

Rational suicide is not defined in the NASW policy (1994). However, an implicit definition may be derived from the description of "voluntary active euthanasia"—"a physician administering a lethal dose after a clearly competent patient makes a fully voluntary and persistent request for aid-in-dying" (p. 59). With this definition in mind, we may describe rational suicide as a self-inflicted death carried out by a clearly competent person who has made a fully voluntary and persistent decision to die.

### Self-Determination

The authors of the NASW policy appear to believe that its thrust is simply an extension of the traditional social work value of self-determination. However, upon closer examination, the concept of self-determination is complex. Many social workers have attempted to simplistically apply the concept without considering its drawbacks and inconsistencies.

Although a thorough review of the concept of self-determination is beyond the scope of this chapter, a number of social work scholars have written about the inconsistencies, contradictions, and complexity of this issue (see Abramson, 1989; Rothman, 1989). Virtually all of the writers on this topic, including those most supportive of self-determination, allow for exceptions to this general policy. Foremost among these exceptions are situations that involve harm or death, such as suicide (Weick & Pope, 1988).

In addition to denying self-determination in instances of danger, there are also numerous everyday examples in which self-determination is not (and should not be) the overriding principle. Many social workers in mental health and substance abuse settings are quite familiar with clients who have little or no awareness or insight into their mental or behavioral disability. Under these circumstances, the social worker's role is rarely to accept the client's definition of the problem, or to help the client reach his or her stated goals as originally presented. On the contrary, the presenting relationship or occupational problem, for example, is often largely due to a mental disorder or a substance dependence problem. Social workers in substance abuse agencies, in fact, frequently take part in "interventions"—group confrontations of the identified client, the goal of which is to coerce the client into accepting treatment. Social workers in mental health agencies often participate in the involuntary hospitalization of potentially dangerous or suicidal clients. Most social workers have no difficulty with these abridgements of the right of self-determination.

In lesser and more subtle ways, clients who come to social workers for assistance often do not know exactly what their problems are, the source of the problems, or how to go about making things better. The role of a professional is to use his or her learning and training to help a client answer these questions and invariably to influence clients to see their problems in clearer ways. Advocates of self-determination appear to believe that clients already possess clear-cut problem definitions and only need help in identifying and carrying out solutions. This is rarely the case.

## Beneficence

Another social work value, not well known or frequently discussed, is *beneficence*. Beneficence is doing what is in the client's best interest, even if the client disagrees with the social worker's position. It is codified as "[p]rimacy of clients' interests . . . the social worker's primary responsibility is to clients" (NASW, 1990, p. 4). The principle of beneficence suggests that a social worker must use his or her own independent judgment about what is in a client's best interest, and that interest may be in opposition to the client's stated desires. I believe that suicide is perhaps the most compelling example of the need to focus on the principle of beneficence.

Social work scholars are increasingly recognizing this principle. One author highlighted the need for "protective intervention" in mental health practice (Murdach, 1996). The proposed revision of the *NASW Code of Ethics* (NASW, 1996) adds a major qualification to its statement about self-determination. In the proposed new code, it is stated that "social workers promote clients' *socially responsible* self-determination" (p. 20; emphasis added). In addition, the specific section on self-determination states that "social workers may limit clients' rights to self-determination when, in their professional judgement, clients' actions or potential actions pose a serious, foreseeable, and imminent risk to themselves or others" (p. 20). Attention to the limits of and exceptions to self-determination adds to our understanding of this complex matter.

Advocates of rational suicide base many of their arguments on the alleged right of a competent, rational person to make decisions for himself or herself. I contend, however, that there are a significant number of instances in which self-determination should not be the primary value. In many instances, beneficence should be our guiding, primary principle. Sometimes a person's stated goal is not in his or her best interest.

## Competence

Rational suicide is closely related to the concept of competence. The NASW policy on end-of-life decisions specifically states that "competent individuals should have the opportunity to make their own choices" (NASW, 1994, p. 60). Competence is defined as "the ability to understand the nature and consequences of a proposed course of action" (Robertson, 1985, p. 562). This seemingly simple definition is elusive in practice, however. In most medical settings, in which competence is far more often an issue than in other settings in which social workers practice, the "test" for competence is simply whether the individual appears to understand, and can repeat back, a simple explanation of the probable outcomes of several proposed treatments. Individuals suffering from dementia, for example, are frequently unable to comprehend the nature and consequences of a proposed course of action and are therefore judged to be incompetent.

But in other cases, such as depression, the individual's cognitive abilities are not obviously affected. It is well known that depression significantly affects an individual's sense of hope, ability to make decisions, and perspective on the future. Depression, which may not produce apparent interference with cognition, can alter an individual's viewpoint on life and the future to one of profound pessimism and hopelessness (Blaney, 1986). Recently published first-person accounts of highly capable individuals with mood disorders amply demonstrate the poor judgement that is frequent in such cases (Jamison, 1995; Styron, 1990). In addition, a study of depressed individuals' perceptions of their prior social adjustment demonstrated that they judged themselves much more negatively and critically while depressed than they did after they had recovered (Morgado, Smith, Lecrubier, & Widlocher, 1991). In other words, when depressed, people see themselves and the world in inaccurately negative and pessimistic ways. This altered perspective is much more subtle, and therefore more insidious, than the more obvious global impairment of cognitive abilities that is defined as a loss of competence. Nonetheless, such a loss of judgment and perspective may lead an individual to feel hopeless and deserving of death, even desiring death, although he or she appears competent.

## ☐  Suicide and Mental Illness

There are several other sources of evidence that suggest that suicide is almost always the result of emotional or mental dysfunction, as opposed to a rational decision. Psychological autopsy studies of completed suicides consistently demonstrate that approximately 90% to 95% of the individuals who die by suicide have a mental disorder at the time of the act, with depression being the most common (Clark & Horton-Deutsch, 1992). The number of people who commit suicide absent a mental illness appears to be very small. Furthermore, such studies have also found that a very small number of individuals who complete suicide have a terminal illness. In fact, in one series of elderly suicides, more suicide victims erroneously thought they were terminally ill than actually were (Conwell & Caine, 1991). This research suggests that suicide is strongly influenced by mental illness, as opposed to being the product of a rational process.

Finally, several studies have shown that terminally ill people are rarely suicidal. In one study of 44 individuals, only 3 were suicidal or had ever considered suicide, and only 7 wished for a rapid death but would not consider suicide (Brown, Henteleff, Barakat, & Rowe, 1986). Significantly, all 10 who wished for death were diagnosed with major depression. None of the other 34 nondepressed but terminally ill patients were suicidal or had wishes for a rapid death. In another study of 200 terminally ill individuals, only 17 expressed a serious and persistent desire to die. Furthermore, depression was found in 58.8% of those expressing a desire to die, as opposed to only 7.7% of those without such thoughts (Chochinov et al., 1995). These studies strongly suggest that it is not terminal illness but depression that leads to suicidal thoughts.

This is not news to social workers who work in hospices or in other settings with the terminally ill. They know that very few terminally ill individuals are suicidal; most cling to life as long as possible (Thal, 1992).

## ☐   "No man [or woman] is an island. . . "

Perhaps an even larger reason why social workers should not support legitimization of rational suicide is the fundamental nature of people's relationships to each other, and the vision of society that social workers hope to bring about. As noted previously in this chapter, social workers have historically focused on the person-in-environment and have long had a vision of a more just, humane society.

I believe that a central concept that emphasizes this attention to the environment is that of community. A community is a group of people who, through geographic proximity or other common bonds, have ongoing relationships with each other, a set of reciprocal obligations, and a sense of belonging. In our highly technological and mobile society, most people no longer feel connected. Many popular writers have addressed the contemporary "loss of community" over the past few decades (e.g., Bellah, Madsen, Sullivan, Swidler, & Tipton, 1985; Slater, 1970). A large variety of technological, sociological, and cultural factors have been identified in explaining this significant change in American life, including such far-flung factors as the inventions of television, air conditioning, expressways, and the automobile. A provocative thesis recently has been advanced by Ehrenhalt (1995), who suggests that it is our idealization of individuality and distrust of authority that has so eroded community. It is clear that Americans are alienated and isolated but long for the sense of belonging that "community" provides.

This lack of belonging has been implicated in the increasing rates of depression that have occurred over the past 40 to 50 years in the United States. Throughout this time, each successive generation appears to have had a larger proportion of members who, at some time in their lives, experience at least one episode of major depression. An impressive number of studies with a variety of different methodologies have replicated this finding (Buie, 1988; Lewinsohn, Rhode, Seeley, & Fischer, 1993). There is no biological process that could produce these shifts this rapidly; the increasing rate of depression is almost certainly due to social forces. Primary among these social forces is the decline of supportive structures in our lives, especially daily personal interactions with other members of the same community. One expert has called this change the "decline of the New England self" and the "rise of the California self" (Buie, 1988, p. 18). That is, the citizen who took his or her responsible role in the community has been replaced by the individual whose primary goals are self-actualization and increased personal choice, unfettered by others' opinions or needs. Americans believe most strongly in "individualism," which includes an underemphasis on the role of other people in our lives. The cost of achieving this self-actualization and increased sense of individualism is the loss of attention to the common good and to community.

A sense of connection makes people less vulnerable not only to psychological problems but to physical ones as well. Living in a community entails being immersed in a complex social network, including sources of support. There is a growing literature that details the positive effects social support has on physical as well as mental health, and the negative effect of social isolation (House, Landis, & Umberson, 1988).

Culturally aware social workers have long known that interdependence and the well-being of the group are more highly valued than individualism in many Eastern societies (Morris & Silove, 1992). In such societies, individuals have fewer choices, and the impact on other people is foremost in everyone's minds when decisions are made. This relative loss of emphasis on the individual good is balanced by a focus on the common good, and people find that such interdependence, reciprocal respect, and community have many rewards of their own.

In this light, it becomes apparent that social workers have, like most everyone else in U.S. society, overvalued the individual and undervalued the group and the community. "Rational" suicide is another example of the inappropriate elevation of individual rights over the well-being of the group.

Realizing that the common good is not necessarily the same as the sum of each person's individual good leads to several clear implications. For example, many well-designed studies have demonstrated that suicide is contagious. Therefore, a person does not have a "right" to take his or her own life, because such an action may influence another to do the same. Highly publicized suicide deaths of famous people lead to temporary increases in the completed suicide rate of others (Gould & Shaffer, 1986; Phillips & Carstensen, 1986). Social workers in schools and psychiatric hospitals are quite familiar with the cluster phenomenon, in which one instance of completed suicide can lead to a rash of additional attempts.

If social workers are really to champion the social good, we must reassess our culturally defined overemphasis on individualism and realize that our individual good is inextricably intertwined with the common good. The formal rejection of suicide as a "right," and the recognition of the harm it does to the common good, would be a step toward an increased sense of community. We must learn that "you find your own good in the good of the whole. You find your own individual fulfillment in the success of the community" (Cuomo, quoted in Ward & Burns, 1994, p. 384).

## ☐ Reconsideration of the NASW Policy on End-of-Life Decisions

With these arguments in mind, let us turn back to the NASW (1994) policy "Client Self-Determination in End-of-Life Decisions." Although the authors of this policy apparently thought that they were focusing on the relatively small number of people who may consider assisted suicide, I believe that the outcome of this policy may prove to be very different. This policy presents a very distorted view of what suicidal individuals are like. The vast majority of suicidal clients with whom social workers come into contact are troubled, depressed, or otherwise not rational. Social workers' general approach—the "default" mode—should be to assume that suicidal thinking is a result of depression or other emotional problems. Social workers should not take a neutral stance, as this policy suggests. To do so would be to overlook many opportunities to address significant emotional and psychosocial problems. Correcting these potential oversights will help social workers intervene in numerous nonrational suicides, which are the vast majority.

## 21
CHAPTER

Deborah Cummings

# In Support of Rational Suicide: A Social Work Viewpoint

Let me begin this chapter by saying that I approach this topic from the point of view of a clinician. My thoughts are based on my knowledge of social work values and beliefs, coupled with my experience as a medical social worker, chair of a hospital bioethics committee, member of the Michigan Commission on Death and Dying, and one of the drafters of the National Association of Social Workers (NASW) 1994 policy statement, on "Client Self-Determination in End-of-Life Decisions." I do not pretend to represent the consensus view of social work, because one does not exist. Given the complexity of the issue, consensus is unrealistic. However, I believe I represent the majority view, as evidenced by the adoption of the NASW policy on End-of-Life Decisions.

I accept Werth's (1996b) criteria for rational suicide as described in Chapter 1 of this book. That is, that the individual has a hopeless condition; is making a choice freely with no coercion; and is using a sound decision-making process. I would add that the decision-making process must include being completely informed of his or her diagnosis, prognosis, and treatment alternatives, and being given access to all appropriate supports and resources. In addition, the individual must be an adult with the ability to make competent decisions.

Having accepted these criteria, I want to emphasize that this discussion deals with persons with hopeless conditions. Hopeless conditions include terminal conditions, situations of chronic, intractable pain; and debilitating or deteriorating conditions of a very severe nature. This chapter does not deal with persons who are considering suicide as a result of a sudden loss or the knowledge of a new diagnosis, or those who are incapable of making a competent decision because of physical or mental illness. It is important to differentiate between these two very distinct situations, and to differentiate the appropriate social work response to each. In the latter situations, and in the vast number of suicides, the appropriate social work response is to take all necessary action to prevent a suicide. This statement was included in the original draft of NASW's 1994 policy statement but was removed later. I believe it is practiced by social workers universally, although it is not included in the policy statement.

The NASW policy statement (1994) in summary defines the social work role as helping people identify end-of-life options, explore thoughts and feelings, and consider various alternatives. Those alternatives include everything from pain management, hospice, and accepting all treatment to refusing treatment, and even assisted suicide. The policy states that social workers are not to act outside the law, nor to personally participate in a suicide in their professional role.

Before presenting the pro–rational suicide position from a social worker's perspective, allow me to describe a personal event from my life that impacted my view of rational suicide. My goal is not to shed light on my personal background but to present a personal situation, one with which I think the reader might be able to identify. In order to do that, I must tell the reader about my mother.

Diane Cummings came from strong German stock. She had lived through the Depression, through very difficult times, and lost her father at an early age. She watched her mother struggle to support and feed nine children during a time when there were no Social Security benefits and no welfare programs. My mother told a story of how they had so little food that she was forced to dig up a potato and eat it dirty and raw out in a field. She said she was thankful to have it. This, I might add, she did not share as one of those "oh, the terrible times I've seen" stories; it was an explanation for her lifelong love of the humble potato.

My mother had six children, two of whom died—one as a young adult, one as a child. My father died of an aneurysm shortly after he retired. As the reader may have gathered, my mother was a person of strength and determination. As is true of so many of her peers of similar background and experience, she had the ability to analyze a situation, to consider options, and to make a decision, no matter how hard that decision might be. Implicit in this was the recognition that life is not always easy or fair.

My mother had a series of health problems including breast cancer, heart attack, bypass surgery, and finally cancer resulting in an ileostomy. An ileostomy is a surgical procedure, similar to a colostomy, that results in the contents of the small intestine being directed outside of the body through an opening in the abdomen. After undergoing an ileostomy, the individual must wear a plastic pouch outside of the body to collect the semiliquid wastes. Difficulties related to this include the routine emptying and changing of the pouch or bag, and ensuring that the bags are properly attached to the body to prevent leakage, odors, and so forth.

I should mention here that my mother was a very private person, and the details of physical functioning were not a topic of conversation at our home. The shock of the cancer diagnosis and the humiliation, to her, and inconvenience of the ileostomy were real burdens. These events in and of themselves were not the proverbial "straw." It was the specter of a lengthy, painful death—a death over which she had little control—that frightened her most of all.

Following her surgery, and learning the news of her widespread and terminal cancer, my mother returned to her home. Upon arriving home she said to me, "I think I had better store up enough pills so that I can take care of things if it gets too bad." I knew exactly what she meant. She had told me earlier in life that she hoped someone would help her die if she were ever incurably ill or in great pain. Later that night I could hear her in her room counting pills into a bottle. My first reaction was to stop her and to take the pills away from her. I could not. Her actions were based on a clear understanding of her diagnosis and prognosis. She was well aware of and had access to all appropriate supports and resources. Her actions were consistent with previously expressed wishes and with how she had led her life. I realized that I did not have the right to interfere in her actions, no matter what my personal feelings were. I believe this situation matches the criteria for rational suicide previously described.

As a footnote to this, my mother never used the pills, never took her life. She lived only a few months after her surgery. She died at home, fortunately virtually pain-free and surrounded by her family. I am convinced that the fact that another option was available to her was of great comfort. I am certain it gave her a sense of control and peace. She had a safety net she could access. One of the reasons I support rational suicide is because I believe that it is important for people to have choices and control. The freedom to choose is liberating in and of itself.

Turning from the personal to the professional, let us examine some of the basic values and beliefs of the social work profession. In 1972, Hollis wrote that "casework has constantly stressed the value of the individual, . . . and has constantly emphasized the right of each man [and woman] to live in his [or her] own unique way, provided he [or she] does not infringe unduly upon the rights of others" (p. 14). Hollis went on to say that two primary characteristics of social workers' attitudes toward their clients are "acceptance and respect of the client's right to make their own decisions" (p. 14). The NASW Code of Ethics (NASW, 1993) states that social workers "should make every effort to foster maximum self-determination on the part of clients" (p. 6). In ethical–philosophical terms, this equates to the principle of autonomy.

A fundamental question related to self-determination, autonomy, and our topic is whether limits exist on self-determination. The answer is yes. Ethics, medicine, and social work all support this view. Self-determination is not an absolute right. Individuals cannot demand things that are illegal or that cause undue harm to others. I cannot, for example, demand that I be given a heart transplant from a healthy, functioning individual. I cannot be permitted to abuse my children or to shoot at my neighbor, even if I think that is what they deserve. The principle of client self-determination must be evaluated within the contexts of law, reason, ethics, and morality. Sometimes these decisions are very clear, and sometimes they are very murky.

Client self-determination must be balanced by other social work values. The NASW Code of Ethics (1993) states that social workers' ethical responsibility is to their client and the client's best interest. This equates to medicine's "do good, do no harm" philosophy. The dilemma this can present lies in defining what exactly is in the best interest of another individual. Social work has traditionally shunned paternalistic and maternalistic approaches that assume someone else can know what is best for another individual. At the same time, the social worker cannot be a passive player or simply "rubber stamp" decisions made by clients. Social workers recognize that at times people need more information, support, or help in analyzing a situation in order to make their own choices. Clients seeking help and guidance are relying on the social worker's expertise, training, and professionalism to help them sort through problems. The social work process is highly collaborative and is sometimes referred to as "loaning your ego" or judgment to another person. The process is also systematic and consists of a series of logical steps: data collection, problem identification, development of a plan, implementation of the plan, and evaluation of the effectiveness of the plan.

Self-determination tells us that people have the right to choose, within appropriate limits, how they live or die. Acting in the client's best interests tells us we need to help clients evaluate needs and options and develop a course of action that best meets their needs.

Applying the social work process to the client who states that he or she wishes to commit suicide, the social worker would first work to confirm the client's real diagnosis, prognosis, and treatment options with appropriate experts. The social worker would then ensure that the client's understanding of his or her diagnosis, prognosis, and treatment options is accurate and complete. A social, psychological, and medical history would be taken. Prior coping patterns, current stressors, and the existence of support systems would all need to be reviewed and evaluated. The social worker would identify all appropriate resources and supports available to the client that might impact his or her desire for rational suicide. Obstacles and barriers to accessing those resources and supports would be addressed. The patient's ability to make an informed decision would need to be evaluated using other professionals as necessary.

The social worker's view of clients and their problems is often different from that of other helping professions. The social worker specifically evaluates the person in the context of her or his entire environment. The person is seen as part of a system, not as an isolated being. The interaction and interconnection between the person and his or her familial, social, economic, and work environment is highly regarded and important to social work. The involvement of the client's social system in the consideration of a rational suicide must be included in any assessment. In the NASW policy (1994), the social worker is directed to "encourage the involvement of significant others in decisions" (p. 60), because end-of-life decisions have familial and social consequences. Social workers also are advised to provide grief work, the process of helping someone deal with their grief, in the event a suicide does occur.

In my own experience on the Michigan Commission On Death and Dying, I had an opportunity to listen to testimony provided by the families of clients helped to die by Dr. Jack Kevorkian. In most of the cases, the family was closely involved in the decision to die, and the planning of the death. It was my observation that these families were extraordinarily supportive of Dr. Kevorkian and appeared to be settled and comfortable with the choices their relatives had made. My assumption is that this supportive reaction is related to Dr. Kevorkian involving the family in the decision regarding the death. This stands in stark contrast to the reaction of most families when a suicide occurs. That reaction typically includes shock, anger, and guilt. Often these feelings are never resolved. The importance of involving families and significant others in a death cannot be overemphasized.

At the same time, the involvement of families should not outweigh the client's rights to privacy and confidentiality, two rights that are identified in the NASW *Code of Ethics* (1993). If a client refuses family notification or family involvement, the social worker needs to accept that decision. However, it would be most difficult to not involve family in a suicide situation, knowing the connections among the person, the environment, and the familial and social systems.

The issue of patient competency as it relates to depression merits comment. My counterpart in this book, Jay Callahan, argued (1994) that persons suffering from advanced disease are often depressed, and their judgement about life-and-death decisions becomes clouded. Clearly a person facing a terminal illness with intractable pain or with great debilitation ought to be depressed. That depression may fall into the category of simply feeling sad or may extend to a depression meeting the *Diagnostic and Statistical Manual, (4th edition)* (American Psychiatric Association, 1994), criteria. I would argue that a lack of depressive symptoms under these circumstances is actually more a matter of concern than the opposite. Depression is the normal response to such situations. Does depression equate to incompetency? I do not think so. Does depression cloud a person's ability to reason and think clearly? Perhaps, although

Lee and Ganzini (1992) studied the effects of depression on elderly patients as it related to their choices regarding lifesaving treatment and found no differences among patients with a poor prognosis—whether depressed or not.

Intrinsic to a thorough social work assessment is the evaluation of the existence of depression, and to what extent the depression may impair judgement. The appropriate action would be to treat the depression and evaluate changes in behavior, mood, or thought processes. If the depression lifts, the client may not wish to consider rational suicide. If the depression does not resolve, or if it resolves and the client continues to request rational suicide, then a judgement needs to be made in terms of the client's right to self-determination and the social worker's obligation to work in the client's best interest. I would suggest that there may be times in which suicide is a rational and appropriate decision.

Callahan (1994) also wrote that assisted suicide is unethical. In his view rational suicide may exist, but it is so rare that a national social policy cannot be justified. The dangers described in the article are those of increasing suicide rates because contagion, and also because of the destigmatization of suicide. *Contagion* refers to the concept of other persons being moved to consider suicide as a result of the example set by the suicide victim. I am not sure that rational suicide is all that rare. *Final Exit* (Humphry, 1991a) was a best seller for many months. A 1992 Harvard survey ("Clinicians and public on care issues," 1994) and all other polls of which I am aware indicate that the majority of people approve of assisted suicide in certain circumstances. Ignoring criticisms of polling techniques, it appears that a great number of people feel that rational suicide is something they understand, support, and might consider for themselves at some point.

One of the arguments frequently offered in opposition to rational suicide relates to pain control. The argument is that pain-management techniques are now so sophisticated and effective that no one need consider ending their life because of unbearable pain. There are two problems with this line of thinking. Pain management technology is vastly improved and quite effective, but not in 100% of cases. Coyle, Adelhardt, Foley, and Portenoy (1990), Hanks (1992), and Sasser (1993) all reported that in 75% to 90% of cases, pain can be successfully managed. I have heard hospice physicians estimate figures as low as 2% to 4% of cases in which pain is very difficult to control. Quill (1993) stated in *Death and Dignity: Making Choices and Taking Charge* that cases of suffering despite heroic efforts by physicians are "not common, but they are certainly not rare" (p. 212). Clearly, to some extent, pain still exists.

The second problem with pain control is that, even armed with effective tools, the medical community does a very poor job of treating pain. In a large survey in Sweden (Rawal, Hylander, & Arner, 1993), some 50% of physicians and nurses admitted they had inadequate knowledge of pain management. A major study published in the *Journal of the American Medical Association* (SUPPORT Principal Investigators, 1995) indicated that 50% of conscious patients who died in a hospital had reported having moderate to severe pain at least half the time in the last days of life. Obviously, a great deal of education is needed to better manage pain.

Those who focus on rational suicide as it relates only to pain are ignoring a major reason individuals consider rational suicide. For many people, the primary concern is not pain, it is the frustration and humiliation of living in a body that does not work. It is the idea of dying in an intensive-care unit with multiple machines and tubes attached to their bodies. It is the potential for confusion, decreasing mobility, and dependency. It is the possibility of having absolutely no control over oneself. There are certainly many resources available for people today, but what if these supports are not enough? What if the quality of life that exists is simply not acceptable for some people? Social work values and ethics support the individual's right to his or her own point of view, and to choices stemming from this perspective.

Another issue raised by Callahan (1994) and many others is the idea that when one condones certain behaviors or practices that may, on the surface, appear acceptable, other behaviors or practices that are more radical and dangerous become more acceptable. This concept is called the slippery slope. This concern is very legitimate. The thought of mass suicide, or of elderly, sick, or disabled persons being encouraged to end their lives early is very frightening indeed.

The flaw in this argument is that it implies that society has no ability to set limits. It suggests, for example, that discussion inevitably leads to disagreement, which inevitably leads to argument, which inevitably leads to fighting, which inevitably leads to assault. The conclusion is that we should not condone the first step of a process, lest we begin the unavoidable march to the final extreme step.

I would argue that we have multiple examples of placing limits, of setting stops along the slippery slope. For instance, we condone disciplining children, but we punish those who go beyond discipline to abuse. As a society we accept the right to defend one's self and one's family, but we do not accept unprovoked violence.

# ☐  Conclusion

The magnificence of human beings is their ability to reason, to apply concepts, and to recognize the difference between what is acceptable and what is not. I admit that this ability is not at all perfect, and that there are those who go beyond the limit of what is generally agreed upon. This is a serious concern and requires that society establish protections and guidelines to avoid abuse. We must act carefully and define exactly what we believe to be appropriate and acceptable and what we find to be inappropriate and unacceptable. We must also define consequences for those who do not act within the guidelines.

Callahan (1994) stated that society should make killing one's self as difficult to carry out as possible. I would rephrase this. Social workers and society should do everything we can to make sure that rational suicide is not the best choice for anyone. We should accomplish this by making pain management available and state-of-the-art. Resources should be accessible and affordable. Supports should meet peoples' needs. Advance directives should provide control over healthcare choices. However, there are those who, due to a terminal condition or the ravages of a chronic disabling condition, would choose to end their lives earlier, rather than waiting for the natural course of events. Rational suicide should be an acceptable option for persons who are fully informed; aware of all options, resources, and supports; and competent to make a rational choice.

And, if a woman of strength and determination who is fully informed, competent, supported, and loved wants to be sure she has "enough pills to take care of things if it gets too bad," then she should have them. Rational suicide should be available, accessible, legal, and without societal editorialization or censure.

## 22
### CHAPTER

David K. Meagher

# The Presentation of Rational Suicide in Death Education: A Proponent's Position

A lesser-known Roman scribe, Gaius Rufus Musonius, wrote that a person's body was only lent to him or her by nature. As such, when the body began to fail, Musonius, in what may have very well been the first example of an advanced directive, stipulated, "I will not therefore delay longer but will cheerfully depart as from a banquet" (Enright, 1983, p. 88). Suicide as a choice, especially in those instances of terminal illness or irreversible loss of an acceptable quality of life, is not unprecedented in history. The right to die by one's own hand is not unique to contemporary society nor is it solely the consequence of a society that worships at the altar of modern medicine and its doctrine of the technological imperative. Admittedly the issue has gained greater public attention with Dr. Jack Kervorkian and his now-famous (although some would describe it as infamous) suicide machine, as well as the various advanced directive options that are included in the package of "patient's rights" along with the assisted suicide propositions that the citizens of the state of Oregon approved. However, it is a dilemma that has perplexed humans for a very long time.

## ☐ Suicide

Before offering a position advocating the inclusion of a positive or favorable attitude toward rational suicide within death education, it is necessary to examine some of the problems inherent in a lack of a clear, concise, and universally agreed upon definition of the word *suicide*. Beauchamp (1978) sees this problem as preceding any debate about the rationality of suicide.

Definitions of the word *suicide* include not only a description of an act but also include an attitude about its moral acceptance. Suicide is defined as: intentionally killing oneself (act), and the destruction or ruin of one's own interests (attitude).

**154**

Nonetheless, this classical definition, an intentional act of taking one's own life in opposition to one's best interest, does not satisfactorily describe the event of suicide nor the real motivation of the person performing the act (Corr, Nabe, & Corr, 1994). There must be a greater understanding of the motivating factors and precipitating events that influence the person to choose to end his or her life. Beauchamp (1978) suggests that for an act to be considered suicide it must include an intention of death by the person with the death being caused by that person and the action being completely self-regarding and without coercion. If the act contains both multiple causation (a terminal illness and an act of self-caused death) and multiple intent (a self-regarding act as well as an attempt to protect others), the distinction between suicide and nonsuicide becomes extremely cloudy.

Shneidman (1980a), in an attempt to create objective criteria that would clearly delineate an act as suicide, offers four ingredients (three components and a triggering process) necessary for an act to be so categorized. A potentially suicidal person is seen as one who is living an unsettled life that includes a pattern of doing things that are not in her or his best interest (inimicality). The unsettled lifestyle may result in the person experiencing increased psychological disturbance (perturbation). In attempting to cope, the person engages in a very narrow cognitive process called "tunnel vision" that reduces the options and resources one will utilize (constriction). In an attempt to resolve the disturbance and to reduce or eliminate the pain, decision choices may be constricted to the point that the act of ending one's life (cessation) may be the only viable option perceived by the person. Rather than simplifying the issue, Shneidman seems to have arrived at a position in which the classification of an act as suicide is at best an ambiguous conclusion. Employing these factors in an attempt to diagram an act of self-inflicted death so as to ascertain a conclusion of suicide certainly demonstrates the complexity of a definition and the reservations one should have about the validity of judgment.

To categorize all deaths in which the deceased initiated the act of bringing an end to his or her life as suicide is not valid. To infer that all persons who die by their own hands did so for exactly the same reason is to fail to understand human motivation and behavior. To equate a teenager's self-inflicted death after a conflict with his her parents, as suggested in the lyrics of the rock song "Try a Little Suicide," with one initiated by a terminally ill person experiencing intractable pain and suffering results in a continuation of society's ignorance about death and the process of dying. The former may be considered an irrational act, the latter appears to be the result of a rational, objective decision.

Should suicide classifications include *rational suicide* as a category? Ingram and Ellis (1992) report that several organizations offering suicide prevention and intervention services do separate suicide into two categories:

1. Emotional suicide or irrational self-murder—a type of suicide that should be prevented whenever possible
2. Justifiable suicide or rational and planned self-deliverance

Some writers (e.g., Ingram & Ellis, 1992; Maltsberger, 1994; Tomme, 1981) have suggested that the term *autoeuthanasia* be substituted for justifiable or rational and planned self-deliverance, as a way of clarifying and further distancing the act of rational suicide from the social rejection of suicide in general.

## ☐ Rational Suicide

What is rational suicide? It is a logical and reasonable decision to end one's life when the alternative, to continue living, is totally unacceptable to the individual. It is autoeuthanasia, a self-initiated act of bringing on a "good death." To better understand the definition, an analytic examination of the belief that rational suicide is an oxymoron is necessary.

*Rational* is defined as the possession of an ability to reason; to be of sound mind; and to engage in logical thought processes. To be considered a rational person implies that the actor employed good judgment criteria in arriving at some decision to act. The issue with regard to determining if an act is rational should be the process employed, not the decision nor its acceptance by others. If a sane person approaches a problem in a logical fashion, utilizing good judgment in arriving at a problem-solving decision, the act must be considered a rational one, even if the decision would be unacceptable to most other people.

Can suicide ever be considered a rational choice? There is sufficient evidence to allow an affirmative response to the question. Heifetz (1975) suggests that there are only two basic groups of people who attempt to commit or do commit suicide. The first group, comprising of those suffering some emotional disorder, does not possess a necessary detached, rational view of life; thus a decision to commit suicide is an excessive or exaggerated reaction to their stresses. In comparison, the individuals in the second group, individuals who are severely ill, or near death or whose whole being is dominated with intractable pain, possess excellent insight and can dispassionately arrive at a rational judgment. Is it rational for a person with a painful terminal illness to commit suicide? For Brandt (1975), an affirmative answer is so obvious that there is not any need to debate the point.

Rational suicide is a deed (intentionally killing oneself) in which the decision to act is a choice made under conditions of optimal use of information, when all of the person's desires are taken into account (Brandt, 1975). Brandt posits that it is a question not just of what a person may prefer now but also of his or her future preferences. If tomorrow is guaranteed to bring even greater pain and suffering, greater loss of quality of life without the availability of any realistic alternatives, the decision to commit suicide would be a rational one.

Corr, Nabe, and Corr (1994) seem to be in agreement with the positions of both Heifetz (1975) and Brandt (1975). They write that emotional disorders are precisely the elements that justify intervention. However, "in the case of a person nearing the end-of-life and [who] has nothing but horror ahead, suicide as 'self-deliverance' . . . is a responsible exercise of individual rights to self-determination" (p. 393).

Lester and Leenaars (1996) argue this point between themselves. Leenaars takes the position that at the moment of taking one's life, the person is "figuratively intoxicated with overpowering emotions and constricted emotions" (p. 169). Lester disagrees and writes that a majority of suicides arrive at the decision logically.

A definition of rational suicide, however, is not be complete unless there is some discussion of the standards that must be met to achieve a rational judgment. Kastenbaum (1995) presents the issue as *rational suicide* versus *suicide as a rational alternative*. The latter phrase seems to be a more acceptable and accurate one for Kastenbaum. The difference between the two is what the person believes she or he will achieve by the act of self-termination. The former category, rational suicide, describes the martyr or the hero; the latter, suicide as a rational act, represents the patient with end-stage cancer or AIDS living a life whose quality seems "worse than evil" (Kastenbaum, 1995, p. 241).

The questions Kastenbaum (1995) raise go right to the heart of the dilemma. He asks:

1. Is life to be valued and fostered under all conditions because it has primary and intrinsic value? Or,
2. Is the value of life relative to the circumstances?

There have been many times in human history when misery was so general and the outlook so grim that it did not require any distinctive individual dynamics to think seriously of suicide (Kastenbaum, 1995).

Ingram and Ellis (1992) elaborate on the concept of rational suicide standards introduced above by Kastenbaum. They write that suicide may be considered ethically justified if the act meets the following conditions: A case of an advanced terminal illness is causing unbearable suffering to the individual, or a case of a grave physical handicap is so restrictive that the individual cannot, after due consideration and training, tolerate such a limited existence.

In a further delineation of the standards, Ingram and Ellis (1992) write that suicide is ethical only if the person is a mature adult and has made a considered decision. A considered decision is one that was not made at the first knowledge of a life-threatening illness and for which the treating physician's response has been taken into account. In addition, the person has made plans that do not involve others in criminal liability, and she or he leaves a note stating exactly why she or he is committing suicide.

Rational suicide, therefore, is characterized by a possession of a realistic assessment of the situation by an individual who is faced with the decision to commit suicide. The individual's mental processes are not impaired by psychological illness or distress, and the person's motivation for the decision would be understandable if presented to objective bystanders (Werth, 1995).

A central theme of the opposition to suicide is that suicide is an ambivalent act. Every person who wants to die also wants to live. A person is suicidal only for a short period of time, and if intervention is instigated, the suicidal crisis often passes and the person changes his or her mind.

This is a reasonable attitude, but it is also possible that a decision to commit suicide can be arrived at through a logical and realistic evaluation of the facts. In addition, two questions arise:

1. Is the suicidal person required to give informed consent prior to the initiation of intervention?
2. If after intervention, the person still is of a mind to die, is it reasonable for designated individuals to restrain the person as an act of prevention?

If the first question is answered in the affirmative, the answer attributes to the person the possession of an ability to exercise the rational thought process that is a prerequisite to giving informed consent. An affirmative response to the second question removes from the individual any and all consideration of personal liberty.

In summary, it appears that many mental health professionals are not satisfied with the definitions and categories of suicide that are commonly employed. Additionally, these professionals seem to be of a mind that accepts the possibility of a rational suicide. Let us now turn to the issue of how this relates to a process that has come to be known as *death education*.

# □ Death Education

Death education is that educational process by which the participant confronts the objective data surrounding the phenomena of death and dying, examines personal attitudes, and develops strategies for dealing with these phenomena as the final stages of life. It is a process whereby each person is helped to develop from childhood through maturity to senescence an acceptance of death as a fact of life (Meagher, 1992). Death education goes beyond the typical high school or college undergraduate class. The planned experience refers also to those educational programs experienced by nursing and medical students, clinical and counseling psychologists, mental health counselors, social work specialists, and clergy preparing to participate in hospital or hospice pastoral care programs. Death education is a resource that permits and helps one to become a better "provider" and "consumer" of the available medical and community services.

Shneidman (1980a) presents two possible goals of death education. First, if one assumes that death is the cessation of the individual and his or her consciousness, the important goal of death education then becomes one of preparation: assisting the participant in the preparation of self and others to face death as the final life experience. Second, if the final act (death) is likely to involve some altered state of consciousness, one would not want to face a totally unexplored region of the self at the last minute. If one assumes that death is a transition to some other form or level of consciousness, the goal of death education then becomes some kind of experience of the self outside of time–space limitations. This then reduces fear and increases one's capacity to cope with the kinds of perceptions and the different order of reality to be experienced, both during the dying process and in the afterdeath, bodiless state.

Wass, Berardo, and Neimeyer (1988) expand on the statement of death education goals. The goals they offer are: to receive information, to develop and improve coping capacities and skills, and to clarify and cultivate one's values.

Additional goals, directed more at the death education of professional caregivers, include the development of skills and behaviors that result in care decisions that are in the best interest of the care recipient, as well as improving communication skills necessary to inform patients of their end-of-life rights. Although competency is generally decided by the courts, there are no clear legal standards for determining whether a person is competent to make medical decisions (Lo, 1995). It is incumbent upon death education to develop informed individuals. The information and materials that are presented should be selected so as to facilitate the development of the skill of making decisions and directed toward an understanding of the issues around autonomy and responsible choice.

End-of-life issues are a major component of a death education experience. At the very least, the program should be directed toward producing an educated "consumer" and public. Werth (1995), in his discussion of the variables that must be present for suicide to be considered rational, identified the essential tasks of death education: the education of the person so as to facilitate an individual's ability to engage in a realistic assessment of his or her prognosis; the education of the public about terminal illness; and the improvement of communication skills that will permit a person to engage in an open and free discussion of choices with significant others.

These goals can be achieved if the medical professional who provides care to patients with life-threatening diseases or terminal illness assumes the role of death educator as an important component of his or her duties and responsibilities. As a death educator, the professional must assist the patient or client to:

1. Understand she or he has decision making power
2. Appreciate her or his medical situation and prognosis, alternatives to the plan of care in place, and all the risks and benefits of the various options
3. Assess whether the patient's decision is consistent with her or his life values and whether the choice is stable over time

The attainment of these abilities are evidence of patient competency (Lo, 1995), which renders a conclusion of rationality upon the decisions the patient makes.

Death-related anxiety and fear are significantly lessened if the terminally ill person has the necessary information and support from his or her significant others and caregivers. Reduction of fear and anxiety allows the person to make more rational decisions around and about his or her own death (Meagher & Leff, 1989).

A review of the literature (Meagher, 1981) suggests that a desired outcome of death education is to influence or change attitudes. The direction of this change is described as being toward acceptance of the idea that dying is an event experienced only by the person who is suffering the process. Inherent in the death education process is a hospice premise; to wit, the process of dying does not remove the right to make care decisions from the patient. In order to make the decisions that would be in the best interest of the patient, death educators need to provide the opportunity and resources necessary for an individual to learn what his or her options might be and to examine the consequences of selecting various available options.

In a study examining attitudes toward euthanasia, Holloway (1994–1995) report that subjects enrolled in a course on death and dying indicated that

1. A person should have the right to choose to die if she or he is terminally ill and is suffering,
2. If the student were to confront a situation of suffering a slow and painful death, she or he should have the right to choose to end life in the fastest and easiest way possible.

The role of death education is not to advocate a single point of view—that everyone who is terminally ill should consider committing suicide. Nor should it be to advocate for coercion on the part of the professional caregiver who, armed with all the facts of the case, would understand the hopelessness of the patient's condition.

# ☐  Conclusion

The ideal time to learn how to swim is not when one is drowning. To wait to do so would be considered irrational. The ideal time to decide whether to choose to continue or not continue with the dying process is not when all recommended treatment has failed and the person is condemned to a life of continual and increasing pain, suffering, and bodily deterioration. To wait for this situation to arise before initiating a discussion of a patient's rights and options should be deemed irrational. The ideal would be to examine the options, assess the consequences of various decisions, and communicate beliefs and wishes before the situation arises. But is that rational?

Death education must make every effort to clearly distinguish between "wanting to die" and "not being able to continue in one's life." There may be times, such as with a patient in intractable pain and substantial suffering with no chance of recovery, when the prevention of suicide may be considered irrational and not in the best interest of the patient.

CHAPTER

Judith M. Stillion

# Rational Suicide: Challenging the Next Generation of Caregivers

The issue of the right to suicide has become more salient in recent years. Indeed, there is growing evidence that the general public as well as some groups of helping professionals are becoming more supportive of this right, at least in situations in which people are terminally ill (e.g., Deluty, 1989; Werth & Liddle, 1994). Discussion surrounding the topic takes place under many labels: the right to die, rational suicide, assisted suicide, passive euthanasia, and active euthanasia. Often these discussions become highly emotional, a sure indication that they are touching core values within the discussants. There is clearly no "right" position on the subject. Highly principled people in every walk of life can and do come to different conclusions on the subject of when and whether people have a right to take their own lives and or to ask for help in dying. Because this is true, it seems imperative that those working in the fields of death education and counseling consider both short-term and long-term consequences of accepting the term *rational suicide*. Moreover, for those of us who are teaching the next generation of caregivers, it seems important to raise all aspects of the issue. In this chapter I briefly review the conditions that have led to the need for courses examining this topic, describe the process I have used to involve students in discussions of rational suicide within such courses, and explain my current position, which argues against rational suicide.

I come to the discussion of rational suicide from the point of view of a psychologist who has served as a counselor in a variety of settings and as a certified death educator, who has been involved in educating prospective caregivers (i.e., nurses, psychologists, teachers, counselors) in death, grief, suicide, and loss across a 20-year period. Death education and death-related counseling are relatively new fields. They were born out of the vacuum created by major changes occurring across the 20th century.

The first change was a shift in the setting in which death occurred. In simpler days, death was an expected, even routine, part of family life. Rural families tended their own sick and, when death occurred, cared for the body and attended to the details of the burial. As life expectancy lengthened by 60% across this century (National Center for Health Statistics, 1996) and medical proficiency grew, death became an event that occurred in an institutional setting attended by specialists who were generally strangers to the family of the dying person. Moreover, as the size of the nuclear family shrank and medical expertise increased, death became a less frequent and therefore less expected event and many people found that they could avoid confronting the reality of death in their lives throughout their childhood and adolescence. The event of bereavement and its subsequent grief and mourning processes also began to be suppressed and ignored in the United States as rituals were deemphasized in an increasingly secular society.

However, in spite of being ignored, death remained a harsh reality for prospective and practicing caregivers, including nurses, teachers, counselors, psychologists, and many other professionals. These professionals found themselves confronted by clients who were attempting to deal with death, loss, and grief without any framework or experience for doing so. What is more, as the space between the terminal diagnosis and the actual death lengthened and the medical profession found ways to prolong life beyond what many people considered reasonable, many in our society felt the need for helping professionals who were comfortable with the subject of dying. At this point, educators, psychologists and other professionals began a systematic study of end-of-life issues, and courses in death and dying began to be offered to prepare preprofessionals students to address the needs of those confronting death, dying, grief, and loss. The nature of these courses has important implications for the subject of rational suicide, because this is generally the first time prospective caregivers encounter the subject.

## ☐  Consideration of Rational and Assisted Suicide in Death Education Courses

I began teaching the psychology of death and dying in 1976. From the very beginning, three observations were evident about the course. First, death education is not a usual academic course. It is heavily loaded with affective material. Students come to it with entrenched beliefs and values and often with unresolved personal grief. Therefore, death educators must be sensitive to individual goals, needs, and values in a way that is not needed in teaching statistics or chemistry. Following from this observation is the second point: faculty teaching death education should be careful not to inflict their values on students. My role as an educator, then, became one of being sure to consider all aspects of each issue studied and to promote open discussion of them within a supportive and respectful climate. The third point that I learned is that students taking death-and-dying courses are often propelled into a semester-long values clarification exercise. Students consistently report that they cannot and do not leave the course material in the classroom. Moreover, they often indicate that at the end of the course, their work in this area is just beginning (Stillion, 1979).

Taken together, these three observations have dictated the mode of teaching that I use. It is an open seminar, restricted to 30 upper-division and graduate students, most of whom are going into the helping professions. All students are expected to participate heavily throughout the course. I first developed the course at the same time that I was teaching group psychotherapy to graduate clinical psychology students. Because

I was teaching both courses simultaneously, it was easy to see that the processes used in the death and dying course had much in common with the curative factors that make for effective group therapy, an observation that I explicated many years ago (Stillion, 1983). Because the course contains so many parallels with group psychotherapy, many of the ground rules of the course are affective in nature. Keeping an open mind is a value explicitly explained in the syllabus, and students are encouraged to reveal their values and beliefs in a safe and respectful environment. Aware of the power that instructors carry with them into the teaching setting, I rarely share my values and attitudes in class, although I am sure that some students may perceive them through questions that I and they ask.

One area that is highly controversial in every death and dying class is that of suicide. Most traditional students enter the course with a negative attitude toward suicide of all types. In order to introduce the case for rational suicide, I use the film *Dax's Case*, which tells the story of a badly burned young man who asked to be allowed to die and was denied that request. Students observe actual treatment of life-threatening burns, and Dax's extreme agony is evident. They hear in his own words of the terrible depression he experienced as he tried to make a life as a blind, severely handicapped, and scarred young man, and of his unsuccessful suicide attempts. In the sequel to the original film, which takes place 10 years after the accident, Dax Cowart, despite adjusting well to his blindness and other handicaps, despite having a happy marriage and a successful business, despite seeming to enjoy his life through music and discussions with friends, still insists that he should have been allowed to die.

This powerful film has predictable consequences. Almost all the students in every class move from a position of being negative toward any type of suicide to supporting an individual's right to take his or her own life. Many even agree that people like Dax should have assistance in dying if they cannot manage to take their own lives. It is then time to bring to their attention arguments against rational and assisted suicide. I raise these arguments by giving students reading assignments and by leading open discussions utilizing probing questions to help them unearth all aspects of the arguments against rational and assisted suicide. The process generally follows the following sequence.

First, students need definitions of such concepts as "the right to die," "passive and active euthanasia," "assisted suicide," and "rational suicide." As they examine these terms, they come to realize that the phrase "the right to die" is the most general of terms used to discuss this issue. They recognize that it refers to a person's right to self-determination and may include such things as advance directives, including a living will and specific directions to doctors and relatives regarding the conditions under which a person would not want to continue living, as well as the request for withholding or withdrawing life-sustaining treatment. Passive euthanasia, students realize, occurs if an individual is allowed to die without attempting resuscitation and with no heroic treatments that might prolong the dying trajectory. They come to recognize active euthanasia and assisted suicide as nearly synonymous terms in that both assume that an individual is given physical and / or psychological assistance in dying. The term "assisted suicide," however, they generally see as more limited because it refers to an instance in which a physician or other caregiver will supply, but may not administer, a lethal dose of a substance. The term, rational suicide is generally viewed by students as referring to instances in which individuals who are not clinically depressed or otherwise mentally impaired come to the decision that their lives are no longer worth living and opt to end them.

As students research these terms, they raise questions such as the following: under what conditions do individuals have the right to terminate their lives? This question opens the door for considering the "slippery slope" argument. If terminally ill people in constant physical pain have the right to take their own lives, do people who are in unremitting psychological pain have that right also? Do elderly people who are physically intact but tired or bored with living have that right? Do healthy young people who are likewise tired of living or feeling hopeless have that right? Do all people have the absolute right to take their own lives at any time?

To begin to respond to these questions, students are asked to read from the works of Szasz (1976, 1986), who has stated that helping professionals have no right to prevent suicide if a person clearly wishes to end his or her life. He also has advocated that suicide should be given the "status of a basic human right" and that the "power of the state should not be legitimately invoked or deployed to prohibit or prevent persons from killing themselves" (1986, p. 811). For the other side of the argument, students read works of ethicists such as Daniel Callahan (1992) who oppose the concept of rational suicide.

Students also raise a second, related question. Under what conditions, if any, do people seeking to die have the right to ask others to help them take their lives? This question generally leads students to investigate legalities surrounding rational suicide and assisted suicide. Students become aware that suicide is no longer viewed as a crime in any state in the union, but that assisting suicide is still considered a crime in several states and those who help individuals take their own lives may be subject to prosecution. This observation generally leads to students raising questions about legalizing assisted suicide. As those issues are raised, model legislation from Oregon, Washington, California, and New Hampshire is made available for the students.

From reading the legislation, students comprehend that in order to safeguard the assisted suicide process, multiple professionals need to be involved in the decision to assist a person in suicide, and that such a decision is the end point in a rather protracted process. Questions then arise about those who will be making the decision. Because some of the students in the course are nursing majors, they help other students understand the specialized nature of medicine today. They point out that decisions to permit and or assist in suicide in the United States are most likely to be made by a group of professionals who have much information about the disease that a person has but very limited knowledge about the human being. As students spend time in further study of the issue, they often observe that our kind of specialized medicine does not lend itself to the type of person-centered decision making that can go on in countries in which more personal medical care is the norm. People who are relative strangers to patients, knowing little more than the diagnosis and prognosis of individuals' situations, would be making the most personal of all decisions for them—the decision to permit and/or assist them in terminating their lives.

A secondary concern is our increasingly litigious society. Some students believe that passing laws to legalize suicide, even under controlled conditions, sets the stage for lawyers to enter the scene. Generally, one or more students express their concern about legalizing a process that will set the stage for lawyers to make money on end-of-life issues.

Economic arguments also arise. Students understand that the process of safeguarding the decision is an expensive one, and they ask if our health system can afford interdisciplinary panels reviewing each petitioner's request. They wonder who will pay the cost of such reviews for those who have no insurance or adequate income? They then raise a different, almost contradictory, issue of equity. In a country in which the quality of medical care one receives is largely dependent upon one's socioeconomic level, would poor people and those living far from medical facilities find themselves more likely to feel pressure to request an early end? And, as the option of suicide becomes more accepted by society, will there be subtle or not-so-subtle pressure to take one's life if a person begins to be a financial or physical burden to his or her family? Might it even become customary that caring elders are routinely expected to take their lives at a certain age, thus ensuring room, opportunity, and perhaps a measure of economic security for the next generation? If this is possible, is it not also possible that others who "drain" society's resources (e.g., severely mentally disabled people) might be expected to make premature exits? Although this is clearly slippery slope–type reasoning, all of these nuances need to be examined by students who will be the next generation of counselors, psychologists, and nurses. Some students in each class begin to take a stance against rational and assisted suicide after following its possible implications down that slope. Indeed, they frequently quote sources like Hendin (1995, p. 194) who stated that

> over the past 20 years practice in the Netherlands has moved from assisted suicide to euthanasia, from euthanasia for the terminally ill to euthanasia for patients who are chronically ill, from physical suffering to mental suffering, from voluntary euthanasia to involuntary euthanasia (called "termination of the patient without explicit request").

Students point out that if this slide down the slippery slope has occurred in a culture in which medical care is more personal, it is very likely also to occur in the United States.

The next question that frequently arises is what core values of our society would change if rational suicide became routine. Callahan (1992) has pointed out that Western culture has been remarkably stable over time in placing a high value on life. Rational suicide, especially in the case of assisted suicide, would provide a third circumstance (in addition to war and capital punishment) in which it would be permissible to take the life of another person. Students who have lived in or studied about cultures in which human life is not valued are frequently loathe to encourage any further incursion on the value of individual life.

As the discussion continues in the course, we generally find ourselves reframing the issue to examine community versus individual interest. Traditionally, in the United States we have opted to stress the rights of the individual above the rights of the community. We continue that tradition as we discuss rational suicide and move to legalize assisted suicide. Basically, we are saying that individuals have the right to decide when and how they will take their lives, and some would even argue that they have the right to ask others to help them die. But is there not an equal obligation of individuals to consider the community in which they live? Does taking one's life diminish the community surrounding the individual? Those who would continue to serve and love and learn from the one who chooses to prematurely leave life—do they not have any rights in the decision? Moving one step away from the central decision circle, the question arises of whether people opting for suicide decrease the value in which all humans hold life as they choose to end theirs prematurely?

To illuminate this point, students tend to reflect on the current values in our culture—instant gratification is a big one. If we are hungry, we tend to grab fast food—the faster the better. If we need sleep, we turn to over-the-counter sleep-inducing medications to provide an instant avenue to rest. If we are in psychological pain, we turn to drugs or alcohol or to "pop" psychology as a way of coping. If we are in physical pain, we demand instant relief through prescription pain killers.

In other cultures and in other days, people have handled these situations differently. They have taken the position that humans can learn from all situations. Facing death promotes a crisis in the lives of most people. Crisis often permits, even induces, growth. Frankl (1963) reflected this view well when he observed that in the final analysis our most basic freedom is the freedom to decide the attitude that we will take toward life's most demanding and demeaning challenges.

In the United States today, however, we tend to regard suffering as a personal insult and death as the final enemy to be confronted. As we discuss this observation, some students begin to view the concept of "suffering as a personal insult" as a type of arrogance. Why, they ask, should our generation of humans believe that they should be exempt from suffering? Can something be learned from experiencing the dying process? They may also view the quest for control of conditions at the end-of-life as further evidence of the need for a quick fix to life's problems. Finally, some students express concern that if rational suicide becomes a reality in our culture, its passage into law might signal a lessening of our efforts to find new drugs to ease the pain of terminal conditions and to create situations like hospice, in which dying people can be helped to cope with end-of-life issues in humane settings.

It is important to note that in every course I have taught, students are divided on the issue of rational suicide when the course ends. It is also important to note that whatever their position, they can defend it using references and logic. More significantly, from the viewpoint of future caregivers, they express respect for other students who do not share their position. They frequently state that the model used in class is the one they would use in counseling dying people and their families. They become committed to providing information and a respectful and open climate, to raising questions that help clients consider all aspects of the issue, and then to accepting the choice made by each individual client.

# ☐ Personal Reflections

I have learned much from watching prospective caregivers wrestle with the nuances of rational suicide over the years. I have reached a personal position on the issue, which is the goal that I hold for my students. I hope that each of them can think through a personal stance on the issues surrounding the right to die and rational suicide from an informed base. I warn them that their stances will need reexamination in the light of their own life experiences, and that they should respect their own right to change their minds on these issues as much as they respect their fellow students' rights to come to a different conclusion. Often students ask me to share my ideas and conclusions on the subject. When I do so privately, it takes the following form.

Can suicide be a rational choice? That is, can people who are "in their right minds" choose to end their lives? There is little doubt that any individual suicide may be viewed by many people as a rational choice. But the term *rational* is a human invention. Certainly, we can develop a definition that will include specific decision criteria enabling us to decide if a particular suicide is rational. Even if we receive perfect agreement that a particular suicide is rational, however, does that necessarily mean that it was the wisest choice? One may choose to die for many reasons—but in the end they all represent the choice to escape from a situation that one views as personally unbearable. Although we may view those who choose such an escape with compassion, understanding, and even agreement that we would do the same in their situation, we must also be aware of the unspoken messages that they are sending as they model suicidal behavior for those around them.

First, they are saying that there is nothing inherently valuable in the act of living. From my personal view, that is simply false. By any measure that we know of, life is the scarcest, most valuable commodity in a universe that is infinitely dark and lonely. It therefore deserves the utmost respect and nurturance. Suicide is not respectful of life. Therefore, I oppose rational suicide partly because it does not recognize the enormous value of life itself.

Second, those who choose to die are modeling escape behavior for others, whereas by choosing not to suicide in the face of adversity, people can be a model of courage and strength. For example, there is the decision made by a middle-aged cancer patient. The mother of three daughters and grandmother to seven, this 58-year-old woman suffered from cancer that had metastasized from her kidneys to her liver, bones, and lungs. A secondary tumor grew to such proportions that it broke her spine. Her pain was extreme in spite of the implantation of a morphine pump in her back. This intelligent, college-educated woman considered and rejected taking her life. She believed that she could continue to teach her daughters by facing death and pain with strength and courage. Moreover, she believed that in helping to care for her, her daughters and husband would be able to work through some of their grief, finish unfinished business, and extend their understanding of the limits of love through service to her. She was right. Her family shared her pain, reminisced with her across the last months of her illness, and even planned the funeral service with her. When she died, they were ready to let her go, and each learned a valued lesson concerning the inestimable worth of life and the reality and inevitability of death. More than those lessons, however, they learned that in spite of pain, an individual can grow and develop and give right up to the moment of death. I learned those lessons too because that woman was my sister.

In my sister's case, the message sent to those who loved her was that life is precious, death is its natural culmination, the dying process can permit growth in many areas and for many people, and the process of living and the struggle involved in dying are meaningful parts of the human condition. Because of these and many other examples, I have also come to oppose rational suicide because by foreshortening our individual journeys, it cuts off all hope for growth and sets a nihilistic model for others to follow.

Rational suicide also raises the question that occurred to some Broadway producers a few years ago: "Whose life is it anyway?" The play and film by that name clearly decided that the protagonist had the right to decide when his or her life was no longer worth living. I question that conclusion. I do not want my grandchildren to grow up in a world in which the miracle of life is discounted or devalued because humans of my generation have demanded to pursue the illusion of control and have succeeded in convincing others to pass laws fostering that illusion. Therefore, I oppose the idea of rational suicide partly because I believe that it encourages people to delude themselves about deeper issues concerning meaning in living.

I also oppose the idea of rational suicide because our knowledge and understanding are finite. Essential to my understanding of the human condition is the knowledge that we come from mystery and will return to mystery. Nothing we do or say will change that truth. In the face of that mystery, I choose to cherish life—and to meet death, in whatever form it presents itself, with as much dignity, trust, and courage as possible.

# ☐ Conclusion

Finally, I want my death to be *my* death. I do not want society establishing laws about it. I do not want doctors, nurses, lawyers, social workers, or psychologists discussing my case and debating my fate. Much has been made of the idea that acceptance of rational suicide and its specialized case, assisted suicide, helps bring about an "appropriate" death. The basic foundation of my appropriate death is privacy, and it is this base that we are in danger of losing as the concept of rational suicide becomes public. Therefore, I oppose rational suicide because it sets the stage for less, rather than more, individual choice in the conditions surrounding my personal death.

# 3

# SPECIAL POPULATIONS

## SURVIVORS

Carol J. Gill

# The False Autonomy of Forced Choice: Rationalizing Suicide for Persons with Disabilities

Two years ago, I confronted the issue of "rational suicide" in a one-day course I took on suicide intervention. All morning, the instructor stressed the importance of protecting people from suicidal feelings. That afternoon, however, she completely reversed position as she discussed the "exceptional cases," namely, people with incurable physical conditions. Extensively and "incurably" disabled myself because of childhood polio, reliant on a nighttime ventilator and on personal assistance for activities of daily living, I counted myself a veteran member of the exceptional group in question.

"Why," I asked, "are persons with incurable physical conditions not candidates for suicide intervention?" The instructor uneasily replied that suicide prevention was not warranted in cases of *rational* suicide. She determined rationality by arguing backward from result to act: if the death "makes sense"—for example, seems preferable to suffering—then the act of suicide must be rational.

Increasingly, it appears that suicide for people with disabilities "makes sense" to a broad spectrum of observers: health professionals, family members, judges, journalists, ethicists and the general public. However, a dissenting minority—comprising disabled persons of diverse ages, backgrounds, and philosophies—protests the automatic attribution of rationality to people with disabilities who wish to die. Many are "grassroots" disability rights activists, such as members of the group Not Dead Yet (Betzold, 1996), who also fight for our community's equal access to education, employment, healthcare, transportation, and the built environment. Others are respected intellectual leaders in our community: policy analysts, historians, social scientists, and attorneys.

## □ Persons with Disabilities Requesting Death

The dissenters originally united in the early 1980s when a California woman with cerebral palsy, Elizabeth Bouvia, petitioned the court for support to starve herself to death. "Right-to-die" proponents lauded her quest as a model of autonomous rational decision-making. She was adult, bright, and persistent. She said she knew her options, had reflected on her circumstances, and had concluded that, because of the physical and emotional pain of her disability, life was intolerable.

Bouvia's story rocked the disability community. Skeptical that a physical condition of 26 years' standing could suddenly and irrevocably render life valueless, disability activists filed an *amicus* brief presenting the hidden Elizabeth Bouvia story. Their account revealed a strong-willed young woman who had waged an exhausting struggle to live despite formidable obstacles deriving not from her body but from an unsupportive social environment. She had weathered childhood separation from her parents, institutionalization, and poverty. Despite emotional swings, including previous suicidal attempts, she established her own household and achieved entrance to a Master's-degree program in social work.

By her mid-20s, however, life stresses intensified. Denied a professional placement because of disability bias, she dropped out of school. She married an ex-convict, became pregnant, and lost her dream of motherhood through a miscarriage. Her brother died and her mother was diagnosed with cancer. The marriage faltered. Within days after separating from her husband, she entered a hospital and announced her intention to starve herself to death while taking narcotics.

To the activists, Bouvia's dying did not make sense. They pointed out that she had opted for death under the cumulative strain of stresses harsh enough to topple anyone's equilibrium, disabled or not. They felt, moreover, that like some racial and ethnic minority group members, she had internalized and buckled under years of social devaluation. Many interpreted her complaints not as readiness to die but as signals of "disability burnout"—the emotional exhaustion described by many individuals with disabilities who struggle to overcome socially constructed obstacles to living. In some newspapers, in fact, Bouvia was quoted as saying she was tired of "the struggle to live within the system" (Hearn, 1984, p. 1). The disabled dissenters read her actions as desperate final efforts to control her destiny. That her suicide plan sounded so right to so many, they asserted, reflected irrational public attitudes about disability.

Indisputably, Bouvia garnered far more public support more quickly for seeking death than for struggling to live. Although she ultimately won court sanction of her "right to die," she has not exercised that option in the succeeding years. The disability activists may have been right to question both the rationality and the suicidal intent of her request to die.

In the late 1980s, David Rivlin, a young quadriplegic man in a Michigan nursing home, requested assistance to die through withdrawal of his ventilator. With the Bouvia legal precedent in place, the court recognized his right to refuse "treatment." Although many nondisabled persons hailed his decision as autonomous and rational, most observers with disabilities mourned it as a pressured escape from unnecessary incarceration. In his last media interview, Rivlin emphasized that he did not wish to die but could find no exit from the restrictions and demoralization of institutional existence. He condemned society's attitudes toward people with disabilities and exhorted the public to help others with disabilities "before it's too late" (Oberman, 1989). Tragically, if Rivlin had lived in one of several states that adequately fund in-home personal assistance, he would have had the option to live, as he wished, in his own home.

Within months of Rivlin's death, a quadriplegic man in strikingly similar circumstances petitioned a Georgia court for the right to turn off his ventilator. Like Bouvia,

Larry McAfee said his disability rendered life intolerable. The court affirmed both his characterization of a ruined life and his right to die. Dissenters with disabilities and their allies publicly denounced Georgia's lack of funding for assisted independent living. Incredibly, at the 11th hour, advocates managed to contact McAfee and offer options for living and working that he had not known were possible. Instead of acting on his option to escape disability through dying, McAfee escaped institutional life. In 1990, he addressed the Georgia state senate, reproaching the state for failing to support citizens with disabilities, inviting the legislators to "imagine a life without control," and urging them to redirect state healthcare funding "to independent living opportunities that can easily be made available . . . throughout the United States" ("Quadriplegic Pleads," 1990, p. 18).

## ☐ Three Arguments Against Judgments of Rationality

The stories of Bouvia, Rivlin, and McAfee present three critical challenges to rationality arguments:

1. Making rational decisions about the worth of life with a disability may be impossible for individuals enmeshed in a social environment that is, itself, irrational on the subject of disability. If people are driven to suicide after internalizing relentless devaluation, are they acting rationally?
2. Suicide decisions for many people with disabilities can be desperate efforts to escape not life but social oppression. If the individual is denied recourse to a thwarted existence or is not informed about all of her or his options, the right to rational suicide becomes a forced solution that is neither "rational" nor a genuine "right."
3. When people with disabilities are maltreated by society, we must question the justice in allowing that society to determine if our death wishes are rational. It is a glaring conflict of interest for society to sanction suicide in any minority group that it helps push to the brink of despair.

## ☐ Pressures to Die

Disparagement of life with a disability is insidious, pervasive, and ingrained in American culture and represents the real tragedy of disability. People with disabilities make up one of the most segregated, undereducated, and impoverished minority groups in the country. Over 70% of working age disabled adults are unemployed (LaPlante, Kennedy, Kaye, & Wenger, 1996). We repeatedly encounter public buildings, programs, schools, transportation, and services that are open to everyone but us. Moreover, the situation is, in some ways, getting worse. Our support programs are being cut. Managed healthcare policies exclude some of our most basic life needs. The Americans with Disabilities Act and other antidiscrimination laws that we struggled for decades to secure are attacked as frivolous. Nondisabled Americans admit in surveys that they are fearful of persons with disabilities (Vernaci, 1991). According to government-funded research, children with disabilities are twice as likely as nondisabled children to be abused (Crosse, Kaye, & Ratnofsky, 1993). Abuse of women with disabilities is more the rule than the exception, a finding that is linked to a high rate of suicidal behaviors (Masuda, 1996). Parents who have killed their children with disabilities have been excused by "sympathetic" judges (Harris, 1996).

Surrounded by invalidation, it is hard not to learn self-hatred. Hatred of the disabled self is an intense *internal* pressure impelling some individuals toward self-annihilation. Disability devaluation fosters *external* pressures as well. I learn monthly of cases in which life-sustaining treatments are not offered to disabled persons unless they assertively press for options; in which families are repeatedly urged to let a loved one "go" because she or he will not recover physical independence; in which depression and despair in people with disabilities are deemed normal; and in which persons with disabilities report substandard healthcare because of their poverty or their health professional's lack of commitment to the needs of persons with irreversible "impairment."

In an environment in which fear and loathing of life with disability is this deeply rooted, I believe it is impossible: to determine the extent to which any individual with a disability is making a "free" choice to die versus yielding to the inner coercion of internalized devaluation or to the external coercion of oppression, exclusion, and blocked choices; and to insure that observers assessing a disabled individual's suicidal message are sufficiently knowledgeable about disability, and sufficiently unimpaired by conditioned prejudice, to act in support of that individual's genuine self-determination rather than in response to their own unconscious fears and revulsions.

## ☐  Applying the Criteria for Rational Suicide

Most established criteria for determining rational suicide are unsuitable or irrelevant when applied to people with disabilities. To illustrate, I summarize criteria presented in Chapter 1 and discuss their shortcomings.

### Mental Competence

The mentally competent *individual* has mature adult status as well as the ability to reason and understand consequences. The competent suicidal *decision* is "considered" (as evidenced by having a living will, joining a right to die organization, etc.) and / or reflects a realistic assessment of the individual's life situation—consistent with views of the surrounding culture.

*Problems*   Although many people with disabilities are mature individuals, discriminatory policies often deny them the rights of adulthood. Like David Rivlin, they are not allowed to have real homes, access to the surrounding community, employment, or even a daily schedule of their own choosing. If personal liberties are limited and skewed by the caprices of social policy, it makes little sense to contend that such individuals act freely as mature adults. Furthermore, long-term social isolation and the pain of an imposed meaningless existence, cited by Rivlin as elements of nursing home life, may erode the individual's capacity to make reasoned decisions.

Moreover, whether or not disabled persons' assessments of their circumstances are judged "realistic" depends on the group doing the judging. Because of disability prejudice, much of society believes it is realistic to conclude that needing personal help is undignified and severe disability spoils life. In contrast, the jury of our peers—most people with disabilities—believes such conclusions are unrealistic. Instead, they feel social barriers and attitudes spoil life.

Particularly misguided is the notion that advance directives signify a careful consideration of dying. Researchers have found that many persons sign living wills without fully understanding what they say. I have talked to competent adults with disabilities who signed advanced directives presented to them in other paperwork, taking no more than a moment to "consider" the decision.

Likewise, prior contact with right to die organizations is no guarantee of rational consideration. Hemlock Society materials have been found beside suicide victims, with and without physical disabilities, who acted impulsively or under the pressure of chronic mental illness.

## Absence of Psychological Impairment

The individual should not act under pressure of psychological or social origins; treatable depression should be ruled out; mental health professionals should assess mental status.

*Problems*   Assessments of simple legal competence are not sufficient to rule out psychological forces that can impel a disabled person toward suicide. A disabled woman victimized by domestic violence, for instance, may score as fully oriented on a mental status examination. Nonetheless, research conducted through the DisAbled Women's Network in Canada indicates that abuse significantly raises disabled women's risk of suicide (Masuda, 1996). No one has yet systematically researched the battering effects of social devaluation on the suicide potential of disabled persons; anecdotal accounts, however, suggest that stigma can, indeed, be deadly. We are rightly concerned about the suicidal impact of social devaluation on gay teenagers and African American men; why not people with disabilities?

Most people with disabilities who gain access to mental health services at all receive them from professionals who are grossly uneducated about disability issues, resources, or hazards. Consequently, professionals either miss signs of psychological distress in people with disabilities or minimize the coercive impact of such distress, assuming that it is normal or reasonable to be depressed by the inherent hardships of disability. Many professionals fall into the trap of presuming that because the disability is irreversible, depression in a disabled person is also irreversible. They are unaware of resources and supports that could ameliorate the distress, usually remaining dangerously oblivious to their own lack of awareness.

## The Individual Is Informed; Experts Are Consulted

A social worker, physician, or other professional can insure that the individual is informed about alternatives; a consultation with other objective experts—such as religious experts—should be sought.

*Problems*   Although it is important to understand how to care for one's medical needs, most people with disabilities say their major problems are social and economic, not physical. Most health professionals are not trained to arbitrate the rationality of suicidal decisions in anyone, much less in persons with disabilities. The majority of medical students are never even rotated through rehabilitation medicine. The principles of curing and acute care learned in medical school translate poorly to chronic conditions. Furthermore, health professionals commonly harbor disability prejudice (Gething, 1992; Paris, 1993). The "in-group" consensus among veteran members of our community is that we learn about our options from each other, not professionals.

Unfortunately, persons who have been disabled for many years often remain outside the information loop. Like McAfee, they may be thrown by the intricacies and inconsistencies of disability policy, unaware of esoteric programs and appeal processes that could yield life-changing supports. If they trust their doctors or social workers to keep them informed, they may succumb to disability burnout before locating the resources that they need to live with quality.

Similarly, religious counselors and other experts are rarely proficient in the life issues of the disability community. In giving advice, they often extrapolate from unchallenged beliefs or limited personal experience with disability. Alternatively, they offer nondirective support that simply recirculates and affirms the disabled person's preexisting notions about disability without adding new perspectives to temper distress. This approach can reinforce despair, as Tough Love founder Phyllis York discovered when she suddenly became quadriplegic; she wrote, "People who tell me they can understand my wanting to commit suicide are not helpful. . . . I hear them silently telling me to do it—that I'm such a mess, I shouldn't want to live" (York & York, 1989, p. 208).

## Persistence of Suffering

Suicide must help avoid the greater harm of hopeless physical or emotional suffering (i.e, suffering that cannot be improved) related to advanced terminal illness, grave physical handicap, pain, or progressive mental or physical condition.

*Problems*    Again, this criterion seems founded on the naive presumption that permanent physical or mental impairments cause permanent emotional distress. In fact, emotional equilibrium is amazingly plastic. Rehabilitation professionals witness the power of human adjustment every day as they watch recently disabled clients navigate periods of shock, disbelief, fear, despair, and anger on their way to accepting and enjoying life with disabilities.

Research on emotional adjustment in persons with disabilities is clear and consistent across studies regarding several important points: (1) There is no significant relation between severity of disability and ultimate emotional adjustment or perceived quality of life. If anything, there is evidence that persons with the most limiting disabilities (e.g., quadriplegics and ventilator users) value life more than persons with lesser impairments (Whiteneck et al., 1985), (2) it is common for people to say their lives are better after becoming disabled than they were before disability (Ray & West, 1984), (3) approximately half of all people with disabilities say they do not wish to be "cured" (Weinberg & Williams, 1978), (4) generally, persons slowly change their priorities about what is most important in life after acquiring disabilities, (5) depression and suicidal behaviors in persons with disabilities are related to social factors, such as social isolation and lack of a meaningful role, not to objective measures of impairment (Fuhrer, Rintala, Hart, Clearman, & Young, 1992). Because there is no evidence linking degree of impairment to suicide, and because the overwhelming majority of people learn, with time, to value life despite extensive permanent impairments, it is invalid to base the rationality of suicide on either the persistence or severity of the condition.

Another problem with this criterion is that it introduces the dilemma of determining how much suffering is required to make suicide a rational option. Many proponents of the "right to die" argue that the presumed psychological suffering of disability can be as painful as any physical trauma. Would it not also be rational, then, to commit suicide to end unremitting psychological suffering owing to chronic depression, anxiety, or painful permanent losses of any kind?

In reality, people recover or fail to recover emotionally from disability in the same way they deal with any severe loss. If time and support heal the suffering of disability as much and as well as they heal the grief of losing loved ones or lifelong dreams, how can the former be accepted as a basis for rational suicide and not the latter? Why is permanent loss of movement in one's extremities more a basis for rational suicide than the permanent loss of children or spouse?

## Persistence of Decision

The wish to die must be enduring and unambivalent.

*Problems*   Contrary to public myth, the persistence of the suicidal wish is an exceptionally poor indicator of rationality, depth of suffering, or gravity of intent. Clinicians who work with suicidal individuals acknowledge that some people rarely, if ever, express the desire to die before committing suicide, while others may express their intent consistently for months yet never act. As a rehabilitation psychologist, I have met many individuals who expressed persistent and intense wishes to die at difficult points in their adjustment to disability, only to change their minds and relish life with time, increased social support, or a shift in life circumstances.

Furthermore, leading suicide experts (Shneidman, 1985) maintain that all suicidal expressions and behaviors contain a degree of ambivalence. Often the ambivalence is denied and remains hidden to all but the most experienced observer—experienced both in the treatment of suicide and in working with the subpopulation to which the individual belongs.

## Lack of Coercion

The suicide must be the result of free will and not coerced by others.

*Problems*   According to suicide authority Edwin Shneidman (1985), suicide results from the pain of unmet needs; that is, people decide to die if they feel they cannot have what they need to make life worth living. It is hard for me to appreciate as "free will" any act engendered by pain and deprivation. It is especially difficult to find real liberty in the suicidal wishes of Bouvia, Rivlin, McAfee, and countless other socially discarded and demoralized individuals with disabilities.

Denied their right to self-determination in critical aspects of life, people with disabilities are literally dying to gain control. Some are dying because they are denied options for assisted living, proper healthcare and pain management, or adequate treatment for depression and suicidal feelings. Some can no longer bear their social isolation and their lack of importance in the world. Some simply cave in to the messages of invalidation they absorb on a steady basis. Lacking resources and alternate viewpoints, they yield to the popular idea that disability ruins life and that they must leave their bodies to find peace.

Although many defend the right to rational suicide as an autonomous act in free-thinking individuals, I am struck by the vulnerability of suicidal disabled individuals to social pressures. The urgency of those pressures can make a decision to die seem more certain than it is. Consider this scenario: A woman with multiple sclerosis seeks Kevorkian's assistance. She sounds adamant about dying. Are we hearing the voice of free will? Or are we hearing a woman's trained conviction that she should not take up space in the world if she is not useful to someone? A recent study of persons with multiple sclerosis found, in fact, that social isolation, not degree of disability, was the common denominator in their suicides. Imagine Kevorkian's client feeling terrified of loneliness, of burdening her loved ones into exhaustion. He offers not only an exit from her terror but a seductive promise to stay by her side until the end. There is even the tantalizing idea that she may be doing something important for others by dying this way. Perhaps until now she has wavered internally about suicide. A medical authority, however, has just put his hand on her shoulder and validated her lowest assessment of her circumstances. If she has been testing the waters to see how others would feel about her death, she has her answer. Although some disagree with her decision, no one stops her. Some applaud her. She is tired and lacks knowledge of other ways out of her pain. No matter how intelligent or mentally competent she is, she is human and her emotions rule. The offer cannot be refused.

Coercion comes in many forms. I have seen clients plunge into depression when a loved one makes a casually disparaging remark about their appearance or uses the word, "burden." Conversely, I have watched persons like McAfee pull completely out of despair when offered an opportunity to feel useful, or persons like Christopher Reeve, who said he decided against dying the moment his children walked into his hospital room and affirmed his importance in the family.

## Consistent with Values

The suicidal decision should be congruent with the individual's spiritual values or philosophy.

*Problems*  The minute a person acquires a disability, he or she acquires a new social status and membership in a new community. In a sense, therefore, the individual becomes suddenly multicultural. Unfortunately, the new values of disability clash with the values of the more familiar nondisabled world. For example, in the ideals of disability culture, people are valuable no matter how differently they function. They are valued for who they are, not for what they can produce. There is no indignity in needing personal assistance. Interdependence is valued over independence, cooperation over individualism. Technology and assistive devices are gracefully accepted as routine aspects of daily living.

Persons with disabilities are often caught betwixt and between these values of disability and the more individualistic production-based values of the American mainstream. In that context, it is hard to judge the "philosophical congruity" of a suicide decision. For example, Elizabeth Bouvia led a full and colorful life as a young woman with cerebral palsy. Was it consistent with her values to accept herself and her life with a disability? Or was it consistent with her values to withdraw from life at age 26 because of her disability? Quite possibly, she, like other minority individuals raised in the majority culture, experienced value conflict. Criteria for rational suicide offer little guidance in sorting out these life complexities.

## Impact on Others

The criteria builders are not in agreement on this dimension. Some stress the importance of not involving loved ones in the suicide; others recommend that significant others be consulted for their agreement. Still others stress that suicide should not harm others.

*Problems*  People with disabilities often have complicated ambivalent relationships with loved ones. Two years ago, I interviewed disabled adults about their recollections of childhood. Many told of being scapegoated as the family burden. It was surprising and painful to hear the invalidating messages some disabled persons heard from genuinely loving family members.

Unlike most nondisabled people, persons with extensive disabilities are often encouraged to believe that, far from damaging their loved ones, their death can be a gift. That conviction is confirmed when loved ones accept the suicide decision and, in some cases, help make arrangements for the dying. The assent of family or friends to one's self-destruction may be one of the most potent of all the forces pushing people with disabilities to carry out ideas of suicide.

## ☐  Using False Autonomy to Rationalize Suicide

Respecting autonomy is not simply accepting at face value whatever a mentally competent adult says regardless of extenuating circumstances. If forced to choose between the lesser of evils or to act in an irrational situation, competent persons make choices they do not prefer. If we are socially responsible, we must do the hard work of listening to and investigating more deeply the wishes of such individuals and helping them secure authentic choices.

Society could create a massive conflict of interest by sanctioning rational suicide for people with extensive, costly disabilities. After withholding the support and options that allow us genuine self-determination, will society offer us the single "choice" that forecloses all other choices? Finding ways to change social values and practices so that people with disabilities can pursue lives of quality is hard. Rationalizing that our suicides are rational may be temptingly easier.

Just people must refuse to view suicide as more acceptable for some groups (e.g., people with irreversible disabilities) than others based on judgments about quality of life. "Right-to-die" proponents often propose this solution: give competent adults the right to decide *for themselves* the quality of their lives and how they wish to die. The reality is, Americans simply will never abide by such decisions without screening them through biases and value judgments. The American Civil Liberties Union (ACLU), for example, has opposed the idea of allowing prisoners on death row the right to suicide, arguing that their limited freedoms and the duress of their circumstances preclude autonomous decision making about death. Although many disability rights activists feel that those arguments apply equally to people with disabilities, the ACLU has nonetheless vigorously supported the requests to die of Elizabeth Bouvia and other nonterminal persons with disabilities.

# ☐ Conclusion

Some of us with extensive permanent disabilities have been fortunate enough to glimpse what is possible for all of us. Bolstered by adequate economic resources and the affirmation of family and friends, we have withstood the assault of prejudice, weathered discrimination, and resisted the forces that limit our life choices. We have been offered the time and support necessary to grow comfortable with wheelchairs, respirators, and other clever devices that frighten the uninitiated; we see they empower us. We have learned to accept assistance as a matter-of-fact aspect of being human, not as an indignity.

It saddens us to realize that support for our lives depends on good fortune instead of social commitment. It frightens us to find that our basic rights to live and learn and work are increasingly questioned as socially burdensome. When we remember that, concurrently, we are being singled out as a group whose dying makes more sense than the dying of people who function more typically, it seems like a bad dream. Unfortunately, we know it is real. We are awakening to the fact that after years of struggle to win equal citizenship, the labeling of our suicides as rational may be the most dangerous form of discrimination we have ever faced.

Karen Hwang

# Rational Suicide and the Disabled Individual: Self-Determination Versus Social Protection

Can a disabled person make a rational decision to commit suicide?

Much has been written, both for and against this idea, by people from many different disciplines. Only a small amount of this material, however, has actually come from disabled individuals themselves. Because this is an issue that could have profound implications on our lives, whether we are disabled or not, it is only fitting that people living with severe permanent disabilities also have a voice in the debate. To be sure, I have never considered myself a disability rights advocate, nor do I profess to be an expert in rehabilitation (except from that which I experienced firsthand). Therefore, the opinion expressed in this chapter is mine alone. However, having lived with a disability for over 10 years, and having interacted with other people with disabilities, I can only trust that my own perspective is not so isolated that it will fail to resonate with other members of the disabled community.

## ☐ Defining Terms

Before we go any further, we need to define our terms. I think most people will agree that the term *rational* involves the application of reason toward the appraisal of a current situation and the evaluation of future options and consequences. *Suicide,* too, seems self-evident enough: literally, the killing of the self. Yet even this definition opens itself up to a wide range of interpretations. Should we always consider it, as some psychologists suggest, an annihilation of the self, an expression of anger in its most self-destructive form (Colt, 1991)? Or can we make a case for rational suicide-that is, a desire for death that is independently attained, stable over time, in accordance with the person's basic values, and free from any perceptual inaccuracies or financial motivations? These criteria are similar to those outlined by Battin (1991).

Our current cultural antipathy toward suicide is largely an outgrowth of the Western Christian "sanctity of life" ethic, albeit with psychological rather than theological justifications. In recent times, however, the unconditional acceptance of this position is beginning to give way to new "quality of life" considerations. The quality of life position does allow that there may be certain cases in which an individual's circumstances are so intolerable that suicide may actually be a sane and dignified option. Because of medical advances, more people than ever are surviving and living longer with permanent, sometimes severe, disabilities. Yet within these ranks there may be certain people who do not wish to continue living, and so for this small subset of individuals we must ask ourselves whether or not the desire to end one's life can ever come as the thoughtful result of reasoned judgment, or whether all thoughts of suicide need be, simply by definition, evidence of some form of impaired judgment.

If viewed in this light, I feel that the answer to the question cannot be anything but the former—that people with disabilities can make a rational decision to commit suicide—simply because denying this possibility does not account fully for the wide range of individual differences among people with disabilities, severely underrates the impact of such factors as intractable pain or physical incapacitation on an individual's quality of life, and is much too unrealistic and patronizing in its presumption that people with disabilities are incapable of making rational decisions regarding their own lives.

## ☐ Self-Determination Versus Social Protection

For a person with a disability, such as myself, this paternalism comes as no surprise; rather, I see it simply as another manifestation of a social mindset that in many ways has not ventured terribly far from the Victorian age in its view of disabled individuals as mentally and physically feeble, in need of protective asylums. The idea that disabled people are incapable of making reasoned decisions to end their lives strikes me as no different from the idea that disabled people are unable to make rational choices to live independently, raise families, or otherwise conduct any other activity that involves thinking for ourselves. Actually, most people with disabilities are just as capable as nondisabled people of assessing their lives and of making rational decisions to live or die. In recent years, the disabled population has made great strides in declaring themselves worthy of political, social, and economic self-determination; accordingly, we also need to respect that integrity with regard to existential matters of life and death.

Human behavior should never be treated like chemistry or physics. In the physical sciences we can be sure of predictability. Create a certain set of conditions and the consequences will always be the same, and a general set of laws can thus be described. In areas concerning human thought and action, however, no two sets of conditions are ever exactly the same, so the same consequences can never be exactly duplicated. Because determining human thought and behavior is not an exact science, we must evaluate each individual on his or her own unique terms. To acknowledge rational suicide, then, is to have respect for individual differences—not between disabled and nondisabled people per se, but among disabled people themselves. I would submit that a reasoned decision to end one's own life rather than continue living with a permanent disability, although unlikely, is nevertheless possible, even if a person is receiving the best care, with no financial pressures, and in the company of supportive, loving family and friends.

It would certainly be unrealistic to discount the physical symptoms of many disabilities as rational bases for suicide. Possibly one of the most compelling of these is chronic intractable pain. Pain is individual in severity, duration, and character, but persistent, overwhelming amounts can greatly affect a person's quality of life (Segatore, 1994). Constant pain also depletes the brain's endorphins, thereby hindering the body's capacity to deal naturally with further pain. Because there is so much variation in the way pain manifests itself, understanding and treating it has been difficult. Courses of treatment generally used for pain associated with progressive, terminal conditions obviously are ineffective, because they do not take long term effects into consideration. Factors such as tolerance, addiction, and narcotic side effects are just as devastating to otherwise medically stable patients. Although new medical therapies are being developed so that the symptoms of chronic pain can be alleviated, many sufferers continue to find no relief.

Even without a universally recognizable motivator such as pain, which everyone has experienced at some point or another, a particular disability may involve an entire constellation of symptoms and complications that are not readily apparent to an outside observer. Long-term ventilator use, for instance, involves an array of related effects that go far beyond the inability to breathe independently, such as the constant discomfort of a tracheotomy tube, need for frequent suctioning to clear the airway of fluid buildup, and increased susceptibility to infection that may result in more frequent hospitalizations. By the same token, constant nausea, incontinence, confinement to bed, or the prospect of becoming a burden to family or community may be so contrary to an individual's values that a permanent state of living under these conditions would be intolerable. The act of suicide may be the individual's ultimate statement of autonomy against a body that has gone completely out of his or her control. I am by no means suggesting that physical pain or incapacitation need necessarily be considered sufficient factors in and of themselves to constitute grounds for suicide in all cases. The psychological impact of physical stressors, however, should never be ignored or underestimated by third parties evaluating a desire for suicide.

Of course, psychological evaluations are, and should be, necessary to weed out those who truly are suffering from distorted perceptions or from temporary depression, but it is undoubtedly wishful thinking to assume that all disabled persons requesting suicide are operating under an impairment in judgment of one form or another. And it would certainly be a mistake for mental health practitioners and suicide prevention specialists to approach disabled people with such preconceived biases about all suicide requests (Battin, 1991). Disabled clients who no longer wish to go on living will refrain from discussing those feelings during counseling or shy away altogether from using mental health services, if they believe that their ideas will not be validated. Being treated as emotionally disturbed could be further devastating to the self-concepts of people who feel that their minds are the only things left within their control. Recognizing that rational suicide is at least a possibility is necessary in order to ensure that suicide requests from disabled individuals are treated in a humane and respectful way. Without first establishing that level of trust, the opportunity for providing further help of any sort is lost.

There is also what I call the "coercion" argument—the idea that suicide requests by individuals with disabilities are a result of society's devaluation of disability, and the internalization of those negative attitudes by those individuals themselves. So pervasive is the incidence of discrimination and victimization in our culture, the argument goes, that coercion is a factor in every request for suicide, even if the individual is unaware of it (Colt, 1991). I find proponents of this idea not unlike those certain radical feminists who equate all heterosexual consensual sex with rape. Granted, the psychological coercion argument may apply in some cases, but it should never be used as grounds for the outright dismissal of rational suicide as a possibility. If coercion is a factor, the evaluator should be prepared to identify the specific areas of coercion or distorted perceptions. If the problem is that evaluating bodies lack a proper perspective on what life after a disability is like, then one possible suggestion might be to involve other qualified disabled people in the evaluation process.

The language of this argument is especially disturbing because it explicitly fosters victimization. Encouraging members of any minority group to think of themselves solely in terms of discrimination, devaluation, and oppression only results in reinforcing feelings of helplessness and vulnerability. By convincing people with disabilities that they are powerless and therefore need to be protected, advocates of this position relegate them to the status of children. Under this model, disabled individuals who express a wish to die are doubly stigmatized as victims of both external discrimination and internal psychopathology. In other words, they are not in charge of themselves and should not be allowed to assume control of themselves—that is, until they have altered their perspectives to reflect ones that meet a sufficient level of social acceptability.

What we need to keep in mind is that attitudes toward suicide are by-and-large culture-dependent, so suicide in itself cannot be used as proof of mental illness. Furthermore, for those who claim that affirming any instance of suicide involving disabled individuals is a form of discrimination, I submit that the denial of individual differences among people with disabilities is an equal or greater form of discrimination. Acknowledging too few alternatives cannot help but paint disabled individuals as stereotypes. Far from affirming the dignity and worth of individual self-determination, proponents of this position still would rather we abdicate control of our minds, bodies, and lives to those who want to protect us from ourselves. However, given the choice, most of the disabled people to whom I have spoken would choose self-determination over this kind of protection.

All other things being equal, it is quite possible that simply acknowledging the validity of a suicide wish may actually enhance a person's quality of life, by reassuring the individual that an end is available at some future point—should it become necessary—and by removing the feelings of guilt, shame, and helplessness that may accompany the desire. This is closely related to a psychological concept called *locus of control*. The principle seems self-evident: the more control we feel we have over our lives, the better we feel about ourselves. Choice empowers and enhances life.

Perhaps the ultimate reason we need to support the idea of rational suicide is a moral one. If we are not allowed the right to define the terms by which we want to live (or perhaps not to live), then we lose an essential quality of what defines us as human. The "value" of life should not be so cheapened as when it is extended past the point at which it is no longer treasured or desired. From this perspective, the choice must be that of the person living the life. Someone who wants to go on living should be able to have access to the widest possible range of resources in order to do so in a fulfilling and dignified manner. A person who does not, because illness or disability has rendered his or her circumstances intolerable, should be awarded the same respect.

# ☐  Medical Ethics and Other Gray Areas

Nowhere is the right to die issue more likely to be hotly debated than in situations in which patients and doctors disagree regarding treatment. Medical science has advanced to the point at which more people are living longer and doing so with a wider range of disabilities. Yet, at the same time, the technological advances of medicine have led to increased specialization among medical practitioners and, with this specialization, there is legitimate concern that doctor–patient attitudes are changing as a result. Physicians often seem more focused on treating the disease, condition, or syndrome than on respecting the overall integrity, values, and goals of the patient (Nuland, 1994). Doctors today, particularly specialists, are less likely to have been personally acquainted with the patient for a great length of time. And yet they are, and will continue to be, the ones who make decisions regarding most patient treatment.

For a disabled patient, it is conceivable that a decision to end one's life may come in the form of refusing lifesaving or life-extending medical intervention. Treatment refusals, especially those made by people with nonterminal conditions, are troubling to healthcare practitioners because they challenge the historic commitment of the medical profession to the preservation of life. They also question practitioners' personal views of themselves as authoritative yet benevolent caregivers. For any patient, demonstrating mental competency when refusing life-sustaining treatment is not an easy business. At times, competency evaluations can sound like "catch-22" nightmares. Patients have the right to refuse lifesaving treatment if they can prove they are mentally competent—but, because no sane person would refuse treatment to save his or her life, a patient who refuses treatment could not by definition be competent. Thus, doctors may be given license to force treatment, often with accompanying dosages of antidepressants or sedatives. Indeed, if the patient demonstrates any sort of ambivalence, it is invariably interpreted as evidence of either incompetency or indecision. Our definitions of sanity, being based on average conditions, do not take into account that it may be a perfectly sane response to wish to die in some extreme situations.

Reidy and Crozier (1991) have found that stereotypic attitudes (i.e., interpreting treatment refusal as a sign of emotional turmoil) are often unfounded in rehabilitation, and that teams in fact tend to overestimate the incidence and intensity of depressive responses to disability. If we were to rule out the possibility that disabled people can choose death rationally, this could set a dangerous precedent with regard to the rights of disabled patients to refuse medical treatment. At the very least, such a position would actually result in exactly the kind of discrimination that it is purported to oppose. By assuming that disabled patients are more subject to coercive pressure and internalized negative attitudes—and therefore less likely to be behaving rationally and independently in refusing treatment—doctors would in fact be imposing a double standard of mental competency when evaluating requests for nontreatment from disabled patients.

In short, protecting the putative interests of a particular group should never be used as grounds for overruling any one individual's right to refuse treatment. For if one individual may be compelled to accept treatment, then so may others—and such a principle could be applied to require treatment for any member of any identifiable group. Further extension of this principle would completely vitiate any patient's right to refuse treatment at all. Rather, as ethicist Howard Levine (1986) points out, "The best way to protect the rights of a group is by protecting the rights of the individual group members" (p. 159).

For example, many in the medical, legal, and psychological professions already do acknowledge that some requests for ventilator removal by quadriplegic patients are, and ought to be, treated as decisions resulting from careful and sound judgment (Maynard, 1991). Healthcare practitioners who automatically treat every such request as a symptom of emotional distress do just as great a disservice as those who unquestioningly accede. Those who misinterpret a thoughtful request as an expression of temporary depression risk trivializing the request and degrading the doctor–patient relationship into a battle of competing wills. On the other hand, it is possible that granting patients some control over their lives by recognizing the right to disconnect might even change their outlooks in the long run.

In addition, I have seen many requests for ventilator removal come within the first few weeks of a disabling injury, while patients are still in the critical-care phase. Sometimes this happens because patients who may have the capacity to breathe independently at some later point feel pressured to take action to end their lives while they are still dependent on a machine. Although we may argue that these particular patients are not acting rationally, there would undoubtedly be fewer such requests if patients were aware that the possibility of rational suicide (including aid-in-dying) could be addressed at a future time.

Before acceding to a wish for treatment refusal, medical and legal professionals should look to the reasons and origin underlying the request and obviously should attempt to address whatever medical or environmental stressors may be contributing to a treatable, reactive depression, if such a diagnosis applies. However, if a person has tested life after optimal rehabilitation or has thoughtfully considered all the outcomes and can make a responsible decision to end his or her life, then these goals can be seen as consistent with those of the medical profession.

## Social Policy Implications

Many advocates for the disabled are extremely insecure with the idea of rational suicide because it completely undercuts the assumption that, because life with a disability is still inherently worthwhile, quality of life issues can generally more or less be resolved by combating societal attitudes and improving access to physical, social, and financial resources. By contrast, every time a Dr. Kevorkian makes the news by aiding a sick or disabled patient in committing suicide, it serves only to send a message to society that a life of disease or disability is "a fate worse than death." This then leads to the "slippery slope," on which the legitimization of rational suicide begins the decline to the mass extermination of the old and frail, as was the case in Nazi Germany. Yet ethicist Peter Singer (1994) has found no evidence to substantiate the slippery slope in the Netherlands, where rational suicide is widely recognized by the medical community. Our society places a high value on individual autonomy. If the commercial success of Derek Humphry's (1991a) suicide manual *Final Exit* is any indication, the majority of people in this country do appear to support maximum control of individuals over their bodies. If we allow the few who choose to die the right to do so quietly, and with dignity, we can then concentrate on shifting public attention back toward addressing the needs of the many more who choose to live.

Of course, society would be sorely lacking if disabled individuals were offered the option of suicide—assisted or unassisted—without first having assessed their needs in other areas. Ideally, no disabled person should ever have to resort to suicide because of inadequate healthcare, economic coercion, or social discrimination, or so that their families can collect on life insurance. Nevertheless, it is a sad fact that many people with disabilities are denied the social resources to live in a dignified manner. National and state policies regarding supportive income and medical insurance discourage productive employment. In this case, suicide may be a perfectly rational response to a system that fails to provide them with the supports they need (Batavia, 1991).

Perhaps the case of Larry McAfee, an institution-bound quadriplegic who filed a court petition in 1989 to commit suicide by disconnecting his ventilator, can serve as an illustration of how acknowledging the right to suicide need not be seen as inconsistent with the goals of disability rights (Maynard, 1991). The Georgia Supreme Court did grant McAfee's right to die, while at the same time the case attracted the attention of various independent-living advocates, who were able to provide him with job training and the resources to move out of the nursing home. Eventually McAfee changed his mind about disconnecting his ventilator. Whether this change of heart was a result of the sudden change in his environmental conditions or because McAfee had finally found legal reassurance that he had ultimate control over his life and death, I believe that this outcome could not have occurred without the achievement of both objectives.

# ☐ Conclusion

I am not denying that there is urgent need to address the social, political, and economic barriers to full self-determination so that all people with disabilities can have the means to live fulfilling and dignified lives. I am not denying the presence of discrimination and its potential consequences on human affect and behavior. But at the same time, we must not allow ourselves to become immersed in a culture of victimization. If we have learned anything from the experience of other minorities, it is that true social inclusion will never be achieved by playing it safe and staying within our own protected sphere. We must empower ourselves to confront discrimination on our own terms, rather than relying on paternalistic third parties to decide what is good for us. To this end, the acknowledgment that some disabled persons may, after careful thought and consideration, choose not to continue living should be seen not as a devaluation of all experiences of disability, but as a recognition that we are all individuals of differing backgrounds and values, and deserving of the right as individuals to determine the course of our lives and deaths.

**26**

CHAPTER

John L. McIntosh

# Arguments Against Rational Suicide: A Gerontologist's Perspective

Although it is my contention and general orientation that the prevention of elderly suicide is desirable, there is anything but total agreement regarding suicide prevention. Arguments and concerns regarding a right to suicide have been advanced by both advocates and opponents. Our society permits the existence of groups that attempt to facilitate or assist those who wish to commit suicide (e.g., the Hemlock Society) and even the offering of workshops conveying how to commit suicide or assist others in their suicides. At the same time, hundreds of communities across the country have suicide prevention agencies (a national directory is maintained by the American Association of Suicidology). Public opinion polls (e.g., Gallup Poll, 1991) suggest that healthy individuals do *not* have a moral right to commit suicide (80% = No, 16% = Yes), nor do those who are a heavy burden on their family (61% = No, 33% = Yes). However, these same respondents indicate that those in great pain (66% = Yes, 29% = No) and incurable disease (58% = Yes, 36% = No) *do* have a moral right to commit suicide. In addition, attitudinal research investigations (e.g., Deluty, 1989) suggest that people find suicide more acceptable when the person's precipitating illness is cancer and when the person is elderly.

This chapter presents arguments against rational suicide. A related topic, physician-assisted suicide, is not addressed specifically, but it is argued here that among several basic issues, a fundamental and necessary condition of physician-assisted suicide is the decision's rationality. Therefore, the arguments presented here are simultaneously applicable to that portion of the physician-assisted suicide debate as well. Detailed writings about the moral, rational, legal, ethical, and philosophical aspects of suicide are available for the reader wishing more information (e.g., Battin, 1995; Battin & Maris, 1983; McIntosh, 1985, chapter 8). For the present discussion, *rational suicide* refers to a self-inflicted death that results from a conscious, deliberate decision by the individual. Further, the decision-making process must be unimpaired by physiological

**188**

or psychological impairment, as well as coercion or the influence of others, and be made with full consideration and awareness of all options available.

To note what may seem obvious, it should be made clear that addressed here is only the issue of suicide. That is, related topics surrounding prolongation of life by extraordinary means (i.e., life-support machines such as respirators), and individuals who are in comas or other circumstances in which they cannot speak for themselves but may have a living will, are not addressed. These issues are, granted, not entirely distinct from those of rational or assisted suicide, but I feel they are different enough, and cloud the issue of suicide sufficiently, so as to be excluded from this discussion (and be left for considerations of other, larger contexts of euthanasia).

## ☐   Religion-Based Arguments

One of the oldest sets of general arguments against suicide includes those that derive largely from religious traditions and judgments. Those arguments typically state that the sanctity of life prevents its taking by anyone, including the self; or that our lives belong not to ourselves but rather to God, who alone can decide when they will end; or that suicide is a sin, which often carries with it codified ramifications (such as denial of burial rights or of burial in consecrated ground). Although these arguments are not dismissed entirely or considered irrelevant to this discussion, they are not the ones around which philosophical or psychological debate has predominantly centered. On the other hand, such arguments may have particular relevance and serve as deterrents for older adults who might contemplate suicide, given the life-long higher levels of religiosity and religious involvement among the current cohorts of older adults compared to current cohorts of young people (i.e., younger cohorts).

## ☐   Right to Die/Suicide Arguments

An essential and key idea presented by advocates of elderly suicide advances a "right to die," a "right to self-determination," and "death with dignity" (e.g., Bromberg & Cassel, 1983; Portwood, 1978). Several arguments surrounding the "right" to suicide and the concept of "rational" suicide have been advanced. Although not often presented as an argument, it can be contended that there is no *right* to commit suicide. Kass (1993) argues in fact that "[t]here is no firm philosophical or legal argument for a 'right to die' " (p. 34). Because the right to suicide or death often implies a right to a pain-free existence, Maris (1982b) points out that there are no guarantees that life will be easy or painless. Indeed, there are no such guarantees about dying either. These elements are part of the unpredictable "human condition," just as the aging process is part of that condition, which requires struggle and adaptation. Harsh conditions do not, therefore, excuse or legitimize suicide.

## ☐   Rational Suicide/Depression/Cognitive Arguments

Perhaps the most discussed of these arguments suggests that suicide at any age is not, or is rarely, "rational" (e.g., Maris, 1982b). Some have argued that the suicidal person may be mentally ill, most often depressed, particularly among the old. Research findings suggest that depression underlies two-thirds or more of the suicides of late life (e.g., Gurland & Cross, 1983). Depression may cloud judgment and affect reasoning abilities. A characterization often made in this regard is that depressed and suicidal individuals have difficulty recognizing or generating alternative solutions to their problems (what Shneidman (1985) referred to as *cognitive constriction* and *dichotomous thinking*). As Brandt (1975) suggests, they may fail to realize their *best* solution. To this extent, therefore, suicide may represent not a rational choice weighed against all possible alternatives, but only a choice from among few, not necessarily representative, alternatives.

This factor, constriction of cognition, is particularly important for older adults. Despite the general maintenance of cognitive functioning in late life, it has long been established (e.g., Botwinick, 1973) that older adults have a tendency to take fewer risks in problem-solving and often may display what has been characterized as cognitive rigidity or cautiousness. Therefore, older adults may be more prone to generate fewer responses to problems or to choose those with less risk involved. The general tendency among older adults may combine in a particularly dangerous fashion with cognitive constrictionistic tendencies typically associated with depression and suicidality. In the case of suicidal elderly individuals, therefore, these mental sets may particularly limit the number of solutions considered while directly enhancing the perception of suicide as an attractive and final choice among the few options actually contemplated. Informed decision making cannot occur if complete and accurate information on alternatives is unavailable to, or not considered by, the individual.

It has also been argued that the suicidal are nearly always ambivalent (Shneidman, 1985). That is, they wish to die, but at the same time they want very much to live. They simply may not see any way that continuing to live, in their present circumstances, is possible. Ambivalence would argue against the absolute, rational, and clear choice being made. The irreversibility of suicide is also noted as an argument against rational suicide. Would the individual choose suicide at a later time? Might the situation improve, given some time? Travis (1991) argues that no one is capable of knowing when his or her life is bad enough or sufficiently meaningless to end it.

Another aspect of these arguments is emphasized by Shneidman (1993). He argues that the cause of suicide is intolerable psychological pain. Determination that pain has reached a level of individual intolerance leads to feelings of hopelessness and the decision to choose suicide because no other solutions are recognized to exist. The pessimism of the suicidal individual produces a view of the future as simply a continuation of his or her present or worse levels of pain and unending suffering. If psychological pain can be lessened, even a small amount in many cases, the individual will choose to live with the psychological pain rather than choose to die. In this context, the clinical message is that we need not entirely eliminate the problems of the individual to lessen suicide risk and wishes. We simply need to lessen the pain load of the person to one that is within her or his personally tolerable level. The goal, therefore, should not be to make the option of death by suicide easier, but rather to confront and lessen psychological pain levels. In the case of older adults, there are likely to be several sources of pain, involving physiological, psychological, and social aspects. Thus, although psychological pain derives from several factors for elders, these multiple sources, at the same time, represent a number of separate targets for pain reduction.

# ☐ Social/Societal Arguments

Although the advocates of a right to suicide suggest that the suicide affects only the one who dies, it has been argued that when a person commits suicide, society loses any benefits he or she might provide to others or that others might gain by providing for the suicidal person (Travis, 1991). Society also loses any skills and special knowledge that the individual might possess. Simply because a person is elderly or retired does not mean that he or she has nothing to offer society and that his or her death is not a loss. In addition, people have obligations to others through social relationships. The diminishment of the social network of older adults is rarely to the point of complete isolation and noninvolvement with others. Further, the act of suicide *does* affect others. The survivors of suicide have often been seen to feel social stigma and perhaps guilt related to the death, and suicide as the mode of death may complicate the grief process in a negative fashion (Dunne, McIntosh, & Dunne-Maxim, 1987). The spouse, adult children, grandchildren, and friends of older adults are potential survivor–victims of elderly suicide.

Siegel and Tuckel (1984-1985) argue that the legal sanctioning of suicide (which is the goal for which most advocates of rational suicide campaign) would undermine societal norms and eliminate clear guidelines in decision making, leading to disorientation and anxiety among those faced with making the decision. Others (e.g., Battin, 1980) have argued that accepting rational suicide may lead to some individuals, and especially the old, being "manipulated" into suicide, perhaps against their will, because they feel obligated (i.e., a duty) to do so in some circumstances. The result then would be to actually *lessen* free choice.

Similarly, Moody (in Battin, McKinney, Kastenbaum, & Moody, 1984) worries that the acceptance of suicide as rational will lead us down the slippery slope to where it is difficult to draw clear delineation regarding candidacy to commit sanctioned suicide. For instance, "Suicide *on the grounds of* old age, not simply during the period of old age" (Moody, 1984, p. 65, emphasis original) becomes one concern. All disabled or elderly persons under such circumstances could be labeled as living a "meaningless" life, and the same might be argued for those who are dependent on others (Post, 1990). Therefore, the issues of criteria, manipulation, and duty become even more problematic. Widespread acceptance of suicide may even encourage suicides that are *not* rational (Mayo, 1980).

# ☐ Argument of Older Adults as Candidates or Beneficiaries

Suicide by the old is often accepted, and the elderly are seen as the primary candidates for rational suicide, partially because they are the group that dies in our modern society, and partially because of ageism—the devaluing of older adults based purely on their age (Conwell, 1993; Moore, 1993). An important issue in this regard is limited economic and medical resources. The primary advocate of the need to control healthcare costs, even if it means rationing care based on age, is Callahan (1987). He argues that limits on the allocation of resources must be set in a society that is aging and in which the elderly utilize and incur a disproportionate amount of healthcare and its costs. His proposals have led to much, often heated, debate (e.g., Barry & Bradley, 1991; Callahan, 1993; Homer & Holstein, 1990; Hunt, 1993).

Battin (1994, pp. 58–79) looked specifically at the issue of older adults, suicide, and rationing in these cost-conscious times. She argues that two options are either to cut costs by denying treatment or to do so by encouraging suicide among the old. The decisions are difficult indeed if these are in fact the only options. This is reminiscent of the world portrayed by Matheson (1969) in his short story "The Test." An elderly man prepares for an examination required every 5 years of all older adults. The test examines a wide range of cognitive, psychomotor, and common tasks of daily living. Failure results in the government putting the elder to death. As this man prepares for the test it becomes obvious he will not pass. Rather than submit himself to the inevitable, he obtains medications from a sympathetic druggist, goes to his room the night before his scheduled exam, and takes the pills, which kill him in his sleep. The extremes of such practices are unsettling, even in the context of fiction.

In a broader sense, the acceptance of suicide among the elderly, simply because they are long-lived and have fewer years left in their lives, leads to a devaluing of the elderly as a group and of the years of life remaining to them. The old are seen as expensive burdens, who contribute little; this is a movement backward in time with respect to ageistic practices and societal attitudes.

Additionally, those who are not old may evaluate the years of late life, along with the chronic physical conditions that many elders possess, and determine that the value of life itself under such conditions is low. Younger persons, or even those of adult ages who do not suffer from debilities or chronic health problems, may fear such conditions and question why anyone would want to live under such circumstances. This devalues the life of such elders and calls into question their decisions and judgment. Again, the outcome may create an obligation to commit suicide under certain late-life conditions, and the assumption of selfishness among older adults who do not choose to end their lives when these conditions prevail. Such elders may feel they are being directed to spare themselves the pain and struggle and to minimize the emotional and economic burdens on their families. In any event, such older adults who do not wish to die may find their options lessened rather than expanded by the societal acceptance of rational suicide. The person to whom suicide appears rational is central in this context.

## ☐ Terminally Ill Individuals as Candidates

Although the terminally ill are most often presented as the example of individuals who rationally choose suicide (and assisted suicide), Siegel and Tuckel (1984-1985) note that cancer patients seem to have no elevated suicide risk compared with the general population. The terminally ill who wish to commit suicide may not be as representative of elderly suicides in general as is often suggested. If rational suicide were widely and legally available, the terminally ill elderly would not likely be the modal utilizers of this "right." In addition, the availability of a hospice for the terminally ill seems more appropriate, if indeed pain management and psychological support are the factors motivating the terminally ill to suicide. Also, it is clear that better education of physicians regarding current pain-management techniques ("comfort care") is needed, along with an alteration of attitudes about the appropriateness, aggressiveness, and dosages of pain medications in the case of terminal illness. The comments made in this chapter regarding psychological pain, and the benefits of even small decreases in levels, could also be applied here for physical pain as a factor in suicide (see McIntosh, Santos, Hubbard, & Overholser, 1994, pp. 106–108).

Even if the terminally ill are considered for rational suicide, research suggests that the desire to die in the terminally ill is highly related to the existence of clinical depression, and that this wish to die decreases over time (e.g., Brown, Henteleff, Barakat, & Rowe, 1986; Chochinov et al., 1995). Those who contemplate suicide are only a subset of the terminally ill who wish to die, but the additional relationship between depression and suicidal ideation and behavior further complicates the issue of rationality of thought. Effective therapies, both psychological and medical, are widely available for depression. The combination of cognitive factors that may affect reasoning, the transient nature of the wish to die or commit suicide, and the availability of treatment for depression and pain, lessen the immediacy of and logical progression to rational suicide decisions by the terminally ill.

# ☐ Questions Raised and Conclusions

Finally, the issue of ethics of rational suicide in late life raises numerous questions. Who is a candidate for rational suicide? Are there age criteria, diagnosis limitations, or time frames? Discussion regarding criteria for rational suicide candidacy (see Battin, 1995, pp. 131–155; Werth & Cobia, 1995) promises to be long and contentious, as it has already been in the case of physician-assisted suicide, in which the criteria for rational decision making (often otherwise undefined, with the exception of the terms "competence" or "unclouded judgment") are virtually universal (e.g., de Wachter, 1992; Orentlicher, 1992; Quill, Cassel, & Meier 1992). Do physicians treating the old and terminally ill receive enough training about depression and mental health to recognize their presences or absences and respond appropriately (see Conwell & Caine, 1991, p. 1101)? Should rational suicide be legalized for the elderly or other groups? If so, should it proceed on a state-by-state basis or should the laws be national in scope? If legalized and accepted, how do we safeguard against abuses and how do we draw the line at appropriate versus inappropriate candidates? The questions are many but the answers are not easy or clear.

It is obvious that debate of this volatile issue has only begun. As in any issue with highly polarized viewpoints and case examples illustrating the extreme end points, there are also the middle ground and the less than clear-cut examples. I believe that acceptance or legalization of rational suicide at this time would benefit few, while potentially harming and opening the possibility for coercion, manipulation, and feelings of obligation among many, especially the old, disabled, dependent, and terminally and chronically ill. The ethics of suicide deserve to be further addressed, and the moral dilemma of suicide remains an unresolved issue.

CHAPTER

Erdman B. Palmore

# Suicide Can Be Rational for Senescent or Terminal Patients

Because the concept of "rational suicide" is relatively new (fewer than a couple of decades old), there has been little research and discussion about it either in the mass media or in scholarly books and journals. There has been even less discussion of how it applies to senescent or terminal patients. This chapter is an attempt to point out that the arguments for rational suicide apply with particular cogency to senescent or terminal patients, and that arguments against it are especially weak when applied to these patients.

Although I believe that suicide can be rational for adults of all ages, I believe it is most likely to be rational among those with intolerable conditions and short life expectancies because of extreme old age or terminal illness. Recent surveys of professionals and of the public show increasing support for the concept of rational suicide, especially in these cases (Werth & Cobia, 1995).

I first define my terms, then present the arguments for rational suicide among senescent and terminal patients, and then refute the arguments against it. At the end I discuss arguments with special relevance to the subordinate issue of physician-assisted suicide.

## ☐ Definitions

By *suicide* I mean the act of taking one's own life voluntarily and intentionally. This includes physician-assisted suicide but does not include euthanasia, which is the act of killing someone else (in a relatively painless way). Whether euthanasia is ever rational or morally justified is another debate, which should not be confused with the question of rational suicide.

By *rational* I mean based on reason and logic: reasonable. This does not imply that everyone would agree with the reasoning or the decision reached, but that the decision is based on logical reasoning rather than on some emotional impulse or illogical thinking.

I agree with Werth and Cobia's (1995) three criteria for judging whether a decision to suicide is rational or not:

1. The person considering suicide has an unremitting hopeless condition, such as terminal illness, severe physical and / or psychological pain, physically or mentally debilitating and / or deteriorating conditions, or quality of life no longer acceptable to the individual.
2. The person makes the decision as a free choice.
3. The person has engaged in a sound decision-making process including consultation with a mental health professional to assess mental competence (and to exclude treatable depression); a nonimpulsive consideration of all alternatives; consideration of the congruence of the act with one's personal values and of the impact on significant others; and consultation with objective others and with significant others.

By *senescent* I do not mean most people over 65 years of age, because the average 65-year-old can expect another 17 or more years of life, most of which will be active years in reasonably good health. Eighty percent of persons over the age of 65 years are healthy enough to do their normal activities (Palmore, 1988). I am not going to discuss these healthy elders, because I believe age alone is not sufficient to make suicide rational. By *senescent* I mean people of extreme old age with a short life expectancy who have deteriorated so far that they find continued existence worthless or unbearable. Senescent people may not yet be terminal, but they usually die within a few years.

By *terminal patients* I mean patients who are so critically ill that they are expected to die within 6 months.

## ☐  Arguments For Rational Suicide

### They Are Dying Already

This is perhaps the strongest argument for rational suicide among terminal patients. Who can object to ending intractable pain and suffering if the patient is dying already? For terminal patients, the question is not "to be or not to be." They will soon "not be," whether by rational suicide or by painful prolongation of the dying process. In such a case, suicide is simply a speeding up of the dying process that has already begun.

For senescent but not yet terminal patients, the choice may be more difficult because they may have a year or more of life left, and some may choose to endure and "hope against hope" that somehow things will improve. But if they are already invalids, suffering from hopeless diseases such as AIDS, Alzheimer's disease, or terminal cancer, who find their lives miserable and their circumstances intolerable, they may rationally choose to end their misery.

## Death With Dignity

After weighing the "costs and benefits," senescent or terminal patients may rationally decide that death with dignity in a manner and time of their own choosing is preferable to a slow, agonizing, prolonged death in which they suffer all the indignities of loss of control and physical and mental function or become a vegetable.

## Reducing the Costs and Waste of Expensive Medical Resources

Because most of the costs of terminal care, especially among the very old, are borne by Medicare and Medicaid, rational suicide among these patients could substantially reduce the projected deficit in these programs. Thus suicide among senescent and terminal patients might even be considered a patriotic act!

There is now a federal requirement that all hospitals ask patients upon admission if they have a living will and, if they do not, give them information and forms to sign if they wish. This was prompted by a desire to both increase patients' self-determination and reduce costs of useless treatments.

Many medical professionals, in the absence of a living will or other directives to the contrary, feel obligated to do everything possible to prolong the lives of terminal patients regardless of how hopeless the prognosis or how expensive and painful the treatment. These professionals may cite the Hippocratic Oath or fear of malpractice liability as justification for their actions (Kapp, 1991).

One study found that even if there is a living will or relatives do not want to prolong the dying, many medical professionals ignore these wishes and proceed with expensive and extraordinary treatments (SUPPORT Principal Investigators, 1995). One certain way to prevent this is rational suicide.

## Reducing the Emotional and Financial Strain on Family and Friends

Dying patients may rationally decide that the most loving thing they can do for their family and friends is to end, through suicide, the financial strain caused by their nursing care and medication, and the emotional pain resulting from the indignities of the dying process.

## Right to Die

Suicide is now legal in all 50 states. The right to die through suicide is as inalienable a right as the right to live. This right is implied by the First Amendment (freedom of religion) and by other amendments that have been interpreted to guarantee the right to do what one wishes with one's own body (as in the right to refuse medical treatment, have an abortion, and so forth) (Matthews, 1987). This right becomes even more cogent for those who will soon die because of senescence or terminal illness.

# ☐   Arguments Against

I will not review the religious arguments against suicide, because these are discussed by Larue and Barry elsewhere in this book. I only point out that it may be "God's will" for senescent or terminal patients to end their suffering through suicide, because modern theologians generally agree that God is merciful.

## Suffering Is Beneficial

This argument asserts that one should not end suffering through suicide because suffering can be beneficial in some strange way, such as by strengthening character, giving one sympathy for others who suffer, giving one a deeper appreciation for the joys of life, and so forth.

This argument sounds particularly hollow if applied to people who are about to die, such as senescent and terminal patients. Although those who have a normal life left may try to make the best of necessary suffering by looking for the "silver lining," it seems heartless to tell dying people that they must not end their misery through suicide because suffering is good for them.

## Suicide is a Result of Mental Illness

This argument simply asserts that by definition no "normal" person would want to commit suicide, that all suicide is the result of depression or some other mental illness, and therefore that suicide can never be rational (Maris, 1982a). A variant of this argument is that suicidal persons have difficulty recognizing or generating alternative solutions to their problems ("cognitive constriction;" Shneidman, 1985), and therefore suicide is not a rational choice weighed against all possible alternatives (Brandt, 1975).

Although it is true that some suicides result from depression or other mental illness, it is also true that many suicides are committed by persons with no signs of any mental illness, who are completely rational in every way, and who give clear and reasonable explanations for their suicide. This is especially true of senescent and terminal patients because their debilitated conditions, pain, and approaching deaths can be reasonable explanations for committing suicide.

## Suicide Is Irreversible

This argument says that suicide is not rational because it is irreversible and a rational person might choose to live at some later point in time if the situation improves, or a cure is found, or the person feels better.

Although this argument may have merit for persons with normal life expectancy, it seems weak, if not irrelevant, when applied to persons who are already dying. For terminal patients, by definition, there is no hope that the situation will improve or a cure will be found before the person's death.

## Pain Can Be Reduced to Tolerable Levels

Shneidman (1993) argues that suicide is often caused by intolerable pain. He says that with modern drugs and counseling the pain can be reduced or the person's tolerance of pain can be increased so that suicide would no longer be chosen.

Although this is true in some cases, there are also terminal cases in which no amount of drugs, short of enough to cause complete unconsciousness, can control the pain, and no amount of counseling can increase pain tolerance to sufficient levels to prevent the desire for suicide.

## Society Loses the Benefits of the Person's Life

This is the social obligation argument that asserts that because everyone has an obligation to contribute whatever they can to others, suicide robs society of the benefits that the person could contribute if he or she continued to live (Travis, 1991). It is argued that everyone can contribute some skill or special knowledge or at least love as long as they live.

This argument also seems irrelevant to people who are dying and helpless, racked with intolerable pain. Rather than contributing anything to society, they are only draining society's resources. They may rationally decide that the most loving thing they can do for their relatives and friends is to end their strain and upset through suicide. This has been called "altruistic suicide" by Durkheim (1951).

## Acceptance of Rational Suicide Leads to Disorientation and Anxiety

If the concept of rational suicide is generally accepted, some say it would undermine the clear prohibition of suicide and force many people to make the choice between life and death. This would lead to confusion, disorientation, and anxiety as to whether someone has made or is making the right choice.

This argument fails to recognize that, like it or not, suicide is now legal in all 50 states. Therefore many people are already forced to consider that option. Indeed, many philosophers (such as the existentialists) and ethicists argue that the basic question facing everyone all the time is whether to continue living or not. This is especially true for senescent and terminal patients who are facing imminent death.

## Acceptance of Rational Suicide May Lead To Some Persons Being Manipulated into Suicide

Battin (1980) has argued that old and terminally ill patients are especially vulnerable to being pressured against their will to commit suicide because they may be made to feel obligated to do so. Some have called this a kind of ageism in which it is assumed that very old people have little value, consume too much medical care, and therefore should be encouraged to end their lives (Moody, 1984).

Pressuring anyone of any age or condition to commit suicide against her or his will is immoral and almost a contradiction in terms. We have defined suicide as the *voluntary* taking of one's own life. However, to single out the aged and say that theirs can never be a rational suicide is just as much a kind of ageism as is saying that they have an obligation to commit suicide.

On a related topic, healthcare should not be rationed on the basis of old age (Callahan, 1987, 1990). If healthcare must be rationed at all, it should be on the basis of efficacy, prognosis, and urgency, not age. If rational suicide for senescent and terminal patients were more widely accepted, it could substantially reduce the pressures to ration healthcare (see the third "pro" argument).

## The Concept of Rational Suicide Leads Us "Down the Slippery Slope"

Moody (1984) worries that the acceptance of suicide as rational "will lead us down the slippery slope" to where it is difficult to draw the line at which it is clear when someone is a candidate for rational suicide. Post (1990) warns that this could result in *all* disabled, elderly, or otherwise dependent persons being labeled as living "meaningless" lives and therefore being encouraged to commit suicide.

This argument is usually the last refuge of the desperate who can find no convincing argument against a specified behavior (suicide for senescent and terminal patients) but attempt to spread the fear that it could lead to other more terrible behaviors. This is like the argument that we should have prohibition against all alcohol because drinking any amount of alcohol may lead to terrible things like alcoholism, drunken driving, murder, and other crimes. Or that dancing can lead to rape. Or that playing cards can lead to gambling and poverty.

Each specified behavior should be judged on its own merit, rather than on fears about what that behavior might sometimes lead to. Therefore, suicide for senescent and terminal patients should be judged on its own merit rather than on fears that it may lead to encouraging suicide among many other persons.

## ☐  Physician-Assisted Rational Suicide

A subordinate question is whether physicians (or other medical professionals) should be allowed to assist a person to commit rational suicide. If we assume that suicide may be rational in some cases, such as with senescent or terminal patients, then there are several additional arguments to support the legalization of physician assistance.

1. Physicians should have the freedom of conscience to determine if assisted suicide is the most humane treatment available. Restricting physicians' right to relieve pain through assisting in suicide is government interference with medical practice. Physicians may feel an ethical duty toward their senescent or terminal patients to help them end their suffering.
2. Legalizing physician-assisted suicide would decriminalize a practice that is already widespread. Many physicians will admit that they have assisted in a suicide, or they know of other physicians who have done so, usually through making a lethal

dose of drugs available (Back, Wallace, Starks, & Pearlman, 1996). Even more physicians will progressively increase various drugs in attempts to cover pain, even though these doses hasten death.

3. Physician-assisted suicide would reduce the occurrence of botched attempts at suicide and all the problems resulting from such attempts. Many patients do not fear suicide; they only fear failure of an attempt, which would make their condition even more miserable.

4. Assisting suicide of a senescent or terminal patient is consistent with the Hippocratic Oath to "do no harm." It does not harm a terminal patient to help hasten the dying process; indeed, it may be the only way to help some patients relieve their pain. (See the fifth "con" argument.)

5. Fears that physicians might abuse a legal right to assist in rational suicide could be allayed by establishing various criteria for judging whether a suicide is rational or not (such as in the section on definitions in this chapter) and establishing review committees (including psychiatrists to detect temporary depression or other mental illness, social workers to counsel the patient, and so forth), which would rule on the rationality of the request for assistance in suicide.

6. No physician would be forced to assist in suicide. Just as some physicians refuse to perform an abortion because it is contrary to their personal beliefs, physicians could refuse requests to assist in suicide if it is contrary to their beliefs.

# ☐ Conclusion

Despite the relative recency of the concept, rational suicide for senescent or terminal patients is gaining more and more acceptance among healthcare professionals, ethicists, religious leaders, attorneys, sociologists, and the public at large. There are at least five arguments for rational suicide that are especially cogent if applied to senescent and terminal patients. The arguments advanced against rational suicide are weak or not applicable to such patients. There are several additional arguments that support the legalization of physician-assisted suicide in such cases.

The wider acceptance of rational suicide among senescent and terminal patients would have many benefits for the suffering patients, their families, the medical professions, and society in general.

# 28
CHAPTER

Patty Rosen

# A Personal Argument in Favor of Rational Suicide

For as long as I can remember I have believed that any person suffering from a terminal or debilitating illness has the right to end her or his life whenever she or he chooses. My religious and moral beliefs have never interfered with my ability to listen and empathize as patients have pleaded their case to die. I have even made pacts with friends who feel as I do, agreeing that if the need should ever arise, we will help each other die. I have also talked with my children about the right to choose, encouraging them to think about it, discuss it, and come to their own conclusions. Then, in one short year, the subject of assisting the suicide of a terminally ill person was no longer a clinical, abstract one for me. It became very personal and up close. The person dying from a terminal illness was my 26-year-old daughter and she asked me to help her die, and I did. I did not have to assist Jody's death; she was capable of giving herself the pills and swallowing them. But Jody didn't want to die alone. She wanted me there with her, to comfort her, and to make sure she died.

It started with Jody complaining of a severe backache. We were in a new city and did not know any doctors so she ended up going from one doctor to another, telling her extensive medical history, showing them where it hurt, and being told it was "no more than muscle spasms." I knew better. I lived with her and knew she could never sleep, was losing weight at a rapid rate, and the pain was all but consuming her. I'm also a nurse practitioner, well trained in the ways of medicine and disease, and try as I might to intervene with the doctors that saw her, I was dismissed as an "overanxious, naïve mother." So, for over a year, with the pain becoming more and more debilitating, Jody was passed around from doctor to doctor, being called everything from a malingerer to a drug addict. Ironically, the only physician I knew in that area did think something was very wrong with Jody but, because she was in a health-maintenance organization, he could not treat or help her. Finally, in desperation, with Jody barely able to move, I flew her back to our former home in California where the doctors knew us, and the fatal diagnosis was easily and quickly made.

Bone cancer. Invasive bone cancer. From her head to her toes she was filled with bone cancer. And then, the final blow. Her bone cancer was a result of medical neglect.

The failure to do follow-up work on an obvious thyroid goiter, first diagnosed when she was 18 years old, had led her, over a 5-year span, to death's door. "All the bells and whistles were ignored" was how the expert witness put it during the malpractice deposition.

Jody was devastated. Angry that she was dying, and furious that it could have been prevented, all trust in the medical community disappeared and she asked me to take her home. She also remembered when she was working as a nurse's aide in a hospital and saw how patients lost all control over their decision making. Now, heavily sedated and dying, she did not want that to happen to her. I was greatly relieved that she trusted me so completely because I was frantic to take her in my arms and somehow "make it all better." Once home, we took it one day at a time, with Jody drugged and sleeping, and me trying to stay rational and not fall apart. Knowing how emotionally dangerous this entire scenario was to both of us I made sure we always had a psychotherapist available, a third party who could listen and diffuse our anger and anxiety.

Nursing care was needed constantly, 24 hours a day. At her request, as I went about the business of taking care of her, I would struggle to hide my feelings of grief. She had stated, from the beginning, "This is bad enough Mom, and seeing you upset makes me even crazier because I can't do anything to help you." So I would put on my "in control, capable self" persona and never leave her side. At the time I did not realize the emotional toll that was being taken on me as I performed procedure after procedure on Jody. I only knew that I was not going to let anyone ever harm her again. Sometimes, while she was sleeping, I would sneak into her room and listen to her breathing, reassured that she was still alive. The medications for pain never gave her relief from the agony and her face, even when sleeping, always reflected the torture she was enduring. Stuffing tissue in my mouth so she could not hear me sob, I would sit for hours wondering how I would ever be able to endure life without her. But also while she slept, I was alone to do battle with my demons of guilt and blame. I berated myself with "I should have" and "why didn't I?" and "it's all my fault." I was sure, in my grief, that somehow I could have protected her, prevented this, and I had failed. She was going to die and leave me and it was my fault. Desperation overtook my life.

However, I was acutely aware that Jody was trapped. No matter how intolerable my own anguish was, it did not even come close to what Jody was experiencing. A sweet spirit, fully alive and functioning, was encased in a totally bedridden, pain-filled body that barely worked. She was dying. There would not be a miracle. She was not going to get better. I forced myself to stay focused on her. Was she depressed? *No.* Was she sad? *Yes.* Was she angry? *Very.*

Friends and family visited as often as they could tolerate, but seeing Jody ravaged by bone cancer was more than most could bear. Mark, her older brother by a year and a half, and also her soulmate, helped me with her care for as long as he could. The helplessness and hopelessness of the situation all but put Mark out of his mind, a condition that took years to heal. Her father, who also adored her, would visit often, staying until he could no longer contain his grief. Then he would leave, totally bereaved because of what was happening to Jody. Even though divorced, we had always remained well-connected about the children, and in this time of crisis he came through like a champion. He might not have been able to stay by her bedside, but he did make sure that we did not want for anything.

About a month after she had heard the "cancer is going to win" lecture from the less-than-sensitive medical-oncology resident, she called me to her room. "Mom, I've been thinking. Now that I know I'm not going to get any better, I want you to help me die." Although tears were running down her face, Jody stated her request in a calm clear voice. She had always been articulate, candid, and concrete, and dying did not alter those characteristics. I fought my impulse to reach for her. The cancer had pretty much eaten away most of her bones and little tumors sat immediately under her skin, making any contact extremely painful. I had learned the hard way that giving her even a little hug or squeeze resulted in her crying out in even more pain, which totally wiped me out. So, as I prepared to answer her request, I merely sat as close as I could get, fighting back the tears, and tried to match her matter-of-fact demeanor. I could not do it. I lost all my composure, lowered my head, and broke into sobs. I felt Jody's hand stroking my hair. "Mom, I hate this. I'm going to miss you so much." How insane! Jody was dying and she was comforting me! I pulled myself together, gave her a quick, gentle, kiss and got her ready to go to sleep. "Don't worry Jody, I'll help you." A little smile crossed her face. "Thanks Mom."

After that, we did not really talk about her request. She knew that I was working up my courage and I knew she was patiently waiting. And then, another turn for the worst. As I was sitting beside her bed holding something for her to read, she asked, in her calm, matter-of-fact way, "Mom, will you read it to me? I can't see much anymore." A feeling of horror swept over me. Was she going to continue to die slowly, inch-by-inch, system-by-system? I thought back two months prior when I had secretly watched her as she had looked at her reflection in the mirror. Tears streamed down her face as her fingers traced the hollows of her eyes, her gaunt cheek bones, and sinewy neck. A little starving skeleton head had taken the place of her beautiful, well-developed facial features with the startling blue eyes that were now sunk deeply into the abyss of dark circles brought about by enduring the constant, acute pain of bone cancer. I watched as she grieved the loss of her beauty and the loss of her body, wondering how I would ever be able to stand the loss of her.

But I could not let my need to hold on to her cloud my vision of her need to die. She had made a decision, a rational decision, and was at peace with it. I had the task of not allowing my own pain, my own fear of loss, to overwhelm me and minimize the reality of her situation. Jody, already trapped in a barely functioning body, was now going blind. She would only wake for a few minutes to take pain medication, or be bathed, or to endure a painful procedure to keep her bowels open. It just was not worth it. "For what, Mom?" "Mom, how long can you watch me suffer?" I did not try to answer those questions. What could I have said? Was I going to tell her she would get better? That this was temporary? What reason could I give her not to die when she was already dying? She was dying, she knew it, and she was ready. Rational. Calm. Ready.

I would think back to all the conversations about dying I had had with patients who were terminally or chronically ill. They all felt so lonely because they could not talk with any of their family, friends, or doctors in an honest way about wanting to die. After everyone had left they would say to me, "I know they love me but can't they **see** I'm ready to die now? They can go home, visit friends, go to dinner, and all I do is lie here, alone in the hospital, and wait to die," and, "Would it be so horrible if I ended it now?" Just like Jody, those people were also rational, calm, and ready. But they knew and I knew that there was no legal, easy way for them to plan their deaths so I could only listen, hold their hands, and hope that death would be swift.

But now it was my daughter. She had asked and I could do something. However, it was still illegal and she knew it. Therefore, no one could know she had asked me for help in dying, and I could not share my horrific burden of grief for fear that someone would try to stop me. "I should be allowed to talk with my doctor and plan this," Jody would say. "Mom, what if you go to prison? What will happen to you?" Worry made her small face with the sunken eyes of the near-dead take on an incredibly distressed look. Once more, in my most convincing style, I reassured her: "Jody, I'll be okay, aren't I always okay? I'll handle it." Her trust and faith in me was humbling and I was determined not to let her continue in agony because of what might happen to me. I found the idea absurd.

Finally, four months after her request, when I could no longer watch her suffer, choking on my tears I said, "Jody, I'm ready." With those words I felt my mind slip into a far removed quiet place. All I could see was Jody's face, feel her pain, and sense her suffering. She had succeeded in making me experience her dilemma. I called her siblings together for a last goodbye. As we encircled her bed, Jody told us how she would miss us, and hated to leave, and she reassured us by saying, "I'll see you all again," and added "Please tell Daddy I love him." We silently wept and tried to make small talk, while Mark, desperate to give comfort, to touch her when he could not hold her, gently massaged her feet. As I looked around the room at the faces of my four children, the scene took on the unreal feeling of a movie, a terribly sad movie with us acting out the parts. We all understood and supported Jody's decision but we were also being forced to say goodbye. It was an absolutely impossible reality to grasp.

But all was not sad. Jody was so relieved that it was soon going to be over that she was almost giddy with relief. As I put the finishing touches on her last bedtime care, she took my hand and held it for a moment, giving it a little squeeze. Quietly, softly, she said: "Mom, this is one of the happiest days for me. I don't have to wake up in this body again. Thank you Mom." Those words, to this day, as I sit and write this, make me sob with my own pain of loss. I miss her so much.

Halloween's Eve was different that year. At the time of her choosing, Jody calmly swallowed everything I could give her, took a few sips of water, kissed me, said, "See you later Mom," closed her eyes, and went to sleep.

I went into a pure panic. What if I failed? What if she regained consciousness? She would be even worse off, but more than that, I would have failed her. I began giving her all the intravenous medications I could pump into her stilled body. I moaned, sobbed, prayed, and kept pushing the drugs. I was as desperate as I have ever been. Alone in the room, I would hold my breath to see if I could still hear hers. Time became a void. My mind started to play tricks. I would look at her and suddenly think I had made a mistake, that she was not terminally ill but was getting better. I fought the impulse to reach for her, to shake her, or to pick up the phone and call for help. I forced myself to stay in the naked reality of the situation, to look at my daughter's withered frame and cadaver-like skull, and to continue my vigil.

Ten hours after we had started the process, the silence came. She had finally stopped breathing. The year and a half of pain, suffering, rage, and hopelessness had ended. I climbed into her bed and gathered her still body into my arms, finally able to hold her without hurting her. Stroking her hair, rocking her gently, I surrendered to my grief. It was over. Jody was dead. A brave and wise young woman, Jody Lynn Grape, age 26, died October 30, 1986, at 1:30 P.M.

I have never felt guilt or remorse for assisting Jody's passing. It was the ultimate act of love that a mother could do for her suffering, dying child. I am grateful that she trusted me enough to ask, made me feel her anguish, and included me in her dying. And I am grateful that I had the courage to help her. I am also thankful that I had had 15 years of clinical experience as a nurse, psychotherapist, and nurse practitioner (with prescription privileges) before Jody became critically ill. I was better prepared than most people for the experience I shared with my daughter. It is also important that throughout my four children's growing up years we had candidly discussed religion, life choices, death choices, and the freedom to govern one's own life. Little did I know that those discussions had established a firm foundation of communication that was going to prove vital with my terminally ill daughter.

When I talk with people about the assist I hear them say that they never want anyone they love to die. Of course not! The pain, caused by the loss of a loved one, is a death within itself. However, I believe, as Jody believed, that the pain of the sufferer takes precedence over the projected pain of loss by the observers. Remember, the observers are not trapped. The observers are still in control of their destinies. They can still go out to dinner, be with friends, take a walk, or make love. The observers can close the door on the terminally ill person trapped in the bed.

I can bring no better argument for rational suicide then the one presented here. I watched it, lived it, and continue to share it. Jody's request was a rational request. She made her decision independently, following her heart and her spiritual belief. When Jody was only 20, years old, she sent me a tape that I still have. On it she says, through her tears, "Mom, [a friend's elderly mother] just died and I'm so glad. She was miserable but was staying alive for the family. Anyone that is that sick should be allowed to die when they want, not hang on because of family."

Each of us, if we so desire, must have the legal right, when the time comes, to plan the ritual of our own deaths without interference from anyone. The mere idea that people think that they can have control over another adult's decision making is totally unacceptable to me. As Jody believed, I believe that only the individual can identify the quality of life he or she wants to live. It is an intimate, personal, decision. Therefore, when Jody said she wanted to die because the quality of her life was dismal, I could honor her. Her life, her decision, even though I was her Mom, was not for me to judge. If I ever find myself in the position in which Jody was, I too will plan the time of my death. I will call family and friends together and, with their loving support, go peacefully and calmly into death's arms.

The day following Jody's death I rushed to the therapist's office seeking any wisdom and comfort she could offer. "Patty, I have Jody's permission to tell you what she said at our last meeting and I want to share it with you now." Leaning forward, taking my hand, she told me Jody's last request: "Please don't let anything happen to my Mom."

## 29
### CHAPTER

Adina Wrobleski

# "Rational Suicide": A Contradiction in Terms

I learned about suicide on August 16, 1979. My 21-year-old daughter, Lynn, got up but did not go to work. In the morning, a neighbor saw her mow the lawn, and around lunch she apparently had some soup. Some time after that, she went down the hall to her bedroom, locked the door, lay down on the floor, and shot herself in the heart. Her husband found her body around 4 P.M.

Since that time, I have talked with and heard from hundreds of suicide survivors—people who are grieving a suicide death. We know what *real* suicide is about. I have never met a survivor of a "rational suicide." That is presumed to be a rational person who sorts through the pros and cons of her or his life and decides to "choose" death. It is deeply offensive to most suicide survivors to hear people talk so glibly about how wonderful suicide is. The advocates seem to enjoy their endless discussions about death.

"Rational suicide" is rather like the question of "how many angels can dance on the head of a pin?" It involves earnest discussions, paper presentations, journal publications, and learned conferences. It is an evanescent pyramid upon which careers have been made, but it is time to tell the "rational suicide" emperor he has no clothes on.

I submit that "rational suicide" is a contradiction in terms—an oxymoron. The beliefs of so many people arguing for "rational suicide" obscure the fact it does not exist. But if there is such a thing as "rational suicide" I am opposed to it; actually, I am opposed to its advocacy.

If "rational suicide" is for people in unbearable pain, why do we reserve it only for old people? "Rational suicide" advocates like to argue that we treat our pets with more compassion than we do old and sick people. By their arguments, would it not be an act of compassion to "help" tiny lives out of their pain? Derek Humphry (personal communication, 1991) says that this is not acceptable "because they are not able to consent." We allow dying children an ordeal we deny our pets. But actually who decides when one dies by "rational suicide?" Who supplies the pressure on the old and sick to die before their time?

**206**

Where is the morality in "rational suicide?" The advocates believe it is moral to help people avoid suffering. But suffering is part of life; going through suffering is what makes most of us stronger and kinder people. Whoever expected life to be easy? I believe that life is random, and almost everyone gets some kind of tragedy. For some, it is the agony of heart disease; for others it is diabetes; and for some, suicide death.

In the past it is understandable that such a shocking and human behavior as suicide should have been wrestled with by philosophers and religionists. But science has proved through 39 years of replicated research that suicide is directly related to biological brain diseases (Murphy, 1995) whether they are diagnosed or not. When there is so much clinical information available about suicide, it amazes me that a sizable number of people are again discussing suicide as a philosophical and hypothetical issue. It is as if astronomers suddenly reverted to astrology for explanations of the universe.

"Rational suicide" has a superficial and facile sense to it. This is because it is normal for all of us to have thought about our own death and under what circumstances we think we could kill ourselves. Combined with the taboo on suicide, which creates a fascinatingly sinister atmosphere, there is a certain siren song of romance about suicide and death that titillates some people. They enjoy speculating on the hypothetical circumstances under which they might kill themselves. This speculation is most enjoyable when one is healthy, and death years away.

The prototypical "rational suicides" are the deaths of Jo Roman (Wickett, 1989), Jean Humphry (Humphry, 1991a), and Janet Adkins (Humphry, 1991a). All their husbands had parts in their wives' deaths. For example, Janet Adkins never talked to nor met Dr. Jack Kevorkian until she got to Michigan; her husband made all the arrangements. Derek Humphry mixed the lethal cup his wife drank, and Mel Roman (a physician) apparently secured the seconal his wife took.

The survivors have appeared on national television shows, describing the "nobility and dignity" with which their loved ones died. They quietly discussed their parts in the death. Real suicide survivors are too shocked and anguished to even know their names, let alone sit up straight and talk on television. Those survivors all continued to be proud of their direct help.

Real suicide survivors are blamed for the death of their loved one, and the blame goes everywhere. Society has taught us to blame people for suicide, and this often creates hostile separations within families and without. It is assumed that survivors somehow "drove" their loved one to suicide. Suicide and guilt are equated. Even the nicest people will say things like, "Oh that poor family, they must feel terribly guilty." Why *must* they? Or we hear, "It must be awful for the family dealing with *all that guilt*." Society has taught us to assume suicide survivors are guilty and in collusion with the deaths (Wrobleski, 1994). Suicide survivors are accused of complicity; "rational suicide" survivors actually are in complicity.

Suicide survivors go through the same grieving process others do, but because of the taboo and stigma they have many extra burdens. Horrible prognostications are made about them (Wrobleski, 1994, pp. 61–62):

- That their guilt will be massive and overwhelming
- That they were in some way in complicity in the death
- That they will be unable to "admit" it was a suicide
- That their marriages will probably break up
- That they and their families are at high risk for suicide
- That they will suffer from it all their lives

- That they will never "get over" a suicide death

The only ray of hope cast to them is that through years of therapy they may "get over it." Even if this were true, there will never be enough therapists to reach all of the suicide survivors. Every year there are about 30,000 suicides, and they leave behind at least 300,000 survivors. This means there are millions of suicide survivors. If all the predictions were true, suicide survivors would be a readily observable, deeply disturbed group of people. Suicide survivors have a right to recover as other people, and they do.

In *real* suicide, there is a strong message that suicide survivors will *never* know *why* someone kills her or himself. However, it *is* known why people kill themselves; they were very sick, and they died. The way people die from biological brain diseases is by suicide. It is as if advocates of "rational suicide" have on blinders that block out the evidence from psychiatry and neuroscience in the past 39 years (Murphy, 1995). But there are thousands upon thousands of therapists who have their feet firmly planted in the psychodynamic past. There's a new disorder named "pathological grief" and many new "grief counseling" specialties. Suicide survivors need to "work through their grief" and "deal with it," they say. Suicide has been with us since the beginning of time, and up until this century survivors have "dealt with it" and moved on to rebuild their lives.

For suicide survivors, there is the assumption that there was a lack of love and understanding of the suicidal person that was at fault in the relationship—that we did not love them well enough, or pay enough attention to them, and were so preoccupied with our own lives that we ignored their cries for help.

A sampling of philosophers (see Battin & Mayo, 1980) show they do not know the *real* world of suicide. For example, Lebacqz and Engelhardt (1980) say: "Persons should be *permitted* to take their own lives when they have chosen to do so *freely and rationally* and when there are *no other duties* which would override this freedom" (p. 85, emphases added).

Who gives this kind of permission? A person determined to suicide doesn't ask permission; she or he does it. Her or his remaining loved ones certainly do not give permission for the devastation in their lives. What omnipotent person decides that such a person's decision is rational? How can anyone know this? Or do they suggest that the suicidal person fill out a form, or make an affidavit attesting to her or his rationality? As to "no other duties," one always has duties, especially to one's family.

Battin (1980) made a chilling statement when she said that,

> Social acceptance of the notion of rational suicide . . . opens the way for both individual and societal manipulation of individuals into choosing to end their lives when they would not otherwise have done so. . . . However, . . . if we accept the notion of rational suicide, we cannot object to the manipulated suicides that do occur. (p. 169)

I find this unusual because she defines "manipulated suicides" very clearly, and the lines from manipulated suicide to assisted suicide to homicide can blur into one another. Suicide survivors are always subjected to a police investigation; it is the duty of the police to determine what happens in a sudden death. A survivor told me of returning home to discover his son dead with his face all bloodied. The police tore up the house looking for a gun. They gave up when they found the family dog with blood all over his face. The man had actually poisoned himself, and the dog had eaten off his face.

There is a great deal of hypocrisy in "rational suicide." A few years ago a woman, named Bertha X, wrote a letter to the *Hemlock Quarterly* (Humphry, 1991b). She told of the "rational suicide" pact she and her husband had. But he suffered a stroke and died in a nursing home. She was writing to warn people not to wait too long to take their store of pills. My question was, "Bertha! if suicide is so terrific, why are you still here?"

In one "rational suicide," an elderly woman wanted the plastic bag removed from her head; her daughter and husband removed it, bathed her face with cool water, and put the bag on again. She died (Humphry, 1991a). Roswell Gilbert "helped" his wife in dying by shooting her in the back of the head—twice. Was it for her relief, or his (Humphry, 1991a; Litman, 1992)?

Then there was the case of Morgan Sibbitt. He declared to Mike Wallace of 60 *Minutes* that he and his wife had a suicide pact, the necessary prescription pills, and the will to kill themselves. He also stated he had "aided" seven people in their suicides. In a follow-up, Mike Wallace said,

As for Morgan Sibbitt, he died seven months ago after a 20-month battle with lung cancer. He was 71. His wife wrote us: "He never took the pills for suicide, despite his pain and breathing discomfort—especially in the final weeks. He died a natural death; I guess his human instincts came through." (Hewitt, 1983)

Like Bertha, she never took the pills either. Similarly, many years ago Elizabeth Bouvia made an international scene over her "right" to not be force-fed, but she is still alive and living quietly in a Los Angeles nursing home (Humphry, 1991a; Litman, 1992).

These are examples of why I believe the advocates of "rational suicide" are talkers, not doers. I know of no evidence, other than anecdotal, that has shown that any members of the Hemlock Society died by suicide, or any philosophers and others who discuss "rational suicide" so earnestly actually killed themselves.

The advocates of "rational suicide" appear not to have concern about the "rights" of the survivors. The rights of those left behind after suicide are not considered. There are degrees of reactions in *real* suicide. It is not true that direct relatives of a suicide are always affected the most. A longtime friend of someone who died may be closer to the person than a sister who is 15 years older and lives across the country. The sister cares but may never have had the time it takes to maintain a close relationship because of distance and time. A wife may not always grieve a husband's death. He may have been an abusive alcoholic for years, and she, understandably, may feel only relief after his suicide.

Relief is one of the only things in grief that feels good. The advocates of "rational suicide" seem to confuse it with feelings that a death was a "blessing." This happens after a long drawn-out death in which survivors suffer from watching the misery of the dying person. This is similar to the reactions of some suicide survivors. Many of them lived under extreme tension before their loved one died. It is not true that all suicide survivors were ignorant of what was happening. Many lived with a chronically ill person who had the "mental cancers" of major depression, manic-depression, schizophrenia, or panic disorder. Some survivors suffered so long watching someone they loved who was so ill that there is hardly any emotion left for grief. Relief comes because their stress is gone, and a long ordeal is finished. This usually is not the case in suicide.

The real world of suicide is that of my friend whose 70-year-old father cut his wrists, and stabbed himself over his whole body. He bled to death in his bed, and his wife found him. The real world of suicide is finding your son hanged to death in the basement. The real world of suicide is the death of your husband who jumped from a high bridge. The real world of suicide is finding your loved one dead from a self-inflicted gunshot.

People shoot themselves, they hang themselves, they burn themselves to death, and kill themselves in many other ways. These deaths are all ugly and undignified, and terribly tragic. "Rational suicide" may be a vain attempt to understand suicide and to make it legitimate. The advocates of "rational suicide" are fastidious; they want people to have a lethal quantity of pills so they may gently sleep away. The Hemlock Society recommends a good dose of alcohol before taking the pills. It also recommends death by placing a plastic bag over one's head "to make sure" (Humphry, 1991a). These combination methods seem hardly more dignified than shooting or hanging.

Reality for survivors is ugly, and people who advocate "rational suicide" have to realize that. "Rational suicide" advocates are silent in the aftermath of suicide; their focus seems to be on a "dignified" death that is an end in itself. The answer to terminal illness is the hospice movement, not suicide. The answer to suicide is not more death, but less. Just because we have not supported hospice or better care to the dying does not mean that we should advocate suicide. And beyond just the "right" to kill one's self, now the advocates want "assisted" suicide.

In "rational suicide" there is no room for grief. The survivors are too busy patting themselves on the back. In *real* suicide, grief is devastating. Because of the stigma and taboo, there is so little understanding of suicide that survivors are completely bewildered; they do not know what hit them. They are in denial—denial before death and after death. Very troubling things they saw or heard before death come tumbling back into their minds as things they should have seen or done. Denial after death helps them get through their initial and continuing journey through grief.

In an effort to make sense of the death, suicide survivors have to make some kind of reconstruction of events—whether it is based on facts or blaming. Recovery from grief entails pulling themselves from the past, which is the only place their loved one still lives, into the present in which they must rebuild their lives. People do recover from suicide grief.

Suicide is not a rational or clearly thought-out action. If there is any kind of a "choice," it is a coerced choice, in which someone survivors loved was unable to see alternatives or consequences. Having said that, it is nonetheless true that it is the person who died who decided *when* all else had failed, *when* everything he or she tried had not worked, and *when* the pain was too much to bear any longer. Someone once said the life of a suicide was like being in a room of unbearable pain where the only door out was marked "suicide." The only decision the person made was that "the time to kill myself is *now*."

Love—as a human, religious, and philosophical issue—is missing from the arguments for "rational suicide." If love were included, the arguments would get all muddied up with grief, despair and anguish. Edwin Shneidman (1980) has written:

> Most suicide is a dreary and dismal wintry storm within the mind, where staying afloat or going under is the vital decision being debated. It is a place where we can't reach them, and their memories cannot save them. (p. 41)

There is a story about the mother of a family talking to John; she is telling him he must go to school. "But I don't want to," he says. "You must," she replies. "I don't want to; all the kids pick on me." "Never mind, you have to go to school." He says,

"I don't want to; all the teachers pick on me too." She says, "John, you're the principal and you *have* to go to school."

The reason suicide survivors go on is because they are the principal in their lives, and they *have* to go on. They plant a stake in the future when they feel least able to do it. They go on for their own sake, for their family's, for their friend's, and for the memory of their loved one.

Real suicide survivors are sturdy people who have lost faith in themselves after a suicide. Trying to make sense of so shocking and tragic a death as suicide, in the face of society's blame, is more than one person should have to bear. Survivors feel they cannot carry on, but they do. They feel it is more than they can bear, but it is not. They feel it is tragically unfair, and it is. They feel they will never get over it, but they do. Why? Because they have to. One way or another survivors do survive, and most do it very well.

I believe the advocates of "rational suicide" are playing at death, titillating themselves, and perhaps, whistling in the dark.

**30**

CHAPTER

Charlotte P. Ross

# Conclusion

*We do not see the world as it is. . . . We see the world as we are.*

(Source unknown)

I have been given the privilege of having the last word. I have chosen to make these concluding remarks just that: remarks, and some observations and reflections, regarding the fourteen pairs of chapters that form the "arguments for or against rational suicide as a viable concept and, consequently, a realistic option for some people."

My first observation is hardly original but glaringly obvious: we each bring our passions and our bias to this issue. We look at this complex, multifaceted issue of rational suicide—and its inevitable kin, physician-assisted dying—and see what we must see. The 28 authors present their viewpoints, each providing exquisitely logical reasoning for maintaining his or her view, citing extensive sources to substantiate his or her position, and sometimes pointing out the fallacies, illogic or dangers inherent in the "other" view. Interestingly, some contributors who hold widely differing opinions cite the same sources (e.g., Freud, Shneidman, Quill, Battin) to make contradictory points. In some chapters, the authors state up-front that the views they present are not the result of scientific study or theory but are based on deeply moving personal experiences, or on fundamental aspects of their religious beliefs, and their comments simply reflect the authors' own values and belief systems. I found these disclaimers to be greatly comforting.

I wonder if such disclaimers should not be used more generously. It does seem that many of us come to this task with life experiences that have shaped our views. We collect the evidence that will justify those views. That is surely understandable, but it is not science. Perhaps there should be a requirement for similar disclaimers on all statements "debating" controversial issues that imply a factual basis but are not based on scientific evidence. I ponder this because the objectivity, reliability, and credibility of science are essential to such debates. An article by Abigail Trafford in the *Washington Post* is entitled, "In Evaluating the Data, Scientists are Only Human" (1997, pp.

4–5). Trafford reports that articles published in two medical journals (*Journal of the American Medical Association* and *New England Journal of Medicine*) looked at the same medical evidence regarding standards in the care of terminally ill patients in the Netherlands, and yet they came to opposite conclusions. She states, "It turns out that supposedly dispassionate medical science is not entirely dispassionate, especially when the subject is controversial" and adds,

> [W]hen those in the medical community are so divided over the results of scientific data, it makes it harder for the public to sort through controversial issues that are as much about morals as medicine. . . . We like to think that facts are cold and hard, with the truth rising up out of a solid foundation of data like Venus on the half shell. But in the real world of medical research, truth is more elusive

Trafford speculates that "one way to evaluate science is to look at scientists and see if they have a stake in the findings." She notes that the authors of one report, which found that legal acceptance of euthanasia "has weakened the moral and medical framework of end-of-life care," are advocates of hospice care who believe that the acceptance of euthanasia has eroded support for hospice care and the use of advanced techniques to relieve pain. The authors of the other report are academic physicians who receive support from government and medical institutions that generally believe that society should allow euthanasia and physician-assisted dying in certain circumstances. She concludes with the observation, "Scientific data designed to enlighten also enflames."

Many if not most of us who speak passionately to this issue have a "stake in the findings." Whether it is to validate one's work, philosophy, or moral integrity or a course of action once taken—or not taken—we *believe*. We, who value life, have feelings about those who "give up" on life. Wallace (p. 49) noted, "The number of grounds on which suicide has been denounced is exceeded only by the passion with which it has been condemned." He cites Becker in offering an explanation for this impassioned denunciation.

> If the "consciousness of death is the primary repression" how threatening must be the willful acceptance of death! To choose to die, "even while knowing that it means oblivion" must create "holy terror"—an anxiety so great that its source must be censured in the strongest terms possible.

Wallace goes on to observe, "Suicide seems to be condemned with special passion by suicidologists."

I do not hesitate to add that I am not immune to bias or passion on this issue. I have dedicated much of my life to efforts to prevent suicide (I believe I am still doing that), and I now work to advocate for improved care and increased choices for terminally ill patients, including physician-assisted dying if suffering becomes intolerable. When asked to write this chapter, I did wonder if my selection was due in some part to my seemingly incongruous career path. That path, which I in fact believe to be entirely congruent, has always focused on listening to those whose situation has left them with only a tenuous hold on life, and who plead for our help. Once again, I believe, there is the challenge for all of us in the helping professions to listen, to refrain from psychologizing another's anguish, and to allow patients to teach us about that which has meaning for them in their lives—and their deaths.

Three decades ago, at Dr. Edwin Shneidman's behest, we "suicidologists" sought to reduce the incidence of suicide by pursuing three basic strategies: educating the public to better hear the suicide victim's "cry for help," making help more easily accessible to those who are suicidal, and reducing the stigma surrounding suicide victims and their families. At that time a prevailing view in our society was that suicide should be condemned as a moral wrong. To do otherwise would be to send the message (presumably to our impressionable youth and other vulnerable groups), that we, as a nation, did not hold life to be sacred; that we condoned suicide and would invite the danger of sliding down the slippery slope into becoming a "culture of death." Then, and to a lesser extent now, some religions held that suicide was a sin; thus they denied the plight of the despairing, just as they subsequently denied the victims of that despair their holy sacraments and burial rites. Medicine, in its determined battle against death, regarded self-destructive behavior as pathological, and the death of a patient a failure. The law, in a number of states, criminalized suicide so as to enforce those views—to prevent suicide by prohibiting it.

Early suicide prevention efforts included launching major education campaigns to help the public better understand and respond to those overwhelmed by suicidal despair, and to try to undo the stigmatizing effect of religious, medical, and legal condemnation of suicidal behavior. Physicians were trained to recognize, assess, and refer suicidal patients for appropriate treatment. Clergy were encouraged to be compassionate of overwhelming but understandable and temporary bouts of despair. (At the same time, Shneidman and Farberow published lists of "Facts and Fables on Suicide" [Shneidman, 1970] which included the following: "*fable*: all suicidal individuals are mentally ill, and suicide is always the act of a psychotic person. *Fact*: Studies . . . indicate that although the suicidal person is extremely unhappy, he [or she] is not necessarily mentally ill." Thus, it was explained by Drs. Shneidman and Farberow, suicide can indeed be rational.)

Regarding legal sanctions, Smith tells us that the primary purpose of organized society, as reflected in law, was to protect the lives of all citizens—including people who, for whatever reason, are self-destructive." (p. 55). He goes on to state that these laws were "changed, appropriately, as mental health professionals convinced lawmakers that suicide was not a crime but, rather, a cry for help." Some of us who struggled to change those laws have a different perception of the law's function, the role of the state in protecting people from their self-destructive urges, and, especially, the effect of criminalizing suicidal behavior on those the law sought to protect.

From a suicide prevention perspective, the laws that declared suicide a crime greatly compounded the problem. Such laws added yet another burden to those already so overwhelmed that suicide seemed their only relief. At that time, those suffering from self-destructive urges would be confessing their intent to commit a crime if they were to tell anyone of their thoughts or plans of suicide. If they attempted suicide and failed to die but required medical treatment, their physician would be required to file a police report detailing the attempted crime. Such efforts to prevent suicide by criminalizing it only succeeded in creating, contributing to, or exacerbating, the fear and withdrawal of those who were suicidal, pushing them even further into deadly isolation.

Smith (page 55) states:

> suicide and attempted suicide were subsequently decriminalized—not because the state had abandoned its interest in protecting the lives of self-destructive people—but precisely because we understood that there are better and more effective ways for the state to perform this vital function.

However, the path to that eventual enlightenment was hardly innocuous. The fear that, to this day, prevents many who are suicidal from seeking help is based on the belief, still held by the majority of the American public, that suicide is against the law. It took years to convince legislatures—state by state—to end those laws. It will take decades to end the legacy of fear, misunderstanding, and stigma created by those well-intentioned but woefully misguided efforts.

I have feelings of deja vu as I reflect on the current efforts to decriminalize physician-assisted dying. This time the prevailing view is that suicide must be condemned as irrational. We are warned that if we allow physicians to assist dying patients to end their lives—or, more accurately, their dying process—we will be facilitating the creation of a societal "culture of death." Once again physicians are pointing to pathology—the terminally ill are most likely suffering from clinical depression (Foley, 1996). And once again legislators are being urged to create laws to prohibit assisted suicide in states in which such laws do not exist, or to tighten the laws in states in which they do. Interestingly, many who pioneered ways to prevent suicide by helping severely depressed individuals find reasons to *go on living* are most passionate about preventing the suicide of those who *cannot go on living*, as though there were no difference.

Although Dr. Werth, in his introduction, clearly differentiated rational suicide from physician-assisted dying, and some authors took pains to elaborate on the differences between the two phenomena, a number of writers seemed to find no distinction between them. Indeed, some of the latter group addressed the dilemma of the terminally ill patient, who suffers a prolonged difficult death, with a discussion of ways to help depressed patients get on with their lives. This gets us back to passion and bias, and perhaps ambivalence.

Leenaars (p. 139) tells us of a debate about the morality of suicide prevention held in 1972 at the University of San Francisco School of Medicine between Edwin Shneidman and Thomas Szasz. He notes that Dr. Shneidman,

the father of suicide prevention in North America, argued eloquently in favor of suicide prevention. . . . Shneidman made the now obvious point that, if a patient talks about suicide, it suggests that he or she is ambivalent. A suicidal person who is ambivalent can often be dissuaded. . . . It should be the psychotherapist's duty to help a person recognize this fact and guide him or her on the side of life.

I served as moderator and cohost of that debate and I remember it well. I especially remember one statement made by Dr. Shneidman toward the end of the program. Looking at the audience, he said, "You always come down on the side of life." And then he added, "Of course, this doesn't apply to me." Paradoxical? Double standard? A heartfelt moment of truth? Perhaps a teasing throwaway line? Or possibly it contained some of all of those things.

This book is intended to contribute to the debate on rational suicide, and also, inevitably, to that "earnest and profound debate about the morality, legality and practicality of physician-assisted suicide" encouraged by the United States Supreme Court (*Washington v. Glucksberg*, 1997). It will likely serve as a resource for some understandably confused members of the public, media, and healthcare professions seeking "facts" and "truths" to guide them as they try to sort through the arguments and rhetoric, and perhaps their own ambivalent feelings about this important, contentious issue. The authors responded to Dr. Werth's invitation to "present their arguments" and then "leave the final decision about acceptance or rejection of the concept up to each individual reader." Thus, my final comments are reflections about the "argument" approach.

In her recent book, *The Argument Culture*, Tannen (1998) urges us to end our society's war of words and start listening to one another. She questions whether the best way to cover news is to find spokespeople who express the most extreme, polarized views and present them as "both sides; the best way to show that you are really thinking is to criticize; and the best way to discuss an idea is to set up a debate. To pursue truth by setting up a fight between two sides can lead us to assume that every issue has two sides—no more, no less. But if we always assume there must be an "other" side, we may end up "scouring the margins of science or the fringes of lunacy to find it." An example of this is the bizarre phenomenon of Holocaust denial. "Deniers" have been successful in gaining television air time and campus newspaper coverage by masquerading as "the other side" in a "debate." Continual reference to "the other side" results in a conviction that everything has another side, and people begin to doubt the existence of any facts at all.

Another example is to pit improved end-of-life care against physician-assisted dying as though they were alternatives. Or to pit individual rights of dying patients against society's responsibility to protect them, as though it were a win-or-lose proposition rather than a balancing act.

Dr. Tannen suggests that there are at least four significant dangers in the argument / debate approach.

*It makes us distort the facts.* A pamphlet distributed in Oregon during the height of the campaign to repeal the Death with Dignity Act carried a grave warning regarding youth suicide. It stated, with an amazing disregard for both facts and logic, that Oregon has the highest rate of teenage suicide in the country and warned parents that, if they failed to repeal physician-assisted dying, the incidence of teen suicide would be driven even higher—to become the number one cause of adolescent deaths.

*It makes us waste valuable time.* We need to be engaging in research, meticulously seeking the answers to important questions, not arguing our opinions. Is it possible to scientifically determine if suicide can be rational? Can the incidence of suicide among terminally ill patients be reduced if they are given greater control over their dying process? How effective are we at assessing clinical depression in dying patients? What could crisis centers, community mental health centers, and other counseling agencies do to respond most effectively to the needs of suffering terminally ill patients who want help in dying? And, finally, after 40 years of investigating countless aspects of self-destructive behavior, perhaps we should ask why we have so few data that address these questions? Is it possible that passion—or bias—can affect not only our interpretation of data, but also which questions we choose *not* to explore?

*It limits our thinking.* The language of extremes actually shapes and misshapes the way we think about things. The power of words to shape perception and invisibly mold our way of thinking about people, issues, and the world in which we live, is well established. The terms *rational suicide, euthanasia, mercy killing, physician assisted dying, compassion, physician-assisted suicide, hasten death, kill, coerce, protect, exploit, democratic,* and *nihilistic* are words that were used in this book to argue a point and influence the reader. Political as well as military metaphors train us to think about, and see, everything in terms of winning, losing, fighting, conflict, and war. Adversarial rhetoric is a kind of verbal inflation. It is not a route to exploration or solutions.

*It encourages us to lie.* If you fight to win, the temptation is great to deny facts that support your opponent's views and say only what supports your side. It encourages people to misrepresent and, in the extreme, to lie. We need look no further than the conflicting reports and interpretations of studies of euthanasia in the Netherlands to see this concept at work. Marie Shear, in a recent book review (1997), chastises an author for describing "rational suicide seekers" as "nihilistic 'death fundamentalists' who advocate a 'death culture' akin to Nazi eugenics and euthanasia" (p. 1). Shear challenges one of the book's misrepresentations by pointing out that "the Netherlands, where assisted suicide occurs under limited conditions, is not really turning huge chunks of its populace into compost at warp speed." Continued misinterpretation of the data does not—and will not—make the charges true.

However, there are encouraging signs that we are finding ways to change the argument approach into a dialogue approach. This book of differing perspectives on rational suicide contains much that can help us along toward that change. One of the most frequently cited ways to defuse antagonism between groups is to provide a means for individuals from those groups to come together to discuss their views. Another is to encourage them to search for areas of commonality rather than differences (Tannen, 1998). The chapters in this book not only provide a forum for the authors to present their views side-by-side with others who hold different opinions, they offer the opportunity for each contributor—and the reader—to learn where those views come together, as well as where they separate.

For example, the authors clearly share a common concern regarding the suffering of suicidal persons and they share a common urgency to address the problem. Jerome Motto's observation (p. 122) offers a useful perspective:

> The question of whether persons of sound mind should be permitted, under specific conditions (e.g., terminal illness), to end their lives, or to be assisted in doing so, is not a scientific question, but a matter of social philosophy. There are thus no "right" or "wrong" positions, only different ways of seeing the problem. Only if one were to insist that suicidal intent is inherently pathological would this philosophical framework not hold. (p. 232)

This book offers an abundant variety of ways of seeing the problem. It does indeed serve as a tool for dialogue on rational suicide and, not so tangentially, the aid-in-dying debate—as is its stated purpose.

# REFERENCES

Abrams, D., Hahn, J., Leiser, R., Mandel, N., Mitchell, T. F., Slome, L., & Townley, D. (1996, July). *Physicians' attitudes toward assisted suicide in AIDS: A five year comparison study.* Paper presented at the 11th International Conference on AIDS, Vancouver, B.C. Canada.

Abramson, M. (1989). Autonomy vs. paternalistic beneficence: practice strategies. *Social Casework, 70,* 101–105.

Admiraal, P. (1987, February 3). *Nightline.* New York: ABC.

Akers, R. (1994). *Criminological theory.* Los Angeles: Roxbury.

'Ali, A. Y. (1994). *The meaning of the Holy Qur'an.* Brentwood, MD: Amana Corp.

American Association of Suicidology. (1996). *Report of the Committee on Physician-Assisted Suicide and Euthanasia.* Washington, DC: Author.

American Counseling Association. (1995). *Code of ethics and standards of practice.* Alexandria, VA: Author.

American Mental Health Counselors Association (1998, May/June). Alaska becomes 45th state to gain licensure. *The Advocate, 21*(5), 1.

American Nurses Association. (1985). *American Nurses' Association Code for Nurses.* Kansas City, MO: Author.

American Nurses Association. (1994a). *Position statement on active euthanasia.* Washington, DC: Author.

American Nurses Association. (1994b). *Position statement on assisted suicide.* Washington, DC: Author.

American Nurses Association. (1995). *Nursing's social policy statement.* Washington, DC: Author.

American Psychiatric Association. (1994). *Diagnostic and statistical manual of mental disorders* (4th ed.). Washington, DC: Author.

American Psychological Association (1992). *Ethical principles of psychologists and code of conduct.* Washington, DC: Author.

American Psychological Association. (1997, July). *Terminal illness and hastened death requests: The important role of the mental health professional.* Washington, DC: Author.

Anderson, J., & Caddell, D. (1993). Attitudes of medical professionals towards rational suicide. *Social Science and Medicine, 37,* 105–114.

Annas, G. J. (1994). Death by prescription: The Oregon initiative. *New England Journal of Medicine, 331,* 1240–1243.

APA on assisted suicide: No go. (1994, October). *Psychiatric News, 23*(10), 30.

Applebaum, P. S., & Grisso, T. (1988). Assessing patients' capacities to consent to treatment. *New England Journal of Medicine, 319,* 1635–1638.

Aquinas, T. (1947a). *Summa theologica, II–II, Question 4, Article 3* (p. 1192). (English Dominican Province of the Order of Preachers, Trans.). New York: Benzinger.

Aquinas, T. (1947b). *Summa theologica, II–II, Question 20, Article 4* (pp. 1261–1262). (English Dominican Province of the Order of Preachers, Trans.). New York: Benzinger.

Aquinas, T. (1947c). *Summa theologica, II–II, Question 64, Article 5* (pp. 1468–1471). (English Dominican Province of the Order of Preachers, Trans.). New York: Benzinger.

Aquinas, T. (1975). *Summa theologica.* New York: McGraw-Hill; London: Eyre & Spottiswoode.

Aquinas, T. (1990). The Catholic View. In J. Donnelly (Ed.), *Suicide: right or wrong?* (pp. 33–36). Buffalo, NY: Prometheus. (Original work published 1266)

Armstrong, S. (1996). CACREP wants your input. *The Advocate, 3,* 7.

Asch, D. (1996). The role of critical care nurses in euthanasia and assisted suicide. *New England Journal of Medicine, 334,* 1374–1379.

Augustine, St. (1972a). *The city of God, Book 1, Chapter 17* (pp. 26–27). (D. Knowles, Ed., H. Bettenson, Trans.). New York: Penguin.

Augustine, St. (1972b). *The city of God, Book 20, Chapter 1* (pp. 31–32). (D. Knowles, Ed., H. Bettenson, Trans.). New York: Penguin.

Augustine, St. (1994). *City of God.* H. Bettenson (trans.) London: England: Harmondsworth, Middlesex.

Bachman, J. G., Alcser, K. H., Doukas, D. J., Lichtenstein, R. L., Corning, A. D., & Brody, H. (1996). Attitudes of Michigan physicians and the public toward legalizing physician-assisted suicide and voluntary euthanasia. *New England Journal of Medicine, 334,* 303–309.

Back, A. L., Wallace, J. I., Starks, H. E., & Pearlman, R. A. (1996). Physician-assisted suicide and euthanasia in Washington State: patient requests and physician responses. *Journal of the American Medical Association, 275,* 919–925.

Ball, J. (1990, November/December). The proscribed prescription. *The Forum, 15*(5), 1, 12.

Baron, C. H., Bergstresser, C., Brock, D. W., Cole, G. F., Dorfman, N. S., Johnson, J. A., Schnipper, L. E., Vorenberg, J., & Wanzer, S. H. (1996). A model state act to authorize and regulate physician-assisted suicide. *Harvard Journal on Legislation, 33,* 1–34.

Barraclough, B., Bunch, J., Nelson, B., & Sainsbury, P. (1974). A hundred cases of suicide: clinical aspects. *British Journal of Psychiatry, 125,* 355–373.

Barry, R. (1994a). *Breaking the thread of life: on rational suicide.* New Brunswick, NJ: transaction.

Barry, R. (1994b). 'Imago dei' and the sanctity of human life. *Providence, 2,* 133–167.

Barry, R. L., & Bradley, G. V. (Eds.). (1991). *Set no limits: A rebuttal to Daniel Callahan's proposal to limit health care for the elderly.* Urbana, IL: University of Illinois Press.

Barry, R., & Maher, J. (1990). Indirectly intended life-shortening analgesia: clarifying the principles. *Issues in Law and Medicine, 6,* 117–153.

Batavia, A. I. (1991). A disability rights-independent living perspective on euthanasia. *Western Journal of Medicine, 154,* 616–617.

Battin, M. P. (1980). Manipulated suicide. In M. P. Battin & D. J. Mayo (Eds.), *Suicide: the philosophical issues* (pp. 169–182). New York: St. Martin's.

Battin, M. P. (1991). Rational suicide: how can we respond to a request for help? *Crisis, 12*(2), 72–80.

Battin, M. P. (1994). *The least worst death: essays in bioethics on end-of-life.* New York: Oxford University Press.

Battin, M. P. (1995). *Ethical issues in suicide.* Englewood Cliffs, NJ: Prentice-Hall.

Battin, M. P., & Maris, R. W. (Eds.). (1983). Suicide and ethics [Special issue]. *Suicide and Life-Threatening Behavior, 13*(4).

Battin, M. P., & Mayo, D. J. (Eds.). (1980). *Suicide: the philosophical issues.* New York: St. Martin's.

Battin, M. P., McKinney, D., Kastenbaum, R., & Moody, H. R. (1984). Suicide: A solution to the problem of old age [Abstract]. In C. R. Pfeffer & J. Richman (Eds.), *Proceedings of the 15th annual meeting of the American Association of Suicidology* (pp. 78–81). Denver, CO: American Association of Suicidology.

Beauchamp, T. L. (1978). What is suicide? In T. L. Beauchamp & S. Perlin (Eds.), *Ethical issues in death and dying* (pp. 97–102). Englewood Cliffs, NJ: Prentice Hall.

Beauchamp, T., & Childress, J. (1979). *Principles of biomedical ethics.* New York: Oxford University Press.

Becker, E. (1977). *The denial of death.* New York: Free Press.

Bellah, R. N., Madsen, R., Sullivan, W. M., Swidler, A., & Tipton, S. M. (1985). *Habits of the heart: individualism and commitment in American life.* New York: Harper & Row.

Benner, P. (1984, October). Clinical nursing expertise: the "hidden" difference. Paper presented at the annual Nursing meeting, National Institutes of Health, Bethesda, MD.

Betzold, M. (1996, June 16). Drop dead, Dr. K. *Detroit Sunday Journal*, section 1, pp. 1, 8.

Blaney, P. H. (1986). Affect and memory: A review. *Psychological Bulletin, 99*, 229–246.

Blolund, C. (1985a). Suicide and cancer: I. Demographic and social characteristics of cancer patients who committed suicide in Sweden 1973–1976. *Journal of Psychosocial Oncology, 3*, 17–30.

Blolund, C. (1985b). Suicide and cancer: II. Medical and care factors in suicides by cancer patients in Sweden, 1973–1976. *Journal of Psychosocial Oncology, 3*, 31–52.

Boldt, M. (1989). Defining suicide: implications for suicidal behavior and for suicide prevention. In R. F. Diekstra, R. Maris, S. Platt, A.Schmidtke, & G. Sonneck (Eds.). *Suicide and its prevention: the role of attitude and imitation* (pp. 5–13). Leiden, The Netherlands: Brill.

Botwinick, J. (1973). *Aging and behavior: A comprehensive integration of research findings.* New York: Springer.

Bowensock, G. W. (1995). *Martyrdom and Rome.* Cambridge: Cambridge University Press.

Bowers v. Hardwick, 478 U.S. 186 (1986).

Bradley, L. J. (1995). Certification and licensure issues. *Journal of Counseling and Development, 74*, 185–186.

Brandt, R. B. (1975). The morality and rationality of suicide. In S. Perlin (Ed.), *A handbook for the study of suicide* (pp. 61–76). New York: Oxford University Press.

Breitbart, W. (1993). Suicide risk and pain in cancer and AIDS patients. In C. R. Chapman & K. M. Foley (Eds). *Current and emerging issues in cancer pain: research issues and practice* (pp. 49–65). New York: Raven Press.

Brock, D. W. (1992, March-April). Voluntary active euthanasia. *Hastings Center Report, 22*, 10–22.

Brody, H. (1992). Assisted death—A compassionate response to a medical failure. *New England Journal of Medicine, 327*, 1384–1388.

Bromberg, S., & Cassel, C. K. (1983). Suicide in the elderly: the limits of paternalism. *Journal of the American Geriatrics Society, 31*, 698–703.

Brown, D., & Srebalus, D. J. (1996). *Introduction to the profession of counseling* (2nd ed.). Boston: Allyn & Bacon.

Brown, J. H., Henteleff, P., Barakat, S., & Rowe, C. J. (1986). Is it normal for terminally ill patients to desire death? *American Journal of Psychiatry, 143*, 208–211.

Brown, R. E. (1970). *The Gospel according to John* (Vol. 2). New York: Doubleday.

Brunier, G., Carson, M. G., & Harrison, D. E. (1995). What do nurses know and believe about patients with pain? Results of a hospital survey. *Journal of Pain and Symptom Management, 10*, 436–445.

Buie, J. (1988, October). "Me" decades generate depression: individualism erodes commitment to others. *APA Monitor, 19*(10), 18.

Byock, I. R. (1991). Final Exit: A wake-up call to Hospice. *The Hospice Journal, 7*(4), 51–66.

Byock, I. R. (1993). Consciously walking the fine line: thoughts on a hospice response to assisted suicide and euthanasia. *Journal of Palliative Care, 9*(3), 25–28.

Byrne, R. H. (1995). *Becoming a master counselor.* Pacific Grove, CA: Brooks / Cole.

Callahan, D. (1987). *Setting limits: medical goals in an aging society.* New York: Simon & Schuster.

Callahan, D. (1990). *What kind of life.* New York: Simon & Schuster.

Callahan, D. (1992). When self-determination runs amok. *Hastings Center Report, 22*(2), 52–55.

Callahan, D. (1993). Response to Roger W. Hunt. *Journal of Medical Ethics, 19*, 24–27.

Callahan, J. (1994). The ethics of assisted suicide. *Health and Social Work, 19*, 237–244.

Camus, A. (1955). *The myth of Sisyphus and other essays* (pp. 3–8). New York: Knopf.

Carlisle, D. M., Leake, B. D., & Shapiro, M. F. (1995). Racial and ethnic differences in the use of invasive cardiac procedures among cardiac patients in Los Angeles County, 1986 through 1988. *American Journal of Public Health, 85*, 352–356.

Cassell, E. J. (1991). Recognizing suffering. *Hastings Center Report, 21*(3), 24–31.

Cassell, E. J. (1995). Treating the patient's subjective state. *Pain Forum, 4*, 186–188.

Cassem, E. H. (1995). Depressive disorders in the medically ill. *Psychosomatics, 36*(2), S2–S10.

Chapman, C. R. (1993). The emotional aspect of pain. In C. R. Chapman & K. M. Foley (Eds.), *Current and Emerging Issues in Cancer Pain: Research Issues and Practice* (pp. 83–95). New York: Raven Press.

Chapman, C. R., & Gavrin, J. (1996). Suffering and the dying patient. In M. P. Battin & A. G. Lipman (Eds.), *Drug use in assisted suicide and euthanasia* (pp. 67–90). New York: Haworth.

Chemtob, C. M., Bauer, G., Hamada, R. S., Pelowski, S. R., & Muraoka, M. Y. (1989). Patient suicide: occupational hazard for psychologists and psychiatrists. *Professional Psychology: Research and Practice, 20,* 294–300.

Chochinov, H. M., Wilson, K. G., Enns, M., Mowchun, N., Lander, S., Levitt, M., & Clinch, J. J. (1995). Desire for death in the terminally ill. *American Journal of Psychiatry, 152,* 1185–1191.

Clark, D. C., & Horton-Deutsch, S. L. (1992). Assessment *in absentia*: the value of the psychological autopsy method for studying antecedents of suicide and predicting future suicides. In R. W. Maris, A. L. Berman, J. T. Maltsberger, & R. I. Yufit (Eds.), *Assessment and prediction of suicide* (pp. 144–182). New York: Guilford.

Cleary, F. X. (1986). Roman Catholicism. In C. J. Johnson & M. G. McGee (Eds.), *Encounters with eternity: Religious views of death and life after-death* (pp. 259–275). New York: Philosophical Library.

Clinicians and public on care issues: poll shows conflict. (1994). *Hospitals and Health Networks, 68*(4), 29.

Cohen, J., Fihn, S., & Boyko, E. (1994). Attitudes towards assisted suicide and euthanasia among physicians in Washington State. *New England Journal of Medicine, 331,* 89–94.

Cohen-Cole, S. A., Brown, F. W., & McDaniel, J. S. (1993). Diagnostic assessment of depression in the medically ill. In A. Stoudemire & B. Fogel (Eds.), *Psychiatric care of the medical patient* (pp. 53–70). New York, NY: Oxford University Press.

Colt, G. H. (1991). *The enigma of suicide.* New York: Summit Books.

Commission on the Study of Medical Practice Concerning Euthanasia (1991). *Medische beslissingen rond het levenseinde* [Medical decisions about the end of life]. The Hague, the Netherlands, Staatsuigeverij.

Compassion in Dying v. Washington, 850 F. Supp. 1454 (W.D. Wash 1994).

Compassion in Dying v. Washington, 49 F.3d 586 (9th Circuit, 1995).

Compassion in Dying v. Washington, 79 F.3d 790 (9th Circuit 1996) (en banc).

Comte, A. (1876). *A system of positive polity* (Vol. 3). New York: Burt Franklin.

Conwell, Y. (1993). Suicide in the elderly: when is it rational? *Crisis, 14,* 6–7.

Conwell, Y., & Caine, E. D. (1991). Rational suicide and the right to die: reality and myth. *New England Journal of Medicine, 325,* 1100–1103.

Conwell, Y., Caine, E. D., & Olsen, K. (1990). Suicide and cancer in later life. *Hospital and Community Psychiatry, 41,* 1334–1339.

Corr, C. A., Nabe, C. N., & Corr, D. M. (1994). *Death and dying: life and living.* Pacific Grove, CA: Brooks/Cole.

Costa, E., Mogos, I., & Toma, T. (1985). Efficacy and safety of mianserin in the treatment of depression of women with cancer. *Acta Psychiatrica Scandinavia, 72,* 85–92.

Cotten, P. (1993). Rational suicide: no longer 'crazy'? *Journal of the American Medical Association, 270,* 797.

Coyle, N. (1992). The euthanasia and physician-assisted suicide debate: issues for nursing. *Oncology Nursing Forum, 19* (7) (Supplement), 41–47.

Coyle, N., Adelhardt, J., Foley, K., & Portenoy, R. (1990). Character of terminal illness in the advanced cancer patient: pain and other symptoms during the last four weeks of life. *Journal of Pain and Symptom Management 5*(2), 83–93.

CQ interview: Arlene Judith Klotzko and Dr. Boudewijn Chabot discuss assisted suicide in the absence of somatic illness. (1995). *Cambridge Quarterly of Healthcare Ethics, 4,* 239–249.

Crane, S. (1898a, Nov. 26). The blue hotel. *Collier's Weekly, 22,* 14–16.

Crane, S. (1898b, Dec. 3). The blue hotel. *Collier's Weekly, 22,* 14–16.

Cross, F. (1970). Cainites. In *The Oxford dictionary of church history* (p. 218). New York: Oxford University Press.

Crosse, S. B., Kaye, E., & Ratnofsky, A.C. (1993). *A report on the maltreatment of children with disabilities.* Rockville, MD: Westat.

Cruzan v. Director, Missouri Department of Health, 497 U.S. 261 (1990).

deFord, M. (1963, June). Do we own ourselves? *The Realist,* 10.

DeHaven, J. (1996, September 9). Woman recalls mother's final battle. *Detroit News*, p. C1.

Deluty, R. H. (1989). Factors affecting the acceptability of suicide. *Omega, 19*, 315–326.

Devine, P. (1979). *The ethics of homicide* (pp. 24–28). New York: Cornell University Press.

de Wachter, M. A. M. (1992, March–April). Euthanasia in the Netherlands. *Hastings Center Report, 22*(2), 23–30.

Diekstra, R. F. W. (1986). The significance of Nico Speijer's suicide: how and when should suicide be prevented? *Suicide and Life Threatening Behavior, 16*, 3–15.

Diekstra, R. F. W. (1992). Suicide and euthanasia. *Italian Journal of Suicidology, 2*, 71–78.

Diener, H. C., van Schayck, R., & Kastrup, O. (1995). Pain and depression. In B. Bromm & J. E. Desmedt (Eds.), *Advances in Pain Research and Therapy. Pain and the Brain: From Nociception to Cognition* (Vol. 22) (pp. 345–355). New York: Raven Press.

Doe vs. Bloomington Hospital, 104 U.S. 394 (1983).

Domino, G., & Leenaars, A. (1995). Attitudes toward suicide among English speaking urban Canadians. *Death Studies, 19*, 489–500.

Donnelly, J. (Ed.). (1990). *Suicide: right or wrong?* Buffalo, NY: Prometheus.

Dorpat, T. L., & Ripley, H. S. (1960). A study of suicide in the Seattle area. *Comprehensive Psychiatry, 1*, 349–359.

Drodge, A. J., & Tabor, J. D. (1992). *A noble death.* New York: Harper.

Droogas, A., Siiter, R., & O'Connell, A. N. (1982). Effects of personal and situational factors on attitudes toward suicide. *Omega, 13*, 127–144.

Dumm, D. (1968). Tobit. In R. E. Brown, J. Fitzmeyer, & R. Murphy (Eds.), *The Jerome Biblical commentary* (pp. 620–624). Englewood Cliffs, NJ: Prentice-Hall.

Dunne, E. J., McIntosh, J. L., & Dunne-Maxim, K. (Eds.). (1987). *Suicide and its aftermath: understanding and counseling the survivors.* New York: Norton.

Dunshee, S. J. (1994, April). Compassion in Dying. *Focus: A Guide to AIDS Research and Counseling, 9*(5), 5–6.

Durkheim, E. (1951). *Suicide.* New York: Free Press.

Ebert, P. A. (1995). "As I see it. . ." *Bulletin of the American College of Surgeons, 80*(11), 4–5.

Ehrenhalt, A. (1995). *The lost city: discovering the forgotten virtues of community in the Chicago of the 1950s.* New York: Basic Books.

Elliott, T. E., Murray, D. M., Elliott, B. A, Braun, B., Oken, M. M., Johnson, K. M., Post-White, J., & Lichtblau, L. (1995). Physician knowledge and attitudes about cancer pain management: A survey from the Minnesota Cancer Pain Project. *Journal of Pain and Symptom Management, 10*, 494–504.

Ellis, A. (1973). *Humanistic psychotherapy.* New York: Julian.

Enright, J. J. (Ed.). (1983). *The Oxford book of death.* New York: Oxford University Press.

*Ethical Times: Newsletter of the Ethical Culture Society of Los Angeles.* Adolph Surtshin, Ed. (1996), March / April). p. 4.

Evans, D. L., McCartney, C. F., & Haggerty J. J. (1988). Treatment of depression in cancer patients is associated with better life adaptation: A pilot study. *Psychosomatic Medicine, 50*, 72–76.

Fear of dying. (1991, January). *Gallup Poll Monthly*, no. 304, pp. 51–61.

Fenigsen, R. (1991). The report of the Dutch governmental committee on euthanasia. *Issues in Law and Medicine, 7*, 339–344.

Fenigsen, R. (1995). Physician-assisted death in the Netherlands: impact on long-term care. *Issues in Law and Medicine, 11*, 283–297.

Fletcher, J. (1942). *Situation ethics.* New York: Random House.

Fletcher, J. (1981). In defense of suicide. In S. E. Wallace & A. Eser (Eds.), *Suicide and Euthanasia* (pp. 38–50). Knoxville, TN: University of Tennessee Press.

Flew, A. (1969). The principle of euthanasia. In A. B. Downing (Ed.), *Euthanasia and the right to death* (pp. 30–48). London: Peter Owen.

Foley, K. M. (1991). The relationship of pain and symptom management to patient requests for physician-assisted suicide. *Journal of Pain and Symptom Management, 6*, 289–297.

Foley, K. M. (1995). Pain, physician-assisted suicide, and euthanasia. *Pain Forum, 4*, 163–175.

Foley, K. M. (1996a). Court decisions challenge ban on physician-assisted suicide. *The Network News, 5,* 1, 15. (Available from Memorial Sloan-Kettering Cancer Center.)

Foley, K. M. (1996b April 29). *Medical issues related to physician-assisted suicide.* Testimony before the House Judiciary Subcommittee on the Constitution, Washington, DC.

Forest, D. V., & Stone, L. A. (1991). Counselor certification. In F. O. Gradley (Ed.), *Credentialing in counseling* (pp. 13–23). Alexandria, VA: American Counseling Association.

Frankl, V. E. (1963). *Man's search for meaning: An introduction to logotherapy* (I. Lasch, Trans.). New York: Washington Square Press.

Friedman, P. (1967). *On suicide.* New York: International Universities Press. (Original work published in 1910)

Freud, S. (1917/1974). Mourning and melancholia. In J. Strachey (Ed., Trans.), *The standard edition of the complete psychological works of Sigmund Freud* (Vol. 14, pp. 239–260). London: Hogarth Press.

Freud, S. (1920/1974). A case of homosexuality in a woman. In J. Strachey (Ed., Trans.), *The standard edition of the complete psychological works of Sigmund Freud* (Vol. 18, pp. 147–172). London: Hogarth Press.

Freud, S. (1921/1974). Group psychology and the analysis of the ego. In J. Strachey (Ed., Trans.), *The standard edition of the complete psychological works of Sigmund Freud* (Vol. 18, pp. 67–147). London: Hogarth Press.

Freud, S. (1933). *Collected Papers.* London: Highgate.

Freud, S. (1939/1974). Moses and monotheism. In J. Strachey (Ed., Trans.), *The standard edition of the complete psychological works of Sigmund Freud* (Vol. 23, pp. 243–258). London: Hogarth Press.

Fuhrer, M. J., Rintala, D. H., Hart, K. A., Clearman, R., & Young, M. E. (1992). Relationship of life satisfaction to impairment, disability, and handicap among persons with spinal cord injury living in the community. *Archives of Physical Medicine and Rehabilitation, 73,* 552–557.

Gallup Poll. (1991, January). Fear of dying. *The Gallup Poll Monthly.* No. 304, 51–61.

Germain, C. B. (1994). Using an ecological perspective. In J. Rothman, *Practice with highly vulnerable clients: case management and community based service* (pp. 39–56). Englewood Cliffs, NJ: Prentice-Hall.

Gething, L. (1992). Judgments by health professionals of personal characteristics of people with a visible physical disability. *Social Science and Medicine, 34,* 809–815.

Gianelli, D. M. (1996, September 2). Major figure in right to die debate dies. *American Medical News.*

Giles, W. H., Anda, R. F., Casper, M. L., Escobedo, L. G., & Taylor, H. A. (1995). Race and sex differences in rates of invasive cardiac procedures in US hospitals. *Archives of Internal Medicine, 155,* 318–324.

Gomez, C. (1991). *Regulating death: the case of the Netherlands.* New York: Free Press.

Gonsalves, M. A. (1990). Theistic and nontheistic arguments. In J. Donnelly (Ed.), *Suicide: right or wrong?* (pp. 179–183). Buffalo, NY: Prometheus.

Gould, M. S. & Shaffer, D. (1986). The impact of suicide in television movies: evidence of imitation. *New England Journal of Medicine, 315,* 690–694.

Graber, G. (1981). The rationality of suicide. In S. E. Wallace & A. Eser (Eds.), *Suicide and Euthanasia* (pp. 51–66). Knoxville, TN: University of Tennessee Press.

Grisez, G. (1980). Suicide and euthanasia. In D. Horan & D. Mall (Eds.), *Death, dying, and euthanasia,* (pp. 742–819). Frederick, MD: Aletheia.

Griswold v. Connecticut, 381 U.S. 479 (1965).

Gurland, B. J., & Cross, P. S. (1983). Suicide among the elderly. In M. K. Aronson, R. Bennett, & B. J. Gurland (Eds.), *The acting-out elderly* (pp. 55–65). New York: Haworth Press.

Hanks, G. W. (1992). Pain management in cancer patients. *Therapie, 47,* 488–493.

Harris, B. (1996, January 10). Mom freed in mercy killing. *Spokesman-Review,* pp. A1, A7.

Hathout, H. (1996). Islam. In G. A. Larue (Ed.), *Playing God: 50 religions' views on your right to die* (pp. 354–361). Wakefield, RI, London: Moyer Bell.

Hearn, L. (1984, February 8). It's more of a struggle to live than die. *Chicago Tribune,* section 5, pp. 1, 3.

Hedge, B. (1991). Psychosocial aspects of HIV infection. *AIDS Care, 3,* 409–412.

Heifetz, M. D. (1975). *The right to die.* New York: G.P. Putnam's Sons.

Heilig, S. (1988). The San Francisco Medical Society euthanasia survey: results and analysis. *San Francisco Medicine, 61,* 21–34.

Heilig, S., Brody, R., Marcus, F. S., Shavelson, L. & Sussman, A. C. (1997). Physician-hastened death: advisory guidelines for the San Francisco Bay Area from the Bay Area Network of Ethics Committees. *Western Journal of Medicine, 166,* 370–378.

Heilig, S., & Jamison, S. (1996). Physician aid-in-dying: toward a "harm reduction" approach. *Cambridge Quarterly of Healthcare Ethics, 5,* 113–120.

Hendin, H. (1991). Psychodynamics of suicide with particular reference to the young. *American Journal of Psychiatry, 148,* 1150–1158.

Hendin, H. (1993). Letter. *American Journal of Psychiatry, 150,* 1903–1904.

Hendin, H. (1995). Assisted suicide, euthanasia, and suicide prevention: the implications of the Dutch experience. *Suicide and Life-Threatening Behavior, 25,* 193–204.

Hendin, H., & Klerman, G. (1993). Physician-assisted suicide: the dangers of legalization. *American Journal of Psychiatry, 150,* 143–145.

Hewitt, D. (Producer). (1983, July 24). *60 Minutes.* New York: Columbia Broadcasting System.

Hill, C. S., Jr. (1990). Relationship among cultural, educational and regulatory agency influences on optimum cancer pain therapy. *Journal of Pain and Symptom Management, 5,* 537–545.

Hill, C. S., Jr. (1995). When will adequate pain treatment be the norm? *Journal of the American Medical Association, 274,* 1881–1882.

Hollis, F. (1972). *Casework, a psychosocial therapy.* New York: Random House.

Hollis, J. W., & Wantz, R. A. (1993). *Counselor preparation: programs, personnel, trends* (8th ed.). Muncie, IN: Accelerated Development.

Holloway, H. B., Hayslip, B., Murdock, M. E., Maloy, R., Servaty, H., & Henard, K. (1994–1995). Measuring attitudes toward euthanasia. *Omega, 30,* 53–65.

Homer, P., & Holstein, M. (Eds.). (1990). *A good old age? The paradox of Setting Limits.* New York: Touchstone.

House, J. S., Landis, K. R., & Umberson, D. (1988). Social relationships and health. *Science, 241,* 540–545.

Huber, R., Cox, V., & Edelen, W. (1992). Right to die responses from a random sample of 200. *Hospice Journal, 8,* 1–19.

A Humanist manifesto. (1973, September / October). *The Humanist, XXXIII,* 4–9.

Hume, D. (1963). *Essays moral, political and literary.* London: Oxford University Press.

Humphry, D. (1987). The case for rational suicide. *Suicide and Life Threatening Behavior, 17,* 335–338.

Humphry, D. (1991a). *Final exit.* Eugene, OR: The Hemlock Society.

Humphry, D. (1991b, April). Letters to the Editor. *Hemlock Quarterly, 24,* 16.

Hunt, R. W. (1993). A critique of using age to ration health care. *Journal of Medical Ethics, 19,* 19–23.

Huyse, F. J., & van Tilburg, W. (1993). Euthanasia policy in the Netherlands. *Hospital and Community Psychiatry, 55,* 733–738.

In re Colyer, 99 Wn.2d 114 (1983).

In re Grant, 109 Wn.2d 545 (1987).

In re Quinlan, 70 N.J. 10, 335 A.2d 647 (1976).

Ingram, E. & Ellis, J. B. (1992). Attitudes toward suicidal behavior: A review of the literature. *Death Studies, 16,* 31–43.

Jaffe, J. H. (1970). Narcotic analgesics. In L S. Goodman & A. Goodman (Eds.), *The Pharmacologic Basis of Therapeutics* (4th ed., pp. 237–250). New York: MacMillan.

Jamison, K. R. (1995). *An unquiet mind.* New York: Alfred A. Knopf.

Jamison, S. (1995). *Final acts of love: families, friends, and assisted dying.* New York: Tarcher / Putnam Publishing.

Jamison, S. (1996). When drugs fail: assisted deaths and not-so-lethal drugs. *Journal of Pharmaceutical Care in Pain and Symptom Control, 4,* 223–243.

Jamison, S. (1997). *Assisted suicide: A decision-making guide for health professionals.* San Francisco: Jossey-Bass.

Johnson, A. (1992). *Human Arrangements.* New York: Harcourt, Brace, Jovanovich.

Jones, E. (1957). *The life and work of Sigmund Freud. Vol. III.* New York: Basic Books.

Jonsen, A. R. (1986). Bentham in a box: technology assessment and health care allocation. *Law, Medicine and Health Care, 14,* 172–174.

Kapp, M. B. (1991). Our hands are tied: legally induced moral tensions in health care delivery. *Journal of General Internal Medicine, 6,* 345–348.

Kass, L. R. (1993, January–February). Is there a right to die? *Hastings Center Report, 23*(1), 34–43.

Kastenbaum, R. J. (1995). *Death, society, and human experience* (5th ed.). Boston: Allyn & Bacon.

Kasting, G. A. (1994). The nonnecessity of euthanasia. In J. M. Humber, R. F. Almeder, & G. A. Kasting (Eds.), *Physician-assisted death* (pp. 25–45). Totowa, NJ: Humana Press.

Kevorkian, J. (1988). The last fearsome taboo: medical aspects of planned death. *Medicine and Law, 7,* 1–14

Koening, H. G. (1993). Legalizing physician-assisted suicide: some thoughts and concerns. *Journal of Family Practice, 37,* 171–179.

Kohl, M. (Ed.). (1975). *Beneficent euthanasia.* Buffalo, New York: Prometheus Books.

Kübler-Ross, E. (1969). *On death and dying.* New York: MacMillan.

Kuhse, H., & Singer, P. (1993). Voluntary euthanasia and the nurse: an Australian survey. *International Journal of Nursing Studies, 30,* 311–322.

LaPlante, M. P, Kennedy, J., Kaye, H. S., & Wenger, B. L. (1996). Disability and employment. *Disability Statistics Abstract, 11.* Washington, DC: U.S. Department of Education.

Larue, G. A. (1992). *Geroethics.* Buffalo, New York: Prometheus Books.

Larue, G. A. (1996). *Playing God: 50 religions' views on your right to die.* Wakefield, RI, London: Moyer Bell.

Lebacqz, K., & Engelhardt, H. T., Jr. (1980). Suicide and covenant. In M. P. Battin & D. J. Mayo (Eds.), *Suicide: the philosophical issues* (pp. 84–89). New York: St. Martin's.

Lee, M., & Ganzini, L. (1992). Depression in the elderly: effect on patient attitudes toward life-sustaining therapy. *Journal of the American Geriatric Society, 40,* 983–988.

Lee, M. A., Nelson, H. D., Tilden, V. P., Ganzini, L., Schmidt, T. A., & Tolle, S. W. (1996). Legalizing assisted suicide—views of physicians in Oregon. *New England Journal of Medicine, 334,* 310–315.

Lee, M. A., & Tolle, S. W. (1996). Oregon's assisted suicide vote: the silver lining. *Annals of Internal Medicine, 124,* 267–269.

Leenaars, A. (1988). *Suicide notes.* New York: Human Sciences Press.

Leenaars, A. (1989a). Suicide across the adult life-span: an archival study. *Crisis, 10,* 132–151.

Leenaars, A. (1989b). Are young adults' suicides psychologically different from those of other adults? (The Shneidman Lecture). *Suicide and Life-Threatening Behavior, 19,* 249–263.

Leenaars, A. (1993). Unconscious processes. In A. Leenaars (Ed.), *Suicidology: essays in honor of Edwin Shneidman* (pp. 126–147). Northvale, NJ: Aronson.

Leenaars, A. (1996). Suicide: A multidimensional malaise [Presidential address]. *Suicide and Life-Threatening Behavior, 26,* 221–236.

Leenaars, A., & Diekstra, R. (1995). Editorial. *Archives of Suicide Research, 1,* 2.

Leenaars, A., Maltsberger, J., & Neimeyer, R. (1994). *Treatment of suicidal people.* New York: Taylor & Francis.

Leinbach, R. (1993). Euthanasia attitudes of older Americans. *Research on Aging, 15,* 433–448.

Lesbaupin, I. (1975). *Blessed are the persecuted.* Maryknoll, NY: Orbis.

Lester, D. (1993). The logic and rationality of suicide. *Homeostasis, 34,* 167–173.

Lester, D., & Leenaars, A. A. (1996). The ethics of suicide and suicide prevention. *Death Studies, 20,* 163–184.

Levine, H. (1986). *Life choices.* New York: Simon & Schuster.

Lewinsohn, P. M., Rohde, P., Seeley, J. R., & Fischer, S. A. (1993). Age-cohort changes in the lifetime occurrence of depression and other mental disorders. *Journal of Abnormal Psychology, 102,* 110–120.

Litman, R. (1967). Sigmund Freud on suicide. In E. Shneidman (Ed.), *Essays in self-destruction* (pp. 324–344). New York: Aronson.

Litman, R. E. (1992). [Review of *Final exit*]. *Suicide and Life-Threatening Behavior, 22,* 517.

Lo, B. (1995). Assessing decision making capacity. In J. D. Arras & B. Steinbock (Eds.), *Ethical issues in modern medicine* (pp. 185–195). Mountain View, CA: Mayfield Publishing.

Loving v. Virginia, 388 U.S. 1 (1967).

MacIntyre, A. (1988). *Whose justice? Which rationality?* Notre Dame, Indiana: University of Notre Dame Press.

Malcolm, A. H. (1990, June 1). Giving death a hand: rending issue. *New York Times*, A6.

Maltsberger, J. T. (1994). Calculated risk taking in the treatment of suicidal patients: ethical and legal problems. *Death Studies, 18*, 439–452.

Maltsberger, J. T., & Buie D. H. (1980). The devices of suicide. *International Review of Psycho-Analysis, 7*, 61–72.

Margolis, J. (1978). Suicide. In T. L. Beauchamp & S. Perlin (Eds.), *Ethical Issues in Death and Dying* (pp. 92–97). Englewood Cliffs, NJ: Prentice-Hall.

Maris, R. W. (1982a). Rational suicide: an impoverished self-transformation. *Suicide and Life Threatening Behavior, 12*, 4–16.

Maris, R. W. (1982b). [Review of *Exit house: choosing suicide as an alternative*]. *Suicide and Life-Threatening Behavior, 12*, 123–126.

Maris, R. W. (1983). Suicide: rights and rationality. *Suicide and Life-Threatening Behavior, 13*, 223–230.

Markson, L. J., Kern, D. C., Annas, G. J., & Glantz, L. H. (1994). Physician assessment of patient competence. *Journal of the American Geriatrics Society, 42*, 1074–1080.

Martin, R. M. (1980). Suicide and false desires. In M. P. Battin & D. J. Mayo (Eds.), *Suicide: the philosophical issues* (pp. 144–150). New York: St. Martin's Press.

Marzuk, P. M. (1994). Suicide and terminal illness. *Death Studies, 18*, 497–512.

Maslow, A. H. (1968). *Toward a psychology of being.* New York: Van Nostrand.

Massie, M. J., Gagnon, P., & Holland, J. C. (1994). Depression and suicide in patients with cancer. *Journal of Pain and Symptom Management, 9*, 325–340.

Masuda, S. (1996). Research summary. In *SAFETY NET/WORK Community Kit: From Abuse to Suicide Prevention and Women with Disabilities.* Toronto, Ontario: DisAbled Women's Network of Canada.

Matheson, R. (1969). The test. In *The shores of space* (pp. 60–78). New York: Bantam Books. (Original work published in 1954)

Matsueda, R., & Heimer, K. (1987). Race, family structure, and delinquency: A test of differential association and social control theories. *American Sociological Review, 152*, 826–840.

Matthews, M. (1987). Suicidal competence and the patient's right to refuse lifesaving treatment. *California Law Review, 75*, 707–758.

Maynard, F. M. (1991). Responding to requests for ventilator removal from patients with quadriplegia. *Western Journal of Medicine, 154*, 617–619.

Mayo, D. J. (1980). Irrational suicide. In M. P. Battin & D. J. Mayo (Eds.), *Suicide: the philosophical issues* (pp. 133–137). New York: St. Martin's Press.

Mayo, D. J. (1983). Contemporary philosophical literature on suicide: A review. *Suicide and Life-Threatening Behavior, 13*, 313–345.

McCaffrey, M., & Ferrell, B. R. (1995). Nurses' knowledge about cancer pain: A survey of five countries. *Journal of Pain and Symptom Management, 10*, 356–369.

McCormick, R. (1981). The quality of life and the sanctity of life. In *How brave a new world* (pp. 383–402). New York: Doubleday.

McDaniel, J. S., Musselman, D. L., Porter, M. R., Reed, D.A., & Nemeroff, C. B. (1995). Depression in patients with cancer: diagnosis, biology and treatment. *Archives of General Psychiatry, 52*, 89–99.

McGowan J. (1968). Jonah. In R. E. Brown, J. Fitzmeyer, & R. Murphy (Eds.), *The Jerome Biblical commentary* (pp. 633–637). Englewood Cliffs, NJ: Prentice-Hall.

McIntosh, J. L. (1985). *Research on suicide: A bibliography.* Westport, CT: Greenwood.

McIntosh, J. L., Santos, J. F., Hubbard, R. W., & Overholser, J. C. (1994). *Elder suicide: research, theory and treatment.* Washington, DC: American Psychological Association.

McKenzie, J. (1965). Judas. In *Dictionary of the Bible* (pp. 462–463). Milwaukee: Bruce.

Mead, M. (1963). From black and white magic to modern medicine. *Proceedings Rudolf Virchow Medical Society, 22,* 130–131.

Meagher, D. K. (1981). Construction and validation of a death attitude scale. In C. Corr & R. Pacholski (Eds.), *New directions in death education and counseling* (pp. 264–273). Manhattan, KS: Ag Press.

Meagher, D. K. (1992). The ethics of death education. In G. R. Cox & R. J. Fundis (Eds.), *Spiritual, ethical and pastoral aspects of death and bereavement* (pp. 3–13). Amityville, NY: Baywood Publishing.

Meagher, D. K., & Leff, P. (1989). In Marie's Memory: the rights of the child with life threatening illness. *Omega, 18,* 177–191.

Meier, D. E. (1994). Doctors' attitudes and experiences with physician-assisted death: A review of the literature. In J. M. Humber, R. F. Almeder, & G. A. Kasting (Eds.), *Physician-assisted death* (pp. 5–24.). Totowa, NJ: Humana Press.

Menninger, K. (1938). *Man against himself.* New York: Harcourt, Brace.

Michigan Commission on Death and Dying. (1994). *Final report of the Michigan Commission on Death and Dying.* Lansing, MI: Michigan Legislative Bureau.

Michigan Nurses Association. (1994). *Position statement on assisted voluntary self-termination.* Lansing, MI: Author.

Miller, F. G., & Brody, H. (1995). Professional integrity and physician-assisted death. *Hastings Center Report, 25*(3), 8–17.

Miller, F. G., Quill, T. E., Brody, H., Fletcher, J. C., Gostin, L. O., & Meier, D. E. (1994). Regulating physician-assisted death. *New England Journal of Medicine, 331,* 119–123.

Minear, J. D., & Brush, L. R. (1981). The correlations of attitudes toward suicide with death anxiety, religiosity, and personal closeness to suicide. *Omega, 11,* 317–324.

Moody, H. R. (1984). Can suicide on the grounds of old age be ethically justified? In M. Tallmer, E. R. Prichard, A. H. Kutscher, R. DeBellis, M. S. Hale, & I. K. Goldberg (Eds.), *The life-threatened elderly* (pp. 64–92). New York: Columbia University Press.

Moore, S. L. (1993). Rational suicide among older adults: A cause for concern? *Archives of Psychiatric Nursing, 7,* 106–110.

Morgado, M., Smith, M., Lecrubier, Y., & Widlocher, D. (1991). Depressed subjects unwittingly overreport poor social adjustment which they reappraise when recovered. *Journal of Nervous and Mental Disease, 179,* 614–619.

Morris, P., & Silove, D. (1992). Cultural influences in psychotherapy with refugee survivors of torture and trauma. *Hospital and Community Psychiatry, 43,* 820–824.

Motto, J. A. (1972). The right to suicide: A psychiatrist's view. *Life-Threatening Behavior, 2,* 183–188.

Motto, J. A. (1994, April). Rational suicide: then and now, when and how. *Focus: A Guide to AIDS Research and Counseling, 9*(5), 1–4.

Murdach, A. D. (1996). Beneficence re-examined: protective intervention in mental health. *Social Work, 41,* 26–32.

Murphy, G. E. (1995). Thirty-nine years of suicide research. *Suicide and Life-Threatening Behavior, 25,* 450–457.

Murray, H. (1938). *Exploration in personality.* New York: Oxford University Press.

Murray, H. (1967). Death to the world: the passions of Herman Melville. In E. Shneidman (Ed.), *Essays in self-destruction* (pp. 7–29). New York: Science House.

Nagel, T. (1970). Death. *Nous, 4,* 73–80.

Nagel, T. (1979). *Mortal Questions.* Cambridge, England: Cambridge University Press.

Nagel, W. H. (1963). The notion of victimology in criminology. *Excerpta Criminologia, 3,* 242–248.

National Association of Social Workers (1990). *Code of ethics: professional standards.* Silver Spring, MD: Author.

National Association of Social Workers. (1993). *NASW Code of Ethics.* Washington, DC: Author.

National Association of Social Workers. (1994). Client self-determination in end-of-life decisions. In *Social work speaks* (pp. 58–61). Washington, DC: NASW Press.

National Association of Social Workers (1996, January). Proposal: revision of the code of ethics. *NASW News, 41*(1), 19–22.

National Center for Health Statistics (1996). *Vital statistics of the United States, 1991* (Vol. ii, part A). Washington, DC: Public Health Service.

Nelson, J. L. (1995). Pain, suffering, and other sources of support for physician-assisted suicide and euthanasia. *Pain Forum, 4,* 182–185.

*New Jerusalem Bible.* (1965). New York: Doubleday.

New York State Task Force on Life and the Law (1994). *When death is sought: Assisted suicide and euthanasia in the medical context.* Albany, NY: Health Education Services.

Nuland, S. B. (1994). *How we die.* New York: Alfred A. Knopf.

Oberman, L. (Executive Producer). (1989, August 6). *The Life of David Rivlin.* Detroit, MI: WDIV.

O'Brien, L. A., Grisso, J. A., Maislin, G., LaPann, K., Krotki, K. P., Greco, P. J., Siegert, E. A., & Evans, L. K. (1995). Nursing home residents' preferences for life-sustaining treatments. *Journal of the American Medical Association, 274,* 1775–1779.

O'Keefe, M. (1995, January 9). The Dutch way of doctoring. *The Oregonian,* p. A1.

Oregon Death With Dignity Act, (1994). ORS 127.800.

Oregon Right to Die. (1994). *Oregon death with dignity act.* Portland, OR: Author.

Orentlicher, D. (1992). Physicians cannot ethically assist in suicide. In M. Biskup & C. Wekesser (Eds.), *Suicide: opposing viewpoints* (pp. 57–61). San Diego: Greenhaven. (Reprinted from *Journal of the American Medical Association, 262,* 1844–1845, 1991)

Palmore, E. B. (1988). *Facts on aging quiz.* New York: Springer.

Paris, M. J. (1993). Attitudes of medical students and health-care professionals toward people with disabilities. *Archives of Physical Medicine and Rehabilitation, 74,* 818–825.

People v. Kevorkian, 447 Mich 436, 527 N.W.2d 714 (Mich., Dec 13, 1994) (No. 99591, 99674, 99752, 99758, 99759).

Perry, S. (1990). Suicidal ideation and HIV testing. *Journal of the American Medical Association, 263,* 679–682.

Phillips, D. P. (1974). The influence of suggestion on suicide: substantive and theoretical implications of the Werther Effect. *American Sociological Review, 39,* 340–354.

Phillips, D. P., & Carstensen, L. L. (1986). Clustering of teenage suicides after television news stories about suicide. *New England Journal of Medicine, 315,* 685–689.

Pierce v. Society of Sisters, 268 U.S. 510 (1925).

Planned Parenthood v. Casey, 112 S. Court 2791 (1992).

A plea for beneficent euthanasia. (1974, July / August). *The Humanist, XXXIV,* 4–5.

Plumb, J. D. & Segraves, M. (1992). Terminal care in primary care postgraduate medical education programs: A national survey. *American Journal of Hospice and Palliative Care, 10,* 32–35.

Pope John Paul II. (1995). *Evangelium Vitae. Origins, 24,* 689–727.

Pope Pius XI. (1930). *Casti Connubii.* New York: America Press.

Pope Pius XI. (1937). *Mit Brennender Sorge. Acta Apostolici Sedis, 29,* 145–167.

Pope, K. S., & Vasquez, M. J. T. (1991). *Ethics in psychotherapy and counseling.* San Francisco: Jossey-Bass.

Portenoy, R. K. (1989). Cancer pain. *Cancer, 63,* 2298–2307.

Portwood, D. (1978). *Common-sense suicide: the final right.* New York: Dodd, Mead.

Post, S. G. (1990). Severely demented elderly people: A case against senicide. *Journal of the American Geriatrics Society, 38,* 715–718.

President's Commission for the Study of Ethical Problems in Medicine and Biomedical and Behavioral Research. (1982). *Making health decisions: A report on the ethical and legal implications of informed consent in the patient-practitioner relationship* (Vols. 1–3, Agency Publisher Publication 82–600637). Washington, DC: U.S. Government Printing Office.

President's Commission for the Study of Ethical Problems in Medicine and Biomedical and Behavioral Research. (1983a). *Deciding to forego life-sustaining treatment.* (Library of Congress card number 83–600503). Washington, DC: U.S. Government Printing Office.

President's Commission for the Study of Ethical Problems in Medicine and Biomedical and Behavioral Research. (1983b). *Securing access to health care: A report on the ethical implications of differences in the availability of health services* (Vols. 1–3, Agency Publisher Publication 83–600501). Washington, DC: U.S. Government Printing Office.

Prince v. Massachusetts, 321 U.S. 158 (1944).

Quadriplegic pleads for dignified life. (1990, February 22). *Chicago Tribune*, section 1, p. 18.

Quill, T. E. (1993). *Death and dignity: making choices and taking charge.* New York: W. W. Norton.

Quill, T. E. (1995). When all else fails. *Pain Forum, 4,* 189–191.

Quill, T. E., Cassel, C. K., & Meier, D. E. (1992). Care of the hopelessly ill: proposed clinical criteria for physician-assisted suicide. *New England Journal of Medicine, 327,* 1380–1384.

Quill v. Vacco, 870 F. Supp. 78 (S.D.N.Y. 1994), *rev'd,* 80 F.3d 716 (2d Circuit, 1996).

Raju, P. T. (1974). Foreword. In F. H. Holck (Ed.), *Death and eastern thought* (pp. 7–23). Nashville: Abingdon.

Rawal, N., Hylander, J., & Arner, S. (1993). Management terminal cancer pain: A nationwide survey. *Pain, 54,* 169–179.

Ray, C., & West, J. (1984). Social, sexual and personal implications of paraplegia. *Paraplegia, 22,* 75–86.

Reidy, K., & Crozier, K. (1991). Refusing treatment during rehabilitation: A model for conflict resolution. *Western Journal of Medicine, 154,* 622–623.

Remmelink Report (1991). *Medical decisions about the end-of-life,* Vol. I: Report of the Committee to Study the Medical Practice Concerning Euthanasia; Vol. II: The Study for the Committee on Medical Practice Concerning Euthanasia. The Netherlands: The Hague.

Robertson, J. A. (1985). The geography of competency. *Social Research, 52,* 555–579.

Robins, E. (1980). *The final months.* New York: Oxford University Press.

Robins, E., Murphy, G. E., Wilkenson, R. H., Jr., Gassner, S., & Kayes, J. (1959). Some clinical considerations in the prevention of suicide based on a study a 134 successful suicides. *American Journal of Public Health, 49,* 888–899.

Robins, L. N., Helzer, J. E., Weissman, M. M., Orvaschel, H., Gruenberg, E., Burke, J. D., Jr., & Regier, D. A. (1984). Lifetime prevalence of specific psychiatric disorders in three sites. *Archives of General Psychiatry, 41,* 949–958.

Roe v. Wade, 410 U.S. Supreme Court 113 (1973).

Rogers, C. (1951). *Client-centered therapy: its current practice implications, and theory.* Boston: Houghton Mifflin.

Rogers, J., & Britton, P. (1994). AIDS and rational suicide: A counseling psychology perspective or a slide on the slippery slope. *The Counseling Psychologist, 22,* 171–178.

Romer v. Evans, 1996 U.S. LEXIS 3245.

Rosenbaum, S. E. (1986). How to be dead and not care: A defense of Epicurus. *American Philosophical Quarterly, 23,* 217–225.

Rothman, J. (1989). Client self-determination: untangling the knot. *Social Service Review, 63,* 598–612.

Sacred Congregation for the Doctrine of the Faith. (1981). Declaration on euthanasia. In D. McCarthy & A. Moraczewski (Eds.), *Moral responsibility in prolonging life decisions* (pp. 290–297). St. Louis, MO: Pope John Center.

*San Francisco Chronicle.* (1995, August 31). Judge throws out murder charges against Kevorkian. p. A6.

Sasser, C. G. (1993). A strategic approach for pain management in cancer patients. *Journal of the South Carolina Medical Association, 89,* 343–348.

Sawyer, D., & Sobol, J. (1987). Public attitudes towards suicide: demographic and ideological correlates. *Public Opinion Quarterly, 51,* 92–101.

Segatore, M. (1994). Understanding chronic pain after spinal cord injury. *Journal of Neuroscience Nursing, 26,* 230–236.

Shavelson, L. (1995). *A chosen death: the dying confront assisted suicide.* New York: Simon and Shuster.

Shear, M. (1997, November 1). Book reviews. *Women's Review of Books, 15,* 1.

Shimberg, B. (1981). *Licensure: what vocational educators should know.* Columbus, OH: National Center for Research in Vocational Education.

Shneidman, E. (1968, July). Classifications of suicidal phenomena. *Bulletin of Suicidology,* 1–9.

Shneidman, E. (1970). How to prevent suicide. In E. S. Shneidman, N. L. Farberow, & R. E. Litman (Eds.), *The psychology of suicide* (p. 130). New York: Science House.

Shneidman, E. S. (1980a). Suicide. In E. S. Shneidman (Ed.), *Death: current perspectives* (pp. 416–434). Mountain View, CA: Mayfield Publishing.

Shneidman, E. (1980b). *Voices of death*. New York: Harper & Row.

Shneidman, E. (1985). *Definition of suicide*. New York: John Wiley & Sons.

Shneidman, E. S. (1992). Rational suicide and psychiatric disorders. *New England Journal of Medicine, 326*, 889–890.

Shneidman, E. (1993). *Suicide as psychache: A clinical approach to self-destructive behavior*. Northvale, NJ: Jason Aronson.

Shneidman, E. (1996). *The suicidal mind*. New York: Oxford University Press.

Shneidman, E., & Farberow, N. (Eds.). (1957). *Clues to suicide*. New York: McGraw-Hill.

Shneidman, E., & Szasz, T. (1972, July 24). The ethics of suicide prevention. *Audio-digest Psychiatry, 1*(2) [cassette].

Siegel, K. (1986). Psychosocial aspects of rational suicide. *American Journal of Psychotherapy, 40*, 405–418.

Siegel, K., & Tuckel, P. (1984–1985). Rational suicide and the terminally ill cancer patient. *Omega, 15*, 263–269.

Singer, P. (1995). *Rethinking life and death*. New York: St. Martin's Press.

Skinner v. Oklahoma, 316 U.S. 535 (1942).

Slater, P. E. (1970). *The pursuit of loneliness*. Boston: Beacon Press.

Smith, R. S. (1993). Ethical issues surrounding cancer care. In C. R. Chapman & K. M. Foley (Eds.), *Current and emerging issues in cancer pain: research issues and practice* (pp. 385–392). New York: Raven Press.

Society for Health and Human Values Task Force On Physician-Assisted Suicide. (1995). Physician-assisted suicide: toward a comprehensive understanding. *Academic Medicine, 70*, 583–590.

Soukhanov, A. H. (Ed.) (1992). *The American Heritage Dictionary*. Boston: Houghton Mifflin.

Special Senate Committee on Euthanasia and Assisted Suicide (1995). *Of life and death*. Ottawa: Author.

Spitzer, R. J., Bernhoft, R. A., & deBlasi, C. E. (1998). *Healing the culture: A commonsense philosophy of happiness, virtue and life*. Proposal submitted for publication.

Stack, S. (1987). Publicized executions and homicide. *American Sociological Review, 52*, 532–540.

Stack, S. (1996, April). *The effect of cultural support for suicide on suicide rates: an analysis of 35 national surveys in 35 nations*. Paper presented at the annual meeting of the American Association of Suicidology, St. Louis, MO.

Stack, S., & Wasserman, I. (1995). The effect of marriage, family, and religious ties on African American suicide ideology. *Journal of Marriage and the Family, 57*, 215–222.

Stack, S., Wasserman, I., & Kposowa, A. (1994). The effects of religion and feminism on suicide ideology. *Journal for the Scientific Study of Religion, 33*, 110–121.

Stephany, T.M. (1993). Hospice-assisted suicide. *Home Healthcare Nurse, 11*(1), 50.

Stewart, K. (1997, July 28). Physician Aid in Dying. *Polling Report*, 1-7.

Stillion, J. M. (1979). Rediscovering the taxonomies: A structural framework for death education courses. *Death Education, 3*, 157–164.

Stillion, J. M. (1983). Where thanatos meets eros: parallels between death education and group psychotherapy. *Death Education, 7*, 53–67.

Stillion, J. M., McDowell, E. E., & May, J. H. (1989). *Suicide across the life span: Premature exits*. New York: Hemisphere.

Stoddard, S. (1978). *The hospice movement*. New York: Vintage Books.

Styron, W. (1990). *Darkness visible*. New York: Random House.

Sullivan, H. (1962). Schizophrenia as a human process. In H. Perry, N. Gorvell, & M. Gibbens (Eds.), *The collected works of Harry Stack Sullivan* (Vol. 2). New York: W. W. Norton.

Sullivan, H. (1964). The fusion of psychiatry and social science. In H. Perry, N. Gorvell, & M. Gibbens (Eds.), *The collected works of Harry Stack Sullivan* (Vol. 2). New York: W. W. Norton.

SUPPORT Principal Investigators. (1995). A controlled study to improve care for seriously ill hospitalized patients. *Journal of the American Medical Association, 274*, 1591–1598.

Szasz, T. (1971). The ethics of suicide. *Intellectual Digest, 2*, 53–55.

Szasz, T. S. (1976). The ethics of suicide. In B. B. Wolman (Ed.), *Between survival and suicide* (pp. 163–185). New York: Gardner Press.

Szasz, T. (1986). The case against suicide prevention. *American Psychologist, 41,* 806–812.

Tannen, D. (1998). *The argument culture: moving from debate to dialogue.* New York: Random House.

Thal, A. E. (1992, May). Should "assisted suicide" be legalized? No. *NASW News, 37*(5), 4.

Tomme, H. A. (1981). Suicide is a sign of civilization. In D. L. Bender (Ed.), *Problems of death* (pp. 106–111). St. Paul, MN: Greenhaven Press.

Trafford, A. (1997, June 10). In evaluating the data, scientists are only human. *The Washington Post,* pp. 4–5.

Travis, R. (1991). Two arguments against euthanasia [Letter to the Editor]. *Gerontologist, 31,* 561–562.

Truog, R. D., & Berde, C. B. (1993). Pain, euthanasia, and anesthesiologists. *Anesthesiology, 78,* 353–360.

Truog, R. D., Berde, C. B., Mitchell, C., & Grier, H. E. (1992). Barbiturates in the care of the terminally ill. *New England Journal of Medicine, 327,* 1678–1681.

Twycross, R. (Ed.) (1994). *Pain relief in advanced cancer.* London: Churchill-Livingston.

Union Pacific Railroad Co. v. Botsford, 141 U.S. 250 (1891).

United States Catholic Bishops. (1980). Statement on capital punishment. *Origins, 10,* 368–382.

Vacco v. Quill, 117 S. Ct. 2293, 65 U.S.L.W. 4695 (1997).

Valente, S. M., & Saunders, J. M. (1994). Management of suicidal patients with HIV disease. *Journal of the Association of Nurses in AIDS Care, 5*(6), 19–29.

Van der Maas, P. J., Pijnenborg, L., & Van Delden, J. J. M. (1995). Letter from Rotterdam. *Journal of the American Medical Association, 273,* 1411–1414.

The Van Dusen case. (1975, February 26). *The New York Times,* pp. 1, 43.

Velcz, C. (1979). Cultural cross-fire. *Human Behavior, 8,* 52–55.

Vernaci, R. L. (1991, October 11). Disabilities scary for many: survey. *Nashville Banner,* p. 5.

Vigeland, K. (1991). Attitudes towards assisted suicide and euthanasia among students. *Nordisk Psykologi, 43,* 1–16.

Von Hentig, H. (1948). *The criminal and his victim.* New Haven, CN: Yale University Press.

Wallace, S. E. (1973). *After suicide.* New York: Wiley Interscience.

Wanzer, S. H., Federman, D. D., Adelstein, S. J., Cassel, C. K., Cassem, E. M., Cranford, R. E., Hook, E. W., Lo, B., Moertel, C. G., Satar, P., Stone, A., & Van Eys, J., (1989). The physician's responsibility toward hopelessly ill patients: A second look. *New England Journal of Medicine, 320,* 844–849.

Ward, G. C., & Burns, K. (1994). *Baseball: an illustrated history.* New York: Alfred A. Knopf.

Warr, M., & Stafford, M. (1991). The influence of delinquent peers: what they say or what they do? *Criminology, 29,* 851–865.

Washington Natural Death Act (1979). RCW 70.122.100.

Washington State Medical Association. (1992). *Pain management and care of the terminal patient.* Seattle, WA: Author.

Washington v. Glucksberg, 117 S. Ct. 2258, 65 U.S.L.W. 4669 (1997).

Wass, H., Berardo, F., & Neimeyer, R. (1988). *Dying: facing the facts.* NY: Hemisphere Publishers.

*Webster's New Collegiate Dictionary.* (1981). Springfield, MA: G. & C. Merriam

*Webster's New World Thesaurus* . (1974). New York: William Collins and World Publishing.

Weick, A., & Pope, L. (1988). Knowing what's best: A new look at self-determination. *Social Casework, 69,* 10–16.

Weinberg, N., & Williams, J. (1978). How the physically disabled perceive their disabilities. *Journal of Rehabilitation, 44*(3), 31–33.

Weinrach, S. G., & Thomas, K. R. (1993). The national board for certified counselors: the good, the bad, the ugly. *Journal of Counseling and Development, 72,* 105–109.

Welty, E. (1963). *A handbook of Christian social ethics* (Vol. 2). New York: Herder & Herder.

Werth, J. L., Jr. (1994). *The effects of precipitating circumstances, stigma, and social support on psychologists' perceptions of suicidal ideators.* Unpublished doctoral dissertation, Auburn University, Auburn, AL.

Werth, J. L., Jr. (1995). Rational suicide reconsidered: AIDS as an impetus for change. *Death Studies, 19,* 65–80.

Werth, J. L., Jr. (1996a). Can Shneidman's "Ten commonalities of suicide" accommodate rational suicide? *Suicide and Life-Threatening Behavior, 26,* 293–298.

Werth, J. L., Jr. (1996b). *Rational suicide? Implications for mental health professionals.* Washington, DC: Taylor & Francis.

Werth, J. L., Jr., & Cobia, D. C. (1995) Empirically based criteria for rational suicide: A survey of psychotherapists. *Suicide and Life-Threatening Behavior, 25,* 231–240.

Werth, J. L., Jr., & Gordon, J. R. (1998). Helping at the end-of-life: mental health professionals and hastened death. In L. VandeCreek, S. Knapp, & T. L. Jackson (Eds.), *Innovations in clinical practice: A sourcebook* (Vol. 16) (pp. 385–398). Sarasota, FL: Professional Resource Press.

Werth, J. L., Jr., & Liddle, B. J. (1994). Psychotherapists' attitudes toward suicide. *Psychotherapy: Theory, Research and Practice, 31,* 440–448.

West, L. (1993). Reflections on the right to die. In A. Leenaars (Ed.), *Suicidology: essays in honor of Edwin Shneidman,* pp. 359–398. Northvale, NJ: Aronson.

WGBH-tv (1993, March 23). Choosing death. In *The Health Quarterly.* Boston, MA: Author.

White, L. (1971). The quality of life. *California's Health, 28–29,* 1–12.

Whiteneck, G. G., Carter, R. E., Charlifue, S. W., Hall, K. M., Menter, R. R., Wilkerson, M. A., & Wilmot, C. B. (1985). A collaborative study of high quadriplegia. In *Rocky Mountain Spinal Cord Injury System Report to the National Institute of Handicapped Research.* Washington, DC: NIHR.

Wickett, A. (1989). *Double exit.* Eugene, OR: National Hemlock Society.

Williams, B. (1976). Persons, character, and morality. In A. O. Rorty (Ed.), *The identities of persons* (pp. 197–216). Berkeley, CA and Los Angeles: University of California Press.

Williams, M. V., Parker, R. M., Baker, D. W., Parikh, N. S., Pitkin, K., Coates, W. C., & Nurss, J. R. (1995). Inadequate functional health literacy among patients at two public hospitals. *Journal of the American Medical Association, 274,* 1677–1682.

Winokur, G., & Black, D. W. (1992). Suicide: what can be done? *New England Journal of Medicine, 327,* 490–491.

World Health Organization (1990). *Bulletin, cancer and palliative care.* Geneva: Author.

World Values Study Group. (1994). *World Values Survey, 1981–1984 and 1990–1993.* Ann Arbor, MI: Inter-University Consortium for Political and Social Research.

Wrobleski, A. (1994). *Suicide: Survivors—A guide for those left behind.* Minneapolis, MN: Afterwords.

Yalom, I. D. (1975). *The theory and practice of group psychotherapy.* New York: Basic Books.

Yarnell, S. K., & Battin, M. P. (1988). AIDS, psychiatry, and euthanasia. *Psychiatric Annals, 18,* 598–603.

York, D., & York, P. (1989). *Getting Strong in All the Hurting Places.* New York: Rawson.

Young, S. H. (1968). Into the sunset [excerpt]. In C. Seaburg (Ed.), *Great Occasions* (p. 240). Boston: Beacon Press.

Zalman, M. & Stack, S. (1996). The relationship between euthanasia and suicide in the Netherlands: A time series analysis, 1950–1990. *Social Science Quarterly, 77,* 577–593.

Zilboorg, G. (1936). Suicide among civilized and primitive races. *American Journal of Psychiatry, 92,* 1347–1369.

# INDEX

# READER'S SURVEY

As Editor, I am interested in your reactions to this book. I would appreciate it if you would copy and complete this survey, and return it to me by way of the publisher. I will compile your responses and use them as an informal survey of your attitudes and how, if at all, reading the book has impacted you. Thank you for your time.

*James L. Werth, Jr., Ph.D.*

1. Gender:    ☐ Female    ☐ Male

2. Age: _____

3. About how many other books have you read on hastened death? _____

4. How did you hear about this book? _____

5. What made you decide to read this particular book? _____

6. How much of the book did you actually read? (If only certain chapters, please list them.) _____
   _____

7. What is your honest evaluation of what you did read? _____
   _____

8. BEFORE reading anything in the book, did you believe that people could make a reasonable decision to hasten their deaths? ☐ Yes ☐ No  Why or why not? _____
   _____
   _____

9. BEFORE reading anything in the book, did you have a definition or set of criteria for "rational suicide?" ☐ Yes ☐ No  If yes, what was your personal definition/set of criteria? _____
   _____

10. After reading the book, how have your attitudes or beliefs or thoughts about "rational suicide" changed, if at all? _____
    _____
    _____

11. Which chapter(s) were most powerful and convincing to you? _____
    Why? _____
    _____

12. What kind of book would you like to see written about the subject of hastened death?
    _____
    _____
    _____

Mail completed survey to:

James Werth, Jr., Ph.D.
C/o Bernadette Capelle
Brunner Mazel Publishers
*A Member of the Taylor and Francis Group*
325 Chestnut Street
Philadelphia, PA 19106

***Thanks for your help.***